THEODORE WIBAUX
PONTIFICAL ZOUAVE AND JESUIT

ThÉODORE WIBAUX

THEODORE WIBAUX
PONTIFICAL ZOUAVE AND JESUIT

By the
Rev. Charles Marie Emmanuel Du Cöetlosquet, S.J.

With and Introduction by the
Rev. Richard F. Clarke, S.J.

Edited by
Brendan Cassell

Published by Papal Zouave International, 2024.

Copyright © Papal Zouave International 2024.

Theodore Wibaux Pontifical Zouave and Jesuit. Is a republication from Papal Zouave International of Charles Marie Emmanuel Du Cöetlosquet S.J.'s book *Théodore Wibaux zouave pontifical et Jésuite.* Published by Retaux-Bray in 1885. An English translation from the London Catholic Truth Society was published in 1887. Two French editions with engravings were also published. One by Lefort Lille in 1885 and another by Société de Saint-Augustin, Desclée de Brouwer in 1890.

The editor has for the first time, republished the 1887 English translation with the engravings from the French editions in 1885 and 1890.

For More information regarding this title and Papal Zouave International please visit:

PapalZouave.com

All rights reserved
ISBN: 979-8-9893230-3-6
Cover design by Brendan Cassell and Bojan Rekovic.

Founded in 2023, Papal Zouave International is a historical society dedicated to promoting and preserving the memory of the Papal Zouaves. A unit of brave Catholic soldiers who came from across Christendom to defend the Papal States and Bl. Pope Pius IX during the 9th Crusade, between 1860–1870.

To learn more, visit PapalZouave.com

Contents.

EDITOR'S PREFACE
.... p. i

INTRODUCTION
.... p. xvii

AUTHOR'S FOREWARD
.... p. xxvi

CHAPTER I.
1849—1864.
Theodore's early days. Family gatherings under the grandparents' roof. His faults. His love of teasing. His good qualities. His mother's influence. Schooldays. Holidays. Boyish pranks. The archery club. His favorite brother. The death of little Francis. .... p. 1

CHAPTER II.
1864—1866.
Theodore a Collegian at Marcq. The prizes he gains. A visit to the Redemptorists. Rome and the September Convention. His desire to become a Zouave. Struggles and sacrifices. Weary waiting. Louis Veuillot is appealed to. The last evening at home. . . . . p. 14

CHAPTER III.
1866, 1867.
Theodore on his way to Rome. Joy mingled with sorrow. Commencement of life in barracks. His letters home. A Zouave's day. Close of the year. Withdrawal of the French troops from Rome. . . . . p. 31

CHAPTER IV.
1867.
Theodore's journal. His piety. His self-sacrifice. His cheerfulness. The Conferences of St. Vincent of Paul. Letters from home. Theodore is no longer a recruit. On guard for the first time. The Abbé Daniel. Correspondence. . . . . p. 44

CHAPTER V.
1867.
Incessant removals. The Coliseum. Feast of the Purification. Beatification of a Capuchin. The Catacombs of St. Agnes. Theodore's eighteenth birthday. The Carnival. St. Joseph's month. . . . . p. 60

CHAPTER VI.
1867.
Sojourn at Frascati. Religion and duty. Spiritual dangers. Easter in Rome. Theodore's quarters in Fort St. Angelo. the Brigands. Camp life. Return to Rome. . . . . p. 72

CHAPTER VII.
1867.
Letters from Roubaix. A grand review. Solemn functions in St. Peter's. Fatiguing occupations. Visit to Religious Houses. Reminiscences. . . . . p. 84

CHAPTER VIII.
1867.

The start for Albano. Orders and counter-orders. The cholera. Theodore's services in the hospital. Death of Cardinal Altieri. Honors bestowed on the 6th Company. Leisure and temptations. Ariccia. Anniversary of Castelfidardo. Return to Rome. . . . . p. 98

CHAPTER IX.
1867

The Garibaldians before Rome. Lieutenant Guillemin. Disturbances in the city. The barracks are undermined. Danger and uncertainty. Arrival of the French troops. . . . . p. 115

CHAPTER X.
1867.

Real warfare at last. Battle of Mentana. Splendid conduct of the Zouaves. Their victory. Moeller and d'Alcantara. Recall of the troops. . . . . p. 125

CHAPTER XI.
1867, 1868.

The effect of twelve months' military service on Theodore. He is made Corporal. His work at the Depôt. Gloomy forebodings. His interview with Pius IX. . . . . p. 142

CHAPTER XII.
1868.

The theater. Good counsel and its results. Theodore's nineteenth birthday. Unwelcome notoriety. Arrival of his brother and cousin. Excursions made in their company. . . . . p. 155

CHAPTER XIII.
1868.

Loretto and Castelfidardo. Month of May in Rome. Theodore's promotion. His quarters at St. Augustine. Another change. The feast of Corpus Christi. . . . . p. 166

CHAPTER XIV.
1868.

Theodore resumes his studies. Military manœuvres. Hannibal's Camp. The Pope's visit. A sham fight. Mentana. Leave of Absence.........p. 179

CHAPTER XV.
1868, 1869.

Three months at Roubaix. A week's retreat. The Golden Jubilee of Pius IX. Depôt at Monte Rotondo. Excursions in the neighborhood. Loulou. . p. 192

CHAPTER XVI.
1869, 1870.

Theodore's new duties. Description of his room. Farewell to Monte Rotondo. The heat in Rome. At Mentana again. Silver wedding of his parents. The Vatican Council. Visit of his father and other relatives...........................p. 207

CHAPTER XVII.
1870.

Acquapendente. Inspection by the General. The Lake of Bolsena. Outbreak of the Franco-German War. Retreat upon Civita Vecchia. Preparations for the defense of Rome. Capitulation. Reluctant departure of the Zouaves. Embarkation on board the Orinoco..........................p.223

CHAPTER XVIII.
1870.

Toulon. Tarascon and Béaucaire. Tours. Theodore's dejection. The re-organization of the Corps. Campaigning. Wearisome marches. Sufferings of the Soldiers. Patay. Col. de Charette. Retreat upon Poitiers........p. 238

CHAPTER XIX.
1870, 1871.

Recollections of Rome. Close of the year 1870. Stephen Wibaux joins the Regiment. Theodore receives his brevet. Willebaud's illness. Theodore's anxiety and distress. He returns home. Last days and death of Willebaud..............................p. 253

CHAPTER XX.
1871.

Return to Rennes. Garrison life. The Zouaves are disbanded. Theodore's hesitation as to his future course. Death of M. Pierre Motte. Theodore starts for Amiens. . . . . p. 269

CHAPTER XXI.
1871.

Retreat at St. Acheul. Struggles between nature and grace. The final victory. Theodore enters the Jesuit novitiate. His devotional practices. First vows. . . . . p. 282

CHAPTER XXII.
1872-1874.

Theodore at recreation-time. At the bedside of the sick. His correspondence. Love for his old regiment. Intercourse with former comrades. General Charette's fête. . . . . p. 300

CHAPTER XXIII.
1874—1880.

In the College at Boulogne. Theodore introduces a military spirit among his pupils. Portrait of Pope Pius IX. Return to Amiens. Tour in Switzerland. Dispersion of the Community at Amiens. Theodore is sent home. . . . . p. 317

CHAPTER XXIV.
1880-1882.

The House in Jersey. Theodore commences his theology. The Apostle of the Sacred Heart. Pilgrimages to St. Matthew. Presentiment and preparation. Illness and death. A Jesuit's last will and testament. . . . . p. 333

EPILOUGE
. . . . p. 350

EDITOR'S PREFACE

THE violent fall of the Papal States and the unification of Italy is a much-overlooked period of history. Even more overlooked are the brave Papal Soldiers who sacrificed their life for the cause of the Church. The following preface will give a summarized account of the events between 1859-1870 so the reader will have a fuller appreciation of this book.

There was a time when the Pope ruled over most of central Italy. Given by Pepin the Short in 754, the Pope's temporal power was called the Papal States. For over 1000 years the Papal States helped secure the sovereignty of the Church, while at times contested and not always sufficient to prevent temporal interference into the affairs of the Church. Nonetheless, the Papal States served as an effective bulwark of the City of God against the City of Man. Without a temporal power, the Pope and the Church would be subjected greatly to the affairs of the City of Man. Imagine the persecution the Church would have faced if they didn't have the Leonine city to defend themselves from the Revolutionary French, Nationalist Italians, and Nazi Germany.

In the mid-19th century, Italy was divided into 10 different territories. In Southern Italy was the Kingdom of the Two Sicilies (its last ruler and his mother are both on thepath to sainthood, Servant of God Francis II and Blessed Maria of Savoy). In Central Italy the Papal States (the last "Pope-King" is also on the path to sainthood, Blessed Pope Pius IX) and San Marino. In Northern Italy was the Kingdom of Sardinia-Piedmont and Monaco, along with Austrian controlled Kingdom of Lombardy and Venetia and the Austrian influenced Duchies of Parma, Tuscany, and Modena.

This time period saw the rise of nationalism, and many revolutionaries on the peninsula got caught up in nationalistic fervor. With the help of secret societies, individuals such as Cavour, Garibaldi, Mazzini, and Victor Emmanuel II, despite conflicting desires for particular styles of government wanted nothing more than a united Italy, even if it was achieved through violence, conniving, and treachery. The Church and the Pope were about to suffer greatly.

Everything came to a head in 1859. The King of Sardinia-Piedmont, Victor Emmanuel II, and his Prime Minister Cavour began their campaign to unite Italy. A secret agreement was signed between Cavour and French Emperor Napoleon III early in the year, and the Emperor promised to help push the Austrians out of the peninsula in return for Savoy and Nice near the French border. In March, the Piedmontese began mobilizing along the border with Lombardy, provoking Austria to mobilize themselves. In April, when the Kingdom of Sardinia refused to de-mobilize, Austria invaded. France quickly joined Piedmont, and together after several months Austria was defeated.

During this time, Sardinia staged uprisings in Tuscany, Parma, Modena, and the northernmost territory of the Papal States, the Romagna, causing them to destabilize. Shortly after the war ended, these territories were annexed by Sardinia-Piedmont. With Austria defeated, they ceded Lombardy to France, who gave it to Sardinia, and in turn Sardinia ceded Savoy and Nice to France. Napoleon III tried his best to influence Bl. Pius IX to accept the annexation of the Romagna to Sardinia-Piedmont. However, the Holy Father held his ground and excommunicated all of those who had taken part in its capture. Now was the time to resist.

There were two options in front of Bl. Pius IX. The Cardinal Secretary of State Giacomo Antonelli wanted to rely on diplomacy, while Monsignor Xavier de Mérode, a private chamberlain of the Pope, believed that diplomacy could not be relied upon, as it was not enough to curb the nationalistic fervor of King Victor Emmanuel II and the Italian revolutionaries. He believed the only way to defend the temporal power was by force, and strengthening the Papal Army would be necessary to protect the Papal States.

This would be a huge undertaking as the Papal Army was very weak and ill-equipped. However, Mérode had a vision that the Army could be revitalized through a multinational force of pious Catholics from around the world, akin to a Crusade. Bl. Pius IX was convinced, he approved of Mérode's plan, and promoted him to Papal Minister of Arms. The volunteers of the Pope would go on to view themselves as soldiers fighting in the 9th Crusade.

The plan was put into effect immediately, with more than 5,000 foreign recruits raised from almost 30 different countries. Most were Irish, Austrian, French, and Dutch. The Austrians formed five battalions of light infantry; the Irish formed the Battalion of St. Patrick; and the French and Dutch formed the Franco-Belgian Battalion. Here is the beginning of the Papal Zouaves; after the 1860 campaign, the Franco-Belgians transitioned into the Papal Zouaves.

Many of these volunteers came from noble lineage. Additionally, many had ancestors or relatives who had fought in other Counter-Revolutionary efforts, such as the war in the Vendée. In fact, the first group of foreign volunteers was the Crusaders of Cathelineau, led by Henri de Cathelineau, the grandson of Vendéen General Jacques Cathelineau. The group existed only a few months before being incorporated into the Franco-Belgian Battalion.

Former French General de la Moricière was selected to lead the Papal Army. Motivated by his Catholic faith, he understood how important the coming conflict would be. In an address given to new volunteers on Easter Sunday 1860, he said:

> At the sound of the grand voice which lately apprised the world from the Vatican of the dangers threatening the patrimony of St. Peter, Catholics were moved, and their emotion soon spread to every part of the earth. This is because Christianity is not merely the religion of the civilized world, but the animating principle of civilization; it is because the Papacy is the keystone of the arch of Christianity, and all Chris-

tian nations seem, in these days, to be conscious of those great varieties which are our faith. The revolution today threatens Europe as Islamism did of old, and now, as then, the cause of the Pope is that of civilization and liberty throughout the world. Soldiers, have confidence, and believe that God will raise our courage to the level of the great cause whose defense He has entrusted to our arms.

La Moricière was also important because he wanted a unit of Zouaves in his army. Having firsthand experience with the effectiveness of this type of light infantry, he had led a regiment of Zouaves in Algeria in 1838. The origins of the Zouaves can be traced back to 1831, after the French conquest of Algeria. The French made allies with the Kabyles, a Berber people living in the mountains. One of their tribes, the Zwawa, were known as fierce warriors and wanted to fight under their new rulers. Battalions of these native Zwawa were formed under the name Zouave. Shortly thereafter, companies of French Zouaves began to form. This type of elite light infantry unit became extremely popular in the 19th century, with units being raised in the Union, the Confederacy, Poland, Spain, and, of course, the Papal States. At the time, the Franco-Belgian battalion was a Zouave unit in all but name, and it wasn't long before their commander, Major Becdelievre, pushed for the adoption of the Zouave uniform.

In front of the Basilica of St. John Lateran, each of the new Papal Army recruits made the following oath: "I swear to Almighty God to be obedient and faithful to my sovereign, the Roman Pontiff, Our very Holy Father Pope Pius IX, and to his legitimate successors. I swear to serve with honor and fidelity and to sacrifice my life for the defense of his august and sacred person, for the maintenance of his sovereignty, and for the maintenance of his rights." Many of those who swore that oath did indeed follow it unto their deaths.

Seeking to continue uniting the Peninsula, Cavour secretly coordinated with Garibaldi for his Red Shirts to seize the Kingdom of the Two Sicilies. By May, Garibaldi's forces had landed in Sicily, and he declared himself dictator in the name of Victor Emmanuel II. By September, the entire Kingdom was under his control, with the exception of over ten thousand holdouts in Capua, Civitella del Tronto, and Gaeta, commanded by Francis II. All eyes were now on the Papal States.

A French garrison was stationed in Rome to help guarantee the Pope's temporal power. However, Cavour had received Napoleon III's blessing to take all of the Papal States, with the exception of the Lazio region (Rome and its surrounding territory), without French interference. With this act, Napoleon III turned his back on his Catholic subjects.

In early September, Sardinia and secret societies began inciting civil unrest in the northern territories of the Papal States. Under the guise of restoring order, Sardinia invaded the Papal States with 70,000 soldiers on September 11, 1860. The Papal States' only hope for victory was if Austria sent reinforcements to bolster the Papal Army through the port of Ancona in the northeast of the Papal States. In anticipation of these supposed reinforcements, the Papal plan was to have the majority of the army maneuver to the city and defend it from siege.

Unfortunately, the majority of the army was routed during the Battle of Castelfidardo on September 18, 1860. The loss was so catastrophic that it became known as a massacre, and the fallen Papal soldiers were seen as martyrs. The battlefield was filled with so many noble Catholic youths from France that an Italian general commented, "You would think this was a list of invites for a ball given by Louis XIV!" On September 29, Ancona fell, and with it, the majority of the Papal States. The Pope's temporal power was reduced to only the Lazio region, which included Rome. Bl. Pius IX protested these losses, but the majority of the world ignored him. While the fighting stopped momentarily, the threat against the Papal States persisted. The revolutionaries would not rest until all of Italy was united.

Over the next few years, the Papal Army grew stronger and became more well-trained. The Franco-Belgian Battalion officially transitioned to the Papal Zouaves on January 1, 1861. A little over a week later, on January 10, 1861, the Papal Zouave battalion gathered at St. John Lateran to swear a solemn oath to defend the Papal States. The Papal Zouave chaplain, Father Daniel, administered the oath, saying:

> So far you have committed yourself individually, but today, all together, we want to solemnly swear fidelity to God, to His service, to the Church, and to her rights. To its kingly head, temporal prince, and spiritual head, we promise to defend his rights and die rather than abandon them cowardly. For my part, gentlemen, in the presence of this battalion which I respect and love, in the presence of God and the Church, I swear to remain always faithful to the Church, to her doctrine and to her rights. I say this oath out of complete fidelity and devotion to serve you and for the salvation of your souls. Now I will hear your oath.

The Papal Zouaves then proceeded to recite their solemn oath.

> I swear to Almighty God to be obedient and faithful to my sovereign, the Roman Pontiff, our very Holy Father, Pope Pius IX, and his legitimate successors. I swear to serve him with honor and fidelity and to sacrifice my life for the defense of his august and sacred person, for the support of his sovereignty and for the maintenance of his rights. I swear not to belong to any civil or religious sect, to any secret society or corporation, whatever they might be, having for its direct or indirect goal to offend the Catholic religion and to corrupt society. I swear not to join any sect or society condemned by the decrees of the Roman Pontiffs. I swear also to the very good and great God to not have any direct or indirect communication with the enemies, whoever they might

be, of religion and the Roman Pontiffs. I swear all of this on the holy Gospel, so help me God. Through our Lord Jesus Christ, Amen. Immediately after the oath was said, the officers raised their swords, and the battalion presented arms. Thus, the Church had new protectors.

The term "Franco-Belgian" and "Papal Zouave" were often used interchangeably as the Papal Zouaves viewed the Franco-Belgians as part of their pedigree and considered them part of their unit. Over 10,000 men would join the Papal Zouaves over the course of its lifetime. The largest the unit ever grew was in 1868, reaching the size of a full regiment with four battalions, totaling almost 5,000 men. However, they started off as a 600-man battalion with six companies.

Unfortunately, due to a disagreement between Mérode and Becdelievre, the latter resigned command of the unit in March. Most of the soldiers wanted Athanase de Charette, the great-nephew of Vendéen General François de Charette, to lead the unit. However, since he was a legitimist, Bl. Pius IX did not want to anger Napoleon III and risk losing the French garrison stationed in Rome. Instead, Swiss Colonel Allet, who had been in the Papal Army for many years, was chosen to lead the unit, and Charette was promoted to Major. Charette's time would come, however, as he eventually led a contingent of French Papal Zouaves during the Franco-Prussian War, and in many ways, he became a father figure among the Papal Zouaves.

Over the next few years, the Papal Zouaves mostly lived a garrison life. The main threats the Papal States faced were brigands and other criminals along the borders and in the mountains, with occasional border disputes with the Piedmontese. The largest of these occurred on August 4, 1862, when 400 Piedmontese soldiers crossed over the southern border of the Papal States and harassed the town of Ceprano, which housed many Neapolitan refugees from the Kingdom of the Two Sicilies. Two companies of Piedmontese soldiers attempted to ford a river to enter the town when a platoon of 17 Papal Zouaves, commanded by Lt. Mousty, engaged them and successfully repelled the assault. The Piedmontese retreated in great disorder, leaving five dead and 25 wounded, while the Papal Zouaves sustained no injuries. The victory at Ceprano showed the Piedmontese that the Papal States were serious about defending their borders.

Aside from military duties, the Papal Zouaves were often involved in religious ceremonies, including processions, masses on feast days, and whenever Bl. Pius IX spoke from his balcony. The unit was defined by its piety and devotion to the faith. To become a Papal Zouave, a recruit needed a letter of recommendation from a priest. All recruits, regardless of social class, began as privates, even among the nobility, such as Prince Alfonso Carlos de Bourbon, the future rightful King of Spain. Pay and rations were meager—half a penny a day, soup, bread, and coffee. Despite the low pay, many Zouaves were generous with their tithes, and most of their free time was spent in churches praying or participating in various Catholic confraternities.

However, the monotony of garrison life did not suit everyone. After an initial boost in numbers following the loss in 1860, recruitment began to decline. This trend was seen in other units as well. For example, the Battalion of St. Patrick was reduced to the Company of St. Patrick and ultimately was dissolved, with the remainder of the soldiers being incorporated into the Papal Zouaves in 1862 By 1863 the number of Papal Zouaves dropped to 300. However, this would soon change.

It started with another backstab from Napoleon III. On September 15, 1864 France signed an agreement with Italy known as the September Convention. It was agreed that Napoleon III would evacuate the French garrison in Rome over the next two years. Additionally, Italy, among other things, promised not to attack the Pope's territory. However, this agreement was merely for show, as it opened the door for Garibaldi and his Red Shirts to invade and cede Rome to Italy without French interference just as they did with the Kingdom of Two Sicilies in 1860. If they failed, Victor Emmanuel II could pretend that they had nothing to do with Garibaldi.

When the agreement was made public in early 1865, there was outrage in Rome at the betrayal of Napoleon III, as it foreshadowed events to come. Upon hearing the news, General de la Moricière, who had been living in France since the defeat of the Papal Army in 1860, prepared to return to lead the army. However, he died and General Herman Kanzler was made Commander of the Papal Army; in 1860 Monsignor Merode resigned as pro-minister of arms, and Kanzler also assumed that position.

There was a surge of Papal Zouave recruits as the threat to the Papal States grew significantly. The unit grew to 1500 men, two more line companies and a depot company were added. Activity with revolutionaries and brigands also increased during this time as they attempted to capitalize off the French exit.

Recruitment swelled again in 1866 after Piedmont passed a series of anti-clerical laws which included imprisonment of bishops, banning of Papal encyclicals, forbidding religious processions, closing of seminaries, subjecting priests to conscription, among many more heinous and anti-catholic acts.

Meanwhile, in the summer of 1866, Victor Emmaneul II joined forces with Prussia against the Austrians in the Seven Weeks' War. The goal of the Kingdom of Italy was to remove the last vestige of Austrian influence on the peninsula. While Italy did not fare so well during the war, Prussia was victorious and the Austrian controlled Kingdom of Venetia was ceded to France who then ceded the territory to Italy, just like what happened with Nice and Savoy in 1860.

By December 1866 the French Garrison had left Rome. All that remained between Victor Emmanuel II and a united Italy was Bl. Pius IX and the last remaining territory of the Papal States. By January 1867, the Papal Zouaves had swelled to a regiment with 4 battalions. Confident in God and His soldiers, Bl. Pius IX announced the convening of the first Vatican Council in October 1869. While the enemies of the Church were plotting to attack the Papal States, a terrible cholera outbreak erupted in the region, hitting the town of Albano just outside of Rome particularly hard. The civil government in the town collapsed, the mayor and most of the residents fled leaving piles of bodies in the street and the sick to fend for themselves.

The only figures that stayed and helped the Sisters of Charity in their care for the sick was the archbishop, Cardinal Altieri, and the vacationing and exiled royal family of the Two Sicilies. The disease would claim the archbishop and the queen mother.

Help arrived in the form of the 6th company of the 2nd battalion of Papal Zouaves. The Lieutenant in charge of the first detachment of Zouaves that arrived was the first to pick up a corpse and carry it to the cemetery. He called out to his men: "I set the example; those who want to work with me stay here, those who don't feel up to it go back to the barracks." The Papal Zouaves followed his example at their own peril. By August 20 the epidemic had subsided but not before claiming two Dutchmen in the unit. One of them, Henri Peters, found consolation in his final moments by holding a crucifix. With his dying lips he kissed it fervently, and exclaimed, "I know that Heaven is before me when all this is past."

With the summer epidemic over, the French garrison no longer in Rome, and Lombardy under Italian control, Victor Emmanul II initiated his plans to capture Rome. The prime minister at the time, Rattazzi and his cabinet, supplied Garibaldi with arms, supplies, and money and allowed him to raise an army. In late September, Garibaldi and his two sons began their invasion of the Lazio region. Their goal was to cause civil unrest and seize Rome, and they hoped that their invasion would cause revolutionaries to rise up and assist them in their takeover, much like what happened in 1849 when revolutionaries seized Rome and forced Bl. Pius IX into exile. He was restored less than a year later with the assistance of France, Spain, and the Two Sicilies. If Garibaldi failed to take Rome the plan was to have the Kingdom of Italy declare that due to the civil unrest, they needed to send their Army to "restore order."

The Red Shirts numbered well over 10,000 while the Papal Army numbered around 13,000, but had an effective fighting force only around 8,000 with over 2,000 Papal Zouaves. Over the next month the Papal Army fought bravely and fended off most attacks that came from the Garibaldians. In late October, the Red Shirts attempted to incite a revolution in Rome, but it failed to gain any traction. On October 22 about 500 Red Shirts infiltrated the city and bombed over a dozen places. One of them was a Papal Zouave barracks at the Palazzo Serritorsi. The explosion destroyed the building and killed 25 Zouaves, most of them from the band and four civilians, including a little girl. The attacks that night from the Red Shirts were repelled by the Papal Zouaves. More attacks occurred the following day, but they too failed. The city clearly was not going to fall to the revolutionary force.

During this time, Empress Eugenie and pressure from French Catholics convinced Napoleon III to denounce the invasion of the Pope's territory and to send him a sizable force to help defeat the Red Shirts. Garibaldi attempted to seize Rome before the French force arrived, but he was unable to do so.

On October 30, the French force arrived in Rome. Garibaldi, hoping to draw France into a conflict with the Kingdom of Italy, pulled his forces back in an attempt to link up with the Italian Royal Army. Realizing his plan, the commander of the Papal Army General Kanzler, with French reinforcements, pursued the Red Shirts and routed them in the town of Mentana on November 3, 1867. The Papal Zouaves were the tip of the spear during the battle, and it was through their efforts that the battle was won. By nightfall, the Papal Army had Garibaldi's Army trapped and surrounded inside the town. The next morning the Red Shirts surrendered, and the Papal and French forces occupied the town. Unfortunately, Garibaldi escaped capture.

He had slipped away during the battle with half his force into the safety of Italian territory. Not wanting to start a war they were unprepared for, the Royal Army did not assist the Red Shirts. Garibaldi himself would never again invade the Papal States. The victory at Mentana is considered the greatest battle ever won by the Papal Zouaves. A monument was dedicated to their victory and to the fallen at the Campo Verano cemetery in Rome.

The victory at Mentana bought the Papal States three more years. Which in turn allowed the First Vatican Council to happen starting on December 8, 1869. Without the heroism of the Papal Zouaves, would the dogma of papal infallibility and other fruits of the Council have been promulgated? The victory at Mentna led to another surge in recruitment with the unit reaching its highest numbers in 1868, almost 5,000 soldiers. Over the next three years things were relatively quiet. That was, until the start of the Franco-Prussian War in the summer of 1870. After the Battle of Mentana, Napoleon III kept a garrison of 4,000 soldiers in Rome. However, his war with Prussia was not going well, and he was getting desperate. He recalled the force in Rome and declared he was returning to the rules of the September convention. On September 2, Napoleon III was captured after his defeat at the Battle of Sedan. With France out of the way and Austria too weak to assist the Papal States, Victor Emmanuel II pounced on the opportunity. Afraid of having Garibaldi invade and risk destabilizing his monarchy, Victor Emmanuel II decided to use his Royal Army to invade Rome.

On September 9, the Royal Army was posed on the Lazio region border. Victor Emmanuel II wrote Bl. Pope Pius IX a letter and sent Count Gustavo Ponza di San Martino to deliver it the following day on September 10. The letter, which really was just a guise to request a bloodless takeover, claimed that due to the removal of French troops from the city, it was necessary for his forces to occupy the Eternal City so that they could maintain law and order from Roman revolutionaries. A strange thing to say since there were no revolutionary uprisings in Rome at the time. Bl. Pius IX did not appreciate the hypocrisy in the letter. He replied to Count Ponza. "What a race of vipers! Whited sepulchers! and wanting in faith!" Count Ponza became so afraid that he rushed out of the room and mistook a window for a door, almost falling to his death. Bl. Pius IX refused to be bullied. He rejected Victor Emmanuel II's offer, an action which certainly would lead to war, one which would be very difficult. The Italian Army had over 75,000 troops stationed on the frontier ready to invade the last of the Papal States, meanwhile the Papal Army had only around 12,000 men. General Kanzler believed that as long as he kept the Italian divisions divided, he could launch a successful offensive strike. However, an offensive attack required approval from the Pope. Kanzler met with Bl. Pius IX immediately after his meeting with Count Ponza.

The Pope disappointed the Papal Army, and he rejected any

offensive operations as he believed the war could not be won. His orders were that, upon invasion, all elements of the Papal Army were to fall back on Rome and wait for the arrival of the Italians, with the exception of the Papal port of Civita Vecchia, so that the Pope could have a potential route to escape if needed. Bits of resistance on the way to Rome were allowed to show the world that Italy was unjustly usurping the temporal power of the Pope by force, additionally a defense of the Holy City was allowed to a point. The invasion began on September 11th, the Papal forces began to fall back to Rome.

Along the way, the Papal Zouaves fought and gave a heroic resistence; a few days later over 8,500 Papal Soldiers were inside the city ready to lay down their lives for their Pontiff. By September 18, the city was surrounded by over 40,000 Italian soldiers, including a large contingent of Red Shirts who came to wreak havoc on the city. Wanting to avoid further bloodshed and believing that a sufficient show of force had been displayed Bl. Pius IX ordered a "surrender at first cannon shot." General Kanzler petitioned the Pope to allow a greater defense to preserve the honor of his army. Bl. Pius IX was swayed and allowed a defense until "a breach has been opened" in the walls.

The Italian attack on Rome began in the early morning hours on September 20. The Papal Army put up a valiant resistance, taking "a breach in the walls" as loosely as possible. After several hours it became clear that a breach had been made. At 10:00 am Bl. Pius IX ordered the white flag to be flown over St. Peter's Basilica. He turned to the diplomats with him and said "Sirs, I give the order to surrender. Abandoned by all, I had to succumb sooner or later. I must not shed blood uselessly. You are my witnesses, Sirs, that the foreigner enters here only by force."

As the Papal Soldiers marched back to the Vatican to await further instruction, anticlerical and secret society members accosted and even attacked the Papal Soldiers. Over the coming days, some were even murdered, and several churches and convents ransacked and destroyed. The Papal Army spent the night bivouacked in St. Peter's Square. The following morning before the military was disbanded and everyone sent home, the Papal Army had one last formation and a final blessing was given by Bl. Pope Pius IX.

An Irish Papal Zouave, Patrick Keyes O'Clery gave this account of the emotional scene:

> When all the soldiers were lined up, facing the Vatican and ready to leave, Colonel Allet stepped forward and, his voice broken with emotion, shouted: "Mes enfants! Vive Pie Neuf!" A mighty cheer broke out from the troops. Just at that moment the Pope appeared on the balcony, and, raising his hands to heaven, prayed: "May God bless my faithful children!" The enthusiasm of that supreme moment was indescribable. With a frantic Eljen! (Hurrah) a Hungarian Zouave drew his sword, and immediately, with a simultaneous scuff of steel, thousands of unsheathed swords glinted in the sun. The scene was absolutely moving. At the thought of leaving the Holy Father, tears of bitter regret ran down the cheeks of those men who had defied death in so many desperate battles. The trumpets gave the order to advance and, as it moved, the head of the column let out a last sad cry of "Long live Pius IX!" which, echoed row after row, was repeated by the whole army and by the crowd gathered to watch the departure.

The Papal Zouaves were put on a train and sent to Civita Vecchia. Under horrid conditions and lack of food they awaited to board steamers to return home. Thus the thousand year reign of the Papal States was over. The final composition of the regiment truly reflects the international makeup of the Papal Zouaves. The unit consisted of the following nationalities after Rome fell on September 20, 1870. 1,172 Dutch, 760 French, 563 Belgians, 297 Canadians, British, and Irish, 242 Italians from various states on the Peninsula, 113 Germans, 37 Spaniards, 19 Swiss, 15 Austrians, 7 Russians and Poles, 5 Americans, 4 Portuguese, 2 Brazilians, 2

Ecuadorian, 1 Peruvian, 1 Greek, 1 Monacan, 1 Chilean, 1 Ottoman Turk, and 1 Chinese. Not included were some nationalities who had finished service contracts with the unit and either failed to return to Rome before September 20 or had moved onto other things. These include but are not limited to Papal Zouaves from the Maltese, South Sea Islands, India, Africa, Mexico, and Circassia.

Having achieved victory, the new United Kingdom of Italy applied its anti-clerical laws of 1866 to Rome. Bl. Pius IX refused to acknowledge the takeover as legitimate. He considered himself a prisoner in the Vatican and refused to step outside its walls for the rest of his life. General Kanzler in solidarity adopted this same position in solidarity. He retained his title as Minister of War honorarily. Subsequent popes remained as prisoners in the Vatican until the Lateran treaty in 1929 between Pope Pius XI and Mussolini, which formalized the relationship between Italy and the Vatican.

For most of the Papal Zouaves, the fight was over. However, the majority of the French Papal Zouaves continued fighting with the unit as they reorganized under the new name the Volunteers of the West. The Volunteers fought to defend France during the remainder of the Franco-Prussian war. They are most well known for their bravery at the battle of Loigny Patay. On December 2, 1870 General de Sonis and Colonel de Charette led the unit in a 300-man charge against the Bavarians. They initially had the upper hand; however, no other French forces came to reinforce them. Upon realizing their true number, the Bavarians pushed them back. Out of the 300 in the charge, 218 died. Their flag had the image of the Sacred Heart of Jesus with the words, "Heart of Jesus save France." After the war the unit was disbanded. Additionally, in 1873, many Papal Zouave veterans joined the Carlist Zouave Battalion under former Papal Zouave Prince Alfonso de Bourbon during the Third Carlist War. Many of the Papal Zouaves held onto hope that one day they would put on their uniform again and retake the Holy City for their beloved Pope. Unfortunately, these events never came to pass. The Papal Zouaves continued their fight against the Revolution in other ways. Such as through missionary efforts, writing in Catholic publications, participating in government, and starting Catholic businesses.

Theodore Wibaux Pontificual Zouave and Jesuit was written by Charles Marie Emmanuel Du Cöetlosquet S.J. and published by Retaux-Bray in 1885. About 3 years after the death of Theodore and on the 25th anniversary of the regiment. An English translation from the London Catholic Truth Society was published in 1887 with an opening introduction by Richard F. Clarke S.J. A popular Anglican convert at the time. Two French editions with engravings were also published. One by Lefort Lille in 1885 and another by Société de Saint-Augustin, Desclée de Brouwer in 1890. The editor has for the first time, combined the 1887 English translation with the engravings from the French editions in 1885 and 1890.

Additionally, the English version did not originally contain the author's foreword, a poem written by Theodore and letter from General de Charette in chapter 22, and the Epilogue. These have been translated using a mix of ChatGPT and DeepL and included in this new release. The English translation has also been changed to reflect American grammar. For example, words like "colour" have been changed to "color".

Finally, while it may seem redundant to have an editor's preface, introduction, and author's foreword, it was important to add so that the reader would fully appreciate Theodore Wibaux. The editor's preface provided you with the neccesary historical background, the introduction will elaborate on the religious importance of Theodore, and the author's foreword will give you a greater understanding of Theodore himself before embarking into his life.

Please enjoy reading the exploits, heroism, and sacrifice of *Theodore Wibaux Pontifical Zouave and Jesuit* re-published for the first time in over 100 years!

INTRODUCTION.

WE often hear it said that the Society of Jesus is essentially a military body. St. Ignatius had been a soldier, and his early life is said to have given the tone to the Order that he founded. The two leading Meditations in the *Book of the Spiritual Exercises* put before us respectively a warrior king summoning his knights around him, and two standards under each of which men are solicited to enlist. The theory of blind obedience which is considered, not without reason, as one of the foundations of the life of a Jesuit, is supposed to be derived from the kind of obedience owed by the soldier to his chief. But in the modern world what is often, though wrongly, regarded as the military spirit is certainly on the decline. In spite of nations armed to the teeth and compulsory military service, frontiers bristling with cannon, and armies counted by hundreds of thousands if not by millions, soldiering is not in fashion now-a-days as it used to be. The commercial spirit has encountered it and vanquished it. Men do not fight for fighting's sake, or lead a soldier's life all their days out of pure love of it. Dueling has gone out of fashion. The military profession is no longer regarded, as it once was, as the only profession worthy of men of high rank. The once despised leech now finds his place in the best society. Nay, the vulgarity which was supposed to attach to trade is fast disappearing, and to be at the head of a large house of business is almost as influential a position as to command a regiment.

It is true that many whose opinions deserve all respect lament this remarkable change which is transforming modern society.

They tell us that the days of chivalry are gone forever: that selfishness rules modern society, that religion, morality, courtesy, culture, the higher education, are disappearing from the world, and that the sordid meanness of the bourgeois spirit is succeeding to the noble, fearless, self-sacrificing generosity of the mediæval knight. This melancholy regret for the days gone by will not stand the test of a careful study of history. We are all inclined to idealize the past. The heroes of chivalry live in the records of their time, but the lawless freebooter, the paid assassin, the oppressor of the poor, the "soldier of fortune," fade away from the memory of ordinary men. If we have lost some heroes, we have, through God's mercy, made the oppressor of mediæval days almost an impossibility. If the poorer class are more independent of their betters, we ought not to grudge them an independence which is a certain recognition of the equality of all men before God our Lord. If our cities are unfavorable to morality, it is not so much because they are large cities, as because they have grown up under the upas-tree of Protestantism. There is many a country village in England which is more degraded than London or New York.

The material conditions of life have improved and are continually improving, and material improvement is a great aid to social and moral advance. When the crowded lodging house, or the hovel where all the family have to sleep in one room, is exchanged for a comfortable cottage, where sanitary regulations ensure sufficient space and enforce the rules of decency, there ensues a very substantial gain to the morality of the inmates.

All this change is mainly the outcome of the growth of commerce, of the commercial spirit, and of the advance in the average intelligence of mankind that has accompanied it. Is it true that this spirit has ousted the military spirit? We do not believe it has really done so. If it had, the spirit of enterprise would be on the wane, whereas it was never more alive than it is now. If it had, men would not be as brave as of yore, whereas we find that the hearts of oak are firm and bold as ever. If it had, England would not have a military organization of tens of thousands of her citizen volunteers, who when their hours of business are over, sacrifice their recreation time to a tedious drill in order to become efficient soldiers, and who in some hour of need hereafter will prove an invaluable addition to her regular army. If it had, America would never have waged the war which destroyed slavery, and in which the sons of commerce fought with a courage which will bear comparison with the renowned exploits of the past. If it had, the Jesuits with their intensely military spirit would find themselves out of harmony with modern life, whereas even their enemies acknowledge their power to advance, *pari passu* (equal footing), with the advancing tide of the cultured civilization of the present century.

The fact is that there is no serious decay in the military spirit. It has only taken another form: its obedience, its organization, its dependence on its chief, its sacrifice of the individual, has assumed a new shape, it has clad itself in a different dress. It has adapted itself to the new civilization. It has not been driven out by the developments of industry and the advance of science; it has changed the paludamentum for the toga, the military for the civil robe. Commerce, so far from proving its enemy, has wedded itself to it and produced a healthy offspring. What has really died out of modern life is not the *military* but the *soldiering* spirit. It is the demoralizing life of the camp which is at a discount, it is the violence, the roughness, the fierceness, the brutality of the forced or hireling service of the middle ages which are gone and gone forever. Our indifference to the sufferings of others has disappeared: the judge no longer watches unmoved the torture of the prisoner who will not confess his guilt. No modern English mob would gloat over the sufferings of brave men, as did too many a mob over the sufferings of the English Martyrs under Henry VIII. and Elizabeth. Few nobles and magistrates of the present day would disgrace their nobility and their high office by the baseness, the cupidity, the wanton cruelty, the dishonesty, the hatred of all that is good, that appears in the corrupt and servile members of the Elizabethan Court.

But while the abuses of military life have disappeared, the true virtues which characterized it are not really lost in the present day. The great trading firms are the regiments of our modern armies. In the manner of their life there is room for most of the true military virtues, save perhaps that form of courage which does not shrink from instant pain or death. Nay, many of the important virtues of the soldier are equally necessary in modern commerce—the promptness in fulfilling commands, the exactitude of unquestioning obedience, the conformity to a strict discipline, the pliable temper which can adapt itself to new circumstances and unexpected contingencies, the persevering refusal tosuffer defeat, the punctuality, the self-command, the courtesy, the subjection, are as indispensable in the factory or workshop as in the camp, in the busy hive of commerce as in the fitful activity of warfare. It is not that certain virtues are dead—they have but changed their shape, and have gained, not lost, by casting their old skin.

This will explain to us why the Society of Jesus, while it clings to the chivalry of mediæval days, is nevertheless intensely modern, and adapts itself so kindly to modern civilization. Its members take a prominent part now, as ever, not only in Catholic philosophy and theology, but also in scientific research and discovery. It is as much at home in the factory of Manchester or Cincinnati as it was on the battlefield of Sadowa or before the walls of Metz. The virtues it cultivates, which are the super natural counterpart of the virtues which are supposed to be characteristic of the soldier, adapt themselves to modern life, just as the corresponding natural virtues transfer themselves from the camp to the house of business.

It may be thought that, if Jesuits are so essentially soldiers who do battle for their faith, a previous military training would have disposed him who had passed through it to enlist in the spiritual army of the sons of St. Ignatius. But in point of fact it is not so: the proportion of those who have been soldiers is no larger in the ranks of the Society ofJesuits than the proportion of lawyers or doctors or men of business. Nor is this difficult to explain, for the obedience to a military chief is essentially an external obedience, whereas the obediencerequired of a Jesuit is essentially and above all an internal obedience of intellect and will. The soldier may go on for years in grumbling insubordination against his captain, so long as he outwardly obeys his commands, whereas a soldier of the Society of Jesus will soon drop out of the ranks, and will have to resign his commission, unless he joins to the outward performance of the will of the Superior the inner submission, the willing subordination without which obedience scarce deserves the name. An old soldier, who had tried his vocation in the Jesuit novitiate and had failed, was once asked how it was that he, who had been trained from boyhood to obey implicitly his colonel, had been unable to obey his Religious Superior. "When my colonel ordered me to do what I disliked," was the reply, "I could come away and vent my indignation, not only in secret grumbling, but in open denunciation of his injustice among my fellow-officers. When my Religious Superior gave an unpalatable command, I was expected not only to perform it in silent acquiescence but with a willing mind."

There is another very important point of distinction between the military government and that of the Society founded by St. Ignatius. Military government necessarily is an absolute and despotic rule, whereas the government of the Society of Jesus is essentially paternal. The Jesuit Superior is bound to carry those subject to him in his heart, to nurse them, so to speak, with tender affection. His relation to them is modeled on that of a father to his children, not on that of a general or colonel to his soldiers. It is essentially based on love. The obedience of the subject is a willing obedience. There is nopunishment for disobedience save one, to have to leave the service. Next to serious sin, the Jesuit considers that dismissal from the army of St. Ignatius is the greatest possible misfortune that could happen to him. A story is told of some visitor who inquired of St. Ignatius where was the prison in which refractory young Jesuits were, after the fashion of the other religious orders of the time, punished for misbehavior. St. Ignatius conducted the stranger down a long corridor, at the end of which was a heavy door all bolted and barred. When the bars had been removed and the bolts drawn and the door thrown. open, the astonished visitor beheld before him-not a dark cell, but the open street! "There," said the Saint," is our prison. A Jesuit unworthy of his high vocation goes out by the back door."

Those, therefore, who speak of the army of St. Ignatius as an essentially military organization, need to explain their words. It is military in its obedience, in the willingness of individuals to lay down their lives for the good cause, in its intimate union with and dependence on its commander-in chief, in its power of rapid mobilization, in its careful subordination of rank to rank.

But it exacts an obedience far deeper than that of the soldier, and on the other hand it lacks the despotic element which necessarily accompanies military rule. But there is a body of modern soldiers who of their very nature have more of the military spirit in its best sense than is to be found in the ordinary soldier. The Papal Zouaves were no mere hirelings, no army of conscripts, no adventurers whose minds were bent on pillage or on violence. They were men who served from an intense love of the cause for which they fought, of the august and venerable Chief who was at the same time the Sovereign of their little army and the Sovereign of all Christendom. Hence their spirit. was no mere spirit of soldiering, it was a spirit of unselfish devotion, it was a spirit of sacrifice to the cause of Jesus Christ. They left home and friends and country to enlist under a Government that was despised and unpopular in the eyes of the world, as it was of old when the mob shouted out in pretended loyalty to their oppressor, "We will have no King but Cæsar!" in order that they might wreak their insane hatred of Him Who was their Saviour, their Captain, and their King. As we might have naturally expected, of the Papal Zouaves not a few earned by their service under the Holy See the far greater privilege of serving during the rest of their lives one or other of the Religious Orders of the Church. Many of them while on service manifested the self-sacrificing forgetfulness of their own comfort and their own safety, in the chivalrous spirit of charity to the poor and the distressed which is regarded as the distinguishing mark of the active Religious Orders. While the cholera was raging at Rome they worked in the hospitals, and nursed the sick with the tenderness and devotion of Sisters of Charity. Their loyalty to the Holy See was worthy of those Religious who take a special vow of obedience to the Pope wherever he may send them, and in whatever duties he may choose to employ them. Their fidelity to their chief, the noble and brave General De Charette, was not the mere external obedience of the ordinary soldier, but more nearly resembled that internal submission of will and judgment which St. Ignatius puts forward as the characteristic of the true Jesuit. Their life was in many respects a difficult one, it had many dangers and many temptations. But it was of its Own nature a life of supernatural heroism, and required of those who lived it as they ought a very high standard of supernatural charity.

From the ranks of the Pontifical Zouaves to the ranks of the Jesuits was therefore a very appropriate transference. The Zouaves fought for the Pope with strong arms and dashing courage, the Jesuits with the higher gifts of cultivated intellects and a self devotion which no one has ever denied them, but which their adversaries have turned into a cause of reproach against them. The Zouaves kept guard over the material interests of the Church, the work of the Jesuits is to further by tongue and pen her spiritual interests; the Zouaves were the objects of the hatred and misrepresentations of the enemies of the Church, so too are the Jesuits.

But the interest of the present memoir does not lie only in the fact that its subject was first Pontifical Zouave and then Jesuit. Let us see what it is that gives its special attractiveness to the life of Theodore Wibaux.

The first point that occurs to us as worthy of remark is that it is a life full of encouragement to the reader. Many religious biographies are rather depressing from the impression they give that the life that we are pursuing is something altogether beyond our level. We may admire the lofty virtue, the absence of faults and foibles and of the ordinary weaknesses of humanity, but this very absence has a disheartening tendency. We are painfully impressed,with our own utter inferiority, and sometimes in a way that produces a feeling of depression rather than the virtue of humility. We are inclined to wish that the holy person whose life we are reading were a little more human. We feel that such persons appeal to our admiration rather than encourage us to imitation. We read how they never slept more than three hours, and that in a sitting posture, and we think how we cannot get along without seven or eight, lying in our comfortable beds; or that their minds were constantly fixed on God, and we reflect how we too often forget Him for long hours at a stretch, and we come to the conclusion that we can never do more than reverence them from a distance.

But Theodore Wibaux was not one of this sort. He was not what we should call a model child, but full of fun and mischief. In his youth he had a fierce battle with temptation. "I am now eighteen," he writes (Feb. 12, 1867), "an age when the passions are strong and many a hard conflict has to be fought," and though God's mercy kept him safe, yet he himself acknowledges that he had terrible battles to sustain, and that he was often on the very brink of shameful defeat. Theodore is no ascetic, indifferent to the innocent pleasures of sense, or to the harmless gaieties of a soldier's life. He entered into them with zest, and enjoyed the amusements around him and the good things of this world that fell in his way.

In his manhood, when the voice of God called him to enter the Society of Jesus, he almost turned aside at the last moment. The light-hearted young soldier dreaded the loss of external liberty and the restraint of religious life, and it was so to speak by a hair's breadth that the victory was won. These narrow escapes, these traits of our common nature, these partial failures, make him one with us who are still inclined to enjoy the world, or who have to fight and struggle against some temptation or other all our lives long. They encourage us in our conflicts, and we say to ourselves "If Theodore gained a glorious victory, why not I?"

The second point which strikes us is the wonderful chain of graces that accompanied him through all his dangers and temptations. He was one of those happy souls of whom we are tempted to say that they are pre-ordained to eternal life, and that God has determined that they shall carry out the plan He has chosen for them, come what may. As we read the various incidents of the biography of Theodore Wibaux, we cannot help saying to ourselves: What strong graces he had, even from the first! Like all good men, he owed them, under God, to his mother's piety, and her influence was perhaps the greatest grace of all. All through his life, when his fate was trembling in the balance, and it seemed an even chance whether God or the devil prevailed, the necessary grace, nay, the efficacious grace, was sure to make its appearance at the proper moment, and to decide the battle in favor of virtue and of right.

The third point, and it is perhaps the most striking of all, is the love of Theodore for our Blessed Lady and the fostering care and tender love she showed for him in return. "Notre Dame de l'Escalier," who stood on a landing near the entrance hall of his father's house, took the child under her protectionand kept him there through all the vicissitudes and dangers that befell him; to her he was entrusted by his mother when he went forth to fight for the Holy See. Our Lady shielded him in temptation and in danger; our Lady brought him safely home; our Lady obtained for him the grace of enlisting in the army of St. Ignatius; our Lady watched over his dying bed. "Every evening," he writes in one of his letters from Rome, "I find rest and refreshment at the close of the day, often one of sharp conflict, at the feet of the Blessed Virgin." In the novitiate his last waking thought was the thought of Mary. "I am resolved," he says in a letter to his mother, "to cling to a fold of Mary's mantle till my latest breath," and again, "I am over head and ears in debt to the Blessed Virgin."

No wonder that so devout a client of Mary passed unscathed through all the dangers to soul and body to which he was exposed, that he escaped the daggers of Italy's revolutionists, and fought without a scratch at Monte Rotondo and Mentana. No wonder that his innocence and simplicity suffered nothing from the ordeal of a soldier's life, or that they found a fitting home at last in the Society of Mary's Son. Truly could Theodore say of the Queen of Wisdom what the Wise Man in Holy Scripture says of wisdom itself: "Forsake her not, and she shall keep thee; love her, and she shall preserve thee. (Prov. iv. 6.)"

We need say nothing in recommendation of this biography. It recommends itself by the varied incidents of a career pursued amid important events and stirring scenes of the last half century; by the simple and easy style in which the book is written. It is a book which those of every age will find attractive. Boys and girls and men and women will read with interest and with profit the story of this brave, loyal, devoted soldier of Jesus Christ.

R. F. CLARKE.

AUTHORS FOREWARD.

To you, my brother Théodore, the honor of these pages; they are yours in a double sense, for you are both the hero and the author.

Yes, everything good that they contain came from your pen, so full of spirit, candor, and youth, or rather from your heart as a loyal son and a Christian.

So much so that, on the day of your departure for a better world, you left nothing to be done for whoever would be tasked with bringing such a treasure to light.

Nothing to do!... except, perhaps, to arrange things a little, to preserve the best of what is excellent, to cut out, alas! many delightful things that make up the charm your daily correspondence, but which would go beyond the scope of a work like this one.

Ah! I now understand the art of the jeweler who, to make an ornament, must choose from a hundred precious stones; I understand his hesitation before such riches, his regrets in the face of the jewels he must sacrifice, his perplexity in deciding which setting to adopt.

And when his work is finished, he cannot help but feel a sense of sadness, for he had envisioned another ideal.... At least, he consoles himself by saying: "My stones are so beautiful that they will make the jeweler forgotten."

This too is my consolation.

May your book perpetuate on earth your apostolate, which was so short but so fruitful; may it prolong the gentle influence of your zeal!

May it teach young people not to extinguish the pure flame of devotion, kindled by God Himself in the hearts of twenty-year-olds. may it give them courage in the fight, showing them how to triumph.

May it remind your comrades-in-arms of the glorious days of that Regiment, where heroism was, in a way, part of the uniform, where everyone's ambition was to suffer for the Church and to die for God.

May it console your family, justly proud of you, as one is proud of all that is beautiful, pure, and great.

Finally, may it reveal to your brothers in religion the riches that the treasure of your humility concealed, and assure them that you are both a model here below and a protector above!

C. DU COËTLOSQUET, S.J.

July 28, 1885.

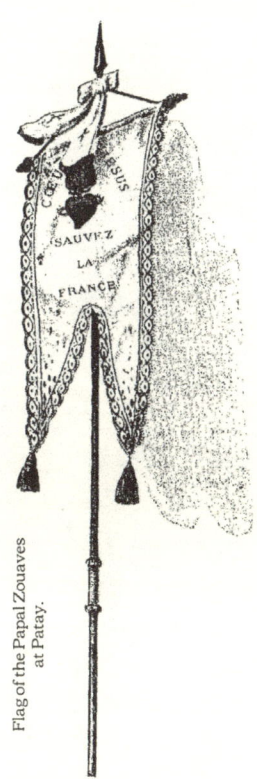

Flag of the Papal Zouaves at Patay.

I, the author declare that I comply filially with the decrees of the Holy See regarding the titles of saint, martyr, and other similar terms, which are used in this work according to their common meaning, and not in any way to preempt the judgment of the Church.

                      C. DU COËTLOSQUET, S.J.

CHAPTER I.
1849—1864.

Theodore's early days. Family gatherings under the grandparents' roof. His faults. His love of teasing. His good qualities. His mother's influence. Schooldays. Holidays. Boyish pranks. The archery club. His favorite brother. The death of little Francis.

THEODORE was born at Roubaix on February 13, 1849. He was named after his uncle and godfather, M. l'Abbé Théodore Wibaux, who spent his strength and laid down his life as a missionary in Cochin-China. Theodore—gift of God—what a responsibility for those who are thus called, if they consider the deep meaning of the word! Neither in the case of the uncle nor in that of the nephew was the name a mere empty one, for the former was truly a gift of God to the heathen, and the latter was not less so to his companions in arms, first in the regiment of Papal Zouaves, and afterwards in the spiritual army of St. Ignatius.

The family of which Theodore was a member was essentially

a Christian family. An atmosphere of religion and piety breathed throughout this happy household; the parents strove to train up in the knowledge and love of God the numerous offspring wherewith He had blessed them, and the children learned to honor and obey their Heavenly Father in the person of those who were for them His representatives on earth.

On a landing, near the entrance hall, stood a large statue of the Mother of God—*Our Lady of the Staircase,* as it was called—and she might almost have been denominated the Lady of the House. On the recurrence of each joyous festival or mournful anniversary, in the hour of grief or the time of gladness, on the departure of any member of the household or his return after a temporary absence, both parents and children might be seen kneeling at the feet of their common Mother, acquainting her with their happiness, or asking her to share in the sorrow it had pleased Providence to lay upon them.

Every Sunday was a feast day, a day of rejoicing as the Lord's day ought to be, when business was suspended and cares were laid aside, according to the custom in manufacturing towns in the north of France. The looms of the factory owned by M. Wibaux stood still, the busy shuttle ceased its hum, the workrooms were deserted by the numerous hands in his employ; and when the morning services were over, there was a family *réunion,* sometimes at Roubaix, sometimes at Tourcoing, where their maternal grandparents, M. and Mme. Motte, resided. From thirty to forty children and grandchildren used to gather round the table for the midday meal, which was invariably preceded by the *Benedicite,* said aloud. Before dessert, M. Motte was accustomed to take off his silken skull-cap; everybody knew the signal and instantly stopped speaking, and if a stranger, unacquainted with the habits of the family, happened to be present, the master of the house would simply say to him: "We always recite the Litany of our Lady now," and then Mme. Motte forthwith began.

It would be absurd to pretend that the juvenile part of the company, at least, had not manifold distractions during these prayers; at a later period Theodore has been heard to own that while the Litanies were being said, many a time he ran his eye over the delicacies spread out before him, and made up his mind as to what he would choose from amongst them. Perhaps it was rather tantalizing for the poor children, but if in very natural impatience, they almost unconsciously hurried over the responses, and uttered them somewhat indistinctly, M. Motte would stop short, and recall the wandering attention of his little flock by slowly articulating in clear, ringing accents: *"Pray—for—us!"*

When the Litanies were ended, those children who were too young to dine with their elders were allowed to come into the room; suddenly a number of rosy little faces made their appearance amongst the guests, putting up their cheeks to be kissed, and asserting their claim to a share in the cake.

Happy household in which, as in the ages of faith, Christian traditions were preserved in all their purity! Fortunate children, who needed not to look beyond their home-circle for relaxation and recreation! Now indeed the grandparents are dead, but the same memories still survive in the hearts of their descendants, or rather they have passed into action, and thus this ideal of family life is perpetuated and handed on.

How would it have fared with little Theodore if his lot had been cast amongst less pious surroundings? In him the beneficial effect of a religious education is strikingly exemplified, since his character was very far from faultless. Self-willed and wayward, he thought his every caprice must be gratified, and if thwarted, he manifested his displeasure by stamping on the floor, and striking the furniture with his fist. One day when something was refused him, he exclaimed: "When I grow up, I will be an Emperor or the Pope, then I shall be able to do just as I choose!"

At the same time, however, his warmth of heart and extreme sensitiveness to reproof, rendered caution necessary in correcting him, for if he saw that he had seriously displeased his parents, he was overwhelmed with despair, so much so that when they had done scolding, they had to comfort him. He was too a very nervous child, and would run away in alarm at the sight of a gun or the sound of a drum.

But the worst fault of all was his inveterate love of teasing his brothers and sisters, especially the ones who disliked it most, for he did not care to waste his efforts on those who were comparatively indifferent to his attacks: it is in human nature to love to strike where it can wound most deeply. Reproofs and chastisements for this conduct were freely administered, but when Mme. Wibaux scolded him, the child would run up to her and put his little hand before her mouth, exclaiming: "No, Mamma, please say no more, I will never tease anyone again." Or sometimes he would anticipate the chiding which he felt he had richly deserved, and openly rebuke himself: "Naughty Theodore! for shame, bad boy! you have vexed Mamma. O Mamma, you will never be able to forget it, and overlook what I have done wrong!" What mother's heart could refuse pardon to such an appeal?

But there were days when gentle means were ineffectual, and stronger measures had to be resorted to in order to curb Theodore's wayward temper. Then M. Wibaux appeared on the scene, and the paternal authority speedily reduced the little rebel to silence and submission.

When Mme. Wibaux took her four eldest boys out, Theodore was the only one who gave her any trouble, indeed she used to say that he alone caused her more uneasiness than all the other three; she continually had to warn him not to give way to his besetting sin, to make him promise to be good if she foresaw that he would be in danger of temptation; but when once the promise was given, she knew she could depend on him, for he was never known to break his word.

One day, however, he had carried his teasing too far, and it was needful to administer a punishment that he would really feel The children were in the habit of presenting themselves to receive their parents' blessing every night before retiring to rest; this was an old custom in the family, and a truly Christian custom, which seemed to shed a ray of supernatural light upon the closing day. That evening, when Theodore in his turn approached, the accustomed benison was denied him; he expostulated, but in vain, he had behaved too badly, he did not deserve his parents' blessing, and was dismissed without another word. The poor child, conscious of his fault, withdrew in tears; but how could he pass the night in disgrace, or sleep with such a burden on his mind? He returned sobbing to the door of his mother's room and remained there a whole hour begging to be forgiven." Mother, I will not go away till you pardon me and give me your blessing; I know I was very naughty; pray do forgive me." Touched by his perseverance, Mme. Wibaux at length gave way, and the experience of that evening taught Theodore what is meant by prayer.

It was owing to the watchful care Mme. Wibaux exercised over her son—a care repaid by the most devoted affection on his part—that she was enabled during his childhood to control and direct his somewhat unmanageable character, whilst the hold she thus obtained over him proved in after life the greatest safeguard to his ardent and impetuous nature. Who indeed could withstand this excellent mother, or resist the thousand little devices her ingenious piety invented? How often one or another of the children found at night by his or her bedside a little note dictated by her thoughtful love, and containing words such as these: "Dear child, remember to say a prayer to our Lady before you go to sleep.—Have you often thought of God during the past day?—Be sure not to forget the coming festival. "Or if the morrow was a day of Communion, she would go from room to room, and read some sentences from the *Imitation*, in order that at this time above all others her children's latest thought, as well as their first moment of waking consciousness, should be given to God.

The number of children wherewith Providence had blessed the union and rejoiced the hearts of M. and Mme. Wibaux was thirteen; but in this fragrant *parterre* He had reserved some flowers for His special use. Some were transplanted, ere their buds were unfolded, to blossom in the heavenly garden; others later on were removed to expand in the sheltering shade of the cloister. Thus this favored family lacked neither protectors in Heaven nor intercessors upon earth; the former were those who were early admitted to the angelic choirs, the latter those who consecrated themselves to God by the vows of religion.

On one point Theodore's character appears strangely paradoxical, and we are inclined to ask how it is possible to reconcile the mischievous delight he took in tormenting others with the extreme kind-heartedness of which he constantly gave proof. The enigma would be difficult of solution were it not that the contradictory qualities we daily meet with in children afford a key to the problem. At any rate, it is undeniable that he was fondly attached to the very persons whom he selected as his victims, and although quarrels with his playmates were very frequent, and some times so serious as to render reconciliation apparently im possible, Theodore was always ready to make the first advances, and five minutes later all was ended with a hearty embrace, both parties being the better friends for the temporary estrangement.

When seven and a half years old he was sent together with his brother Joseph, who was his senior by one year, to the day-school at Roubaix. The little fellow was put in the ninth class; the first step must always be on the lowest round of the ladder. Theodore was not naturally studious; he loved to run wild, to scamper about in the open air, and play all manner of pranks; restraint of every kind was irksome to him; he would never put himself out for any one, and when anything good was to be had he would appropriate the lion's share, as if it were his right. But a laudable pride impelled him to exert himself; by no means indifferent to success, and conscious of his own powers, he had no intention of leaving the first places to be taken by others. Without the stimulus of this healthful emulation he would very probably have trusted, as boys so often do, too much to his own abilities, and would never have risen above mediocrity, the miserable portion of many a young man who flatters himself that talent without application will carry him through.

Thanks to diligent and assiduous *study,* Theodore got on so well that he was almost always at the head of his class; during the eight years he attended the day-school at Roubaix, he gained no less than twenty-seven prizes and thirty-one *accessits,*[*] a harvest he might well be proud of, the more so as the *prix d'excellence*[**] was invari-

---

[*]   Honorable mention.

[**]   Prize awarded to the top student in a class.

ably awarded him. And yet he never seemed vain of his triumphs, nor did he betray the slightest jealousy towards a more successful rival. To be first was, it is true, always his aim, but he bore no ill-will towards those who outstript him in the race; he was not conceited as to his own powers, and consequently was ready to acknowledge the superiority of others. On one occasion after the distribution of prizes, when he was returning home laden with books and wreaths, he begged one of his brothers to relieve him of a portion of this welcome load, in order that persons who saw them go by might think that the honors had been equally divided between the two boys.

Sundays and Thursday afternoons were holidays, and the freedom of home life seemed all the more delightful when it was no longer an every-day matter. M. Wibaux's house was open to all his boys' school-fellows, and the large garden attached to it attracted many visitors. Sometimes as many as thirty friends would assemble there on Thursday afternoons, turning the place upside down with their noisy mirth. Nothing was wanting to contribute to their enjoyment; ample space for their games, a large lawn, spreading trees, not to speak of the high spirits of the merry lads themselves, and last, not least, a wide expanse of blue sky overhead, no small boon in the midst of a town bristling with tall factory chimneys.

"My dear garden!" Theodore wrote after he had become a Zouave. "I never can think of it without affection; indeed the tears often come into my eyes when I recall the pleasant memories of my childhood connected with it. I remember how I used to like to see my dear father and mother looking so happy as they sat chatting together under the trees. Even now whenever I hear the bells out in the open air I think of our garden. Do you remember the Easter eggs? What fun that was! And the noisy romps we had with our school-fellows, and the. afternoons spent in the company of our chosen friends. "God grant we may meet again one day in the gardens of Paradise!"

"The Wibaux always made us welcome at their house," writes one of their former school-fellows. "There was an air of hearty friendliness about it, and one always felt better for having been there." No one could resist the influence of that happy home. Mme. Wibaux showed gentle motherly kindness to all her guests; M.

Wibaux made himself one with his boys, willingly joining in their sports and sharing in their pleasures. The eldest son, Willebaud, occupied a position between parents and children; he was four years older than Theodore, and at the close of a brilliant career at college, had become his father's right hand, and exercised a sort of paternal authority over the younger members of the household, a position which might have been invidious, had not his authority been exerted with affection and judgment. He was consulted by his elders and gave advice to his juniors, and no one thought of calling in question what he said.

It will readily be imagined that in all the merry games of which his father's garden was the theater, Theodore was the life of the party, for, although there was always about him a certain awkwardness of manner which he himself was ready to acknowledge and to join in ridiculing, he excelled in every kind of active sport. The originality of his tastes too, distinguished him from the generality of boys, still more so the wonderful aptitude he possessed for finding out occasions of making a good hit, or playing some ingenious trick. The neighbors learnt this to their cost, not to speak of the masqueraders in carnival time, on whom the frolicsome school-boys used to shower down a perfect hailstorm of pellets of hard clay, their greatest delight being to observe that the clowns and harlequins were quite at fault as to the quarter whence the annoying missiles proceeded.

If he thought matters looked threatening, Theodore exercised great discretion as to his own share in the mis chief, whilst he urged the others on, trusting to his long legs to get him out of a scrape. One day, in order to take reprisals for something or other a neighbor had done to offend the boys, Theodore suggested that the gate of his poultry-yard should be set open, thus giving free egress to sundry rabbits and chickens, who lost no time in availing themselves of the opportunity afforded them of disporting themselves amongst the flower-beds. The instigator of this malicious act meanwhile posted himself on the wall, holding a ladder whereby to ensure the speedy and safe retreat of the messenger whom he had charged with the execution of the errand. Shortly after the door-bell sounded; a servant brought a letter addressed to M. Wibaux. The culprits were on the watch and they undertook to deliver the letter. It is needless to say that it never reached its destination, and the complaints of the irate owner of the poultry-yard did not meet M. Wibaux' eye.

Amongst the favorite sports archery held the foremost place, and the cousins of Roubaix and Tourcoing, desirous to give definiteness to their meetings for its practice, determined to form a club. A dozen members were soon found, then a president had to be chosen; it was agreed that this office should be the prize of the best marksman, and should be open to general competition. Theodore carried off the palm, and was duly installed as president of the new club, which was called by the name of St. Sebastian, the special patron of archers.

This little society existed for several years. Tourcoing and Roubaix, rivals in days of yore in the archery-field, revived their ancient antagonism, and the cousins merged the ties of kindred in their anxiety to maintain the credit of their respective townships. The Tourcoing party being more numerous, naturally scored more points, and shouts of Hurrah for Tourcoing! rent the air. Then Theodore would encourage his side to make greater efforts, and a victory for Roubaix would be the signal for fresh cheers. On St. Sebastian's day this modern guild of archers, like their medieval forerunners, devoutly heard Mass, and afterwards met in solemn assembly, when the youthful president gravely delivered an address, and all present joined in singing some verses expressly composed and set to music for the guild by one of his uncles, M. Pierre Motte.

When examination-time approached, Theodore knew that in order to gain, as he was ambitious of doing, the prize for memory, he must put his shoulder vigorously to the wheel; but then it would be necessary to sacrifice to extra work the happy hours of recreation, and this he was not prepared to do. How could a compromise be effected? Ever fertile in expedients, he bethought himself of a plan, namely, that of inviting all those amongst his comrades whom he considered as formidable rivals to join in the Thursday afternoon sports, and thus prevent them from spending their free time in study. If they accepted, there was no reason for Theodore to curtail the period usually devoted to pastimes, since he was confident that his great facility in learning would give him the advantage over his school-fellows. But if so much as one refused, neither the attractions of a game at "prisoner's base," of a pleasant walk, nor of the society of his friends, could tempt him to leave his room; the whole of Sundays and Thursday afternoons were then given up to study, and even some hours of the night, too, for he would sit up late and rise early, feeling he could not enjoy himself freely in the playground or sleep quietly in his bed, while he knew that a more studious competitor was preparing to snatch the coveted prize from his grasp.

Not unfrequently on holidays, yielding to his love of liberty and of the open air, he would start the first thing in the morning for a long country ramble, carrying with him, after the example of laborers, a homely but substantial lunch, in order to enjoy to the full the pure air and the exhilarating sense of perfect freedom. Or still better, he would take with him his little brothers, Léon and Francis, who were only too proud to be permitted to accompany their big brother *Todore*, as they called him.

Francis was the Benjamin of the family, and Theodore's especial friend and favorite; indeed, no one could help loving the little fellow, with his curious old-fashioned ways, and his decided character, so unlike a child of his tender years. One day he had heard a great deal about the soldiers in garrison at Lille; without saying a word, he left the house, and set off walking down the street with an air of great determination. Someone who was sent after him, asked him where he was going? "To Lille," he replied, "where the soldiers are." On another occasion he saw a boy much bigger than himself being beaten, and instantly, forgetful of his diminutive size and puny strength, he threw himself on the one who appeared to be making unjust use of his superior power. If at meal times Theodore began to tease either of the others by throwing at him tiny balls of bread-crumb, little Francis would clamber down from his high chair, and with the most resolute mien, place himself in front of the one who was thus assailed, with outstretched arms trying to protect him from the missiles aimed at him. His chief happiness was to listen to the music in church, and he was often heard singing the melodies to himself in an undertone when alone at play. He was like a little robin, always merry, always warbling, giving pleasure to all around him.

But alas! Léon fell ill with a quinsy sore throat, and the two unseparable friends had to be separated. Francis, who could not understand the reason of this, managed to elude the vigilance of the nurse, and ran to throw his arms round Léon's neck. "Surely I may kiss my own little brother!" he exclaimed, as he was hastily removed from the room. This affectionate embrace did its fatal work; almost immediately he was attacked by the same malady, which turned to croup, and in a short time his life was despaired of. The little fellow himself was aware that his days were numbered: "I am going to die," he said, "and they will put me into the ground, but I shall not stay there, I shall go at once to Heaven to see God." Being thirsty he asked for something to drink, "something nice," as he used to have when he was out with Theodore. It had been the habit of the big brother, on occasion of their long walks, to have some lemonade by way of refreshment for himself and his little companion, and what made it doubly delicious to the latter, he used to pour it into a large glass for Francis, that he might "do just like Theodore." A similar beverage was therefore brought at the request of the sick child; he sipped it, and then said: "It tasted much nicer when *Todore* gave it me."

On All Saints' day, during the High Mass, just as the first words of the *Gloria* were being sung, Francis' innocent soul winged its flight to Heaven, to rejoin Jean and Angèle, a brother and sister who had both died in infancy, and mingle his voice with theirs in the joyous strains of a never-ending *Gloria*.

Shortly before this, Theodore, with his brother Joseph, had been sent to school at Marcq, near Lille. How he counted on the first holiday when he should be allowed to go home, and see his dear little Francis again! A long walk had already been planned for the day, which was to be spent in playing, singing, and talking together. Instead of this, M. Wibaux went himself to break the sad news of their brother's death to the two boys. They shed many tears: Theodore especially seemed at first as if he could not submit to this trial, it was too hard to think he should never see Francis again! But the faith and resignation of the Christian Father suggested consolations fitted to soften "the grief of his sorrowing children, and two days later, Theodore and Joseph went over to Roubaix to be present at the joyous songs of the Mass of the Angels. To their regret they found that they were not allowed to see their little brother again, since for fear of contagion, they were forbidden to enter the room where his mortal remains were laid; they therefore, by means of a ladder, climbed upon a wall, whence a view of the apartment could be obtained, and Mme. Wibaux wheeled the crib, all decked and wreathed with flowers, close to the window, in order that the brothers might have the mournful pleasure of gazing once more on the beloved features of their darling. In their name she silently pressed her lips once more to his cold cheek, then, raising her eyes, she pointed upwards to the Heaven whither he had gone; a touching tableau, which M. Wibaux witnessed amid fast-flowing tears.

As soon as Theodore had heard the sad tidings, he had written to comfort his mother. In imagination he already saw his little brother entering the regions of eternal bliss, and in his letter he expressed his gratitude to God on that account. "We ought to bless God's Holy Name for having vouchsafed to take Francis to be an angel, we ought even to sing songs of thanksgiving. . . still I cannot restrain my tears when I think of the dear little fellow. He often talked to me of God and of Heaven, and often asked me whether God always did what was right. Since I cannot have the melancholy satisfaction of giving him a parting embrace, I will offer to our Lord the additional pang this costs me; and I have charged my good Angel with my last messages to my sweet little brother.

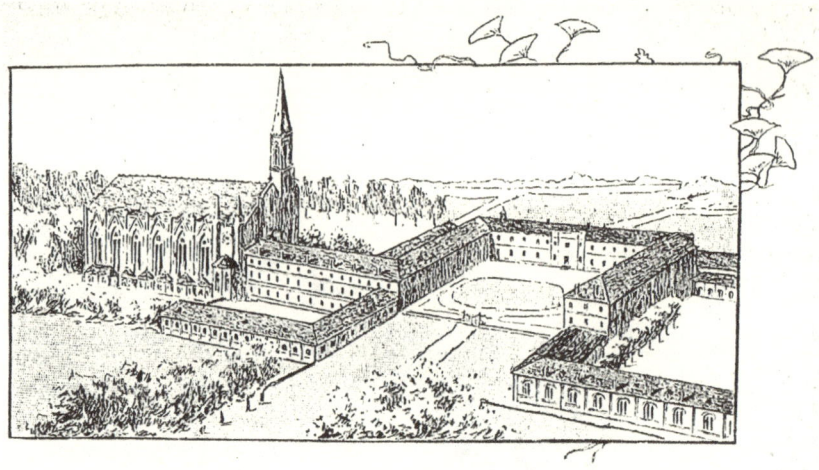

CHAPTER II.

1864—1866.

Theodore a Collegian at Marcq. The prizes he gains. A visit to the Redemptorists. Rome and the September Convention. His desire to become a Zouave. Struggles and sacrifices. Weary waiting. Louis Veuillot is appealed to. The last evening at home.

THE training Theodore received at the College of Marcq, where he was sent to reside as a boarder, with a view to the completion of his education, was well calculated to carry out what was already begun, and to form his character; to finish in a word, the solid Christian education so happily commenced under the parental roof. The heads of the College did not merely desire to form accomplished scholars and good Christians, they further aimed at training Apostles, and with this object encouraged their pupils to take an active part in works of charity.

Theodore at once requested to be admitted into the Confraternity of the Blessed Virgin, and also to be allowed to become a member of the Conference of St. Vincent of Paul, which latter had this advantage, namely that the charitable works connected with it were entirely managed by the pupils themselves, the feeling of responsibility thus imparting to everything a double interest. Our student gave every penny of his pocket-money to the poor, and by this free handed proceeding constantly left himself with an absolutely empty purse; nor did the gentle remonstrances which were addressed to him ever avail to restrain his lavish generosity with regard to the needy. When he met poor children on the country roads, he used to question them, make them repeat their prayers, and then recompense them with a gift of money; sometimes he would make them run a race, promising a prize to the one who should first reach a given goal. But when on such occasions he had bestowed the reward upon the conqueror, he too often, touched by the suppliant glances of the rest, wound up by giving a *largesse*[*] all round.

Alms, however, which take the shape of money, are comparatively easy to bestow; the members of the Conference used furthermore to occupy themselves during their walks in distributing presents of bread and meat or articles of clothing for the body, as well as words of edification for the soul, thus gradually initiating themselves into the difficult art which consists in giving that most precious of all gifts, namely oneself. On Sunday afternoons Theodore, with some of his fellow-pupils, superintended the Patronage which had been established in connection with the College; about two hundred children were present at these lessons in reading, writing and arithmetic, given by a young gentleman who used by way of variety to assume in turn the character of a pedagogue and that of a leader of sports. No words can express the trouble this unruly assemblage gave Theodore, he found it no easy task to carry out the rules without stifling the promptings of his kind heart, and in the course of his Sunday labors he at least reaped a rich harvest of acts of patience, thus making ample atonement for his own schoolboy escapades.

Never did he know what it was to waver in anything connected with his religious practices, he looked neither to the right hand nor to the left, being equally free from ostentation and from human respect. He would never have thought of going to sleep without

---

[*]   A gift.

Chapel at Marcq College.

having hung his rosary round his neck, and placed upon his breast a large copper crucifix familiarly termed at home *Theodore's big cross.*

During the vacations he made a point of hearing Mass every day, and of reciting a number of self-imposed prayers; this exactitude on the part of one who so dearly loved amusement and independence, proves him to have been possessed of no common energy, and must doubtless have been the means of procuring for him graces neither few nor small.

Yet, side by side with these admirable qualities, his old faults existed in full force; his aversion to restraint, his habit of teasing, his love of ease, formed a darker side to the picture, though they did not prevent his kindness of heart from making him an universal favorite. His character presented a singular mixture of good and evil; no one could have been further removed than he was from being one of those youthful pieces of perfection which too often settle down in after-life into mere common-place mediocrity. His virtues had to be won at the sword's point, and it will be seen later on that they were on this account all the more brilliant and none the less solid, since in this fallen world everything which is really worth having must be purchased at a high price.

His success as a rhetorician was greater than ever during this year, at the close of which he carried off the first prize, and as constantly happens in the case of one who is beloved. by his comrades, a perfect ovation of shouts and wild acclamations followed his steps as he triumphantly passed down the long hall bearing to his mother his splendid gold medal. This truly pious woman, fearing lest pride should mar her son's triumph, took occasion to whisper in his ear as she kissed his cheek, "Thank God for this."

"I have done so already," promptly rejoined Theodore, and his mother afterwards said that this answer had given her more pleasure than all her son's prizes could bestow.

About this time Joseph and Theodore accompanied their grandparents to Téterchen, where the Redemptorist Novitiate is situated; the reason of the journey being the wish of M. and Mme. Motte to visit one of their sons, who had recently been enrolled in the Order of St. Alphonsus. M. Motte amused himself on the way with a copy of Virgil, from whose poems he could repeat long passages by heart, inviting his grandsons to compete with him in these exercises of memory, out of which he invariably came triumphant. When the party reached their destination, the two boys were much impressed by all they saw within the walls where the youthful novices were being trained for the labors of the Apostolate. There is something mysterious about a religious house when beheld from without, but when viewed from within, it is seen to be irradiated by heavenly light. Our travelers found in the abode of the Redemptorist Fathers that open-hearted hospitality and Christian simplicity which puts everyone at his ease, and that unstudied joyousness which belongs of right to every novice, since it is the spontaneous effusion of a heart which rejoices in having given itself altogether to God. At the sight of such a life, which reminds one of Heaven, Theodore remarked to Joseph: "What an advantage it is to be at peace with one's own conscience!" And as the two brothers sauntered in the garden, they proceeded to discuss the future; Joseph already saw a place marked out for himself in this family of apostles, while Theodore confessed that he did not think he should ever be a religious, but would like to be a missioner, as was his uncle the priest. The beauty of sacrifice was already beginning to dawn on his youthful vision, but he was fain to surround the Cross with a poetic halo, being ignorant as yet that every Christian soul must need to learn to gaze steadfastly upon it in all its stern reality.

In October 1865, at the commencement of a fresh year of study, a higher course of instruction in rhetoric was arranged for the pupils who had made most progress in this branch of learning. Theodore put down his name at once, being desirous of filling up the outlines of what was as yet but a mere sketch. And indeed in spite of the brilliant success he had achieved and the prizes he had won, he could not flatter himself that he had, in the brief space of a single year, so studied his models as to know them thoroughly well, and to have acquired for himself that mastery of style which can only be the result of much reading, and long practice in composition. He was just in a stage to profit by such instruction, and it is mainly to this second year's study that he owed the marvelous facility wherewith he handled the pen, and the power he possessed of saying just what he wanted to say in the most attractive manner without ever appearing to aim at effect.

In the early weeks of 1866, however, thoughts of a very different nature began to present themselves to him in the midst of his engrossing studies. Every Catholic eye and heart was turned towards Rome, for it was impossible to witness the crafty manner in which the Convention lately seized between France and Italy was being put into execution, without a thrill of well-founded alarm. It will be remembered how, on September 15, 1864, Napoleon had promised to withdraw the French troops from the States of the Church within a period of two years, on condition that Piedmont should respect the territory of the Holy See, and not oppose the organization of a Papal army. It is unnecessary to do more than mention the imperfectly masked treachery in which this Convention was so fatally fertile; the eagerness of France to observe the treaty on the one hand, on the other the effrontery with which Italy violated the terms of the contract, and neglected no means of stirring up sedition in the provinces belonging to the Pope; the interminable parlaying between the two Cabinets; the incessant protestations uttered in Paris against the manner in which the levying and equipment of troops was carried on in broad daylight around the States of the Church; the answers returned by Florence, staving off the timid but troublesome demands of French diplomatists by means of the false coin of empty protestations signed by M. Batazzi with one hand whilst at the same time he offered the other to Garibaldi. In presence of this gradual but barefaced violation of a treaty which guaranteed to the Sovereign Pontiff at least some remains of liberty, Catholics uttered a cry of alarm, and in reply were informed by the French Government that all must necessarily be going on for the best, since the Italian Government declared that it was so.

Thus placed between these two powers, Pius IX. did not fail to protest; but how can a Sovereign effectually resist injustice when he is both surrounded by treachery and deprived of military forces? Nevertheless, his appealing voice was heard all over the world, from every side Catholics pressed forward to occupy that post of honor which France was about to vacate, for the hour was alas! fast approaching when her national flag would no longer be unfurled for the protection of the Pontifical tiara.

Theodore, too, felt himself carried away by the stream of generous feeling which was flowing Romewards; he went to his father, and asked permission to repair to the Eternal City. He doubtless expected that some objections would be made to his proposal, but far indeed was he from anticipating the reply he actually received from the lips of M. Wibaux, who was a man of prudence and practical sense. "You a Papal Zouave!" he exclaimed, "what an idea! You who do not know what self-denial or suffering is! You who are so dainty about your food, who cannot sleep if your bed is not arranged to your fancy, who cannot go without so much as a cigar that you wish for! My dear boy, you must begin by conquering yourself; show me in the course of the next year that you can do what is distasteful to nature. You dislike mathematics, set yourself to learn them; you are full of faults, make it your business to correct them; then I shall I think you fit to encounter the hardships and privations of a soldier's life."

M. Wibaux spoke like a man of judgment, like a Christian, and like a father anxious to promote the welfare of his son. Nevertheless his firmness disconcerted Theodore; the task which lay before him was no easy one, the time wherein it had to be accomplished was brief, whilst the points to be reformed were numerous. The prospect moreover to have to conquer himself, to encounter foes on every hand, to be perpetually on his guard, was not attractive; but he desired the end, and therefore he accepted the means necessary to that end, and set to work without delay. His brothers Joseph and Stephen, all his school-fellows and his teachers, knowing nothing of his plans, were greatly puzzled by the change in him, for he was no longer the same person, or rather he was still his old self, minus his faults. Theodore had grown obliging, he did not try to tease, he had given up his favorite crotchets, he no longer, sought his own ease, and so rapid a transformation caused universal astonishment. One of his masters, who knew the real state of the case, seeing him on one occasion talking during the hours of study, said to him: "If you intend to be a Zouave you ought to understand and observe the rules in a very different manner." The admonition had not to be repeated, since Theodore never again failed to keep silence at the appointed times.

But whence had he obtained the strength which seemed unaccountable even to himself? The secret lay in the fact that he was not alone in his painful and unceasing struggle, but had thrown himself headlong into the arms of his dear Immaculate Mother, and had begged and implored her to aid him. The room which he and his brother Joseph occupied looked out upon the play-ground, and opposite to the window was a statue of our Lady; in the evening he used to remain long upon his knees gazing upon it, his eyes sometimes. being full of tears; and all this seemed very mysterious to those who saw him. When the hours of study were over, instead of joining in the sports of his companions, he would hasten to the chapel, and there renew his pleadings at the feet of her whom he loved to call his Mother. The secret struggle of Theodore with his old self made him feel the need of seeking courage and perseverance outside himself, and no one is so strong as he who is equally convinced of his own weakness and of the power of prayer.

He drew up a list of those who died a martyr's death at Castelfidardo, placing the name of Pimodan at the head of the list, then he ook these Christian heroes for his chosen patrons and favorite models. But he was fully alive to the fact that the prayer of the lips will not, if it be indeed sincere, arise towards God unaccompanied by that other prayer, the prayer of action; and without dreaming of high-sounding mortifications, he set himself to do as well as possible all that school-life required of him; the practical character of his religion being shown by the rules he laid down for himself. "I will try to learn my lessons perfectly. . . I will not begin to read until my work is quite finished. . . I will go without lunch" (a resolution which is certainly very meritorious for a hungry lad of seventeen), "I will not take my recreation with—or with—." On the other hand he determines to take his recreation at least once every day in the company of a fellow-pupil for whom he feels an extreme antipathy. He resolves to say his beads daily, offering one decade for the intention of a boy from whom he has to put up with a great deal of annoyance.

Yet there are not wanting those who imagine that virtue is to be won without striking a blow, that sanctity is the free gift of Heaven, a gift which can be obtained by the mere fact of wishing for it!

Theodore deeply felt the need of aid from on high to enable him to sustain his daily struggles, and he made out a list of his favorite saints, adding the following prayer at the end of his litany: "Offer to God, I beseech you, my poor sacrifices, help me in my confessions, enable me to profit by my Communions. I want to become altogether different from what I am, and my needs are so great; yet I am full of hope."

He considers the month of May an admirable opportunity for making progress in his new path, for taking Heaven by storm. "My dearest Mother," thus he addresses our Lady, "thou knowest how sad I feel, my hearts inclined to evil, my soul is full of gloom and destitute of fervor. I do not love God, I do not love thee as I ought, yet I am not wanting in confidence, for I have been told again and again that thou canst change the greatest sinners into the greatest saints. I entreat thee to obtain for me the gift of fervor, and of all those other virtues which thou dost love, and to make me by the end of this month, a worthy servant of Holy Church and a worthy soldier of the Holy See. O, my good Mother, hear and grant my petitions!"

Saint-Martin Church, in Roubaix.

Not content with saying his beads every day, he resolves to recite the Office of the Immaculate Conception, he multiplies his self-denials, both his waking and sleeping thoughts are full of nothing but sacrifice, and from this period his piety never ceased to be characterized by tender feeling and generous self-denial.

In August 1866, the long vacation was once more at hand, and Theodore dreaded the prospect of so much liberty, for though he never lost heart, he mistrusted his own weakness. "The slight victories I have gained," he wrote at this time, "inspire me with courage. I have been arming for the conflict during the last five months, and I am anxious to prove to those about me the reality of my intentions." He goes on to provide against even the most trifling occasions on which his old faults were likely to reappear. "I must remember how weak I am, how easily dazzled and led astray. It is only by unceasing watchful ness and the practice of continual mortification in regard to my every word and deed that I can hope to keep in the right path and to acquire the seriousness which is expected of me."

The result was that during these holidays everything testified to the greatness of the change which had passed over him. Each act, each word, bore the impress of the process at work within, and revealed the manner in which he realized the unseen and had learned to delight in sacrifice. No longer was he a light-hearted child, careless and sportive, indulging every playful whim; he was a man who knew how to keep himself in check, and for whom the path of duty was illumined by light from Heaven. "Take courage, Theodore, take courage and persevere," thus do we find him apostrophizing himself about this period, "by a voluntary acceptance of trial and sacrifice thou hast chosen the better part. How high a place wilt thou win for thyself in Heaven, if one day thou dost become a Papal Zouave, if thou art brave, patient, and chaste."

He lays down a strict rule for himself during this season of relaxation he will rise early, spend an hour in church, hear as many as three Masses on Sunday, give up all amusements which interfere with the service of God; his time is to be spent in working, reading, and in helping others, his walks sanctified by a visit to some church; morning and evening he will make a meditation and examine his conscience. One mortification which suggests itself to his mind is of a specially difficult nature, and he generously embraces it; Theodore liked smoking, not so much from the force of habit, for this he had not yet had time to acquire, as for the sake of doing as others do and appearing manly and independent. How many lads of his age think that their emancipation from tutelage dates from the day they smoked their first cigar! However that may be, Theodore resolved that thenceforward tobacco should be a forbidden luxury; and although the sacrifice sometimes cost him dear, it was on that account all the more welcome to him, for a breath of the supernatural had passed over his spirit. It could not be said that for him the idea of entering the Papal service was a whim, a mere passing fancy, or a *pis-aller*;* it was a true and genuine vocation. "If I work more earnestly than ever at my sanctification, it is with a view to the fulfillment of my schemes for the future. I know that disappointments, sufferings both moral and physical, dangers of all kinds await me, but the prospect does not dishearten me. Love of God, of the Church, and of Pius IX, the desire to win Heaven by means of suffering, to die a martyr's death, may these be the only motives which actuate me. "Who can help admiring the loyal and brave sentiments of a soul attracted by the beauty of the ideal and transformed by its power?

When, two years later, during a leave of absence, the youthful Zouave re-perused these resolutions, long since carried out into action, he was astonished himself at the fervor and fortitude with which he had prepared to follow his vocation, and it was with sincere satisfaction that he recalled this year of struggle and of conquest, for nothing is sweeter to look back upon than a sacrifice which has been courageously made. On the margin of the page containing the rules he had then marked out for himself, he wrote: "How much it cost me to bear the humiliations to which my self-love was exposed, and to crush out my instinctive love of liberty! How painful I found it to mortify myself! But nothing is lost which is done for God, and as a mother guides the first tottering steps of her little child, so have I been guided and upheld. May I always correspond to the grace which has been vouchsafed to me!"

The conditions imposed by M. Wibaux upon his son. had now been fulfilled; the former had acted with firmness and determination, the latter had shown himself worthy to be a soldier of the Pope. Yet it happened that during these very holidays certain influential persons counseled delay, and thus the whole matter was rendered doubtful once more.

When Theodore saw the fair vessel of his hopes thus founder at

---

*   A last resort

the moment when it seemed to be in the very act of entering port, he could not refrain from giving free vent to his grief and disappointment. But he submitted nevertheless, and this fresh trial brought his virtue into brighter relief. He spent his time in studying philosophy and mathematics, subjects that were the reverse of congenial to him, yet he never allowed a single murmur to escape his lips. It was a hard struggle, but he obeyed. "I cannot help crimsoning with anger, impatience and regret when I read the newspapers," he wrote to a friend who was, like himself, awaiting the permission of his parents to set out for Rome. "My desire," he goes on to say, "is to offer my youth and strength to the Holy Father; I first began to think of doing so three years ago, but those were mere childish dreams. I have this year been inspired by God to devote myself to fighting for the Church, and the inspiration was so real as to effect the greatest changes in my whole being, and indeed entirely transform my character. Since that period the idea of martyrdom has been the mainspring of my actions; but I am still doomed to uncertainty and disappointment. Do you therefore unite your prayers with mine, that we may both be comforted and strengthened."

Meanwhile the march of events at Rome was a very rapid one; the last contingent of French troops was to quit the Papal territory in December. In vain did Pius IX. renew his protests against the policy of Florence, and Catholic hearts perceived with horror that the moment was approaching when the Head of the Church would have to depend upon his own handful of troops to stave off the encroachments of Italy. Fruitless efforts were made in France to obtain from the Imperial Government a respite in the withdrawal of the troops, but that unhappy country was, alas! doomed to sink lower and lower, dragged downwards by the anti-Christian policy of its ruler.

In the midst of these various delays, under which his ardent spirit could not but chafe, Theodore tried to think of someone who would sympathize with his aspirations, and whose opinion might turn the scale in his favor. With this view he wrote to Louis Veuillot, unfolding to him his wishes, stating the faults of his character, and, with that simplicity which is at once so charming and so rare,. asking whether it was indeed too great a piece of presumption on his part to aim at the supreme honor of serving the Pope. Louis Veuillot wrote in reply the following admirable letter, every word of which is replete with truly Christian feeling, and might have been uttered by some warrior of medieval times, whilst pointing out to his son the road to Jerusalem, and exclaiming: "Depart, my child, such is the will of God!"

"Paris, November 23, 1866.

"My dear young Friend, In less than a month, unless God should decree otherwise, and His designs are not yet revealed to human ken, the political Head of France, the eldest daughter of the Church, will re-enact the parricidal conduct of Philip the Fair, or may we not rather say of Judas. Though the unanimous voice of the nation does not call for the perpetration of this crime, this atrocious sin against God and against the whole human race, the eldest daughter of the Church will acquiesce in it with a good grace, if not with a good will.
. . .

"It is not because St. Peter wants soldiers that I would counsel you to go to Rome, but because we want to offer them to him, we want to offer our blood in order to atone for the disgraceful defalcation of France. Should God permit some of our fellow-countrymen to fall fighting under the banner of St. Peter, in reality they will fall fighting for France, for their country which will ere long, in all probability be overtaken by a terrible humiliation. The father who devotes his son to the cause of the Church, really gives him to France; all the blood that is not shed for the Church, will be shed in vain.

"Who can say whether a final struggle will give dignity to the disaster now impending over Rome, and which will be for the chastisement of the world? Will there be a second Castelfidardo to redeem this treachery? I scarcely venture to hope it, for the men with whom we have to deal would be afraid to found their edifice in the blood of martyrs, they prefer to construct its walls with the foul mire of apostasy. They consider themselves strong enough to attain their end, and we have perhaps, indeed, sinned too deeply to be permitted to expiate our transgressions at the cost of our blood.

"I cannot give you any decided opinion as to whether you ought to offer your services to the Pope, but I incline to the side of your doing so. At any rate it is something to have had the will to do so, and it cannot fail to bring down a blessing on your whole future life.

"I commend myself to your prayers.

"Louis Veuillot."

This forcible language, and the turn events were taking, put all doubts to flight; no hesitation was henceforth possible, the permission so long waited for and so well deserved, was granted at last.

One cloud remained on Theodore's horizon; he feared lest his youth and apparent delicacy might cause him to be pronounced unfit for military service. But he waited for the decision of man in full confidence in God, "who," as he said in a letter written about this time, "will carry on and complete His own work."

Preparations were now set on foot for the journey, the real object of which was kept secret, because there were certain formalities to be gone through, and on the result of these the final decision must depend. It was given out that M. Wibaux was about to take Theodore to Paris, for a pleasure trip, and when the future Zouave sat down for the last time at the family table, the younger children were more than usually merry, being delighted at the idea of the pleasure their elder brother was to enjoy. Meanwhile the poor mother could hardly restrain her tears, and tried to smile in order that her grief might not be perceived. The innocent unconsciousness of the junior members of the family imparted a peculiar coloring to the separation; Theodore preserved a serene exterior, and said to every one *au revoir*,* though he knew full well that this farewell might be forever.

When the last moment arrived, Mme. Wibaux took her son by the hand, and led him to the feet of *Our Lady of the Staircase*, saying with no outward sign of emotion, "I entrust you to her care; Mary, I give my son to thee." Then came the dreaded parting, and the final kiss; and when all was over, the courageous mother with-

---
*   Goodbye.

drew into her oratory, in order to let her tears flow freely at the foot of the crucifix, uniting her grief with that of Our Lady of Dolours.

But ere long Christian courage triumphed over maternal weakness, so that she could sing a *Te Deum* in the depths of her heart, and the next day she wrote as follows to her husband:

"I feel the need of keeping very near to God, Who has asked of me my child, and the thought that he is given up to Him, enables me to rejoice in the midst of my sorrow. Do you not feel that this sacrifice of our son calls upon us to lead a more Christian, a more edifying life? Three of our children are already in Heaven, and our dear Theodore is walking along the road which leads thither. Our other children too are full of promise, and we may surely count ourselves among the rich ones of the earth when we think of these jewels which will one day adorn our crown in Heaven. How vain is all the world values when compared with the treasures which we can take with us to our eternal home I am writing at Theodore's table in his little room, so rich in associations. *Fiat!* I cannot describe what I feel, my heart is full of conflicting emotions, grief and hope, love and happiness. Our Lord loved us even unto death, let us offer our sacrifice in union with His sufferings."

During their stay in Paris, M. Wibaux and his son called on Louis Veuillot; the conversation naturally turned on the cause of Rome and the attitude of France, and the champion of the Church, with almost prophetic foresight, spoke of the evil days in store for his country. Theodore sent the following account of the interview to his eldest brother, Willebaud. "The crown," M. Veuillot said, "will not have been snatched from the head of Pius IX. with impunity. The punishment will fall most heavily upon France, because she is the most guilty. Trials and humiliations will be our lot, indeed, I can see no other explanation of the sudden elevation of Prussia and the abasement of Austria. When I beheld the cowardly conduct of that Catholic power, I foretold its ruin on the very day of Castelfidardo, and I now do the same in the case of France."

Then speaking of Napoleon III, he went on to add: "That man will come to a miserable end. As for us who are Christians, we must be prepared for everything; we shall be treated with ignominy, imprisoned, threatened with death." He certainly had a keen eye with regard to futurity who could thus speak four years before Sedan, and the advent of the Commune.

There are chosen souls in whose case God causes the pain of sacrifice to be more acutely felt, in order to enhance their merit. Not until mother and son were separated for the first time, did the former become aware how great was her love for the child whose training had required so much patience and occasionally given cause for so much anxiety; she felt almost tempted to wish that he might not pass the examination, and yet, so thoroughly did she feel the mysterious sweetness which ever mingles with the bitterness of sacrifice, that from the depths of her bleeding heart she called upon M. Wibaux to rejoice. "I wish you could read my inmost soul, for though I cannot but feel acutely the wound I have received, I am full of gratitude for having been the mother of Theodore, the precious *gift of God*. I dare not tell him all the love I feel for him, lest by so doing I should increase twofold the pain of his sacrifice. . . I therefore constantly commend him to our Lord. The younger children are very merry, being in complete ignorance about their brother. Stéphanie looks everywhere for Papa and Theodore, and sends you plenty of kisses for him. Pray do not leave our dear boy until the last possible moment, and bid him farewell again for me when you are really obliged to say good-bye. I am persuaded that you will come back alone, but we have given him up to God; it is only this thought which enables me to bear the idea of seeing you return without him."

Then she allows herself one look at the past, and recalls the delight—a joy which only a Christian mother can appreciate—which she had often felt when in church at her husband's side, surrounded by their nine children, she united with them in singing the praises of God. "Those were indeed happy days," she writes, "which can never return, but which I can never forget! How many of them I have enjoyed, and how fervently, O my God, do I thank Thee for them all!"

On the 5th of December, she wrote as follows to Joseph and Stephen, who were then at Marcq: "Your father has come back this morning, alone. May God's will be done! Theodore started in good spirits, after having paid his devotions to Our Lady of Victories. May God keep him free from contamination! My dear boys, do beg some prayers for him."

God had accepted the sacrifice so generously offered, and the separation was now an accomplished fact. Hence forward we must no longer regard Theodore as a child, but as a Papal Zouave, as the representative of his family in Rome, as one towards whom many loving thoughts will be directed, for whom many prayers will be offered day by day, and who will be sustained in his exile by the recollection of the beloved home circle he has left.

CHAPTER III.

1866, 1867.

Theodore on his way to Rome. Joy mingled with sorrow. Commencement of life in barracks. His letters home. A Zouave's day. Close of the year. Withdrawal of the French troops from Rome.

AT length Theodore is on his way to Marseilles, with about thirty other volunteers, French, Belgian, Dutch, and German. Whilst they amuse themselves with smoking and singing, he withdraws as much as possible into himself, to think of God, and of the dear ones he has left, to raise his heart to Heaven in silent prayer, wondering that his companions care to do anything else. Accustomed as he is to look only on the supernatural side of the Zouave's life, he does not allow himself to diminish the sacrifice by any satisfaction conceded to nature. He steadily refuses himself the little privileges which a well-filled purse could procure him; he is not traveling for pleasure, the third class is quite good enough for him, whether on the railroad or the steamboat. His last act before leaving France was to visit the shrine of *Notre Dame de la Garde*; then, fortified by the consciousness of her powerful protection, he went on board the steamer with a hopeful heart.

"We were all crowded together upon the deck," he writes, "and our table and lodging was not the most luxurious! At meal times we were divided into companies of twelve, and to each group was given some bread, three spoons, and a large saucepan. It was really laughable to see the ravenous way in which the big Dutchmen fell on their food. "The strongest and boldest helped themselves first, and our friend, not being one of those, had to go without his share of the contents of the cauldron, and console himself with a piece of cheese which he ate with his bread.

At night they all laid down on the deck, entirely without protection from the pouring rain and rough wind; it need hardly be said that sleep was impossible; after this fashion their apprenticeship began. At last, on Saturday the 8th of December, the feast of the Immaculate Conception, they landed at Civita Vecchia, and on the evening of the same day Theodore entered Rome, under the immediate auspices of her to whom for many months past he had confided his hopes, his fears, and his plans for the future, and who now seemed to welcome him with out-stretched arms, as, on this her feast-day, he arrived within the gates of the Papal City.

Military life does not at the outset present a very attractive aspect; rough work, strange faces, orders which demand implicit obedience, and, continually suspended overhead, that Damocles' sword, which is known as confinement to barracks. Theodore, looking around him, found nothing that in any degree could alleviate the pain of separation. In spite of this, the dominant feeling of his heart is that of thankfulness.

"At last I have put on the uniform of a soldier of Christ, and have fully entered on the path of sacrifice. God be thanked for having in His mercy chosen me to be one of the defenders of His Church! And I thank you too, my dear parents, for having turned a deaf ear to what the world said, and listened only to the voice of God. As for me, natural affection often speaks only too audibly to my heart, especially during the last three days, when I think that now the sea rolls between us, and I may perhaps never see you again, I feel quite heart-broken. But above and beyond all this there is devotion to the Holy Father, and the consciousness of having done one's duty. Who would ever have dreamt of Theodore being a soldier! I can hardly believe in my own identity as I march about with a sword at my side, or a heavy rifle in my hands. I tell myself I am not a soldier, but a son of Pius IX. I am obliged to repeat this to myself over and over again, for I always felt an aversion to military life. Still I am not destitute of interior happiness, far from it, indeed I sometimes am tempted to exclaim aloud: Welcome suffering, since it is for Jesus Christ! And if the natural man has to make many bitter experiences, the spiritual man enjoys true content."

When, on the first morning, he is introduced to his new quarters, vivid memories of the past throng in upon him. "The barracks make a strange impression on one, especially on an unfortunate recruit who has just left a pleasant little room, fitted up for him with a mother's kind care; but still I slept soundly, quite oblivious of the fact that I was in Rome and in barracks, indeed I made up for the three sleepless nights I had had previously.

"The next morning the call to the recruits to turn out made us all spring from our beds; it was a very different signal to the musical sound of my alarm, which on Sundays only roused me to a delightful sense of enjoyment in my comfortable bed. We had to march in rank to some barracks at a considerable distance, where we were to receive our rations and our uniform; then we were ordered to peel potatoes. I would have given anything for you to see me, dressed in my nice great-coat, with my hat on, handling the knife—you may guess with what dexterity!— you would have laughed heartily at me.

"After the doctor's examination, I put on my uniform, but not without a little help. I cannot describe what I felt in laying aside my civilian's clothes, one after another, it was like parting from old friends. I had already met with a great vexation on the deck of our vessel, for during that miserable night I had the misfortune to lose my rosary, the dear and inseparable friend and solace of so many years. At any rate, however, I still have the cross that I always wear close to my heart, and I trust I shall keep that until my latest breath. About three p.m. we were free to amuse ourselves. The first thing we did was to go to St. Peter's and the Vatican, that is all I have as yet seen of Rome, and it is certainly what I most cared to see. The square of St. Peter's was lit up with the most brilliant sunshine. How much I thought of you my dear parents, it was just our dinner-time at home! No doubt you too thought and talked a great deal during the day of your Zouave son, and Mother went to Communion for my intention at dear old St. Martin's, where we have all prayed together so often; meanwhile here was I all alone in this vast city of Rome, very uncomfortable in my new dress, hundreds of miles away from Roubaix. But it is for the love of God! I hear the Angelus ringing all round, I must kneel down and say it. . . .

"Dear Father and Mother, dear brothers and sisters, I can only tell you how much I love you, I repeat this over and over again all day long. Do not be anxious about my spiritual life. Never before did I experience so strongly the need of prayer; never did I feel so great a love for our Lord. Now that I have not you any longer, I seek my consolation only in Him. Yes, I miss you sadly, I feel it more every day, and although I made the sacrifice freely; the cross weighs heavily upon my shoulders, and cuts me to the heart. Instead of my quiet, regular life at home, my parents' counsels, the friendship of my dear brother, I have peremptory orders, hard work, the pain of separation from all I know and love. It is true I foresaw all these things, but still I feel them keenly. May God's holy will be done! I am present in Rome, but I do not live there, I live in Roubaix. By day, in the midst of my most unpleasant tasks, at night, when I lay down in bed, my thoughts are continually with you. This morning, a little before nine, you were at breakfast, and at the same time I was eating my dry bread and coffee. Every morning when I get up, I ask for your blessing, just as I used to do when I knocked at Mother's door on my return from Mass at half-past six."

Thus did prayer and the life of faith soften the asperities of a life at once new to him, and utterly at variance with his tastes. Then too, he saw Pius IX, being so fortunate as to meet him in the streets of Rome; and the youthful Zouave arose with renewed courage after kneeling to receive the Benediction of the Father of Christendom for whose sake he had left all. Poor Theodore! it was the will of God

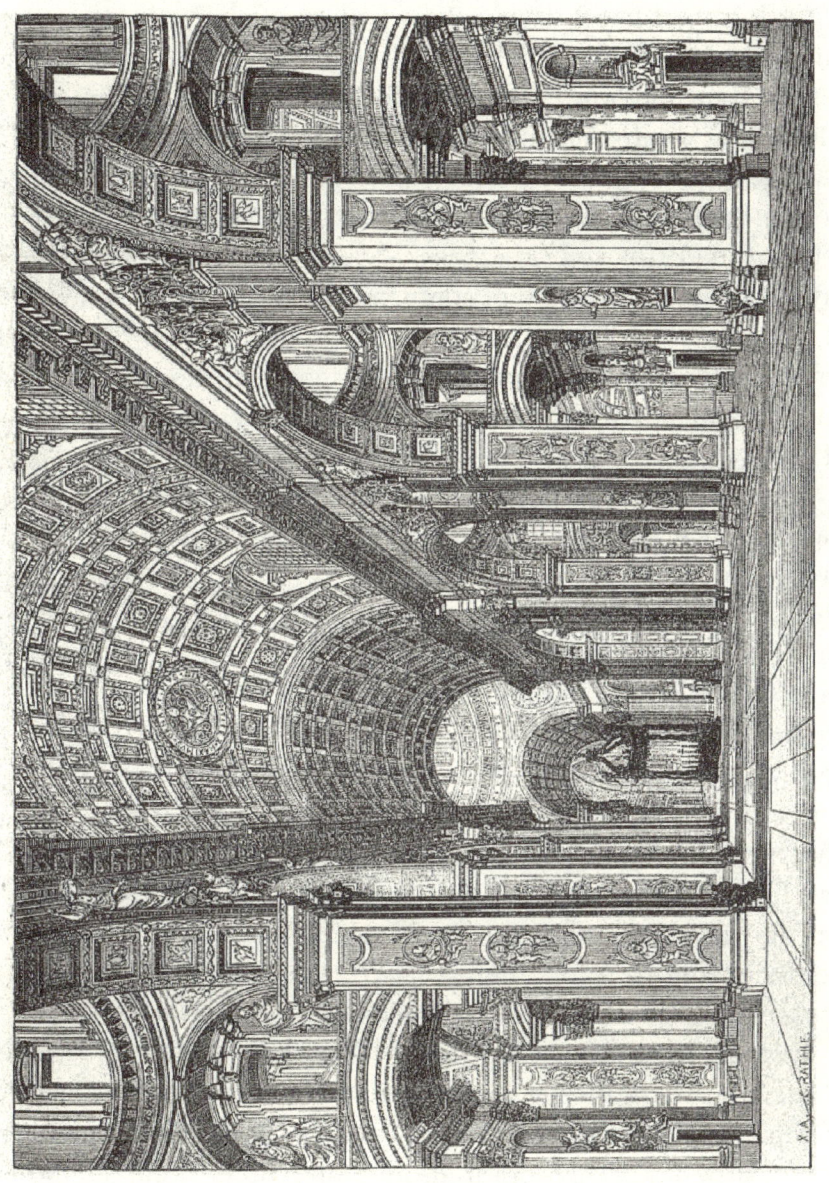

Saint Peter's Basilica in Rome.

that he should for a lengthened period experience all the bitterness of absence and separation! His first letter home is the outpouring of his simple, loving heart; it concludes as follows:

"A fortnight ago I was in Paris with my father. My dear, good father! I have not done half enough to prove how much I love and respect him, and how I regret the trouble I have been to him. When I look back on my parting with you all, I feel quite remorseful for having shown so little affection and gratitude. Forgive me, dear brothers and sisters, and you, Willebaud, in particular, for the poor return I made for your kindness. My love to Joseph and Stephen, my sisters, and my constant companion, Léon, dear little man! He at any rate will not forget me. I like to go over all your names. Do write to me soon, I am longing for letters from Roubaix. For my part, I mean to write my journal every day, and send it off at the end of each week.

"Before bidding you good-bye, I must once more beg your blessing, and once more say how dearly I love you. Do not imagine that I repent of my project for a single moment, far from it! but I cannot help feeling the separation acutely. After all I am little more than a child, not yet eighteen, and this is the first time I have been away from you; it is only natural that I should miss you all sadly. But I trust to God's help and to your prayers; I do not believe that I could keep up were it not for the thought of Heaven as my reward. I hope I may always prove myself worthy of my good parents, that I may always be steadfast, chaste, courageous. It must be allowed that the first few days of a soldier's life are very much the reverse of pleasant, and I find my uniform an awful worry. But these things are but externals, and from my inmost heart I can thank God for having chosen me to be a defender of a good cause!"

It would be untrue to say that no tears were shed over this letter at Roubaix, but they were tears of joy, not of sorrow. All the members of the family were justly proud of their representative at Rome; all spoke of their gratitude and sense of the honor conferred on them, not of the sacrifice wherewith it was purchased, and yet in each heart there was an undercurrent of pain, for the satisfaction derived from the fulfillment of duty is a flower abundantly set with thorns.

The letter containing the first impressions of one for whom he had expressed so brotherly an interest was sent to Louis Veuillot.

"I return the delightful letter you were so good as to send me," he wrote in reply to M. Wibaux. "I could not have been more touched by it had the writer been my own son. I wonder whether you would let me have a copy of that letter; it is worthy of a place in the *Acts of the Martyrs;* the whole spirit of it is truly Christian and truly ingenious. I can understand how much you must have suffered, but I am sure that you must have rejoiced amid your sufferings. Give my respectful compliments to Mme. Wibaux; it is not necessary to be personally acquainted with her in order to have the highest esteem for her, since the sentiments expressed by her son are an index to the piety and virtue of his mother."

The expression *truly Christian and truly ingenuous,* applied by M. Veuillot to Theodore's letter, shows how true an estimate he had formed of his character.

A few days later it is Mme. Wibaux's *fête,** and the absent member of the family again joins in spirit the happy circle he has left. He writes:

"Darling Mother, you know how grieved I am not to be with you today. God has permitted that mother and son should be thus roughly torn asunder, and He does all for the best. Dear Mother, you know my heart, you know I love you fondly, and if I have not always shown this by my conduct as I ought to do, forgive me on this your feast. The remembrance of your name is always united with Papa's. I cannot think of you apart, for to you both equally we children owe the deepest affection and gratitude, in fact to you both after God, we owe everything. How thankful we ought to be that you have brought us up to be good Christians! You need not fear that we shall ever be otherwise than dutiful children. You have taught us to cherish and preserve the inestimable treasure of purity, and have set before us in your persons an example of Christian virtue. Has not God already rewarded you, by choosing one of your children to be a defender, however unworthy, of His holy cause?

---

*   Honor.

"I am afraid my last letter may have led you to think that I was out of spirits. Pray dismiss all apprehensions on that score, for I can assure you that I am quite happy. It is only natural that a vague feeling of sadness should creep over me at times, especially when I first wake in the morning. But on these occasions I turn my thoughts at once to God; I invoke my patrons, our Lady, and dear little Francis; I call to mind the honor God has conferred upon me, I entreat Him to forgive my weakness, and thus I soon recover my habitual frame of mind, which is peaceful and resigned. I can truly say that I rejoice in suffering; my strongest incentive is the thought of you all, and one grace I specially ask is that I may not lose, while so far away, my love for the simple pleasures and familiar customs of family life. Write to me often therefore, about all I have loved and left; tell me all that goes on at Roubaix, in our dear, quiet little house.

"As my present on your feast, I offer you a pure and loving heart, and the promise that I will always remain what I am now. You can hardly believe, dearest mother, what an attraction I experience for prayer. I seek God everywhere and in all things. Pray often for your child, and ask others to pray for him too in order that, if God should require of him the sacrifice of his life, he may be a pure offering, well-pleasing in His sight.

"I am writing these lines seated on my knapsack, in a very uncomfortable position; one drill is just over and I am expecting the bugle to sound for another every moment. I am quite aware that I have not expressed a quarter of what I feel, but it is enough to tell you how much I love you, and how entirely I share in the family rejoicings."

What more welcome gift could be offered to a Christian mother on her feast-day, and what separation would not be alleviated by so much affection and confidence?

The hundred and one occupations of the conscript do not prevent him from thinking of everything and remembering everyone. For instance, when the 26th of December comes round, the feast of his brother Stephen, Theodore writes beforehand to send him his greeting and good wishes. He lets his pen run on freely:

"Today is Sunday, is just half-past two by the time here, but at Roubaix it is only two o'clock. You, dear Stephen, are probably amusing yourself in the large playground at Marcq; and in a quarter of an hour the bell will ring for study before Vespers. You will pray for your Zouave brother in the chapel where I have so often implored the blessing of God on my projects. As for myself I am comfortably installed in a little room, with a worthy fellow-countryman; we have hired it for ten francs a month, but it has to accommodate four of us, which considerably diminishes the expense. Exactly under our window is a grove of splendid orange-trees, wherein hundreds of birds are singing; opposite to us is a church which stands out finely on the back-ground of a deep blue sky. In the heart of ancient Rome, listening to the sound of innumerable bells, my mind's eye turns to Roubaix, and the dear old school-house at Marcq. I would not part with such moments as these for anything, and when I want to strengthen myself for duty, and encourage myself in virtue, I think of the dear ones at home, and of you, my beloved brothers, who are so pious and good.

"A week ago we began drill. At six o'clock in the morning the bugle sounds the *reveille;* there is not a moment to be lost; we have to adjust our wretched gaiters and leggings, which seem to have been invented for the express purpose of teaching us patience; then each man has to wax his cartridge-box and belt, polish his saber and rifle, and all this half in the dark. A second bugle-call summons us to go downstairs, and then 'quick step, forward, march!' and we defile on to the square of St. Peter's.

"It is no small privilege to be drilled opposite to the vast Basilica; three times already we have had the gratification of presenting arms to Pope Pius IX, and his blessing has, upon each occasion, awakened within our youthful hearts a more ardent longing to live and die in his service. Oh, if you could only see the Holy Father and behold the charming expression of his countenance, combining as it does gentleness with majesty! I feel the strongest conviction that I am engaged in the service of a great saint.

"Nothing is more amusing than to see with what eagerness all the Zouaves, both high and low, attack their rations at mealtimes, certainly no lack of appetite is observable. My health is excellent, and I sleep extremely well, though what we lie on is little better than sacking, and we have only a single coverlet. What has become, I wonder, of my nice eider-down quilt? There are eighteen of us in our quarters, to reach which we have to mount six flights of stairs; the floor shakes at every step, and our apartments are under the leads; but on the other hand I can look towards St. Peter's when I say my evening prayers; I can even wish good-night to Pius IX, whose suite of rooms I can see lighted up, and I feel happy in being thus near to him. Up to the present time I have, so to speak, breathed too constantly the atmosphere of the barrack-room and too seldom that of Rome, yet every day my heart receives fresh impressions when I revisit St. Peter's. The first time I entered it I was not nearly as much struck as I expected to be, for every part is in such perfect proportion that one cannot realize the immense size of the whole, but since that first visit my admiration has been ever on the increase, for every kind of beauty is united there. Each morning and evening we have a quarter of an hour's rest between our drills, and I make a point of spending it beside the tomb of the great Apostle. One day we went up into the vast cupola; at the very top is a globe, which from below does not look larger than the footballs at Marcq, yet eight of us could get inside. And oh, what a splendid view we had! At our feet lay Rome, with her memories of the past, and what future destiny God alone knows; then there was the Campagna, with its rich verdure, and further still the sea and the snow-topped mountains. I can assure you that from such an elevation one does indeed feel ready to proclaim the goodness of God.

"I like to be with you so much, dear brothers, that I would fain remain longer in your company; but I am anxious not to miss Vespers. This morning I had the privilege of receiving the martyr's God, and I feel calm and prepared for whatever may happen."

Christmas comes with its festivities and rejoicings; and the soul of our pious Zouave is stirred to its depths by the solemn ceremonies of that holy season: "I felt as if I should never be able to prepare myself with sufficient care. On Christmas Day I heard two Masses, and went to Communion in the Jesuits' Church. As such times how one's heart seems to glow with love towards God! If I had a hundred lives, I would willingly have given them all to Him. As I knelt at the foot of the crib, I offered up my heart with all its affections, all its memories, and I arose strong and hopeful. On coming out of church we went to St. Peter's, and found that immense basilica thronged with people. The Holy Father made his entry, borne beneath a canopy and surrounded by a splendid retinue of Cardinals, Ambassadors, and Princes. The service lasted quite three hours; the Holy Father sung the Preface in a tolerably strong voice, and at the moment of the Consecration, some trumpets concealed within the dome gave forth a few notes which seemed to come from heaven. Pius IX. held the Sacred Host in his hands for some minutes; how pure the Victim, how holy the High Priest, and how glorious the temple! the time did not appear long to me, and I quite forgot that I had been up since six o'clock in the morning. It was mid-day when the Holy Father left the church; his countenance wore a somewhat sad expression, and he did not smile as usual whilst giving the blessing. This may have been the result of fatigue; it is astonishing that he should preserve his strength as he does in spite of all his troubles.

"On the 31st of December the Holy Father went in state to the Jesuits' Church, in order to sing the *Te Deum* as a thanksgiving. I also had my *Te Deum* to sing; I had to thank that Divine Providence which had led me by the hand and guided me to Rome, and entrusted to me, whilst still so young, a sacred mission and a noble task. Marvelous indeed are the ways by which God leads us; and when I pass in mental review this year 1866, my lips can utter nothing but words of gratitude and praise.

"On New Year's Day, I was able to receive Holy Communion at eleven o'clock; I felt that this first day of the year ought to be given to God, and I trust that all the rest may be likewise dedicated to Him. Since I have been in Rome, I have felt an ever-increasing longing for the Bread of Angels, and I always leave the holy table with renewed strength and greater love for the cross and suffering. The Abbé Daniel, our chaplain, whom I have taken for my confessor, advises me to go weekly to confession, and I mean to comply with his advice.

"In this pious manner did Theodore begin the new year, a year of anguish and triumph, a year marked by dark plots and revolutionary intrigue, yet brightened by many a glorious Ideed of Christian heroism. Our Zouave had arrived at a fortunate moment, for the very day when he first set foot on Italian soil was that which witnessed the withdrawal of the French troops from Rome. "Go my children," Pius IX. said to them on their departure, "go, with my blessing, go in peace. If you see the Emperor, tell him I pray daily for him. I pray for his bodily health, for they tell me it is not good; I pray for his spiritual health, for they tell me his mind is not at peace. The French nation is Christian, and it ought to have a Christian ruler. Do not imagine you are leaving me alone, for God is always with me."

And since God is pleased to employ human instruments to do His work, He awoke in the hearts of Catholics a spirit of generous devotion, so that from all lands they flocked to the standard of the Pope. The Company of Zouaves, scattered throughout the States of the Church, had already been recalled to Rome to take the place of the French troops, and had made their entry into the city, with bands. playing at their head, amid an immense concourse of people. "To see them march past," said Theodore, "made one feel proud to belong to so fine a body of soldiers."

Some apprehension was felt lest the departure of the French troops should be a signal for the outbreak of disturbances; the Revolutionists were on the lookout, watching for the favorable moment, but the presence of the Zouaves held them in check. Inflammatory placards were posted up, exciting the people to revolt, but they had no effect, and the year closed quietly. "The tranquil state of Rome is a mystery to everyone. God only knows whether it is the lull preceding the storm, but precautionary measures have been taken in view of a possible outbreak. Five discharges of artillery from the fort of St. Angelo are to be the signal for all the Zouaves to regain their several barracks; upon a second and similar discharge every man is to repair to his post. We are forbidden to go about the town alone after nightfall. We are all of us filled with an indescribable longing to meet the Garibaldians face to face; as for myself, I hope I shall, if need be, fight and fall like a true Christian."

Saint-Martin Church, in Roubaix.

CHAPTER IV.

1867.

Theodore's journal. His piety. His self-sacrifice. His cheerfulness. The Conferences of St. Vincent of Paul. Letters from home. Theodore is no longer a recruit. On guard for the first time. The Abbé Daniel. Correspondence.

"I PROMISED to write my journal every day, whatever efforts it may cost me, in spite of all difficulties, and however great the disinclination I may feel; and I will do it too, for I know the interest attaching to every little detail in connection with those we love when they are away from us. However, I must beg beforehand that both penmanship and style may be leniently criticized. As a matter of fact, I shall generally be obliged to write sitting in some uncomfortable posture, under circumstances by no means conducive either to bodily ease or mental tranquility. So you must only think of the intention, and accept my good will."

Promises are easily made, and often rashly given time alone can test their sincerity and their worth. Theodore was faithful to his word, and thanks to this habit of writing every day, he still lived amongst his home interests, and kept his family acquainted with all he did, and all that befell him in the course of his daily life, by means of an uninterrupted series of charming letters, wherein he showed himself just as he was, pious, gentle, generous, affectionate.

In these voluminous pages, written as fast as his pen could travel, we see how he prayed and how he suffered, we hear his merry laugh and song, we feel the very throbbings of his heart, we are brought face to face with all the occurrences, important and unimportant, which make up a soldier's life. He is so glad to think of the pleasure that his letters give to his relatives, and he himself finds so much relief in this familiar intercourse, that he allows no difficulties to hinder it. He will find time to write, even if he has to get up an hour earlier in the morning, or sit up for an hour at night when he is tired; in the guard-room, during the intervals of rest at drill, or when a halt is made, he manages to scribble a few lines, although his knapsack, a large stone, or the top of a wall, is the only available place whereon to rest his paper.

The inmost thoughts of his soul are revealed in these pages; never having had any secrets from his parents, concealment of any kind would have been a difficulty to him. And if his adherence to his promises evinces at the same time the strength of his affections, and a force of will such as is rarely met with, it also proved the chief safeguard of this singularly attractive young man. The slightest backsliding, the least deviation from the path on which he had entered, could not fail to betray itself in these daily outpourings; and in spite of any effort he might make to dissimulate or disguise the truth, a father's discerning eye, a mother's loving heart would know how to read between the lines, and perceive the change that had come over the child of their affections. Of this Theodore was fully aware, and he loved his parents too well to cause them this pain; he determined to tell them everything, and to conduct himself in such a manner as to have nothing that he would be ashamed to tell them.

In looking over these memorials, the difficulty is how to choose from amongst them; everyone knows that the great charm of letters consists in their freedom and spontaneity, which enables the reader to catch the mood and tone of thought of the writer, whether it be grave or gay, according as circumstances influence it at the time. These letters have been treasured up by his family, but they can hardly be said to belong exclusively to them, they are rather the property of his regiment, since Theodore has unconsciously assumed the character of an historian, and given, as no other Zouave has done, the history of the Papal army. Other pens have traced its main outlines, and given a general view of the whole; but he has depicted things as he saw them, as they really were; here we have history written while its drama was yet enacting, a series of charming sketches from nature, wherein scenes of every description find a place.

We have heard what he said about the various trials which beset him at the outset; ere long we find his high spirits and joyous nature regaining the ascendancy; and the breath of prayer, ascending upwards, drives away the heavy clouds.

"At last I have got the better of all my childish weaknesses, and am thoroughly happy in my work, looking up to Heaven. Just at the beginning, I confess, my heart at times utterly misgave me; my great sensitiveness, my youth, the fact of my having so recently left home, the fond recollections which thronged in on me, the complete change in my manner of life, the strangeness of my surroundings, all combined to depress and agitate me; but I had recourse to prayer, and my good Mother in heaven hastened to my help. I told you all my troubles in my first letter, for I thought that if I did not get rid of them altogether, I should at any rate feel them less if you shared them with me. Now there is not one of the Papal Zouaves as happy as myself; not that I begin to find anything attractive in military life, I certainly have no ambition to become a general, God forbid! It is the consciousness that I am helping to further the most sacred cause in the world, that I am fulfilling the Divine will, which imparts to me a supernatural strength.

"Every morning my first thoughts are for the friends I have left; I offer to God my heart with all its affections, pray Him to watch over and bless those whom I love; I ask myself what has brought me here, who it is for whom I am willing to shed my blood, and what my reward will be. I keep a careful guard over the purity and fervor of my heart, for these are virtues essential to a Zouave; I remind myself that Jesus Christ, omnipotent and sinless as He was, carried His Cross, to Him I completely give up my own will and my own ease, and I go my way with a light heart. Whither my path will lead me, I know not, and no one can tell me. God has His own means of bringing about the future triumph of the Church. I feel that I am well off here, at the Holy Father's side, and I would not give up my place for any consideration. Whether I fall with him, or whether I share in his victory, I shall have done what filial duty requires of me, and I shall not go unrewarded."

Our Zouave had not as yet had time to become thoroughly conversant with military life, he had still much to learn which surprised and sometimes shocked him, but his comrades had already been able accurately to take his measure. To be on good terms with all, and to make friends with few, was the maxim he laid down, the rule to which he adhered; thus, without giving offense, he avoided exposing himself to the contagion of bad example. There was something remarkably winning about this great, stalwart youth, with his gentle and almost childish countenance, his broad, good-humored smile, his simple piety, his frank manner; no one could help loving *the holy young man,* as many thought fit to call him. In fact, who could resist a genuine liking for one who did not know what it was to bear malice, or to speak bitter words, who thought others good because he judged of them by himself, and who held on his way unflinchingly, as if the beaten path of sacrifice were the only one on which a Zouave could walk?

Never did he allow the exigencies of barrack life to stand in the way of the pious practices to which he had been accustomed from his earliest years, and in the performance of which he seemed, as it were, to breathe again under those distant skies, the pure air of his childhood's home. Nor was he ever deterred by considerations of human respect; why should he mind the presence of his comrades, were not they too soldiers of Holy Church? The Zouaves were all required by rule to say night prayers, but every evening, however tired and sleepy he was, Theodore might be seen kneeling at his bedside, continuing his private prayers when the other men were already asleep. In the early morning he hastened to the nearest church for his devotions, only too happy if he could induce someone to accompany him, and before meals he never omitted saying the *Benedicite*. Whenever the duties of the service and drill left him some hours free, nothing gave him greater pleasure than to set out with two or three of his special friends, to explore the streets of Rome or the environs of the city, in search of the basilicas dedicated to our Lady or erected in honor of different saints or martyrs. If he espied some far-off tower, or the spire of a distant church, without any hesitation he would make a long round to reach it, returning well pleased at having found a new object for a walk, a fresh link to bind him closer to the unseen world.

There was so much youthful freshness about him, so much elevation of thought and feeling, that every one who came into contact with him caught some measure of his enthusiasm. There is a salutary contagion in a holy life, and in the company of one who was so good it was impossible not to feel oneself better. According to his ideas, the Papal Zouaves were a sort of military Order, who must be blameless as the Saints in order to be brave as the Knights of old; an ideal theory too beautiful not to suffer sadly when confronted with reality. On this point many a disappointment awaited Theodore, but he was not one who would allow the example of others to authorize his adoption of a lower standard, or consider it as warranting less generous effort on his own part.

When he was present none of his mess-mates ventured to indulge in unseemly jests, and if occasionally, from a mischievous desire to tease him and amuse themselves at his expense, someone in joke made use of a coarse ex pression, the poor boy's face assumed such a piteous look, that out of compassion for his distress the conversation would be dropped. Incredible as it may appear, barrack life did not rub any of the bloom off his innocence, which arose from the innate purity of his soul. One of his friends states that he remembers perfectly well hearing several Zouaves express their amazement at the wonderful manner in which he was preserved from harm. All about him felt an involuntary respect for innocence such as his, and even the least scrupulous knew that they must be careful what they said before him.

Fully aware as he was from the first that the ordinary routine of daily life, if viewed aright, offers abundant opportunities for suffering and for merit, he refused to avail himself of any privilege or exemption. What could be a better preparation for giving his life for God on the field of battle, once for all, than to offer it to Him piecemeal, as it were, each and every day?

"Most of the men who can afford it have engaged the services of some worthy native of Holland or Flanders, who in consideration of the daily pay and rations of bread, will brush your clothes, keep your kit in order and make your bed. This is very pleasant, but I think it is rather effeminate, and hitherto I have resisted all temptations, and done everything for myself. What is the good of sparing myself? My very weariness will earn a blessing for you as well as for myself."

Theodore would also gladly have dined regularly at the restaurant, as many of his comrades did, yet he did not allow himself to do so unless by way of exception; thinking it better to keep to the soup and rations served out to the men. Only this fare being insufficient to satisfy his hunger, he found himself compelled to procure an additional portion. "You would be astonished," he writes, "at the prodigious proportions my appetite has assumed; it must be confessed. my present manner of life tends to develop this fortunate weakness in an extraordinary manner. We have drill twice a day. In the morning we are frozen with cold in the Square of St. Peter's, but the steel of my rifle feels almost warm to my touch when I think that it is for the sake of Pius IX. that we are there. In the afternoon we are bathed with perspiration; at any rate we get variety. It is frightfully fatiguing to shift about the heavy rifle, especially when one has to wheel round. I hope it will make me strong."

Can this possibly be the same Theodore who but a year ago was so fastidious in his tastes, who consulted his own pleasure, and was so keen on getting the best of everything for himself? Can it be that he who was sensitive to a fault, who was miserable if in any way slighted or neglected, or even greeted with less friendliness than usual, is now found in the foremost rank whenever a sacrifice has to

Saint Peter's Square in Rome.

be made, self-denial to be practiced? Rather let us ask to what sublime heights is not man capable of rising, if the energy of his nature is only roused to action by the animating impulse of grace.

At fixed times the soldiers were confined to their quarters, and forbidden to leave the barracks under any pretext whatsoever; on those days games were got up, stories told, and tricks exhibited. Theodore willingly contributed his quota to the general entertainment, sometimes by singing songs, or inventing fresh additions to the exploits of the legendary *Sergeant*. "We are excessively merry," he writes, "only yesterday evening I had great fun, singing *The two blind men* with another Zouave."

At other times when allowed to go out, they assembled in a room which they had hired in the town. What happy hours they had there, and with what pleasure those of the company who are still alive can look back on those evenings!

"To make you understand how we enjoy ourselves, I must take you up three flights of stairs; my dear mother would find them rather steep to climb, but they are nothing for a Zouave's long legs. We ring the bell, and a kind, fat old lady opens the door, her countenance radiant with smiles. She is a motherly old soul, an excellent Christian, by the way, and she makes it her delight to look after the well-being of the Zouaves who lodge with her. Three of her rooms are occupied by Lieutenants Desclée, Wyart and Lefebvre; the fourth is ours, it is naturally not such a nice one, but it looks out on St. Andrew's Church, which is close by, and we have abundant opportunity for enjoying the bright sunshine." Here the Zouaves used to talk together about their homes, and play cards, or repeat the ballads of their native land, and recall the merry songs of their school days, laying in a store of mirth to keep up their spirits on days when distasteful and toilsome work made everything wear a gloomy aspect, and stripped military life of all its poetry by ruthlessly exhibiting it in its stern and unattractive reality.

Friendship, which supposes a community of interests and the absence of individualism, must have flourished to the ull amongst the Zouaves, coming together as they did from all parts of the world to devote themselves body and soul to one and the self-same cause.

Without having ever met before they understood each other perfectly, and comrades who had not as yet exchanged a single word, felt at once completely at home with one another. Still Theodore was extremely cautious, especially at first, as to his choice of friend; but after a time he found the circle of his acquaintance enlarged in consequence of his becoming a member of the Society and attending the Conferences of St. Vincent of Paul.

A meeting of the Confraternity of the Blessed Virgin, presided over by the Abbé Daniel, was held every week in a convent chapel. "You cannot think," Theodore writes, "how happy I feel there, at the feet of my dear Immaculate Mother! How I love those meetings! they seem to give me fresh strength and courage, whenever I possibly can I mean to go to them." After an instruction to the members given by the chaplain, there used to be some singing. The organist was Lieutenant Guillemin, whom his men familiarly called *the angel guardian,* and who later on fell at Monte Libretti shouting, "Forward, hurrah for Pius IX." It was worth hearing how Theodore, standing at his side in the little chapel, used to lead the hymns to our Lady, singing out of the fullness of his heart. "It is a real delight to me to repeat those beautiful and comforting words. I fancy myself back at Marcq, singing with my brothers and the other boys in the school-chapel, or at St. Martin's at my dear mother's side."

The Conference of St. Vincent of Paul had begun its active labors in 1861, by a distribution of soup to the poor. The battalion was then stationed at Anagni; when the Zouaves received their pay, as they did every five days, they used to put a certain portion aside for works of charity, and with the funds thus accumulated they opened a soup kitchen in the town, presiding over it themselves in the character of cooks. The soup appears to have been excellent, at any rate such numbers of would-be recipients thronged to the kitchen, that the Bishop suggested that it should be diluted, because the beggars were getting to despise the simpler fare of which they had formerly partaken with gratitude.

In 1863, when the battalion was occupying Rome and Frascati, the Conference was formally organized, and one year only subsequent to its foundation, it already numbered one hundred and forty-six members, having afforded assistance to sixty families and given away a sum amounting to £120. Under the able direction of the President, Captain de Gouttepagnon, it continued in existence until the disastrous days of 1870, holding its meetings every week, counting three hundred members annually, and distributing alms to the amount of £240.

Yet those who thus spent their leisure time in visiting the poor, and the contents of their purses in relieving their necessities, were regarded by the Italians in the light of mere mercenaries, hirelings paid to be false to their own convictions!

Theodore was one of the most assiduous attendants at all the meetings of the Society, he would have made any sacrifice rather than fail to be present at the customary gatherings, where his zeal and piety soon rendered him conspicuous, and led to his being chosen to occupy the posts of honor, or rather to fulfill the most onerous duties.

But let us return to January, 1867; four weary weeks had passed away, and as yet no letter from Roubaix had reached our recruit, much as he longed for news from home; nor were his repeated entreaties of any avail, they did not procure a single sign of remembrance, a single word of comfort. "Dear parents," he writes, "if I did not know you so well, I should be tempted to call you very unkind. Do pray write and tell me how you all are, and give me some encouragement in the path of virtue. I have to steer my bark all alone now, and I need your wise counsels in order to keep clear of the rocks; a few words from Father or Mother, or indeed any one, would be the greatest boon to me. I really am quite at a loss to account for your silence."

Not one letter, but several letters from Roubaix had alas! been lost, and the poor boy had long to wait. God has His secret way of dealing with souls who are destined to acquire great merit; happy he who gladly avails himself of every opportunity of gathering these celestial pearls! At last, on the 8th of January, a breath of his native air came to revive the Zouave's heart. "How delightfully I spent a whole hour last night, seated on my bed, heedless of the noise around me! I read and re-read Papa's two notes, the two long letters my dearest mother wrote me, and the letters from my brothers also; I quite forgot where I was; I seemed back at Roubaix, with all of you again, who are so good and dear to me. . . . It is just noon now, and I must go off to drill directly; I have to wear my knapsack on my back all the time. How much there is that I should like to tell you! About three o'clock we shall have a few minutes' rest, I shall go to St. Peter's and pray for you all. The bugle is sounding; good-bye. . . .

"Our drill is just over, we have had a hard time of it. From twelve till four we have not had our knapsacks off for a single moment. Special thanks to dearest mother for her two letters. Never fear, Mother, tell me all about home, you need not be afraid of paining me by reminding me of the happiness in which I can no longer share. I am a Zouave now, and of my free-will I renounced everything to take up the cross. If nature spoke rather too loudly at first, she is pretty well silenced by this time. I am very well and in good spirits. Why should I be otherwise? Hitherto God has preserved me from harm. It is most providential that since I have been in Rome, I have never once been assailed by temptations of an impure nature. I owe this mercy to my Mother in heaven, who proportions her grace to my great weakness. I am not afraid of death, quite the contrary; I have far more dread of suffering. Pray for your son, my dear parents, that he may be a true Zouave, in the most Christian, the highest sense of the word."

It is almost as if a kind of rivalry existed between the absent son and the friends he had quitted as to who should walk with most fortitude and generosity in the path of sacrifice. The following passage occurs in one of Madame Wibaux's letters:

"I am writing in your little room, at your desk, where your crucifix hangs; all is still just as it was when you left. Let us have recourse to prayer, my dear boy, to keep up our courage. The cross is heavy, but you have our Lord ever with you; comfort yourself too with the thought that all your trials will bring down blessings on your family. To us a smile of approval from our beloved Holy Father is worth more than all manner of worldly distinctions. Like you, we too thank God for having chosen you to suffer for His sake."

Theodore on his part would not be outdone, and he determined to be faithful in the least things; for these, transfigured by the light of faith, seemed no longer unimportant to his eyes. For instance: some months previously to his departure for Rome, he had promised his father to give up smoking, and although the circumstances were altered by his entrance into the army, he still adhered to his promise: "I have not so much as touched a cigar, nor indulged in a single whiff of tobacco; I can assure you this has not been at all easy, for at times it is a great privation not to smoke, when one is on guard, for instance, and on a hundred other occasions. No matter, please God, I shall keep my word. When once one goes in for sacrifice one may as well be thorough about it."

Somewhat later he thinks it only just to let his father know what it costs him to keep this promise, which he considers binding upon him until he has been expressly released from it.

"Last night was spent with about forty comrades in the guardhouse, in the middle of a long corridor, through which there was an incessant drought. I own that I longed for a cigar or a good pipe. It is almost impossible to abstain from smoking when one is shut up with a lot of Dutch fellows whose language one does not understand. It is really too stupid, especially when one is not able to while away the time with reading. Sometimes I have been on the point of giving way. Thank God, I have resisted so far, but over and over again I have vowed I would ask you for your permission.

"On the 12th of June Theodore was drafted into the battalion. "I am no longer an unfortunate recruit, whom everybody excuses out of pity and to whom it is a mockery to give the name of soldier; I am now enrolled in the 6th Company of the 2nd Battalion. Farewell to drill; harder work and severer discipline await me now, but in compensation, from this day forward I have a right to call myself a Zouave. My God, I resign myself entirely into Thy hands."

Meanwhile new recruits flocked freely in to place themselves at the disposal of the Holy Father; numerous promotions took place amongst the officers of the Zouaves, and the battalion was transformed into a regiment. The Revolutionists thought the time had come for stronger measures than the publication of manifestos and the utterance of menaces; they wanted to make some startling demonstration, that would intimidate the people, and strike terror into the defenders of the Holy See. The partisans of the Revolution were true to their principles; in their opinion all weapons are legitimate, and on this occasion they employed the poignard. "The Zouave who taught me how to manage the rifle has been assassinated on his way back to the barracks; only the other day I shook hands with him on parting, and said: I shall see you again. How mysterious are the ways of Providence! The murderer has been arrested; he is a Neapolitan, who, it appears, pledged himself to kill three soldiers of the Papal army, an achievement which was to obtain for him liberation from the galleys. The fatal blow was aimed with skill, evidently by the hand of one who was an adept in the art of destroying his fellow men; the affair has aroused the greatest indignation amongst right-minded people.

"At the roll-call this morning, the Colonel recommended us all to keep quiet and be very prudent. He reminded us that we were strictly forbidden to go about the streets alone after night-fall. Today for the first time I have been sentry at San Salvador. It is 10 p.m., I am shut up with a corporal and two men in a horrid hole, dark and smoky. I shall have to wrap myself up in my cloak presently, and sleep as best I can on the bare boards; I have been four hours on duty already in a frightful wind. . . . My comrade is calling me to take his place; good night, I wish you all a better night than I shall have.

"I am just off duty, having been on guard for two hours, my rifle on my shoulder and my rosary in my right hand; that is how I like to pass these solitary hours, alone with God, and thinking of home. When midnight struck, I said to myself: Now everyone is asleep at Roubaix and at Marcq. I said as many decades as I could for those I love, and for them I offered to God all the discomforts of my lot, every step I took on my beat, and the time did not seem long. At 1 a.m. I went back to my boards, but at 5 a.m. I had to be roused from a sound sleep to go on guard again. Altogether I have been eight hours on duty. Such is a soldier's life! A painful and toilsome life, entirely destitute of earthly compensations. Still this life, accepted in a Christian spirit, is not without its attractions. What a consolation to be able at night to offer to God a long day's work, performed for His sake, and His alone! What happiness to think one is a step nearer to Heaven, that one has earned a fresh blessing for others! May I ever regard it in this light, O my God! Away with all human consolations I wish for nothing but to rest in Thee, and love Thee only."

Nature, however, will assert herself even in presence of the most generous resolutions; there must be a struggle if there is to be a victory. After this first experience of a sentry's duties, Theodore lets his mind wander beyond the walls of the barracks, and dwell wistfully on the rest and comfort of his far-off home. The rosary does not make the wind less cutting or the boards seem soft for weary limbs. "This evening I went to see M. Daniel, as one goes to a friend for sympathy, I felt I must unburden my heart to him. I was quite out of spirits, an unusual thing with me, and I cannot account for this depression, I felt the need of prayer, and yet I could not pray; I could not help contrasting my past with my present life. I confess these weaknesses to you, my dear parents, as I confess them to God; you will pardon them in me, as He pardons them. It must be owned that for a few moments my heart failed me as I thought of the drudgery to which I must now look forward—in all probability I shall not get more than three proper nights' rest in the course of a week. If I could have gone to a church it would have done me all the good in the world, but unfortunately I could not leave the barracks. However, I came away from the chaplain a changed man; his blessing and the good advice he had given to me, speaking in God's name, had set all right. You need not be afraid that when I grow faint-hearted I shall keep my troubles to myself. They are a temptation, of the devil, and prayer is the best means of resisting them. Through prayer I shall be preserved, strengthened, and made a true Zouave, of this I am confident. Do not forget to pray a great deal for me.

"January 20th, St. Sebastian's day.
"My first waking thoughts this morning were of this illustrious Saint to whom, for several reasons, I have a great devotion, and

whose name awakens so many pleasant recollections. I was on duty this morning; at 9 a.m. I was free, but it was 11 a.m. before I could go to Communion at the Church of St. Sebastian. I did not forget a single one of the members of our little club. After I got back to Rome I heard another Mass."

Here are indeed well-spent days! The morning hours are consecrated to God, those of the afternoon are devoted to charity, for Theodore passes them in a hospital, by the bedside of a Zouave who is sick; and in the evening he joins a few friends at a restaurant, where they call for one of the dishes peculiar to the country, and give themselves up to light-hearted mirth.

The letters from Roubaix arrived safely now, very frequently too, and the delighted recipient, as he read the affectionate messages and wise counsels they contained, could almost fancy himself listening once more to the dear familiar voices of the writers. Madame Wibaux was indefatigable in recording, for the benefit of her absent son, all the trifling incidents which make up the sum of family life, and which she knew had an especial relish for him. She told him how many earnest petitions were daily addressed on behalf of the beloved Zouave to *Our Lady of the Staircase,* how little Stéphanie would kiss her baby hand to her for Theodore as well as herself, and how Léon, at the end of the holidays, had declared he would not go to school again, until she had set before him the example of his soldier brother, asking him if he thought Theodore ever refused to mount guard, or do anything else he disliked; then the child had become quite tractable, taken his books, and announced himself ready to set off at once.

Thus all day long Theodore was never absent from the thoughts of those whom he had left, and all day long the remembrance of them was present to his mind, acting as an incentive to the practice of virtue. "How many times a day do I ask myself: Would father and mother approve of this? or, What would Willebaud do in my place? And in this way I generally come to a right decision. I want your advice about spending my money. Mother always said I had no idea of its value. One fault I must own to, namely, a weakness for good dinners at the restaurant, but I really think my wonderful appetite is principally to blame for this. However, I am not without scruples on this head, and I think it better to say everything openly to you, then I have nothing left on my conscience."

CHAPTER V.

1867.

Incessant removals. The Coliseum. Feast of the Purification. Beatification of a Capuchin. The Catacombs of St. Agnes. Theodore's eighteenth birthday. The Carnival. St. Joseph's month.

EVERY picture has its dark side, and though nothing could be more delightful than the relations existing between Theodore and his friends, the cordial intimacy which lightened the load of his daily life was, on the other hand, the means of causing him fresh suffering whenever any one of these loved companions was sent out of Rome with the rest of his Company. Our youthful Zouave found difficulty in accustoming himself to this coming and going, this perpetual change of comrades and barracks. As soon as he was stationed anywhere he tried to make a home for himself there, attached himself to the people and things around him, to the Madonnas and churches, and even to the very barrack-room itself, if the windows happened to command a view of some fine point of the Roman Campagna. An order from his Colonel, a few notes of the bugle, and all the framework which was to give regular shape to his life, fell to the ground; the habits adopted but yesterday, yet which already seemed to have grown familiar, had to be abandoned, and everything had to be begun over again at the cost of fresh pains.

"The very walls of the room where I have slept for some time, even a knife I have used, everything grows in time to wear the face of a friend for me, and consequently prepares fresh regrets for me amid the ceaseless shifts and changes which make up a soldier's life. . . . Some people cannot understand how it is possible to grow fond of the barracks where one has done so much hard work, and borne so much fatigue, but is just on account of what I have suffered there for God, the prayers I have offered there, that I love the place."

At such times he would ascend to Heaven on the wings of prayer, and when looked down upon from such an elevation, the petty miseries inseparable from his profession were lost to view, or if seen at all, their somber hues served but to introduce some variety into the monotonous uniformity of life in barracks. An *Ave* repeated before some image of our Lady, a visit to the Church of St. Agnes, a walk in the Coliseum, speedily restored the tone of his mind.

"It does me so much good to visit the Coliseum," he writes, "only the other day I spent three hours there. I was more impressed with the glorious associations which hover around that hallowed place than even by the beauty of the ruins themselves. What a lesson the world might learn there, and what encouragement is there afforded to us who suffer! The persecutors have passed away, the crowds who shouted their angry threats from those innumerable tiers of seats have long since become dust, but the saints who fell upon this arena are crowned with unfading glory! Every stone, every corner of this vast amphitheater seems to have a voice; a simple cross stands in the center of the arena, I knelt before it for some time, and prayed for you, my dear parents, as well as for myself, who have so much need of prayer. At the foot of this cross one feels one is not praying alone, but that the voices of Virgins and Martyrs are uniting themselves by thousands with one's own. The Zouave who kneels here does indeed kneel upon ancestral soil. Finally I seated myself upon a broken pillar, and slowly read over all your dear letters, abandoning myself to recollections of the past and thoughts of the present, and joining in spirit the merry group which gathers around the dinner table at home. Then I climbed upon the ruins, in order to gather some flowers, which I enclose for my mother; they come from the Coliseum and have borrowed their hues from the martyrs' blood.

The Colosseum.

"There were a great many visitors, apparently indifferent, for the most part, to the associations of the scene around them; the English amused themselves by climbing from one row of seats to the other up to the very top, without so much as looking at the cross, or uttering a word of prayer. It was a melancholy sight. I was obliged to tear myself from this hallowed place in order to return to the prose of military life. That same evening I was appointed to form part of the patrol.... It is a singular duty, and a very fatiguing one; it consists in marching during part of the night behind a gendarme, who steps along gravely, like a physician followed by four members of the faculty, through the darkest and most tortuous streets of Rome, listening to every sound, and arresting every one whose appearance can be termed in any way disreputable.

"There were two of us Zouaves accompanying our leader, who, since he knew no language but Italian, remained more silent than Pandora herself; he was, however, quite aware of his dignity, and by no means insensible to the comfort afforded by a *petit verre*.* Can you not fancy us marching along, my comrade at the gendarme's

---

*   A quick drink.

side, I at the regulation ten paces behind, and this for five mortal hours, walking at a snail's pace? The sky was studded with stars, and one might well give oneself up to dreaming, humming over and over again:

> The moon is bright, this cloudless night.
> The vault of heaven is filled with light.

"But my thoughts were otherwise employed, and whenever we passed a Madonna at the corner of the street I repeated an *Ave*. During the whole time our patrol lasted, the worthy gendarme kept treating us to wine and coffee, so that more than once I was obliged to throw away the wine; I contrived to do this without being noticed. What else could I do, since it was impossible to drink all that was offered me, and equally impossible to refuse to accept it? The civilities of these good gendarmes certainly do not cost them very dea; they merely have to call for a bottle of wine in a wine-shop which happens to be open after hours, to drink it in some dark corner, and then ask for the bill as a matter of form only, since they know perfectly well that they will not be allowed to pay for it. After this fashion they charm away the weary hours while making their rounds."

"February 2.

"Today is kept as a great festival in Rome. The chaplain gave us a very good sermon this morning; amongst other things he said: 'If I look towards the Temple of Jerusalem I behold a twofold sacrifice going on there, that of a Mother who offers up her Son, and that of a Divine Child Who offers up Himself. And if I look down from this pulpit, I behold an actual renewal of the same sacrifices; sacrifices, moreover, no less pleasing to God, and no less replete with merit. I am certain that the thought of all which took place this day, has been for the mothers of my present audience a source of ever new strength and courage. It is for you, dear brethren in Jesus Christ, to renew the offering of your lives, and above all of your hearts, in order that they may belong entirely and forever to God.' Dear parents, is not the example of our Blessed Lady a great encouragement for us? Rome wears quite a festive air today, for the feasts of the Madonna are observed here, not in name alone, but in reality. The Square of St. Peter's presents a splendid sight, filled with gay equipages, the gorgeous trappings of which flash and glitter in the bright Italian sun."

"February 6.

"I am going to ask you, my dear parents, to say a prayer for me at a special time. I always feel rather depressed when I first wake in the morning, and think of the hard day's work before me; my thoughts turn in voluntarily in the direction of home, and I realize how far I am from all I love. I repeat prayer after prayer, and renew all my sacrifices, and before long my usual cheerfulness comes back to me. Yet I hope you will always think of me about half-past 6 a.m., and you may be sure I am praying for you.

"I am writing in a gloomy guard-room, but in my dark corner I can hear the joyous bells of St. Peter's ring out. There is to be a solemn ceremony tomorrow; a Capuchin Father is to be beatified. This evening when I was on duty, with my rifle on my shoulder, I said my beads in his honor, and I have the greatest confidence in his intercession."

"February 7.

"The sun rose today in unwonted splendor, and all nature seemed to have donned its festive garb, as if in sympathy with the joy that filled each heart, on account of the beatification by which another protector is given us in Heaven. When I entered St. Peter's I felt a foretaste of celestial happiness. In the vast nave the light was subdued by means of curtains, innumerable tapers were suspended from the roof; the pillars were draped with rich hangings, and four large pictures represented four of the miracles worked by the Blessed Benedict of Urbino. At the end of the nave was a picture of the lowly Capuchin going up to Heaven. During the service, voices which sounded almost unearthly in their beauty sang hymns celebrating the praises of him who had been pure and humble of heart. What glory for an obscure monk to be thus proclaimed Blessed by the representative of Jesus Christ, in this splendid basilica, in the presence of so vast a throng! I was carried quite out of myself, and in my enthusiasm kept repeating to myself that I too ought to become a saint, while to the newly-beatified Capuchin I addressed the following petitions: O thou who art now so glorious in Heaven, be not selfish in the midst of thy felicity! I expect a miracle at thy hands, for thy power is only equaled by thy compassion. Look down on a poor Zouave who has to fight and struggle, as thou didst during thy life on earth; make me a chaste and worthy soldier of Christ, detach me from this world, in order that I may be united to God. I desire to love the cross now, that I may win Heaven hereafter."

Who can doubt that the prayer of the young soldier, mounting upwards as the wreaths of incense from the golden censers floated upwards slowly to the vaulted roof of the Church, reached the ear for which it was intended, and that amid the songs of triumph which sounded that day in his honor in the capital of Christendom, the Blessed son of St. Francis distinctly heard the voice of him who implored his help that he too might become a saint!

At the conclusion of the ceremony, a small party of Zouaves, Theodore among the number, descended into the catacombs of St. Agnes, in order to pray at the burial-place of the martyrs. "I fancied," he says, "I could hear the voices of those who had been persecuted, chanting in solemn accents: Blessed are they who suffer for justice sake; blessed are the clean of heart. We frequently noticed a tomb with the cavity for the phial which marked the resting-place of a martyr, and we made a longer pause there. Surrounded by these sacred remains, which in the darkness and silence were eloquent with a language peculiarly their own, I thought of my beloved parents; in fact when do I not think of you!

"Leaving the catacombs, we turned our steps to the beautiful little Church of St. Agnes. One might think the Saint had erected this sanctuary for herself, and made it fragrant with the rich perfume of her gentleness and piety. Every portion of it is simple, yet costly; both the pillars and altars are of the rarest marble, and no meretricious ornament is anywhere to be seen. All the virgin-martyrs are represented there; the dim light which prevails seems to aid devotion. Lamps are kept burning constantly before the statue of St. Agnes, and it is pleasant to recall the touching story of her unshaken courage and spotless innocence. She was pleasing to God because of her eminent purity, and on this account He preserved her from her enemies. I besought her to keep me pure, and I have a firm belief that she will do so."

"February 11.

"I cannot tell you how much delight your letter gave me, my dearest Mother, I can think of nothing else. You say that you cannot express what you feel, and in this I am like you; God alone knows the love I bear my parents, a love too great to be embodied in words. How well you know how to find the way to my heart, and how to tell me just what I want to know about those I have loved, and now love more than ever! I am sure you often go to Communion for your soldier son; as for myself, when I grow weary on duty, I betake myself to Roubaix, enter unperceived into our little house, and by the help of my watch, know all that is passing there. I cannot imagine how it was that the same idea occurred to us both, but I had already entrusted my guardian angel with the same affectionate messages you had whispered to yours. A thousand thanks for your eight closely-written pages, whenever I have an available moment, I shall employ it in writing to my beloved parents. I find this habit so consoling that I should indeed be loath to discontinue it.

"This is the last letter I shall write while I am seventeen. Tomorrow I shall wake with the weight of eighteen years on my shoulders. How old I am getting! Tomorrow you will all be thinking of me. I shall fancy you drinking. my health, and in the evening saying a prayer together for my intention. Before concluding my letter, I ought to say how grateful I am to God for the many and great favors He has bestowed on me during this seventeenth year of my life. Where shall I be a year hence? Farewell."

"I am now eighteen," he writes on the following day, "an age when the passions are strong, and many a hard conflict has to be fought;

an age when one cannot too earnestly commend one's innocence to the safe-keeping of Heaven." Theodore, accordingly, rising at a very early hour, contrived to go to Communion. After drill was over, a pleasant surprise awaited him in the shape of a feast got up in honor of his eighteenth birthday, by a small party of select friends, who all enjoyed themselves thoroughly, and many were the amusing stories that were told of home life, or the wild pranks of their school-boy days. "Really," says Theodore, "to see and hear us was enough to make the stern old statues of Rome relax their gravity."

Just at this time an excellent opportunity presented itself to Theodore of placing himself in a position to take part more freely in excursions and pilgrimages, and cultivate the society of his friends. If it is true that circumstances make great men, they may be said in another and a higher sense to make saints; for God, in His all-foreseeing mercy, ordains that some chosen souls shall, on their way through life, find themselves, by what men call chance, in circumstances calculated to try their virtue, and out of which by His grace they will come triumphant.

M. Mouton, who was then adjutant to the regiment, had more than once offered Theodore a place as one of his secretaries. A more desirable appointment could not be imagined, the only duties connected with it being an hour's work daily copying despatches, in consideration of which the lucky secretary could claim exemption from fatigue-duty and from sentry-work. Moreover, Theodore had in M. Mouton a fellow-countryman and a friend, thus everything combined to make the offer attractive, and he accepted it. "No sooner had I taken my seat at the desk, than my conscience began to upbraid me. I could not stifle its reproachful voice, a feeling of shame came over me, and I asked myself what had I done? I grew quite bewildered. Look here, I said at length to myself, I did not come here to kick my heels in an office. It is ungenerous to shirk the drudgery of military life; I am a soldier, not a clerk. Let me have suffering, and the more of it the better, provided it is with God and for God, for my friends and for Heaven. My appointment lost all attractions for me, I determined to go at once to M. Mouton and resign it. It went very hard with me to make all his kindness go for nothing.

I told him my story frankly, gave him back the papers in the same condition he had given them to me, and returned to private life."

"February 19.

"The whole morning I have been cleaning my accouterments; tomorrow there is to be a grand review, and everything must be as bright as a mirror. So till three in the afternoon I was busy with this dirty work. These reviews and parades are a regular bugbear to me, you know how incredibly awkward I am. My comrades laugh at me, and tell me I have a perfect mania for polishing, but the fact is I am less handy than they, and therefore longer about it. If ever I go back home, you may give me the boots of the family to black, I will undertake them all. It comforts me to think that every brush I give is counted by my Angel guardian, as was the case with the good religious who had to go a long way in the desert to fetch water, and who heard a voice beside him saying, 'one, two, three. . . .' It was his good angel counting all the steps he took for the love of God."

The Carnival time had come now, bringing with it the usual accompaniment of merry-making, processions of carriages, and showers of *confetti*. In spite of the threatening attitude of the revolutionary party, the people of Rome could amuse themselves at will, thanks to the presence of the Zouaves, who remained under arms all the time. "All the houses on the Corso, without a single exception, were hung with red cloth, and the balconies crowded with beauty and fashion. We marched by proudly, and I am sure many a revolutionist must have felt his heart misgive him, as he saw the bright steel of our bayonets glittering as we passed. My battalion was stationed on the Square San Lorenzo. Everyone was awaiting the signal to begin; the boxes of *confetti* were filled, the bouquets were ready, the ladies had put on their wire masks to protect their faces, and were preparing themselves for the fight. At last the gun was heard; the solemn-looking senators appeared in their splendid equipages, the populace followed them in. crowds; it was a singular sight.

"The mock hostilities were soon in full swing. The maskers disporting themselves in carriages or on foot were assailed by showers of *confetti,* which they returned vigorously. You know the *confetti* are small sugar-plums which break to powder at a touch. Everyone is at liberty to do what he pleases; if you do not want to receive your share of the missiles, you must stay indoors, it is useless to get angry, nobody will heed you. There was one car full of Zouaves disguised as clowns, with high hats like a sugar-loaf. I do not know what their bouquets cost, at any rate they distributed them very freely. All the play consists in going slowly up and down the Corso ten or twelve times, throwing *confetti,* and having them thrown at you. These good Romans are mere children after all; one is glad to see them amusing themselves after so innocent a fashion. The festivities of the day closed with horse racing; there were seven competitors who galloped at full speed from the Piazza del Popolo to the Piazza di Venezia, amid hisses, cheers, and all possible uproar. Such was the first day of the Carnival, and I expect all the others will be pretty much like it; in the evening we returned to our barracks, worn out and famished."

These days of public rejoicing were anything but pleasant for the defenders of the Holy See. "I am on guard with three Dutchmen; it is impossible to make them understand a word I say. I have before me the agreeable prospect of standing sentry for six hours, and to-night, again, I shall have no sleep. Thank Heaven, tomorrow I shall be under arms all the afternoon." The Carnival closed without any bloodshed or disturbance of the peace. Not only had the Zouaves kept evil-doers in check, they had also, by some of them taking an active part in the festivities, rendered good service to the public cause; "for the revolutionists would have liked a dull and gloomy Carnival, that they might with some show of truth, proclaim aloud that the good days were done; now it could not be denied that the Zouaves had themselves been at pains to contribute to the popular amusement.

"On Ash Wednesday, I went to Mass at St. Louis of France. I bent my head to receive the ashes, as the priest said: *Memento homo quia pulvis es.* I do not think these words are gloomy or depressing, on the contrary, they seemed to breathe hope into my heart, for they reminded me that we are not destined to suffer always. I must be brave; all will come to an end at last.

"February 28.

"Francis' birthday. The first thing I did this morning was to ask my angel-brother to pray for me. Happy little boy my companion in so many walks, how fond we all were of him! He is seldom out of my thoughts; I tell him all my troubles and entreat him to intercede for me. Many a time I fancy myself calling him and taking him in my arms as I used to do. I tell him my needs, and I doubt not that he obtains many graces for me."

"March, 1867.

"Today St. Joseph's month begins; we shall often unite in prayer to the kind protector of Christian families. You will invoke him of an evening, kneeling before the statue decked with flowers, and I, wherever I may be, out walking, on guard, or hard at work. I have been anxiously longing for this month to come, for each year hitherto it has brought me spiritual favors and blessings. I made a novena in preparation, as I did last year, and on the 1st, I got up much earlier than usual, and hastened to our chaplain; I was in time to serve Mass and go to Communion. Every morning I go to the Church of the Holy Ghost, close by our barracks. And while you are at breakfast, my dear parents, if you say to each other: 'Now Theodore is praying before the image of St. Joseph,' you will not be far wrong."

About this period, Louis Veuillot visited Rome, as was his wont from time to time, in order to draw fresh fervor from the fountain-head of Catholicity, fresh charity from the paternal heart of the Father of the faithful. The Pope had given a special blessing to the writer whose pen was always employed in the service of the Church; now the *Univers* was to be published again, Pius IX. being himself strongly in favor of the re-appearance of this uncompromising advocate of truth. Theodore had not forgotten that it was in great measure to M. Veuillot that he owed the happiness of being a soldier of the Church; and he lost no time in calling on him. Veuillot warmly welcomed his young friend, and invited him to dinner; but, alas! this invitation could not be reconciled with the requirements of military service. If Theodore had consulted his own pleasure, he would have jumped at the proposal; but duty bade him rejoin his comrades, who had to remain under arms all the evening doing nothing. He found some compensation in the pleasure of meeting M. Veuillot occasionally in church, a slight one, it is true, but may not the converse of the heart, when Christians unite in prayer, be more eloquent than the language of the lips?

"I was present in St. Peter's, when Pius IX. accompanied by all the Cardinals, came to pray before the Altar of the Blessed Sacrament; it is his habit to do so every Friday in Lent. I was within arm's length of him, so I had abundant opportunity to observe the serene and lofty expression of his countenance. He prays most fervently. He never took his eyes from the altar, while his lips moved so that I could almost catch the words he said. How many things he has to ask for, both for himself and for his children! When I see him like that on his knees, I feel tempted to address a prayer to him in my heart, as if he were one of the Saints. M. Veuillot was close to me; he was praying very devoutly, and I am sure he could scarcely restrain his tears. The other day at the *Gesù,* when the Holy Father went there for the Forty Hours, a loud voice, which, however, betrayed the emotion of the speaker, kept exclaiming 'Long live Pius IX, the Pontiff-King!' This cry, which the people took up and re-echoed, was the utterance of our good friend's filial piety."

The Colosseum.

CHAPTER VI.

1867.

Sojourn at Frascati. Religion and duty. Spiritual dangers. Easter in Rome. Theodore's quarters in Fort St. Angelo. Pursuit of the Brigands. Camp life. Return to Rome.

WHENEVER the strict routine of military life allowed the Zouaves a day's holiday, those of them who had a taste for country excursions, used to go to a distance in order to breathe the fresh air of the Roman Campagna. Theodore loved to make one of the merry band which set out on such excursions, a favorite place of resort being Frascati. "It is a little gem of a city, consisting of rows of handsome old villas rising one above another, open to the mountain breezes, shaded by spreading trees, and commanding a view of the finest panorama in the world. On one side is a range of snow-covered mountains; on the other stretches the sea, smooth as a silver mirror; in the midst is the grand old city, with the lofty dome of St. Peter's, gleaming in the sunlight. I never feel so happy as when gazing on a beautiful landscape; my soul rises to Heaven, and I long to make others share the delight and admiration which I vainly strive to express in words."

On reaching Frascati he always made a point of going first of all to pray before the miraculous image of our Lady, belonging to the place, and also of paying a tribute to the memory of the Zouaves who were buried in the Cathedral. Afterwards a visit would be paid to the Zouaves quartered in the Jesuit College at Mondragona; "they are twelve fortunate fellows, whose duty it is to defend the house against brigands. The more I see them, the more I envy their good fortune; to be there is almost enough to make one wish to begin one's studies over again, the more so when I heard the voices of the boys singing in the chapel at Benediction. To think that the Zouaves who are stationed here have close at hand, not only the woods and country walks, pianos, and billiard-tables, but what is much more valuable, the example and counsels of the Fathers!"

When his leave of absence allowed him to take a wider range, he would wander hither and thither, visiting the monasteries, ascending Monte Cave, riding through Castel Gandolfo and Albano, roaming along the shores of the lakes or beneath the shade of the forests, sometimes on foot, sometimes mounted on a donkey. He describes himself as looking like a second Don Quixote, since his legs touched the ground on either side of the animal he bestrode. Those were happy days, free, healthful, and sunny, days which elevated the soul and expanded the heart, and enabled the group of friends to forget the toils of their daily life by means of harmless hilarity and innocent gaiety.

It must be obvious to the reader that the piety of Theodore Wibaux was not of that severe and solemn type which restricts itself to the performances of a certain round of narrow observances, or the utterance of a certain series of appointed formulas. The fulfillment of his daily duties constituted his primary and most important act of devotion, whilst Masses, Communions, and visits to churches held but a second place; and yet thanks to the kindness of his comrades, who knew his tastes, he was seldom obliged to deprive himself of that spiritual food whence came all his strength. "This morning a good-natured Dutchman had the charity to arrange my knapsack for me, thus I was enabled to receive that Bread of Heaven which teaches one to love the Cross. Whilst writing these lines, sitting in a corner of the guard-room, I feel an interior peace which I would fain make you share, for I know God dwells in my heart in all the fullness of His compassion and His love, and I am conscious that I love Him, and desire to live for Him." During the month of March, whenever his duties permitted it, he spent some time each day before the statue of St. Joseph, his dear saint, as he called him. He went to Communion several times in a week in his honor, sometimes fasting until mid-day on this account, and in the evening before returning to barracks, he would pay another short visit to the church in order to ask an evening blessing from his illustrious Patron and Protector, who could not, he thought, fail to bestow an abundant benediction upon one who was so far from all the sweet charities of home.

"March 19, St. Joseph's day.

"My first thought on awaking was of St. Joseph, and my first words were a prayer to him. The depression I formerly experienced in the early morning never troubles me now, and it was certainly in no gloomy mood that I awoke today. I went betimes to church, and heard three Masses.

"It is midnight now, but our whole company is under arms, it is to keep watch in honor of Messrs. Garibaldi and Mazzini, whose feast the Revolutionists may take it into their heads to celebrate after their own peculiar fashion. One of their proclamations has been seized, in which it is said that while the bishops and clergy are shut up in the churches keeping the feast of Joseph of Nazareth, they would keep the feast of Joseph Garibaldi and Joseph Mazzini, the only true defenders of liberty. The manifesto wound up with an appeal to the Roman people, urging them to shake off the foreign yoke. However, nothing came of all this fuss except an attempted assassination on the Corso. The man was taken just as he had succeeded in pinning a Zouave to the wall. I try to lead as holy a life as possible, without troubling myself about what passes around me."

Truly, he had need to watch and pray, for the dangers to which the soul was exposed were more numerous and more terrible than those which beset the body. During the retreat which the Zouaves made before Easter, they were told that the members of the Revolutionary Committee had been discussing how they could best get rid of the Zouaves, who formed the principal obstacle to the execution of their plans. It was finally resolved that, since the soldiers of Pius IX. would not yield to force, no pains were to be spared in order to corrupt them, and many sad instances might be quoted in proof of the assertion. Persons then living in Rome, or in the garrison towns of the vicinity, well know that such was indeed the line of action adopted by those miscreants, their endeavor being to lead the Zouaves to turn aside from the path of virtue, in order to make them a more easy prey. It is the old story of Samson and Dalila over again, we know that the Philistines have never lacked imitators. It is all very well to serve the Pope, and to fight like heroes, but beneath the Pontifical uniform human nature is human nature still; Theodore was well aware of this, and he therefore kept watch with most jealous care lest perchance the priceless jewel of purity should be stolen from him.

"March 25.

"*Ave Maria!* This is what all the bells of the city are ringing out, all the birds of heaven echoing in their songs. It is now 10 a.m., our guard is nearly over. I am writing on an old cannon, in a plot of greensward almost under the Pope's window. Before me Rome lies outstretched, with its dome and resounding belfries; beyond is the bright background of many-hued mountains. Never has the sun been brighter, the sky clearer, nature more joyous, than on this day of the Incarnation. The air is filled with the warbling of feathered songsters. . . . The day is done. What a splendid festival, what a procession! I have received the Papal blessing several times, for you and for myself. The Holy Father traversed the city in his state carriage drawn by six black horses, with an escort of dragoons and guards, and followed by all the Cardinals; every minute cries of 'Long live Pius IX. Long live the Pope-King!' rent the air. I have never seen the Pope look so happy, he smiled on every one, and his hand was constantly raised to give his blessing. About twelve of us Zouaves, bareheaded and bathed in perspiration, pressed close to the wheels of the Pope's carriage. The Cardinals could not repress a smile at our enthusiasm.

"On Holy Saturday the loud booming of the cannon on Fort St. Angelo resounded in honor of the glorious Resurrection. With what delight I repeated the words of the *Regina Cali,* and joined in singing *O Filii et Filia.* Then there came Easter Sunday, a happy day, when joy was in every heart, on every countenance, on the whole face of nature. I will not attempt to describe the effect produced on me by the solemn benediction from the balcony of St. Peter's. It is impossible to imagine anything more impressive; the breathless silence of the immense multitude; the voice of the Supreme Pontiff speaking with power. When he appears, every head is bowed, every voice hushed; it is as if the whole universe waited in expectation of the blessing his venerated hands are outstretched to bestow. I rose from my knees with a strange emotion that brought the tears to my eyes. In the evening the vast basilica was all lighted up, even to the top of the cross on the summit; the effect was like a scene in a fairy tale."

Whilst Rome was keeping these gala-days, the Revolutionary party was organizing detachments of brigands, who were to prepare the way for the Piedmontese army by creating disturbances in the vicinity of the city. These highway robbers intended to begin by carrying off sheep and cattle, in the hope that they might at a later period succeed in confiscating whole provinces. The Zouaves on their part were constantly on the alert, eager to fight, full of plans for the future and dreams of battles to come. But unfortunately a piece of mystification put an end to these campaigning schemes.

"A week ago we were told that we were soon to start for the mountains, an order to this effect had even been given. We all rejoiced to think of varying our monotonous life by means of this excursion, and I, who am so fond of beautiful scenery, was especially delighted. After all we were only made to shift our quarters, being sent to Fort St. Angelo, where the work is hardest. I confess that it was

Fort Saint Angelo.

with a heavy heart that I bade adieu to my old Serristori barracks, to the Church of the Holy Spirit, where I had been so often, and to my mess-mates, who were Dutchmen. I could not understand their language, but they were very fond of me, and showed their affection in a hundred different ways, though *goed Wibaux* was all they could say. They used to say their prayers together very devoutly every evening; I have pasted a picture of St. Joseph on the wall of our room, to the no small delight of the honest fellows.

"Now I am occupying a very lofty nest, under the feet of St. Michael, having to mount two hundred and forty-six steps to reach my rooms, being without water for washing, and obliged to do most toilsome work. "But the unpleasantness of his first impression soon wore off: "I can hardly tear myself from my window, which looks towards the east, since from it I can see Rome and its cupolas, and listen to the sound of the church bells, which never cease their chime. I have placed a very nice picture of our Lady in my new mess-room, and I have given to it the name of Our Lady Help of Zouaves. It is most edifying to see the good Dutchmen saying their prayers before it of a night, and when I wake in the morning my eyes fall upon it the first thing, and I fancy my Mother is smiling on me. A few more hours and April will be done. . . . Tomorrow the fair month of Mary begins; surely she cannot fail to bless one who is both a Zouave and her child. At any rate I shall not lose anything for lack of prayer. I shall see you from afar when you assemble of an evening for prayers in the chapel, which will be full of flowers, the statue of our Lady being surrounded with roses. In spirit I shall be there singing the sweet hymns with you; my good Angel must make the pilgrimage to Marlière in my stead." But the Zouaves too, had their month of Mary; they had erected an altar in the little chapel of the Trappist Fathers, where the members of the Confraternity met every evening, to pay homage to the Queen of Heaven, and sing her praises. And when Benediction was over, Theodore would regain his quarters at St. Angelo, and, leaning out of his favorite window, continue his pious songs by himself.

But ere long the scene suddenly shifts, and the time comes to take leave of Rome and Fort St. Angelo, for the hour of action has struck.

"Corneto, May 15.

"I am writing on the edge of a rock, in full view of the Sea. While I was on guard yesterday, our captain came and ordered me to make ready to leave at once, as we were going to Civita. I was almost beside myself with delight, and the enthusiasm was general. We set off with our knapsacks on our backs; we amused ourselves with singing as we went along in the train, and at 10.30 p.m. reached our destination. We marched out of the town at midnight with loaded rifles, with a countryman for our guide. General de Courten brought up the rear with a piece of artillery. We numbered about ninety men, I formed part of the vanguard. A band of about forty brigands is occupying the mountain, they are fully armed with double-barreled guns, revolvers, and poignards. There are four wide outlets whereby they might effect an escape; our business is to guard these, for the rogues, thus shut in, must die of hunger or carry the position by storm. For some time our route lay along the sea-shore; the water looked beautiful in the brilliant moonlight. It was very tiring to march continuously for six good hours, in the most absolute silence. When we arrived at the foot of the mountain, where the legionaries had already taken up their position, we were made to deploy, in order to act as sharpshooters. A regular brigand-hunt was organized; I made the sacrifice of my life, like all the rest, and prepared to fire. We beat several woods, and exchanged a few shots; I saw quite enough to make me feel certain that I should not acquit myself badly in action. The troop of brigands is surrounded on all sides at present.

"I like this style of life immensely, in spite of all its fatigues. Shall I try to describe our little camp? In the distance the general sits, surrounded by four or five officers; nearer the mountain, the Zouaves belonging to my company are scattered about, some asleep, others laughing and talking. In the meadow a huge cauldron is steaming, it contains a large sheep, for which we have to thank the generosity of the brigands, who last night celebrated a very St. Bartholomew as far as sheep go, for they massacred eleven hundred. As for our beds, they are worthy of a king; we cut down a great quantity of leafy branches and made excellent mattresses by covering them with hay; a throughly rustic sort of accommodation. To-night the greater number of us will no doubt be stationed at the entrance of the wood, to prevent anyone from escaping."

"Monte Romano.

"At last I am able to snatch a spare five minutes in the midst of a march, in order to send you a few words of affectionate greeting, but lately I have more than once felt as if I should never be able to do so again. How much I have been through during the last few days! I ought indeed to be grateful to God and to our Blessed Lady for having thus supported me through so many dangers and fatigues. It has been a rough apprenticeship, for a war with brigands is no ordinary warfare. They are good walkers, thoroughly at home amongst the mountains, and one has to give proof of powers not inferior to theirs. Since my departure, I have spent all my nights in the open air, lying on the damp ground, in the solitary woods. It was our duty to watch the path to the grottoes; we had to listen in silence, holding our breath, our fingers on the trigger of our guns. Every sentinel had orders to fire without a previous challenge; it is frightful to think one might kill a man in this way, a comrade perhaps, for the sentries have been repeatedly on the point of firing on the guard coming to relieve them. I have myself over and over again knelt down, and then just as. I was about to fire, my sharp eyes enabled me to perceive that the supposed foe was but a phantom after all. It is all very well to be courageous, and offer to God the sacrifice of one's life, but there is something very gloomy in thus lurking in ambush at night; it would be far preferable to encounter three times the number in the open field. The beauty of moonlight, the ceaseless song of the nightingales, and the memories of home which grow more vivid with the growing danger, were strangely out of keeping with the incessant and vigilant watch which it was necessary to maintain. On the one hand was the voice of nature, which would be heard, and never did the familiar fireside appear more attractive, or more worthy of regret; on the other hand were firm faith, lively hope, and a perpetual renewal of one's sacrifice, combined with those thoughts, prayers, and aspirations, which when exchanged between the soul and her Creator, become the source of ineffable consolation. At such times the eye and heart turn frequently to the star bespangled firmament, as if to seek there a pledge of the fulfillment of God's promises. On one of these occasions a comrade said to me: 'Who knows whether tomorrow we may not sing our Sunday Mass in Paradise?' Under such circumstances, nature with its stores of affections and memories, and religion with its treasures of faith and self sacrifice, seem as it were, to divide the heart between them, and by means of this division, to expand and enlarge it.

"The three first nights the attempts made by the brigands against the legionaries were without result. We heard the firing at a short distance from us, and the balls whistled over our heads; the fourth night they had recourse to stratagem, and succeeded in reaching the outposts unperceived. A bearded giant knocked down the two sentinels, his companions rushed after him; the troops, taken ùnawares, sent after them a well-sustained platoon-firing, they fancied they heard the cries of a wounded man, but that was all. Their prey had escaped from their grasp, and it is impossible to describe the annoyance they expressed when we saw them next morning. After beating the woods to no purpose, we were obliged to leave. We have just arrived at Monte Romano, a picturesque little village which I have thoroughly explored, only to find a bad pen and some bad ink. I went first of all to the church, for I feel the need of prayer more than ever, and my greatest privation has been the impossibility of continuing my visits to the Blessed Sacrament. Yesterday we went to hear Mass in a village at some distance, the priest received us with open arms. My health is excellent, I am very merry, I constantly think of you, and in spite of the short allowance of sleep I have had lately, I feel quite fresh.

"I passed a very good night at Monte Romano; it seemed quite luxurious to me to sleep once more under a roof, on a bed of straw! The next day we were up at 4 a.m. and by the evening had reached the banks of a charming little stream, whose cool clear waters were refreshing to look upon. Twenty of us, under the command of a sergeant, spent four days there, sleeping in tents, and leading the life of recluses. At night we took it by turns to act as sentinels, in order to guard the spots where the river was fordable; but we had no surprises of any consequence, one of us killed a horse. In the day time we were free to bathe, dream, philosophize, or spend our leisure hours in the peaceful sport of the angler. This life thoroughly suited me; I kept so entirely to myself that whenever I saw a strange face I felt inclined to ask whether the world was still going on the same, and whether men were as wicked as ever? As the brigands did not put in an appearance, we at length bade adieu to these scenes of enchantment, and set out for Corneto, one of the most charming old towns I have ever seen. It overlooks the sea, from which it is about three miles distant, and the inhabitants appear to be very hospitable. I was greatly astonished on my arrival to receive an invitation to dine with a Canon who was desirous to make my acquaintance, and I certainly spent a most enjoyable evening. Picture to yourself a small garden with a view of the sea, and in this garden an aviary, some choice antiquities, and an arbor shaded by vines, with a model host to do the honor of it all. Canon Angelo, who is perfectly in keeping with his charming surroundings, is quite fanatical about us Zouaves; he kept squeezing our hands as he showed us over his house, and pointed out the best views from the garden. Dinner was served in the open air, and we were able to watch a splendid sunset over the water. It was a very pleasant party, composed chiefly of sergeants, and I am truly grateful to our chaplain for having procured this introduction for me.

"On the 25th of May we returned to Rome, covered with dust and perspiration. Thus ends my first campaign; how many of our comrades envy us! Our expedition has not been fruitless, if it has shown our chiefs what they may expect of their men, and besides this, will not the fatigue and want of sleep we have endured for God's sake, bring down blessings upon us? I have never found anything unbearable all the time, and my severest privation has been want of sleep. Yesterday when I was on guard, I actually dozed off while standing sentry. As to my marching powers, I may say I have done credit to my name, and shown myself worthy to be my father's son."

The boy of eighteen is a soldier now; in his case piety and courage go hand in hand; he can pray, but he can fight too, and he has learned the secret of preserving under all circumstances that union of the soul with God, which divinizes duty, and also gives courage to fulfill it without flinching.

CHAPTER VII.

1867.

Letters from Roubaix. A grand review. Solemn functions in St. Peter's. Fatiguing occupations. Visits to Religious Houses. Reminiscences.

MANY pleasant surprises awaited Theodore on his return. First of all he found one of his friends, M. Carlos Cordonnier, had enlisted in the Papal army; having come to Rome as a tourist, he remained there as a Zouave. "It was not altogether unexpected," says Theodore, "but I am so glad! He is such a good marksman too, no fear that he will waste his cartridges. "From that time forward the two compatriots were inseparable friends; the new comrade was a fresh confidant for Theodore, a brother in heart and affection, destined to become a brother in reality later on by means of closer ties.

Then too, while he had been away hunting the brigands, a pile of letters from Roubaix had accumulated, containing photographs of various members of his family; and with these precious likenesses in his hand, the big Zouave fancied himself a child again with his little sisters; a schoolboy with Joseph and Stephen. He too wanted to send a nice portrait of himself home to his friends, and so he went to be taken, but the result was rather disappointing. "You will see for yourself that I have not much of the soldier about me," he says. "In fact, I am convinced I shall never make one.

"Everyone in the barracks is asleep now, taking a siesta; but I do not care for this, and would rather spend the time with my dear parents. Our collegians from Marcq will be at home now, what a large party you will be at dinner! I can see the happy faces and hear the merry laughter. The absent Zouave will not be forgotten, you will be wondering where he is, what he is doing. Or perhaps you have just received the account of his terrible campaign, and are drinking his health. . . .

"What return can I make for your kind letters? Dear Mother, it seems the more you write to me, the more you love me. I too feel keenly and love warmly, but I have not the power of putting on paper all the secrets of my heart, while your letters are just like a delightful conversation between a fond mother and her loving child. Once every week you draw me to your side, you take both my hands in yours. I seem to be present with you, to hear you counseling me, encouraging me, inspiring me with confidence. When I look into the future, I scarcely dare to cherish the hope of one day seeing you again. I have thrown myself blindfold into the arms of Divine Providence like a child who is weak, helpless, forlorn; God is leading me, and I follow, calm and trustful. And when passions, regrets, memories of the past, threaten to disturb my inward tranquility, a merciful hand holds me back from giving way to them. Oh! if the time should ever come for me to leave the Zouaves, I should say from the bottom of my heart: From military life, good Lord deliver us! I continue to struggle and to pray, for every day I see more plainly that in order to become a bad Christian, it is enough to leave off making any effort to be a good one."

The month of June was to witness a glorious triumph for the Church and her Chief Pastor. The anniversary of the coronation of Pius IX, the eighteenth centenary of St. Peter, the canonization of several saints, the beatification of two hundred Japanese martyrs, all combined to attract thousands of the bishops, clergy, and laity to the metropolis of Christendom. For a time everything wore a tranquil aspect; hostile menaces, evil prognostications, pusillanimous fears, all were for a time hushed to silence.

"St. Peter's is being completely transformed; everywhere hangings, wreaths and pictures are being put up; it is a labor worthy of the ancient Romans. One shudders to see the numerous *San Pietrini* suspended in mid-air, as cool as possible and apparently entirely in their element. For my part I much prefer the church without these decorations; its majestic beauty in itself is quite enough, and needs no superadded ornament. There is a perfect swarm of French priests in Rome, and every day their numbers increase. One meets them at every turn, walking about with their heads in the air, a breviary under one arm and an umbrella under the other; whenever they encounter one of the 'brave Zouaves,' as they call, us, they invariably accost him. I do like to see them so much."

On the 21st of June a salute of fourteen guns was fired in honor of the saint of the day, one of the patron saints most dear to the people of Rome. At an early hour in the morning Theodore repaired to the lowly chamber where St. Aloysius drew his last breath. "The walls are the same, and the same ceiling and door are left, but it has been decorated and made into a beautiful little chapel. There, in the very room where the holy youth toiled and suffered and held communion with God, one feels the need of being chaste and fervent, and one gains fresh strength for the spiritual combat. I saw the crucifix before which he prayed, the Madonna on which he used to gaze with filial affection. I did not forget you, my dearest parents, in this hallowed sanctuary, nor in that of the Blessed Berchmans, close by. It is as if Providence had purposely ordained that the cells of these two angelic beings should be near together. Can you not understand how it soothes and helps one whose heart is agitated by passions of all kinds, to come and pray, in this atmosphere of purity and peace, for grace to struggle and strength to conquer? I left with the firm resolution to be more brave and generous in future."

On the same day a review was held of the Pontifical army; the eight thousand soldiers of the Pope marched into the grounds of the Villa Borghese, in the midst of a closely-packed crowd of spectators, all eager to see and greet with hearty cheers these noble volunteers, whose life was one long act of heroic devotion to the cause of the Church. Amongst them were many members of noble houses side by side with heroes of lowlier birth; and amongst the bystanders too were many prelates, priests, and simple laymen, who also fought for Christ, though with less deadly weapons, with word and pen, with acts of charity and pious deeds. They were the chosen defenders of the Church militant, a living embodiment of her Catholicity, the bloom, as it were, of her perpetual youth. And when, as the long lines of the Pontifical army marched past, the Zouaves appeared in their turn, with their bright equipments and soldierly bearing, smooth young faces like Theodore's contrasting with the bearded visages of veterans, when these troops, so varied in their nationality, yet united in a common faith, closed their serried ranks around the flag they defended with such splendid courage, the enthusiasm of the spectators knew no bounds: shouts of "Long live Pius IX! Long live the Zouaves!" seemed to rend the very heavens. It was a magnificent spectacle in every way, and the Zouaves had just cause for pride. Various dioceses vied with each other in generous contributions towards the support of the little army. Theodore might well feel proud, for the diocese of Cambrai alone paid the expenses of two hundred and forty soldiers of the Pope.

Three days later Pius IX. addressed an allocution to the bishops and priests then in Rome, in which he gave notice of a General Council to be held in 1870. It belongs to the Church of God alone to speak thus confidently about the future, even at a time when it appears as if she were scarcely certain of the morrow. But of all these festive celebrations, the most brilliant was that of the 29th of June, the eighteenth centenary of the martyrdom of the first Pope. Pius IX. had fixed upon that day to bestow upon the Church a fresh phalanx of saints and protectors, amongst whom Germaine Cousin, the simple French shepherd-girl, was destined to shine.

"As a son of the Church, and a defender of her sacred cause, I felt my heart beat high with joy and pride at witnessing the accomplishment of one of the greatest miracles of faith. This venerable assemblage of bishops and clergy, the tranquil serenity of the Holy Father, the universal rejoicings that nothing has occurred to disturb, are to me, in this year 1867, a sight no less marvelous than that of Peter walking upon the water. It is to be feared that troublous times are close at hand; but however that may be, we shall at least have seen the triumph that was foretold. We Zouaves have to pay rather a heavy price for the pleasure of witnessing these grand ceremonies, but we do not grumble. Today, for instance, I have only just come off duty, and in an hour I must be under arms again. Nothing can go on without the Zouaves being present, the sight of us seems to give everyone a sense of security. I will not attempt to describe the ceremony itself. I was posted in St. Peter's from eight in the morning until one, to keep back the crowd. From 4:30 a.m. a countless multitude thronged the steps of the church, and when the doors were opened, a perfect torrent streamed in. The procession passed first through the streets, I was prevented seeing it, being on duty, but how could it be otherwise than most imposing, seeing that nothing which contributes to the external beauty of religion was wanting? The new saints were represented in it, and there was a banner of St. Germaine, preceded and followed by the bishop and priests of the diocese.

"It is a solemn moment when the Cardinal Procurator three times in succession asks the Pope to consent to the canonization, first *instanter,* then *instantius,* finally *instantissime,* and when the Pope, at the third request, expresses his compliance, a fresh band of intercessors—in this case twenty-five in number—is given to the Church, a fresh constellation added to her firmament. At the same moment a loud *Te Deum* of thanksgiving bursts from the lips of all present, expressive of the joy and gratitude filling every heart. The *Tu es Petrus,* composed by Mustafa, the choir master of the Papal chapel, was sung; it was very fine, the singers being divided into three choirs, the soprano voices from their places in the cupola seemed to be wafted down from Heaven itself. I saw and heard the whole under most disadvantageous circumstances, holding my rifle all the time, squeezed by the crowd, and obliged every moment to call the unruly multitude to order. I was fairly used up, but it was a satisfaction to think that I too had had a part in the ceremony, and surely St. Germaine will remember the poor Zouaves who took so much trouble in her honor. I did not forget to pay due homage to St. Peter; if it is true that he holds the keys of Heaven, is it likely that when he sees my uniform, he will make any difficulty in letting me in?"

These grand functions were followed by other services, less solemn and less imposing, perhaps, but more touching. Every day one or other of the best preachers among the prelates whom this occasion had brought together, ascended the pulpit to proclaim the glories of the Church. Theodore would fain have multiplied himself so as to have been in several places at once; we are told how he went to hear Mgr. Mermillod preach the panegyric of St. Paul; how he followed a triduum held in honor of the new French Saint, whose praise Mgr. Berthaud celebrated with all the poetic charm and grace of his eloquence; how he was present at the solemn coronation of Our Lady of Perpetual Help, the special treasure of the Redemptorist Fathers, before which he loved to go and pray. Nor was the little Confraternity of the Zouaves overlooked; Mgr. de Cambrai said Mass for them, and Theodore renewed his act of consecration, already made at school, and received Communion from the hand of his Archbishop. Later on in the same day, he went to call on him, and reminded him how, a year before, at the College at Marcq, one of the rhetoricians, who had been appointed to deliver the address of welcome, had in his speech on the occasion, made his desire to enter the Papal service very apparent. That school-boy's wish had been realized to his heart's content; was there one of all the Zouaves as happy as Theodore?

Ere long the heat, the cholera, and the fever rendered Rome an undesirable place of residence for the thousands of visitors who had flocked thither to witness the solemnities of which we have been speaking. But before their departure, those who had come from the north of France gave a farewell banquet to their fellow-countrymen whose duties kept them in Rome; Theodore, with other French Zouaves, was invited, and, seated by his friends and teachers of former days, revived the associations which still united him closely to his home, and seemed to revisit once more the scenes where his childhood and early youth were spent. But the illusion did not last long;

the toils and duties of every-day life had to be resumed without rest or respite, or rather with the prospect of exchanging the hard work of the past for still harder work in the future, since the period of tranquility, occasioned by the festivities in Rome, and the freedom from all apprehension of immediate danger, had induced the military authorities to grant leave of absence to many members of the Pontifical army, and thus a double portion of work fell to the share of those who remained. The latter, however, did not complain; for, as Theodore said: "If the Revolution were to break out suddenly, or the Garibaldians to come down on us, the absentees would never cease to regret their temporary desertion of their post. I wish to remain where I am, near the Holy Father, and I prefer to do double work, provided I have the encouragement afforded by his presence, and the consciousness that I am ready at any moment to shed my blood for him. My health continues excellent, but the heat is stifling. If my good angel had to count and treasure up every drop of perspiration which stands on my forehead, he would have enough to do. It is a great privation to get no bathing, what would I not give to be able to take a good header into the water! The worst is that one cannot employ oneself to any purpose in the guard room this hot weather; it produces a certain drowsiness both of mind and body, which unfits one for everything. You must accept my goodwill, and the proof I give of my affection.

"I have consecrated July to St. Anne, and inaugurated the month by going to Communion. I now fully understand how this Sacrament gives courage to martyrs, solace to the afflicted, and makes suffering attractive and desirable. Though I am far from feeling the ardent love and holy transports of St. Gertrude and St. Mechtilde, and have only the goodwill of my heart to offer, I always come away from the Holy Table fortified and consoled. Would that I could approach more worthily!

"I have good news to tell you, dear parents; I shall now be able to hear Mass daily, and say my prayers at the same time as my dear mother. Just fancy, we were forbidden to leave the barracks before 10 a.m. But I knew that would not last long. Henceforth we are free to go out before the roll-call, and I can tell you I do not doze away all the morning in bed. When I have not to go on duty, I drink up my coffee with all speed, and make my way through the dirty winding streets of the Ghetto to my favorite church. I am never at a loss to know where there will be Mass, as a bell rings to tell one when and where to go. seldom go alone, being generally accompanied by two comrades, one of whom is a Vendean of Pius IX, just what one would fancy the Vendeans were in Louis XVI's time; the other a capital fellow, a Dutchman; I could not have a more devoted friend, or one more thoughtful in anticipating my wishes. I really believe there is nothing he would not go without for me. He is a well-educated young man, and has devoted a good deal of time to study. We take long walks together, and I find him a most agreeable companion."

The burning heat of the sun did not deter Theodore from pursuing his peregrinations in and about Rome, which offers so much that is curious, interesting, and attractive to the visitor. He wishes to make himself thoroughly acquainted with the Eternal City, with its religious history, the legends of its saints, the transformations its noble edifices have undergone. To him it appears in the light of a vast museum, wherein everything has a special significance to the eye of the Christian. "I am enthusiastically fond of Rome," he writes, and can readily understand how to many it becomes a second home." Pagan Rome, he acknowledges, has no interest for him, but he ascribes this to his ignorance of history, for he finds that the monuments of antiquity do not lack majesty and importance when viewed in connection with the glory of God, and the triumph of the Church.

For a time it appears to be his object to go the round of all the countless religious houses in the city. Accompanied by a few other Zouaves, as pious and fervent as himself, he visits one after another, inspecting the buildings, examining the pictures, asking to see the treasures of the house, to have the relics displayed to him; he will not be refused admittance anywhere, even finding means of penetrating into precincts whence visitors are as a rule excluded, for what difficulties will daunt a Frenchman when once he has set his mind on anything? "I am never so happy as when I am with these good Religious, in the abode of piety and prayer, where sanctity is something real that can be felt and seen. The very site of these sweet solitudes adds something to their charm; by a coincidence not unfrequently met with, places once given up to debauchery, ostentatious display, and vainglorious pride, now purified and transformed, are become the home of chastity, self-denial and humility; evidently Providence permits this for its own wise ends."

This indefatigable sightseer takes care that his friends at home shall share in the pleasant impressions he receives, and many charming incidents from the lives of the Saints are found interspersed in his letters. His correspondence really forms an excellent guide to the city of Rome, one too, replete with life and Christian sentiment, which does not merely contain a dry statement of facts, but whose every page breathes poetry and love. It cannot be denied that in all the convents the Zouaves were treated like spoiled children, the uniform they wore formed the best of introductions, and the Religious were only too delighted to make as much as they could of the soldiers of the Church. At the Convent of the Sacred Heart, Theodore and his friends saw the celebrated picture of the *Mater Admirabilis,* and knelt a few moments before it in prayer. The Mother Superior was enchanted to receive them, and gave them each a medal. The monks of St. Jerome showed them the cell occupied by Tasso, the tree beneath which he used to sit and dream, and the magnificent monument Pius IX. erected over his tomb. At the monastery of St. Bona venture they venerated the sacred remains of St. Leonard of Port-Maurice, canonized on the previous 29th of June; and at the House of the Thomist Fathers, the body of St. Alexis, whose resting-place is close to the staircase beneath which the lowly Saint for so many years lived the life of an angel upon earth. In the church of the Dominican Fathers they saw the large stone which the devil hurled at St. Dominic, and which for all his clumsiness he must have grasped firmly, since the deep mark made by his claws is still to be seen on it. Some French novices accompanied the visitors over the house; Theodore remarks how well the white habits looked side by side with the bright uniforms of the Zouaves.

He kept the 31st of July in honor of St. Ignatius, and indeed spent almost the whole day at the Gesù. "The small and shabby rooms," he writes, "are left much as they were in the Saint's lifetime. The walls are papered with letters, the presses are filled with most valuable relics. Here it was that St. Philip Neri and St. Ignatius used often to confer together; here St. Francis Borgia many a time offered the Holy Sacrifice. How many good and useful undertakings were planned within these walls! How many fervent prayers sent up to Heaven! In what was formerly the Saint's study, a patriarch was saying Mass; a good many bishops were present, I went to Communion. How happy and pure one feels in such surroundings! Another Zouave was with me, a man of exemplary life, a second Guérin, the habitual serenity of whose soul nothing ever ruffles. One of the good Fathers spied us out, and insisted on our having some breakfast; we did not refuse, and our Zouave appetites did credit to the hospitality of our kind entertainers. We went again in the evening, as there was solemn Benediction; the altar looked magnificent. Tell me, do you not think I had reason to thank God for a very happy day? I love these festivals beyond everything, they are the true joys of my exile; above all, I like to carry the thought of you about with me everywhere, to unite my prayers with yours, to implore grace and blessings through the medium of the same intercessors.

"August 2nd, Feast of St. Alphonsus.
"I was on guard yesterday, and again last night; no sooner was I at liberty this morning, than I hastened to pay my homage to the Father of the Redemptorists, as I did to the Father of the Jesuits on his day, and rejoice in the glory of the saints."

Thanks to such untiring activity, Theodore ere long became familiar with every nook and corner of Rome, and his good offices as cicerone were often called in request by French tourists. The majority of these visitors being newly-married people, his good-nature had the result of obtaining for him the *sobriquet** among his comrades of *Cicerone for the wedding tour,* or the *Honeymoon guide.*

Theodore must indeed have possessed an iron constitution to bear the life he led. To be on one's feet all day long in the height of summer, to run about in one direction or another in all the intervals of military service, and employ every spare minute in letter-writing, requires a superhuman energy. "Excuse my style," he says in one letter, "in weather like this one feels little inclination for writing; from morning till night I am bathed in perspiration."

About this time cholera and fever wrought sad ravages amongst the Zouaves. Not a day passed by but one or other of the men on guard was struck down, and had to be taken to the hospital. Nevertheless, in spite of the burning sun and fatiguing service, Theodore kept at his post; the only thing he complains of being that he found it so difficult to say his prayers while on guard, with his rifle on his arm. "Thank God with me," he says. "Far from hankering after my dear Roubaix, I feel every day more strongly that my place is in Rome, and I hope I may never be tempted to forsake it. As the heat

---
*   A nickname.

Church of Gesù.

gets more intense, and the departures more numerous, the more proud I feel of being able to hold up. We have had a time of severe trial lately; it is no exaggeration to say that we have 20% sick, there is not a single Company in which several deaths have not occurred."

Amongst other victims of the pestilence, one of Theodore's friends was suddenly carried off. He speaks of him in the most affectionate terms, and remarks how well they always got on together. Although feeling very ill, this intrepid young man continued to do everything as usual, up to the day when his strength finally gave way, and he had to be taken to the hospital. The Sisters nursed him with unremitting attention, no petted child could have had greater care; the Chaplain was frequently heard to call him an angel. The only thing that caused the sick man uneasiness, was the thought of his mother's grief; "I am an only son," he said, "and she is a widow. What will my poor mother say when she hears that I am dead? Tell her that I am going to Heaven, and it is to her that I owe it." Shortly before he died, his cheek being flushed with the fever that was consuming him, the Sister said to him, "Come, I really think you are a little better." "Oh no, I am not," he replied, "besides, it is for the best that I should go now, or I should have to go through this all over again."

Theodore had found in this friend that which always had a peculiar fascination for him: purity and generosity of heart. "When I recall the miseries and hardships we had to encounter at the outset, I like to remember how, with his unselfish kindness, he tried to supply my wants. On board the boat, when we suffered so much from the cold and rain, he insisted on lending me his fur-lined coat, saying he was much more accustomed to exposure than I was. He and I began military life together, and the constancy he displayed encouraged me to persevere in a career which was at first strange and distasteful to me. Pray for our sick, for they are not all as pure in heart, as well prepared to meet death; happily the number of cases is on the decrease now. Our future is in the hands of Providence; what God keeps is well kept."

And truly what else remained to be done in face of the dreadful disease which mowed down the good, in face of the machinations of the wicked who were weaving new schemes, but to abandon oneself to Providence, and go on in the plain path of duty? This was Theodore's favorite doctrine, and one which he constantly put into practice. "My dear parents," he writes, "let us trust in Providence, and say again and again, Thy will be done; nothing more effectually soothes and tranquilizes the soul when it is tortured by the tempest of passions, torn to pieces by conflicting hopes and fears."

No wonder if, to one of so warm and affectionate a nature, life often appeared dull and wearisome, especially when August came, reviving as it did in the breast of the quondam schoolboy recollections of keen enjoyment, of the varied amusement of the holidays, the blissful meeting with fond friends at home: reminiscences painful and yet pleasant, which, while they make the disagreeables of the present stand out in harsher prominence, yet by a singular contradiction, facilitate the task of bearing them in patience.

"Do you remember the prize-day, dear Mother, that happy day when we were so completely one in thought and feeling? Do you remember how we knelt at our Lady's feet, to implore her blessing on the work of the past year, on the pleasures of the coming holidays? Nothing marred the happiness of that day, bright with the golden sunshine of cloudless youth! My chief delight is thus to live in the past. What a contrast it forms to the dreary realities of the present, a barrack-room with all its unbeauteous associations; there remains to me, however, the supreme consolation of knowing that in all this I am doing the will of God."

The Vatican.

CHAPTER VIII.

1867.

The start for Albano. Orders and counter-orders. The cholera. Theodore's services in the hospital. Death of Cardinal Altieri. Honors bestowed on the 6th Company. Leisure and temptations. Ariccia. Anniversary of Castelfidardo. Return to Rome.

"August 6th.
"THIS is the last day that I shall spend in my beloved Rome, and God alone knows how long a time will elapse before I see it again: perhaps a fortnight, perhaps three months. Tomorrow we start for Albano, a town delightfully situated between two lakes, in the midst of fine mountains, opposite the sea. Were I going to a less pleasant place of abode, I should be dreadfully sorry to leave Rome."

These lines were written in the guard-room, during the night. The next day, after numerous orders and counter orders, and weary alternations of hope and disappointment, they set off at last, with their knapsacks on their backs, and a great quantity of baggage. "Every time a start is made the same question has to be considered, namely how to get the greatest amount of things into the least possible space, that is to say, how to cram all one can into a very small knapsack. The sergeant called me out of the ranks, with four other men, in order that we might go with the baggage; I did not much regret the departure of my comrades, because I hoped to rejoin them the next day. We left the barracks mounted aloft on wagons, drawn by very fine artillery horses, and in this guise we traversed the whole city, to the no small amazement of the Romans, who knew not what to make of these proceedings. We carried our cartridge-boxes, our rifles, and our bread-bags slung crosswise. When we reached Maccao, a halt was called in order that we might take a short rest in the splendid barracks built there by Pius IX. At midnight we were suddenly aroused by M. de Charette, who forbade us to proceed. This was a new annoyance, involving fresh sacrifice, but the order must have been of importance, since the Lieutenant-Colonel came to the extreme end of the town, and at such an hour, in order to deliver it in person. The following day was spent in weary waiting, and in the evening we were politely requested to return whence we came. Such unexpected moves as this make up a soldier's life!"

The reason of all this coming and going was fully explained as soon as it transpired that the cholera was raging with great violence at Albano. Carts, baggage, and men, all went back to Rome, and there patiently awaited the return of the rest of the Company. "We do not know what they are doing, but we are sure they will be greatly vexed, since they will have seen the promised land without being allowed to enter it. We are expecting them this evening." Poor Theodore! how little he dreamed as he wrote these lines what a keen disappointment was in store for him, and what need he would have to repeat that *Fiat,* which assuages the grief of those whose trembling lips can scarcely utter it.

"My very dear parents, I really must tell you what a terrible vexation I have had, I do not know when I have felt anything of the kind so much. To think that forty five men of my corps have had the opportunity of displaying the most heroic devotion, whilst I was doing nothing at all in Rome, only waiting about uselessly, seems almost more than I can bear. The very day they reached Albano the cholera broke out with unheard-of violence. In an incredibly short space of time the place was deserted; not a soul was left to do anything for the sick or bury the dead. Our gallant Lieutenant de Résimont was the first to act; he lifted a corpse in his arms and carried it to the cemetery, all the rest followed his example; our men of the 6th outdid one another in self-denying deeds. On the field of battle the smell of the gunpowder, the excitement of the scene, makes one forget danger; but when one finds oneself face to face with a dead body, or a sick man in his last agony, then no ordinary amount of determination and superhuman courage is required! Just think of these Zouaves lavishing the most devoted care and attention on people who were perfect strangers to them, nay more, who hated them. The inhabitants of the place were thoroughly hostile to us, and had even resolved to oppose our coming; now the detested Zouaves appear in the character of angels of consolation. The General declares that the behavior of our men was quite heroic: it has been reported to the Holy Father, and an address presented to him speaking in highest terms of the 6th Company of the first Battalion; they will all be decorated.

"Oh, why has God required of me such a sacrifice? Unless I believed that it was ordained by some special design of Providence, I should be utterly miserable. It is really too much to know that our comrades are sacrificing themselves thus, and be prevented joining them: I hardly know how to contain myself for vexation. At the very moment of starting, we were told off to look after the baggage; three times we were on the point of setting out, and each time we got a counter-order to stop us. These are to all appearance trifling incidents, but the finger of God may be seen in all. It was not His will that we should receive the medal of the Holy Father, He has denied us the privilege of giving public proof of our devotion; He has reserved for us what is perhaps a more painful sacrifice, hidden sufferings, which if accepted in a Christian spirit, will merit as great a reward. We have had terribly laborious work in times past, which has taxed our powers of endurance to the utmost. For my part I have sought a refuge in the Sacred Hearts of Jesus and Mary, and to them I willingly make the sacrifice of this medal which I should have been so pleased to win and so proud to wear. Good-bye, dear parents; I have but poorly expressed my real feelings-they are too strong for words. Pride in belonging to the 6th, admiration for the conduct of my comrades, regret at being excluded from a share in their labors, confidence that I have fulfilled the holy will of God all these various emotions struggle within my heart.

"My best love to all. Please remember me often in your prayers.

"P.S. Heaven be praised! I am to start for Albano in half an hour, with the remainder of our gallant band; God has ordered all for the best. I trust I shall do my duty bravely."

Worthy indeed of admiration was the sight to be seen in Albano at that time, namely heroic charity spending and being spent amid scenes of horror and death. Those amongst the inhabitants who were not struck down by the scourge, fled from it in hot haste, or were paralyzed by fear; the Gonfalonier had already crossed the frontier, the members of the Commune had all disappeared, so that there was no one invested with sufficient authority to make arrangements for attending to the sick, who, left to themselves, lay helpless in the deserted habitations; whilst unburied corpses, some of them nearly naked, and in an advanced state of decomposition, were to be seen in the empty houses and even in the public thoroughfares.

In the midst of this dire confusion, beneath a scorching sun, and in an atmosphere laden with pestilence, the soldiers of Pius IX. divided amongst them the work which had to be done. Some took up their post in the cemetery, where by day and by night they were occupied in digging graves and burying the dead, ninety corpses being brought to them in the course of the first night. The Lieutenant Colonel, who came over from Rome for the purpose of encouraging his men, heard that two of the Zouaves, who were busy digging graves, had not even paused to break their fast, although it was already late in the morning, and nothing short of an express order from their chief could induce the brave fellows to take some refreshment. On the other hand, those Zouaves who remained in the town were incessantly engaged in caring for some hundreds of sufferers; they undressed them, waited on them, rubbed them, assisted them to die like Christians, and it might have been thought that they had spent their lives in nursing the sick. Around them many courageous souls vied with each other in carrying on the work of saintly charity; several priests succumbed to the malady whilst exercising their sacred functions, and the Daughters of St. Vincent of Paul were, as usual, an example to all; the King of Naples, who refused to quit the place, himself attended to the wants of his brothers, his servants, and the other members of his family, the Queen-Mother being one of the first victims. Two of the Zouaves, natives of Holland, caught the dire disease from carrying on their shoulders corpses in a state of putrefaction, and expired within twenty-four hours, full of joy. One of them, Henri Peters by name, had not even straw to lie upon, but in the crucifix he found abundant consolation amid all his sufferings. Holding it in his hands, he forgot earth and its sorrows; with his dying lips he kissed it fervently, and exclaiming: "I know that Heaven is before me when all this is past," peacefully expired.

It was at this conjuncture that the rest of the 6th Company received orders to leave Rome. Theodore and his companions went by train to Albano, and marched merrily from the station to the town, covered with dust and perspiration. It took an hour and a half to accomplish the march, for a considerable distance had to be traversed, and the heat was overpowering; in order to beguile the way they sang as they went along, as if going to some festive entertainment. Theirs was the joy which is born of sacrifice, the serene content which the Christian alone can feel when confronted with the King of terrors.

"Why should we feel sad? We have freely offered up our lives to God, it was His will that we should come here, and surely He will not forsake us now. A gloomy stillness broods over the town; I remember seeing it *en fête*,* and the contrast strikes me not a little. I will not attempt to tell you how delighted we were to see our dear comrades again, they looked worn, but their enthusiasm was unabated. I was hard at work all the evening, and went to bed tired out. The next morning, before entering upon the work for which I

---

*   Celebration.

was sent here, I had the happiness of hearing Mass, and receiving Holy Communion. I felt the need of prayer, and of union with Him Who gives strength for self-sacrifice. What would become of me were I left to myself? Even as it is, I must confess that, being totally unaccustomed to the sight of suffering, I felt a certain dread of the task which lay before me."

While Theodore was making his thanksgiving, fresh courage seemed to animate him; on leaving the church he went to the hospital, tied on a white apron over his uniform, and in order to make a good beginning, spent eight consecutive hours amongst the sick. "Our duty was to attend upon fifteen cholera patients, all very difficult to please, extremely ungrateful to all appearances, and repulsively dirty. But when one remembers that they are suffering members of Jesus Christ, one's natural repugnance disappears at once. We have to lift them up, give them drink, and do everything for them which may be necessary. Some of the Zouaves are so tender and kind that they might be taken for modern editions of St. Vincent of Paul, and they seem quite to understand how to say a word season, and direct the thoughts of the sick to Jesus Crucified. You cannot think how fond one gets of these poor creatures; I was present when two of them breathed their last, the second was a very aged man, who suffered terribly. We prayed beside his bed while he was in his agony, and just as I held the crucifix to his lips, he breathed his last.

"We have no merit of our own, for in the first place it is God Who works in us, and besides this, the example of our chiefs is the greatest encouragement to us. Lieutenant Colonel de Charette comes over from Rome nearly every day, the captains and lieutenants belonging to all the several companies take it by turns to spend a day or two here, and our brave Lieutenant de Résimont encourages us in every way by his words and still more by his example. General Zappi, and Kanzler, the Minister of War, pay us frequent visits; the Holy Father sends us his blessing, and he has carried his paternal solicitude on our behalf yet further, by making a present of some excellent wine to the Sisters and the Zouaves, in order that they may keep up their strength; in fact, we are like spoiled children. Some of the Zouaves carry their devotedness to an extreme; for instance, the one who sleeps next to me, invariably spends part of the night in burying the bodies of those sufferers who have died during the day."

There is one detail however which Theodore passes over in silence, since it is a thing too praiseworthy for him to tell of himself, and under such circumstances his habitual frankness was overruled by his humility. When the supply of linen ran short, he employed several hours of the night in washing out the soiled and infected garments which had been removed from the bodies of the dead, overcoming all the disgust which so repulsive a task could not but excite, in order that he might obtain a change of linen for his beloved cholera patients. Could the devotion of Elizabeth of Hungary and John of God have gone further than this?

Whilst the cholera was at its height, an affecting ceremony took place at Albano, the funeral of Cardinal Altieri, the Bishop of the place, who was loved as a father by all its inhabitants. He was in Rome when he first heard what a grievous visitation had overtaken his children; and in spite of his feeble health and the remonstrances of all around him, he set out at once in order to employ his little remaining strength in the service of his flock. All day long he was busy hearing confessions, consoling the bereaved, administering the last sacraments to the dying; and when night came, the only rest he took was to watch beside the sick in the hospital. When on his death-bed, he gave his blessing to some of the Zouaves whom he perceived to be kneeling around him, commended the sick to their care, and promised to pray for them. In order not to increase the prevailing panic, it was decided that the funeral should take place at night, but news of this arrangement got wind, and the consequence was that the people thronged together in crowds, the men pressing eagerly forward to draw the hearse, before which the Zouaves marched in double file; indeed, almost the entire population may be said to have escorted the body of their benefactor to the grave, bearing torches in their hands and chanting a solemn Requiem as they moved along. It was a mournful and yet a soul inspiring sight; the expression at once of deep grief and fervent gratitude.

"August 13th.

"I have just received your welcome letters, to cheer and encourage me. We were busy attending to our dear patients when a sergeant brought them to me. A thousand thanks for them all, you do indeed know how to speak to my heart. How good God is to me! Not only has He brought me here, but He gives me strength to do my duty. I owe it all to Him and to Him alone, for with a disposition so weak and impressionable as mine, I should have done nothing left to myself. I must take courage and persevere, giving all the glory to God. Ours is a noble mission, every one envies the 6th Company, and I really think the townspeople are beginning to attach themselves to us. I pray God to enable me to keep Him ever in my thoughts, and to do everything as in His presence, for sad indeed would it be, if through indulging some petty vanity, or falling into any other snare of the devil, I should lose the little merit I may be able to acquire.

"On the Assumption, our Lady took from us one of our brothers' in arms, she wanted him with her on her feast. In the morning he went to Communion in the church, and when evening came he was in Heaven. It was an unusually rapid case, he was carried off in a few hours.

"I wonder how you have all been spending this glorious feast, which used to pass so happily in our family circle. I have not forgotten the processions we had in the morning, and the happy afternoons which followed. Here tapers were lighted before all the Madonnas, and in the streets cries of *Evviva Maria* sounded on all sides; the effect was quite touching. The atmosphere is fresher than it was, the swallows have returned, and I think we are going to have some really fine weather."

In fact, the disease disappeared all at once, and the Zouaves were bidden to cease from their work as sick-nurses, and take some rest, in order that they might be ready to fight the Garibaldians. But before taking leave of their patients, the infirmarians wished to compensate to themselves for being no longer able to serve them; they clubbed together therefore, and caused to be handed over to them a sum amounting to about £9, and in so doing crowned the saintly charity of self-sacrificing deeds with the shining gold of bounteous alms. "Our recent campaign," Theodore writes after leaving Albano, "has graven in our hearts memories which can never be erased. Will it not be a great consolation for.us when we come to die, to think of those whom we assisted in their last agony? I feel sure that some of them are already praying for us in Heaven. Had we not known that we were working for God, we could never have had courage to do all we did. Those of the inhabitants who remained in the town did not attempt to do anything for the sick, but contented themselves with uttering unmeaning cries. If we had met with the slightest gratitude, the case would have been altered; but some said we were paid by the Commune, others that we acted under compulsion. Some of us were sent for to bury a woman, while her male relatives sat in the house doing nothing, and when expostulated with, said they were not undertakers' men, it was the Zouaves' work to bury the dead. In the midst of it all however, our cheerfulness was unabated, indeed the more tired we were, the merrier we grew, because our inward content became all the greater. We used to joke with one another, and pretend we were nurses, apothecaries, or doctors. A young woman having been attacked with cholera, her baby was in danger of being starved to death, but the Zouave who was nursing the mother took charge also of the child, and fed it with milk in the kindest manner possible. God rewarded him who thus acted a father's part, by taking the nursling to be with the angels in Paradise: and I assure you that the loss of their pet was quite a grief to the Zouaves."

"August 20th.

"This is a glorious day for our Company. The Minister of War, assisted by our Colonel and several official personages, conferred the cross of Pius IX. on our gallant Lieutenant in presence of all the townspeople. He thoroughly deserved it, and tears filled his eyes when it was pinned on to his breast. Our Sergeant-Major was created a Knight of St. Gregory, and two other sergeants Knights of Sylvester; then came thirty-six privates of the 1st detachment, each of whom received from Kanzler a large sized gold medal, bearing the inscription *Bene merentibus*.* The General congratulated the whole company on the part of His Holiness in the warmest terms on the manner in which they had conducted themselves. I felt quite proud of my comrades. However, I could not help thinking what delight it would have been to me to have had one of these beautiful medals to display to you; and it was only by a mere chance too that I lost it! Well, it is not really lost, for God, to Whom I offer all my actions, takes everything into account, and will one day give me something far more precious. We should indeed be to be pitied, if we only looked to man for our reward. Henceforward the 6th takes the precedence of all the other Companies. You may fancy what an effect these shining medals produce."

This simple avowal plainly reveals the hopes that had lain hidden in the heart of our Zouave. To be decorated when only eighteen years of age, what a daring dream for a soldier to indulge! And what a disappointment to see this dream dispelled! For a long time afterwards, whenever the name of Albano was mentioned, Theodore had to resign himself anew to the sacrifice of that fondly cherished hope, for the heart cannot easily forget, even though no feeling of embitterment adds a pang to the past.

After all their labors and exertions, the men of the 6th had a period of rest and leisure, which the brave infirmarians greatly needed in order to recruit their strength. And as freedom from restraint is requisite to real relaxation, they were allowed ample liberty to amuse themselves, each in his own way, by excursions into the country, the companionship of friends, the sweets of *farniente*.**

"I spend my time in long walks," says Theodore, "our duties are a mere nothing, and this easy-going life reminds me of home. We go about Albano just as we please, without our sabres, and carrying a short stick which we have cut, each for himself, in the forest. Some go shooting, some fishing, others join in a picnic. For my part, I have made good use of my legs hitherto. I generally set off with a

---
*   A medal given to Papal Soldiers for exceptional service.
**   The relax feeling you get while being idle.

light walking-stick in my hand and a book under my arm, and I amuse myself with reading, all the while reveling in the beauties of the fair scene spread out before me. I have found a delightful place of resort under an old tree, whence one obtains a fine view of Rome, Castel Gandolfo, the lake, and all the most lovely spots in the neighborhood. No one ever comes to disturb me there. Occasionally I go to see a good Jesuit Father, whom I have chosen as my confessor, or I pay a visit to the Sisters and the sick in the hospital.

"As I write, shouts of boisterous laughter reach my ears. One of the Zouaves, a Dutchman of gigantic stature, in the style of Don Quixote, is calmly riding up and down on a donkey, heedless of the owner's expostulations. Each time he passes the kitchen window, he gets two or three buckets emptied on his head, which drench both him and the animal he bestrides, to the infinite amusement of the by-standers. At the same time another Zouave is rocking a chubby-cheeked child in his arms, just like an experienced nursemaid; it is really altogether a laughable sight. Unfortunately, it is impossible to use one's mind with all this noise going on, and if I find it difficult to write, I fear you will find it no less difficult to read what I have written."

Such a life was doubtless full of attractions, but it was equally replete with danger in the case of one who, like Theodore, was young, enthusiastic, and somewhat given to dreaming. Albano had resumed its festive air, and nothing but gay songs and merry laughter were to be heard within the walls of the little town, where many members of the Roman aristocracy had already arrived for their annual summer stay. Might it not be termed a second Capua as far as the Zouaves were concerned? In vain did Theodore seek refuge in reading, and in studying Italian; fierce storms of temptation swept over his soul. Hitherto he had not known such struggles, because never until now had he been brought face to face with such temptations. He was astonished to find himself no longer like a child who does right without exactly knowing why; it was the will of God that for him virtue should in future be the result of conflict and of victory. In view of the shipwreck which apparently threatens him, he seeks in all directions for a plank which may afford him a chance of safety. He unbosoms himself to his prudent director, who cheers and consoles him; he entreats his parents to advise him and pray for him, but above all, he casts himself into the arms of God's mercy, and prays without ceasing.

"To all appearances I am leading the most easy and pleasant life, but I must confess to you, my dear parents, that never have I had to struggle as I have now to preserve myself from contamination. Happily religion affords plenty of objects on which to fix my affections. Every morning at Mass I renew my power of resistance and my desire for self-conquest; every evening at Benediction, I find rest and refreshment at the close of a day—often one of sharp conflict—at the feet of the Blessed Virgin. I am resolved that whatever my liberty and whatever my temptations, the virtue that especially distinguished St. Aloysius shall be the chosen virtue of my youth."

In writing to his brother Joseph, who had just completed his studies, he speaks quite openly, recalling the past with all the buoyancy and freshness of youth, though a strain of melancholy is perceptible when he speaks of the present. "I think of you very often, my dear Joseph, and I remember you especially before God. I can quite understand what your feelings must be, now that the time has come for you to make an important decision. On leaving school for good one cannot help looking back on the years spent there, and it is not without more or less of a pang that one bids farewell to school-life, and the work which was coupled with so much enjoyment. Would that we could be boys all our days! I never used to look forward to the hour when I should be released from the yoke, or long for the time when I should be grown up, and my own master. Even now I hold fast my departing youth; I do not like to think of losing my simplicity and becoming hardened. Do you pray for me, as I pray for you; believe me, one cannot be a child at eighteen years of age. Sometimes I have terrible battles to sustain, and I cannot have too much strength to enable me to resist. May God help and direct me!"

Theodore had not to look far in order to find the sympathy for which he craved, the counsel of which he stood in need, for he had made some real friends amongst the Zouaves. One of these, whom he acquainted in writing with the anguish he endured, the interior conflicts which rent his soul, replied with the true candor of a Christian, and as one who thoroughly understood his comrade's state of mind. When fifteen years had passed away Theodore still remembered with gratitude the friend who had given him a helping hand on the path to Heaven. M. and Mme. Wibaux too did all they could to cheer and encourage their son, not filling their letters with useless reproaches or tedious sermons, but reminding him that temptation is not in itself an evil, and expressing their confidence that he would never do anything to disgrace them.

"I do not know how to thank you, my dear Father. Your words, suggested by your kind heart and your own experience, make me more than ever resolved to go on struggling, to be generous to the last. I am quite aware that I shall have to suffer, but your example will be a powerful incentive to me. Happily, the satisfaction resulting from a conquest over one's passions is greater than the pleasure derived from sinful indulgence. This is what a Zouave, one of my friends, was telling us the other day as the teaching of his own sad past. He is rather excitable, and very imaginative, but a very good fellow for all that. I was with him the first night I slept in the barracks, and since then, strangely enough, we have hardly been separated a single day, both being in the same company, the same barracks, often the same room. I shall always be grateful to him for one service he rendered me; it was the second night, and I was feeling rather awkward, not knowing exactly whether or no to say my prayers before going to bed, when he noticed it, and coming round whispered to me, 'Take my advice, my dear fellow, and don't ever forget your prayers at night.' Well, I was going to tell you, on the 11th of September we had a delightful excursion, which he had planned, to keep the anniversary of what he said had been a memorable day for him. We provided ourselves with an ample supply of provisions, found a shady place by the waterside to serve as a dining room, and sat down to a good spread. Beefsteaks, ham, crayfish, cheese, butter, dessert, all tasted excellent, our high spirits being the best sauce. It was an enchanting scene; a splendid sunset, perfect seclusion, a circle of chosen friends. When our repast was ended, we formed a group round a tree on the top of a hill, in the light of a brilliant moon, while our friend told us his history, and the reason why that day was a happy one for him, in the most frank and pleasant manner. It was on the 11th of September, 1853, whilst he was leading a dissolute life, that the thought of the immortality of the soul was brought home to him. through something said by a friend, whose presence was un welcome on account of his superior sanctity. Since that time, by slow degrees and incredible efforts, he had arrived at the knowledge of the truth. He then proceeded, for our admonition, to descant with much warmth on the deceitfulness of worldly pleasures, alleging that when all possible gratifications were within his reach, he felt disgusted with everything, and would often abruptly quit some scene of festivity or guilty indulgence, asking himself where it was possible to find happiness."

Little by little, Theodore recovered his wonted composure. Later on, under somewhat similar circumstances, the wild winds of temptation will again stir his soul to its depths, but he will outride the storm safely, since, made strong by his weakness, he has anchored his bark securely under shelter of the Most High.

For the time being, his duty was to hold himself in readiness for any emergency, and, as he said, keep his mind at rest. Everyone was talking of Garibaldians, of disturbances, of insurrection; every hour brought some fresh alarm. Twenty-five men, under the command of a sergeant and two corporals, were sent from Albano to Ariccia, some *fonctionnaires-caporaux** being attached to this band, amongst whom Theodore was one. "I am now invested with the rank of a corporal," he writes, "though I have not the stripes. My new dignity empowers me to hurl thunderbolts, assign the fatigue-duty, issue commands, keep order, and make myself feared or loved. Mine will be a short-lived reign, for as soon as this detachment has done its work, I shall again become the insignificant individual I was before. Certainly I have no ambition beyond that of remaining a private in my beloved 6th; I have not enough of the soldier in

---

* *Fonctionnaire-caporal* is the name given to a soldier who fulfils the duties of a corporal, without having the rank of one.

me for a corporal, and my inexperience makes me prefer common duties and the ordinary routine to any position of authority, however slight its responsibilities. I should dislike having to punish, and should not know how to command."

The 18th of September was duly observed by the Zouaves, as it was the anniversary of the memorable battle of Castelfidardo; and the twenty-five men at Ariccia attended Mass in full uniform. The sergeant in command had fought like a lion at the side of Joseph Guérin, who had been his companion and friend. "I should have been sorry," says Theodore, "if I had not been able to go to Communion on that day, one is glad and proud to think that amongst the martyrs whose intercession one implores, are some who wore the same uniform as oneself. I always invoke Joseph Guérin with confidence, he can refuse me nothing, for I have many claims on him, not the least being my great need of help. "The whole day was kept as a holiday; wine was served out to the men, and better rations. As for the staff, all the corporals, even the supernumeraries, were invited by their sergeant to a special banquet. The seniors in the service revived the reminiscences of the famous battle, and as if to recall the circumstances more vividly to mind, a frightful storm, accompanied by hailstones of the size of walnuts, broke over the assembled company. "When," asks Theodore, "will it be given us to act over again the gallant deeds of our brethren? We all long impatiently for the hour for action to strike."

With that common sense which was one of his distinguishing characteristics, he thus expresses in plain and simple words what he thinks of the Pontifical army. "We soldiers of the Pope are no ordinary army. No doubt some who are young and wealthy are sometimes apt to forget that they are here as the defenders of the holiest cause on earth. But if anything occurs to remind them forcibly of their duty, the spirit of the Crusaders revives within them, they are one in heart, in mind, in aspiration. This love for Pius IX, and for Holy Church, covers a multitude of imperfections; it inspires them with a keen desire to fight and to die. Such contempt of death is not natural to any man; but these all look forward to the day when they will be required to make the sacrifice of their lives as to a day of rejoicing. We have many enemies before us, but few friends at our side, and traitors all around breathing out menaces; the very atmosphere we inhale is tainted, so that we suspect everyone to be an enemy in disguise. Only yesterday the station-master and the head of the telegraph office at Albano were arrested, they had engaged to intercept the despatches of the Pontifical Government, and only forward those of the revolutionary party. Garibaldi was to make good his entry at Velletri, and the trains were to be placed at his disposal for the transport of troops; we were destined to have the honor of receiving his first shots. Few and despicable though we were, we should have sold our lives dearly! It is a great happiness to me to think that this is the month of the holy Angels Guardian, who are our most faithful friends, always ready to sympathize in our afflictions and present our prayers to God; we have every reason to hope for great things."

The twenty-five Zouaves stationed at Ariccia continued to lead a happy and united family life. As may be imagined, in such complete seclusion the most trifling occurrences were magnified into events of importance. One day a parcel arrived for our friend the newly-made corporal; on being opened, it was found to contain a pair of slippers, and inside those slippers were letters from Roubaix. This caused quite a commotion in the barrack-room, in an instant Theodore became the center of a group; at first the shape and pattern of the slippers were admired, then someone discovered a charming photograph hidden among the papers. "I recognized my dear Stephen with his beaming smile, dressed like an elegant gentleman, with a fashionable little hat. The likeness passed from hand to hand sergeant, corporals, Dutch and French, all pronounced the same verdict on it: 'What a swell! Anyone can see it is your brother.' I assure you I felt quite flattered by the compliment. What a pleasure for me, dear Stephen, to see you again after ten months' separation! The last time we really saw one another was in the long avenue at Marcq. I seem to have before me your merry face, which is enough to call a smile to the gloomiest countenance; and hear that loud voice of yours, with which Willebaud finds such fault. You manage to escape the blows, while Joseph gets them, and if I remember aright, Willebaud has a heavy hand, which comes down on one like a lump of lead. I dare say Joseph can bear witness to this. With you, my merry lark, all must be blithe and gay. Well, well, laugh while you may and enjoy your youth."

After this fashion the days slipped by at Ariccia; it would have been a delicious life for mere tourists, but the Zouaves had other work to do. An order from headquarters suddenly broke in upon this charmed existence, recalling the 6th Company to Rome, and summoning its members to exchange dreams for reality, sweet repose for stern fatigue! The Revolution was breaking out on all sides, the Garibaldians were massing their forces, treacherous deeds were being done everywhere, and the Pontifical troops, though few in number, had to make a stand against all this. The First Vespers of the feast of Mentana had already begun to ring

CHAPTER IX.

1867.

The Garibaldians before Rome. Lieutenant Guillemin. Disturbances in the city. The barracks are undermined. Danger and uncertainty. Arrival of the French troops.

ALTHOUGH the frontiers of the Papal territory were still said to be guarded against invasion by the army of Victor Emmanuel, bands of Garibaldians constantly made inroads into the States of the Church, attacking villages, robbing the public treasury, extorting money from the inhabitants, desecrating the churches. Their design in pursuing these tactics was to draw the Papal troops away from Rome to the frontiers, so that in the absence of its defenders, they might make themselves masters of the capital. And when these Garibaldians, harassed and repulsed on all sides, found themselves in want of supplies, they had no difficulty in again passing through the Italian lines and re crossing the frontier, to raise recruits, and lay in fresh stores of ammunition. It was agreed that the Piedmontese army should wink at all these proceedings, that watch should be kept, but nothing seen of what went on, nay more, that the invaders should be actually furnished with the sinews' of war; and no great acuteness was needed to perceive that the Government privately encouraged what it publicly pretended to prevent. Hostilities went on throughout the whole province of Viterbo; and at Acquapendente, Valentano, Bagnorea, Subiaco, Monte-Libretti, besides many other places, the Papal troops gained great applause for the gallantry they displayed in the field.

"I have come back alive," writes Theodore, on his return to Rome, "so you may set your minds at rest on that score. During the last week our men have won laurels everywhere. Let us hope our turn will soon come, our Colonel said everyone would have a chance. with deep emotion that I re-entered the city of Saints, the center of our spiritual life, the city of St. Agnes, St. Aloysius, St. Stanislaus, and St. Cecilia. On seeing it again I feel as happy as a child returning to its mother's arms. Now I have become a private soldier once more, and hurrah for hard work! there will be no lack of that now."

The reports which reached Rome daily of fresh feats of arms achieved by the Zouaves, made their life of un ostentatious self-sacrifice and laborious drudgery all the harder for the troops who were retained for the defense of the city, and whose only field of glory was the dull round of military duty, whose only foes were secret conspirators lurking in dark places. "I have been mounting guard over the Garibaldian prisoners; their forlorn appearance and frightful rags excite one's pity. May I have strength to bear this irksome, and in some senses, degrading toil. Farewell now to all sentiment; my letters will, I fear, for the present, be rather devoid of interest; the prosy routine of my life seems to weigh me down; but courage! is it not all for God?"

The brilliant exploits of the Pontifical forces had to be purchased at a heavy price, that of the lives of many of their best men. Amongst the killed and wounded, Theo dore read the names of several of his friends, and oh, how bitter to him was what he called his inaction! To one whose only ambition is to be foremost in sacrifice, how hard to stand by, and see others on the arena of conflict! Lieutenant Guillemin had fallen at Monte Libretti, completely outnumbered. "It was a great shock to me to hear of his death," writes Theodore, "I felt as if tears would have been a relief, but what consoled me most was the thought that this brave young officer was in Heaven. God daily adds to the number of those who will be our intercessors, who will pray for us, and watch over us in the conflict that awaits us. My God, if blood must be shed in order to procure the future triumph of the Church, here it is, take ours; I freely make the sacrifice of all the friends I love, henceforth I will bear their loss without a murmur. Guillemin was a pattern to all, and universally beloved; death did not take him by surprise, he was already ripe for Heaven. On the morning of the day he died, he said to the chaplain, 'I am quite willing to go to confession, but really I have nothing on my conscience.' One can readily believe that a soldier who goes to battle thus prepared will shrink from no deeds of heroism; death has no terrors for him, since even if vanquished, through it he becomes a victor.

"A visit from Pius IX. has been a great comfort and help to our wounded in their sufferings. The Holy Father had a kind word and some little remembrance for each one, he looks more calm and placid than ever. Such consolation would make a bed of suffering seem like a couch of roses to me!"

While disturbances prevailed throughout the Pontifical territory, the state of affairs in Rome itself appeared as tranquil as in the happiest times, until suddenly, on the 22nd of October, the Revolution broke out in every quarter of the city. At six o'clock in the evening the call to arms caused all the Zouaves to turn out. "Our company went immediately to station itself on the Piazza Colonna. The stillness there was quite oppressive, all the shops were closed, and the streets of the Corso, which usually present such an animated appearance at this hour of the day, re-echoed only to the steps of the patrol. Until two in the morning we kept guard outside the vast palace Piombino, within which some officers and gendarmes were carrying on a search for Garibaldi, who, it was said, lay concealed there."

During this night, the guardhouse and barracks were attacked by ruffianly bands, who fell on the Pontifical soldiers with mad fury, and attempted to make their way to the capital, to sound an alarm; but on all sides the assaults of the insurgents were repulsed by Zouaves, Rifle men, and gendarmes. In the distance reports were heard from time to time which sounded very ominous through the darkness. All at once, a tremendous explosion shook the city to its foundations; the Serristori barracks, undermined by the treacherous enemy, had been blown up. This building, to the height of three storeys, presented a confused heap of rubbish, broken timber, and scattered furniture, and the piteous cries of those who were buried beneath the ruins could be distinctly heard. The Revolutionists wanted to get rid of the Zouaves, and in their choice of the expedients to be adopted, gave the preference to those which would perform the work on a large scale. Amidst the general confusion, Mgr. de Mérode, M. l'Abbé Daniel, and Colonel Allet organized a rescue party; twenty-two dead and twelve more or less hurt were got out, the others all escaped without injury. By this cowardly action the Garibaldians exhibited themselves in their true colors; the means they made use of were unworthy of civilized beings, but by employing them they were sure of attaining their end, and of doing so without risk to themselves. It was thought that several other barracks were undermined, and orders to evacuate two of them were consequently given.

During the remainder of the night a body of troops patrolled the city; a great number of knives and cartridges. were picked up, and some arrests made. "At ten a.m.," Theodore writes, "we returned to barracks; no sooner had we got there than I was named orderly to the General. Without pity for our tired limbs, at half-past four, our gallant Company was again called out; we went to support some riflemen who were occupied in besieging a house full of Garibaldians. It was there that the Orsini bombs were manufactured, and nothing could have been easier for the miscreants than to take these missiles which were ready to hand, and throw any number of them amongst the besiegers; but the latter, unintimidated by any such consideration, forced open the doors, entered the rooms, and always merciful, even to traitors, spared the lives of forty men, who fell on their knees and begged for quarter in the name of Pius IX.

"We spent the night before last keeping guard at the Porta del Popolo, in a thick and icily cold fog. Last night we were under arms on the Piazza Colonna, so you may fancy by this time I am so sleepy and tired that I can scarcely hold up my head. I have an hour at my disposal which I mean to devote to you, for I know how anxious you must be just now, and I, too in these days of excitement and agitation, am glad to find rest and comfort in the remembrance of my peaceful home. We spend the day time in making excursions outside the city, for the Garibaldians would not dare to show themselves in broad daylight; in fact, a stranger visiting Rome would not suspect that there was anything wrong. But when evening comes, there is reason to dread blows struck under cover of the darkness; the city becomes as silent as the grave, at six o'clock you might fancy it was already midnight. The live-long night we go shivering up and down the streets, the tedious hours pass so slowly. A fight in open day would be hailed with joy; even if the enemy were ten to one, we should go out against them right cheerily, but no enthusiasm can withstand the depressing effect of being shut up in the heart of a great city, enveloped with darkness, and surrounded by treachery. How constantly, under such circumstances, my thoughts turn to you! It is necessary to keep reminding oneself that all these disagreeables are endured for God, and if one were to lose one's life, one would gain Heaven. None but supernatural motives would ever give me the courage to kill a man, or expose myself to be shot down, or even to bear fatigue and encounter dangers. At Mass of a morning I lay in a store of strength to draw on during the day, for in the time of action it is very difficult to collect one's thoughts, and fix them on God. The only thing to be done is to raise one's heart once for all in a few words of fervent prayer, and say: All for Thee, O my God!

"You would not believe what ingenuity the Revolutionists display in inventing deceitful devices. Several Garibaldians have been going about disguised as Zouaves, between them they killed a gendarme. We arrested one man whom we caught throwing Orsini bombs, he said he was only doing it for amusement! What a sweet and innocent pastime! He was a Post Office *employé*. Another Garibaldian was overtaken by the judgment of God; he was carrying two bombs when one of them accidentally exploded. He was killed on the spot, we found him bathed in blood, his face having been literally blown away. Pius IX. still displays his accustomed intrepidity, the other day he drove through Rome amid crowds of people."

Outside the walls the invaders were daily gaining ground, but their advance had at least one beneficial result, in that it caused many a mask to be laid aside. The hero of Caprera, though a prisoner in his island, and guarded by seven Italian men-of-war, contrived to elude the feigned vigilance of his gaolers, and as if defying the fulminations of Victor Emmanuel, made straight for Florence. From thence he traveled by special train to the Roman frontier, where his two sons were awaiting him at the head of his followers. This connivance on the part of the Italian Government was a little too barefaced; France, weary of listening to the plausible pretexts put forward by Signor Ratazzi, had recourse to threats, and an expeditionary force was assembled at Toulon, with the view of reminding Victor Emmanuel in a practical manner, that the terms of the September Convention were still binding. As a matter of fact, had not Italy bound herself by the terms of its first article to prevent, even by force if need be, any attempt which might be made from outside upon the States of the Church? The French fleet several times received orders to weigh anchor and proceed to Civita Vecchia; but

Monte-Rotondo.

on each occasions, explanation put forward by the Cabinet of Florence brought about a temporary understanding between the two Governments, and a counter-order prevented the departure of the fleet. No more absurd farce could possibly be imagined.

Garibaldi, however, little heeding all this parleying and chicanery, applied himself to the more practical task of acquiring territory, and on the 27th of October established himself at Monte Rotondo, five leagues from Rome. In vain did the brave Pontifical Legionaries hold the place for twenty-seven hours; how could three hundred and fifty men possibly be a match for ten thousand of the enemy? Henceforward the appearance of Garibaldi beneath the walls of Rome was hourly expected, and in that case nothing short of prompt and decided action on the part of France could avail to save the city. "Day by day," Theodore writes on the 29th of October, we hear that France is about to interfere, but she does not do so, though it is high time that she gave some sign. Our position has become untenable; we are all worn out, and the final acts of the drama must be close at hand. We can only trust that God will protect the Church. One thing encourages us, and that is the arrival of men who formerly served as volunteers, and now come in crowds to occupy their old places in the ranks; they can hardly give themselves time to exchange their civilian's dress for the uniform.

"Together with fifteen of my comrades, I am at present occupying a bastion near the Gate of St. Pancratius. Our post consists of a low wall, capable of being defended without the aid of artillery. The whole of the troops are distributed in this manner along the feeble fortifications of Rome; our power of resistance is but limited, we are few in number, and if left to ourselves cannot hold out long. We fulfill our trying duties as well as we can, and wait to see what will happen; our time is spent in acting as sentinels, in the bitter cold and unceasing rain. Between times we sleep in a barn, without undressing, thinking ourselves lucky to have straw to lie on, for we have long been unused to any such indulgence, and for the last week have not once had our clothes off. But though I look rather worn and hollow-eyed, I do not feel tired, and never have to give in.

"Sometimes I gaze with admiration on Rome that I love so well, and I feel a sudden pang when I think that with all her beauty and all her sanctity she may be standing on a vast mine, which may be ready to explode at any moment. Yet though the cry of battle is heard on all sides, and the very air seems full of revolutionary terrors, how can one believe that the Vatican itself, and all the time-honored sanctuaries and historical monuments which adorn the city, will become the prey of the Garibaldians? People say that nothing short of some general revolution, some terrible crisis of fate, will avail to regenerate the world, and force it to return to the true Church, and that of this revolution, Rome will be the center. If such things must happen, may Thy will, O God, be done! and may we be enabled to promote Thy glory according to the measure of our strength.

"Whilst writing to you, I am conscious that at any moment the alarm may be given, and I may have to lay down my pen and take up my rifle. In the short space of an hour, or even less than that, the battle may have to be fought between truth and falsehood, between the most sacred of rights and the most odious of wrongs. My soul is at peace, because my trust in the mercy of God is unbounded. I feel that I am very weak, and that were I to die so young I should leave many joys and sweet affections that life offers me. I also feel how unfit I am to appear in the presence of God; nevertheless I do not cease to hope. My good angel will guide me in the fight, my uniform, my sufferings will plead for me, and my blood, if freely shed, will cleanse my soul from its stains. Thou, O my God, hast promised that Heaven shall be the reward of those who suffer for justice' sake; accept me therefore, since I have, as far as my imperfections will allow, offered up my blood in union with that which Thou didst shed, and united my sufferings to Thine."

It is impossible not to admire these soldiers of the Church, whom neither hard work nor weary watching could daunt or dishearten, and who yet had nothing in prospect but defeat and death. But the horizon, gloomy and lowering as it was from a merely human point of view, shone with celestial light when the beholder turned his gaze from earth to Heaven.

Such of the Pontifical troops as were located in country districts had been recalled to Rome, in order that as strong a force as possible might be concentrated at the point against which the enemy was about to direct his attack. Crowds of vagabonds resembling wild beasts rather than men, immediately swooped down upon the places thus left unguarded; Subiaco, Velletri, Valmontone, Viterbo, saw their walls invaded by wretches who called themselves Garibaldians, and who, undercover of this designation, forming as it did an excellent cloke for unprincipled adventurers, enacted the part of conquering heroes, appointed municipal officers of their own way of thinking, raised taxes, levied imposts on the clergy and the religious houses, committed every kind of sacrilegious atrocity in the churches; indeed, one might have fancied that a horde of demons had escaped from Hell

"If France would only send us her flag!" Theodore exclaims over and over again. But fresh despatches only awakened new hopes to be repeatedly and cruelly doomed to disappointment. It was a long and weary waiting, and the heart of the French Zouave deeply felt the painful situation, both as a patriot and a Christian. The feast of All Saints dawned sadly for Rome and for her defenders. "This year I shall not even be able to go to Communion. Happy those who are spending this feast in Heaven, where sorrow is unknown! I shall offer up my own trials for the greater glory of the saints and the relief of the souls in Purgatory. I am prepared for whatever may happen; I accept beforehand the humiliation of defeat; yet I need increased strength, and I beg you to pray the holy martyrs to kindle in me some spark at least of their glowing zeal. I cannot say how much I should like to see you again, dear Father and Mother; eleven months seems a long time to have been parted from you, but in Heaven there will be no more separation, and I hope that one day we shall all be united there."

On the 30th of October the soldiers posted on the heights of the Janiculum caught the sound of military music in the distance, and after awhile they could plainly distinguish the joyous strains played by the bands of the advancing French regiments; Rome was saved: *Vive la France!* One day more, and it would have been perhaps too late; but as it was, gloomy apprehensions were scattered to the winds, and at the sight of the tricolor flag hoisted on the Castle of

St. Angelo beside the Pontifical ensign, a thrill of gladsome hope pervaded the Holy City.

The time was come to free the Roman territory from the bandits who were infesting it, for as France was occupying Rome, it was now possible to strike a decisive blow, and attempt a sortie. The soldiers rejoiced at the prospect of a real battle, especially those who for the last month had been constantly threatened with Orsini bombs, assassination, and all the various underhand expedients employed in revolutionary warfare. While every preparation was being made for attacking Garibaldi at Mentana, the Piedmontese army crossed the Roman frontier near Viterbo, and openly fraternized with the Garibaldian hordes. As the crowning act of his long course of disloyalty to the Holy See, Victor Emmanuel signified to France, and to the other Courts of Europe, that the sole object of this occupation was *to promote the maintenance of order*. Difficult indeed would it be to imagine an instance of more shameless and impudent falsehood.

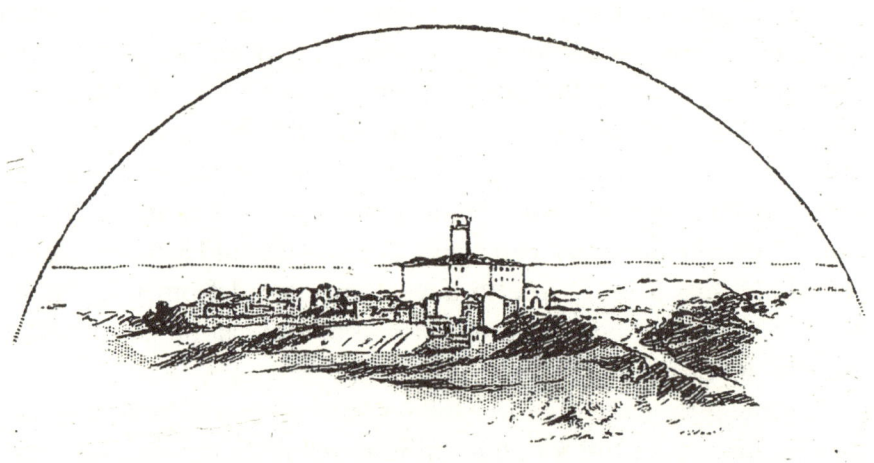

Monte-Rotondo.

CHAPTER X.

1867.

Real warfare at last. Battle of Mentana. Splendid conduct of the Zouaves. Their victory. Moeller and d'Alcantara. Recall of the troops.

"Rome, Nov. 7th, 1867.

"My dear Parents—I can never be grateful enough for the honor God has conferred on me in permitting me to take part in the glorious battle of Mentana. It is no mere dream; I have in very deed been fighting for His sake. For five consecutive hours I was in the midst of a hailstorm of bullets, and over and over again I was in danger of losing my life. God has not, it is true, seen fit to accept a single drop of my blood, but the fact of my presence on the field attested my readiness to shed it all for Him. I wish I could make you realize all I have passed through; I will do my best to give you an account of our expedition.

"We set out in the night between Saturday the 2nd and Sunday the 3rd of November; it was very dark, and the rain fell in torrents; we were nevertheless in the highest spirits. The whole of the regiment of Zouaves was there; the Legionaries and the corps of Swiss Rifles marched with us; and, what is more, we were to have the

French under the command of General de Polhès for our companions in arms. It was a fine sight to see this imposing column, consisting of five thousand men, deploy upon the Nomentanean Way. The Zouaves, five hundred strong, formed the vanguard, behind them marched the other Papal troops, whilst the rear was brought up by the French, who acted as a reserve force, their infantry, artillery, and companies of the line, amounting in all to two thousand men."

It was only right that the soldiers of the Pope, having been so long alone in their arduous task, should on this occasion have the post of honor assigned to them, and the respective commanders had therefore agreed that the French should allow the Pontifical troops to take the initiative, whilst they held themselves in readiness to come to their assistance should occasion require.

On leaving Rome, the troops marched slowly for four hours along a muddy road, until a halt was called upon a vast plain near Capo Bianco. Amidst general excitement, Theodore had the delight of meeting again with his friends, Lieut. Wyart, MM. Vittrant, Cordonnier, Moeller, and others; it was a solemn moment, for they all felt that they were perhaps spending their last hour of converse together on earth. During the battle the friends were not separated, and were always in the foremost rank. Moeller had formerly been an officer in the Zouaves, but he had just enlisted a second time in the capacity of a private, having requested to be enrolled in the 6th Company of the 1st battalion, in order not to be parted from Theodore, with whose family he was acquainted. On the evening of Saturday the 2nd, before the troops left Rome, the two friends had supped merrily together. "Moeller was then," Theodore relates, "tired out from a long expedition he had made in the morning; his feet were extremely painful, but he cheerfully shouldered his knapsack. I could not admire him enough, for when one has never been accustomed to carry anything heavier than an officer's sword, a knapsack must seem an intolerable load, and I would gladly have carried two to relieve him."

An hour and a half was passed in friendly intercourse, the soldiers and the chaplains walking up and down together; a slight refreshment was partaken of; the wet clothes were dried at blazing fires made of brushwood; some of the men entrusted their intimate friends with commissions to be executed in case of their death; then all at once the rain ceased, the sun shone out brightly, the clarion sounded, announcing the moment of departure, and its joyous notes woke an echo in many an eager heart. But our hero shall tell his own tale.

"I embraced M. Wyart, shook hands all round with my friends, then in a few words of earnest prayer, I entreated our Lord and those saints to whom I have a special devotion to remember my sufferings and my good will, and show themselves merciful to me. My thoughts next turned to you, my dear parents, and I implored my guardian angel to convey my farewell greeting to you, and bid you pray for me. As we set off we sang the old refrain familiar to our battalion, beginning thus:

Forward, Zouaves, forward go; be the first to face the foe.

These verses had been composed by some Zouaves in bygone days, and sung by them as they marched across the rough roads of the Apennines. The sole merit of the lines consists in the sentiment they express, but what better claim to excellence could they have, than the fact that they breathe forth the firm confidence of a soldier who is prepared to fight, a Christian who is prepared to die? The two companies who preceded us soon deployed to act as skirmishers, while we were made to wait."

Garibaldi had displayed consummate skill in the choice of a position; his army, at least ten thousand strong, occupied the oblong plateau on which Mentana and Monte Rotondo are situated. These two towns, with their forts, their white houses and their thick walls, stand out clear against the sky, perched as they are upon the crest of the ridge which separates the valleys of the Tiber and the Anio. The slopes of the mountain are broken on either side by streams, waterfalls and ravines, so that, owing to the rugged nature of the ground, it is no easy matter to gain the summit. In the immediate vicinity of the two little towns, olive groves, vineyards, thickets, and enclosures furnished the Garibaldians with excellent hiding-places which concealed their movements, and whence they might sally forth unexpectedly and fall upon their assailants.

"The Companies of Zouaves who had been sent on in advance, climbed a wooded hill, and disappeared from sight amid profound silence. The heart of every one beat fast. It cannot be denied that there is something very solemn in the prospect of an impending battle; the soul left to herself for a moment realizes how short is the distance which may perhaps separate her from eternity. At last we heard a single shot fired; then several more in succession; and a welcome cry sounded in our ears ordering the 6th Company to advance to the support of the right hand division. We mounted the slope with agile and rapid steps, while the Garibaldians, screened by the bushes, sent us plenty of bullets, without however doing us any harm. One could not help feeling a certain pleasure at seeing the red-shirts before us at a distance of about two hundred yards, especially as their brilliant hue made it easy for us to take aim. They were the pick of the Garibaldians, young fanatics, more deluded than wicked, who had been led astray by the seductive dream of national unity; many of them were Bersaglieri and Piedmontese. More than one who was found dead upon the field was evidently one of those favored soldiers to whom the Italian Government had been graciously pleased to grant an indefinitely long leave of absence, on the understanding that they should take service under Garibaldi. The remainder was a mere assemblage of brigands and good for nothing fellows attracted by the hope of pillage.

"The exchange of shots lasted for some time, but this style of proceeding ill-suited the impetuous nature of Lieutenant-Colonel de Charette. At last he dashed up, heedless of the bullets flying around him: 'Boys,' he cried, 'try and drive them out at the point of the bayonet!' Putting spurs to his horse, he shouted, 'I will go alone,' well knowing we should follow him. Everyone threw off his knapsack, in order to advance more rapidly; the various Companies became mixed up together and dispersed in all directions. We were obliged to pause for a moment in our eager progress before the Vigna Santucci, an enclosure planted with vines, and surrounded by a low wall, of which the adjacent buildings served as a place of entrenchment for the Garibaldians. It was soon taken by assault; the plateau was swept clear, and some pieces of artillery were planted there by the Pontifical army. We resumed our headlong pursuit of the Garibaldians, who were driven out of house after house and vineyard after vineyard."

What Theodore described was in fact a bayonet charge on a large scale which extended over a wide area and forced the enemy to fall back upon Mentana. Officers and men ran on *pêle mêle*,* the only word of command to be heard being: Forward, forward! The rallying call was no longer obeyed, impetuous daring supplied for the nonce the place of strategical skill. Throughout the engagement Theodore had, thanks to his long legs, managed to be always in the van; beyond the Vigna Santucci he fell in with Carlos Cordonnier, and the two friends with some of their comrades hastened along the road which led to the village. It seemed almost foolhardy to go on, so thickly were the bullets raining around them, but their excitement was so intense that they could think of nothing but how to advance as far as possible and kill as many of their foes as they could. On reaching a pathway, the opening to which was disputed by the Garibaldians, who had been lying in ambush behind a brick-kiln, Carlos fired for the first time; Theodore instantly handed him his own gun, saying, "Take it; it is loaded; you are a better shot than I am. Hardly were the words uttered when a Garibaldian came within range, and Cordonnier fired: "He is down," cried Theodore, highly delighted.

This anecdote is intensely characteristic. Too many men grow bewildered by the din and excitement which is ever to be found on the field of battle, they lose their head and waste their cartridges. Indeed a soldier was once actually heard to excuse himself to his commander for his random method of firing by saying that he must be doing something. Theodore was one of those whose self possession and presence of mind never desert them; his companions in arms even now perfectly remember the collected air with which he proceeded along the road to Mentana, heedless of the bullets whizzing around him, and how from time to time he drew up his tall

---

*   Confusion.

figure to its full height, took aim, and fired as coolly and deliberately as if he had been shooting at a target. Then he would step behind some brushwood in order to reload, and go through the same performance without moving a muscle of his face.

Meanwhile the enemy had made a hasty retreat upon the village, from the walls of which they were pouring a destructive fire upon the Pontifical troops, who were close behind. Fortunately the Zouaves were able to entrench themselves behind some stacks of hay and straw at a short distance from the ramparts, and in this position they continued to fight for another four hours. The struggle grew fiercer and fiercer, repeated attacks being made upon the houses, but this method of warfare cost the lives of so many brave men, that it had to be relinquished. The Garibaldians being undercover, could take aim at their ease, while their opponents were obliged to show themselves each time they fired, and the enemy, taking advantage of the opportunity thus afforded, did deadly work.

"I was close to Moeller when he was wounded at the conclusion of the engagement, a ball having struck him on the shoulder just as he was entering the town. He sank to the ground, behind a large barrel, which protected him. In a moment however, he got up without assistance, his countenance expressing a strange mixture of suffering and pleasure; 'I am delighted,' he said, 'to think that I was the first to enter the town.' His courage was wonderful, amounting almost to recklessness; he was always in the van, and seemed absolutely unconscious that the bullets were flying thickly around him. I hope his wound will not prove serious, but in any case we cannot but envy him. In the evening he told me he felt quite prepared to appear in the presence of God.

"Paul Doynel also fell at my side, exclaiming, 'It is all up with me!' Two bullets had passed through his body, and he could only drag himself along by supporting himself on his gun, as one would use a crutch. When the surgeon mentioned to him the possibility of an amputation proving necessary, he merely replied, 'I am quite willing to part with an arm for the sake of the Church.'

"About half-past three the French made their appearance before the walls of Mentana, announcing their arrival in a peculiarly significant

Mentana.

manner, namely by five minutes' consecutive firing; one might have thought it was drums beating the tattoo. These chassepots are terrible weapons, it is a good thing that our soldiers should try their effect for the first time on the enemies of the Holy See.

"Darkness at last put an end to the combat; the army encamped on the surrounding heights in order to be able to command all the roads. Cold, hunger, fatigue, the joy of finding some of one's comrades safe and sound, grief at learning the death of others, all this, together with short snatches of broken sleep, made up the history of that night. If I had time, I would try and exhibit to you the bright and amusing side of war, the stir of the camp, the blaze of the bivouac fires at night, the harmless acts of plunder. Every one of us had something in his hand, a first-rate revolver, a bayonet, or a cap taken from a Garibaldian. As we expected a still more severe engagement on the morrow, I merely took possession of one of the enemy's bayonets, but some men contrived to appropriate the horses which belonged to the officers of our opponents."

Upon the field of battle heroism was still to be seen in active exercise; the form was changed, but the spirit was the same. On the spot where so much soldierly courage had been displayed, Christian charity was now at work, and all night long ladies who had volunteered to act as infirmarians, rivaled the Sisters of St. Vincent of Paul in the tender care they lavished on the wounded, making no distinction between friends and foes, whilst the chaplains continued to administer spiritual aid to the dying, as indeed they had never ceased to do in the thickest of the fight. At sunrise on the following morning the Garibaldians, who had had time to realize the completeness of their defeat, hastened to surrender, and by so doing, completed the triumph of the good cause.

"The prisoners, under the escort of the French troops, were conducted in a long file to the Castle of St. Angelo, the remainder, who had fled during the battle, succeeded in reaching the frontier. The enemy left eight hundred killed and wounded on the field, while about two hundred men belonging to the Papal army were put *hors de combat.** As for Garibaldi, not even a glimpse of his white plume

---

* Incapable of combat due to injuries sustained in battle.

was anywhere to be descry; he told his followers they could drive out the foreign mercenaries with the butt end of their muskets, then, when the struggle was at its hottest, he escaped to the frontier. Some of the Zouaves saw a carriage which at their approach suddenly turned and drove off in an opposite direction; it is quite possible that this vehicle may have contained the high-souled hero. His favorite cry had been: Rome or death! Finding he could not obtain the former, it did not, I imagine, cost him a very severe effort to relinquish all idea of the latter.

"As to myself I cannot make out how it is that I am still on my legs, when I think how many balls whistled round me, and how many wounded fell beside me. Once a carabineer stumbled up against me and knocked me down just as I was in the act of taking aim. It would be no easy task to convey to you all my new and strange experiences. At first the firing produced no effect at all on me, at the end of five minutes my face and hands were already black with powder, and in my haste I had swallowed half a cartridge. We went along so quickly that we covered three quarters of a league before we knew what we were doing.

"At times, even in the midst of the fray, a rush of feeling seems to come over one and make one very sad. If you knew how heartrending are the groans of the wounded, and how terrible it is to see a friend covered with blood or perhaps fearfully disfigured! The next day I went all over the battlefield, the dead were still lying where they had fallen, so that here and there I recognized a comrade or an acquaintance, and the ground was covered with the *debris* of various weapons. The corpses of the Garibaldians were scattered over an extent of several miles; their wounded died like dogs, refusing all spiritual aid and declaring openly that they preferred to go to hell. How beautiful was the contrast presented by the Christian soldier! I shall never forget the sweet expression on the face of Watts Russell, one of the Zouaves. He was only seventeen, and was the youngest, and perhaps also one of the most innocent among all those who fell upon this glorious field. Struck towards evening on the forehead by a bullet, he dropped down dead without having had time to utter a single word; I saw him stretched on the ground near the hayricks, looking like an angel, and faithful unto death to his favorite motto which he always wore about him: *Ama et fac quod vis.*[*]

"On the 4th of November we made our entry into Monte Rotondo. The hapless little town had had much to endure. For a whole week the Garibaldians had comported themselves like veritable Vandals; no provisions were to be had, and desolation reigned everywhere. It was very painful to see the churches, and especially the Cathedral, in which the tabernacle door had been perforated by a bayonet. The altars were stripped of their ornaments, the images and statues horribly defaced, nothing had been spared from outrage. The Dutch Zouaves kissed, amid many tears, the spots thus desecrated; one of us found a ciborium and twelve Hosts on the corpse of a Garibaldian. Such are the men who style themselves liberators, and such the dispositions wherewith they go to battle! An altar was erected in front of the Cathedral, and the chaplain said Mass there, at which I assisted in a spirit of reparation. We spent about two days at Monte Rotondo, deprived of absolute necessaries.

"Yesterday we re-entered Rome, receiving a splendid ovation. Our company headed the column, and the road to Monte Rotondo was thronged with carriages which had driven out to meet us. After we had passed through the Porta Pia, the enthusiasm knew no bounds, even the most timid ventured to show themselves, and everyone shouted, *Viva i Zuavi! Viva Pio IX!* In this chorus of applause our ears recognized the accents of many a French voice, and several persons rushed forward to shake our hot and grimy hands. Colonel de Charette sat his horse—which, by-the-bye, had been taken from the enemy with an air of conscious triumph, and looked what he really was, the hero of the day. Many of our soldiers wore Garibaldian caps instead of their own *képis,* which they had lost during the battle, others had one of the enemy's bayonets

---

[*] It's possible Wibaux got this phrase mixed with a different phrase that was popular with Watt-Russell. The phrase *Ama et fac quod vis* translates to "Love and do what you will." This is typically associated with St. Augustine and is about doing all of your actions out of love of God. The phrase *Anima mia, anima mia, Ama Dio e tira via* is probably what Wibaux meant to write. This phrase translates to "My soul, my soul, be this thy song, love thy God and speed along." This was a popular and original saying by Watts-Russell. After his martyrdom, the English and Canadian Papal Zouaves adopted this phrase into their unit songs.

fixed on the end of their rifles. We carried our heads very high as we marched along with our spoils; it was a proud moment. I tried to raise my heart to God, Who alone gives the victory.

"The Garibaldians have received so severe a blow that they can hardly hold up their heads again; and tranquility has been restored to Rome which was when we left in such a disturbed condition. The French soldiers, who at first treated us Zouaves as if we were children, now esteem us and like us, so that we get on capitally together; they were far from expecting to see what they actually witnessed, and cannot help expressing their surprise. They say we marched along in first rate style, and are worthy to be placed at their head. After marching for six hours with my knapsack on my back, I was immediately told off to mount guard at the Capitol. How times have changed! In former days the conqueror was conducted thither in chariots drawn by four white horses, in order to receive a brilliant ovation; now they only do duty there as sentries, in the most prosaic manner, exposed to the cold and to the four winds of heaven. We still have to sleep on straw, in the draughty passages of the Ara Coeli; I find it very different to my comfortable room and good fire.

"P.S.—The battle of Mentana began on St. Hubert's day; a nice hunting-party for us!"

Such is Theodore's description of the battle; a description given by a soldier who is altogether ignorant of the successive phases of the struggle, and of the various manœuvres executed by the Pontifical and the French troops, and who confines himself to a straightforward narration of what came under his own observation. It is not our business to play the historian's part any more than it was his; here, as elsewhere, our duty is to follow him step by step, and strive to place before our readers a faithful portrait of this loyal Zouave and pious Christian.

A few years later, whilst engaged in arranging and completing his reminiscences, he took occasion to express his appreciation of the part played by the French army on the day of Mentana. His words are only a commentary on the well-known saying of General de Failly: "The chassepots worked wonders."

"The chassepots poured their fire upon a group of houses, and the Garibaldians took good care to remain invisible all the time that this fearful discharge lasted, so that the walls alone had the benefit of it; they bear traces of it to the present day. Far be it from us to detract from the credit of the French army, or deprive it of a single particle of the glory it so hardly earned, yet it is only right to show up the injustice of those who persist in ascribing to it all the honor of the day. The flag, unfurled upon the field of battle, had the effect of a threat, and struck terror into the hearts of the Garibaldians, while at the same time the presence of the French troops stopped the advance of the Piedmontese soldiers, who had encamped at a short distance from the theater of conflict; they also, by means of skilful maneuvers executed in the vicinity of Monte Rotondo, intercepted the enemy's reinforcements. Nevertheless it is only fair to repeat, that before the French took any active part in the affair, the positions had all been carried. The conquered deemed it less humiliating to ascribe their discomfiture to the marvelous doings of the chassepots, and the enemies of the Church found some measure of compensation for defeat in refusing the Pontifical army any share in the triumph which its bravery had won."

The victory of Mentana was followed by a spell of unbroken sunshine. A breath from on high had dispersed the storm-clouds which had long been hanging over the Eternal City, and the Church shone forth with added luster, proud of her gallant defenders, prouder still of her newly made martyrs. The acclamations with which the entire Catholic world hailed the victory of its Supreme Head, the cries of disappointed rage uttered by the enemies of the truth, blended in a strange chorus, each in its own way doing honor to Jesus Christ. The defeat of the Gari baldian hordes inaugurated a period of comparative tranquility, which reached its apogee three years later, on the occasion of the Vatican Council.

It was only natural that the day after the battle Theodore should seek to spend a little time in thinking quietly over the past. How many opportunities had the last year afforded him of proving his affection for the Church! Weariness, fatigue, and disappointment had been his portion in no scant measure, but did not the very recollection of them amply reward him for all he had undergone? And after Mentana, what more had he left to wish for? His gratitude seems to overflow as he pens the following lines: "God has ordered all for the best, and when one looks back upon the history of the Revolution, one can see in it nothing but a continuous miracle. It is only necessary to compare the vile hypocrisy of the conspirators with the loyalty of the defenders of the Church. As for us poor Zouaves, even now we still wonder how there can be any of us left. The plan of the Garibaldians was to bury us alive under a heap of ruins, and none other than the hand of God could have frustrated their evil design, and brought us safe out of many perilous situations, where, humanly speaking, we were certain to be overwhelmed by an army ten times superior to our own in numbers. Our two months' campaign will leave behind many a precious memory, and we are fully recompensed for all we have undergone by the satisfaction of knowing that we have done our duty, the pride of having served the Holy Father, and the edification of having witnessed so many holy and happy deaths, which really make one quite long to become a martyr."

But for all this rejoicing our hero still retains a lingering regret which he, as usual, confides to his parents. "When I think of Mentana, I am half sorry that I was not left on the field, it seems rather inglorious to have come off without a single scratch, the more so as my height makes me conspicuous. Another time I hope I shall either not come out of the fight at all, or else do so minus a limb, or at any rate as an occupant of the ambulance." And his mother so fully sympathizes with the ardent aspirations of her soldier son, that in her reply she expresses herself as follows, showing that she too, under similar circumstances, would have acted as the mother of the Maccabees acted. "I can quite enter into your feelings, my dear boy, and understand that you would have deemed it an unspeakable happiness to lay down your life for God, and enter upon the enjoyment of His presence in Heaven. You may be sure, however, that He will accept your good will." Both mother and son were no friends to compromise in the question of sacrifice, and the mere mention of it awoke a corresponding echo in each of their hearts.

Theodore meantime devoted himself to those of his friends who were among the wounded, and whenever he had a free moment, hastened to the hospital to see how Moeller and his companion in suffering, Carlos d'Alcantara, were going on. It was most touching to hear these two mutually encourage one another from their sick beds; Moeller termed these days the happiest of his life, and when any one asked him how he was, he would answer: "I am gradually sinking;" while d'Alcantara, in the midst of agonizing pain, consoled himself by repeating: "The greater the suffering, the greater the merit."

The atmosphere of that sick-room had something quite supernatural about it, for Christian peace and resignation shed a celestial perfume there. These two sons of Catholic Belgium, who had been united in sacrifice, were united also in death; the same day saw them both expire. "I am overwhelmed by the news," Theodore writes, "I could not believe it until I had heard it from several different persons, for I thought Moeller was quite convalescent. I longed to go and pray beside his body, to press a last kiss upon his forehead, I felt too that I owed this to our long friendship, but in a soldier's life even the most reasonable wishes must yield to stern necessity. I tried in vain to find someone who would take my place, so as to set me free for a short time; I offer the sacrifice I had to make for the repose of his soul. I really must be present tomorrow at his funeral and I trust God will make a way for me to do so. Shortly before Moeller's death, a comrade said to him: 'Look here, Moeller, I am full of health and strength, while you are stretched on a bed of suffering, and are soon going to die. Would you exchange your lot for mine?' 'Not for worlds,' he answered, and the expression of his countenance told more eloquently than any words could do, how confident was his expectation of future bliss."

The lull which followed the victory of Mentana was of brief duration. The Revolutionists gnashed their teeth for rage, whilst eagerly anticipating the hour of revenge. A mine was actually discovered beneath St. Peter's; the miscreant who had undertaken to blow up the San Francesco barracks, having been seized with remorse as he was in the act of firing the train, gave information to the authorities. "We literally sleep over mines, and go to bed at night with the agreeable prospect of waking to find ourselves perched aloft on the dome of some church, or of never waking at all Whilst at Ara Coeli we were told on three successive days that we were to be blown up that very night, and consequently were much astonished to find ourselves safe and sound the next morning. It is a fact that a large quantity of powder was discovered beneath the Capitol, and for this reason our removal was determined on. It has been a great boon to the 6th Company, for we have the honor of being lodged almost in St. Peter's, beneath the spacious. vestibule which forms the continuation of the colonnades on the left. The Holy Father desired to have some of his Zouaves near his person, like a parent who in the hour of danger gathers his children closely round him; and consequently he caused the vestibule in question to be converted into a splendid barrack-room, the finest in Rome, nay more, in all Europe, and occupying the best situation in the whole world. We are lodged like princes, having bedsteads, with paillasses and mattresses, good fires, and in short all that we can need. Having thus been selected to form a guard of honor, we are obliged to keep everything as bright and clean as possible, for we receive many distinguished visitors. And then it is delightful to fall asleep every evening at the very feet, as it were, of St. Peter, under the windows of the apartments of Pius IX. We no longer fear that we shall be blown up. Good night, my dear parents."

During the closing days of November Theodore's thoughts naturally reverted to the events of the preceding year, and he re-read what he had then written in his notebook, in order to live over again in spirit the last happy days he had spent under the paternal roof. "It was exactly a year ago yesterday that I bade my dear mother farewell. I thought of this last night when I was on guard at the Capitol. What a change from last year! At Mass this morning I renewed the sacrifice of all that I then gave up, and I hope that you, sitting by the warm fireside and at the well-spread table, will remember a poor absentee, who begs you will say a few prayers for him."

Whilst looking through his note-book, he comes across the following passage, after an account of a walk with his eldest brother:

"When we got back, we sat talking together for a long time, and Willebaud told me that mother could not at all accustom herself to the thought of my going. When I heard this, my eyes filled with tears." "What a pleasure it is to me," he goes on, "to read these pages, written while the thought of separation was still new to me! I am able to recall the anxiety, the misgivings I felt, and at the same time to see how the merciful hand of Providence directed all things for the best."

If he thus loved to recall the past, it was not in order to give way to enervating regrets, but rather in order to draw from the fount of memory strength to accomplish in a generous spirit the duty of each day, beset as was that duty with weariness, fatigues, midnight watchings. "God only knows how arduous I find the sentry work; for the last week I have literally lived in the guard-room, being on duty for twenty-four hours at a time. There is work enough to be done, and continually increasing cause for anxiety. Tomorrow the French will finally evacuate Rome, it is a miserable farce for which a heavy reckoning will have to be paid some day."

The French troops were in fact recalled, and the tricolor ceased to float over the Castle of St. Angelo. At the earliest sitting of the French Chambers, however, the Imperial Government could no longer postpone a definite declaration of the policy it intended to pursue in regard to the Temporal Power, and M. Rouher, pressed on all sides by the majority, stated in his master's name that Italy should *never* be permitted to take possession of Rome. Many may yet remember with what an outburst of delight these words were hailed by all Catholic hearts, the positive character of the assurance they contained seeming to leave no room for disloyal evasion. No one rejoiced more heartily than Theodore: "At last France is resuming her rightful place; M. Rouher found great difficulty in uttering that *never,* but on that account Catholics will remember it all the better. Poor Italy! unhappy Revolutionists! The *Galantuomo** is placed in a pretty predicament.

"Could there possibly be a finer sight than that presented by this great struggle, the diabolical hatred on the one side, the sublime

---

*   A respectable gentleman.

devotion on the other, and all these surging waves of opposing feelings breaking at the foot of a tottering throne? An apparently feeble and helpless old man is in reality a great motive power, influencing not only the whole world, but each individual conscience, and Pius IX. is the chief personality of the age. Conquering or conquered, in triumph or tribulation, he always preserves that supremacy which is the prerogative of eminent sanctity and unselfish devotion, and he is worthy indeed to be the chosen representative of God upon earth. Whilst all is agitation around him, it is our privilege to form a wall of living stones for his defense."

Mentana.

CHAPTER XI.

1867, 1868.

The effect of twelve months' military services on Theodore. He is made Corporal. His work at the Depôt. Gloomy forebodings. His interview with Pius IX.

It is interesting to note what changes of twelve months of military life have wrought in the subject of this memoir. Is it possible that the barracks, the guard-room, the seductions of pleasure and the absence of restraint have not tended to destroy the freshness and simplicity which formed one of his most attractive features when he first came to Rome? Shall we find in him the same sincere piety, the same generous devotion, the same child-like affection for home, that characterized him a year ago? Will not the hard work and rough companionship to which a soldier is exposed have vitiated his palate, so that he no longer relishes the simple pleasures in which he formerly took delight ? Let him answer for himself; the following letter, written on Sunday, December 15th, 1867, will serve to dispel all doubt, and set all apprehensions at rest.

"Guard-house at the Coliseum, 7 p.m.

"I must write a few lines to my dear parents at the close of a day which has been spent in a very different manner from what I should have chosen. I have thought a great deal of you ever since I woke in the morning. I always think more of home on Sundays than on other days, because then I feel more acutely the privations my absence imposes on me. I remember the early Mass at which my mother always went to Communion, the High Mass, the prayers said in common, the family gatherings, the many pleasures that were all the more enjoyable because they were so simple and pure. Thus I have been taught in all sincerity to consider Sunday a holy and happy day; happy it cannot fail to be where God is never forgotten. Scarcely a night passes without my dreaming of you. I go the round of my relatives and friends, and when morning comes I feel quite angry with the bugle which dispels my illusions. Of all things, I detest passing the whole day in a guard room, there is nothing more wearisome. One fancies one will spend the time so usefully in reading, writing, learning Italian: not a bit of it! All these excellent intentions are put to flight when once one gets in this horrid prison, and one finds there is nothing to be done but to keep up an idle conversation with the sergeant, or the men, if they happen to understand French, to eat, drink, and try to kill time.

"Luckily for me, I am at the Coliseum, the best place I could be in. Despite the frightful cold, I have been able to pray at the foot of the Cross both for you and for myself, and that has in some measure sanctified the day. Just at the time you were, as far as I could guess, at Tourcoing, in front of a blazing fire, whose warmth would not be unacceptable to me at this moment. A little more, and we shall have to go on duty in skates; one's hands ache so terribly that it is difficult to fix the bayonet in its place. The other day, in the Square of St. Peter's, I slid on the ice by the large fountains; a fresh reminder of home, which gave me the greatest satisfaction."

It must be acknowledged that if Theodore has altered at all, it is that he has become strengthened, in virtue, and has learnt to regard self-sacrifice no longer in the light of a stranger of stern and forbidding aspect, but in that of an old and familiar friend. His heart is indeed unchanged, but changes have taken place around him; his friends, Crombé and Cordonnier, have been promoted, and Theodore rejoices in their advancement all the more because he does not desire the same thing for himself. "Hurrah for the Roubaix corporals!" he writes. "We drank their health with a hearty good will, for they have not got their stripes for nothing. It has been agreed that on the day that any one is promoted, he shall give a dinner to the others, and I think we may look forward to a good many such entertainments.

"As for me, apart from the drawback of my boyish appearance, I am quite destitute of the deportment, the authority, the indescribable something one sees in a corporal. I could never punish the men, nor could I ever make them respect me. It would be just the same thing as in the Sunday-school at Marcq, where I had a class of boys to manage. We who come from Roubaix like nothing so well as to get together; if one of us is at all out of spirits, he soon recovers his tone in the company of the others. What greater pleasure is there than talking about home?"

But Theodore's turn came for promotion; he, too, like the rest, had to mount the first round of the ladder, though it cost him a painful effort to do so, so far was he from courting military distinctions. Had he been merely made corporal, he would not have complained, but the functions. assigned to him presented themselves before him in such somber hues, that the usually light-hearted soldier could not refrain from indulging in bitter lamentations. It is impossible to repress a smile on reading the letter he wrote on the occasion, in which he heaps Pelion upon Ossa to an extravagant extent. One might suppose some terrible mis fortune had befallen him, so greatly does his imagination, always over active, exaggerate and magnify the disagreeables connected with his new post. These proved in reality far less formidable than he anticipated, but the undue estimate his fancy formed of them was at least a means of procuring him an occasion for the exercise of virtue and submission to the will of God.

"Almighty God has sent me one of the heaviest crosses I have as yet had to bear. I have been definitely appointed corporal, but alas! I have to pay a heavy price for my stripes, for I am sent to the depôt to teach the newcomers. I feel quite stunned by this unexpected announcement. Before you can enter into my trouble, you must let me give you an idea of what is in store for me. Picture to yourself a large gloomy building, the St. Calixtus barracks. Within all is in direct confusion and incessant bustle, a crowd of raw recruits, without equipments and ignorant of discipline, are going to and fro in the greatest confusion; you never saw such a queer lot of men! My business is to drill this motley crew, and what is harder still, get them into some sort of shape; a delightful pastime! Twice a day I must knock into their heads by dint of shouting, the meaning of *Portez armes** and a great many other equally interesting things. Fancy me standing in front of a score of these individuals, who look as if they came fresh from the tower of Babel, me of all people, with my ungainly proportions, not knowing what to do with my legs, or where to put my arms!

"Between times, I shall have to set them their work, study the theory of drill, etc. This is not the worst; think into what company I shall be thrown! Generally the corporals sent to the dépôt are older men, who are half brutalized. What an attractive circle of friends for me! Besides, one great qualification for a drill-master is to be rather surly, and this is quite foreign to my nature. As for the instruction, I ought by rights to take the place of the taught rather than the teacher; and then when one has gained a little ground, one has to begin all over again, for every week a fresh batch of recruits is sent one. I am afraid lest the drill should absorb all my thoughts and stifle what little fervor and devotion I have. Perhaps I shall not even care to write to you any more. There will be no going to Mass of a morning, I shall have to give that up, and it was just that which was my greatest support. What I really dread most of all are not the disagreeables of my work, the humiliations, the isolation from my friends; the truth is, I tremble for myself, so young as I am, and exposed to so much danger! I must now lay aside my pen to go to Vespers, and unite in prayer with you.

"Today I am writing to you with a couple of stripes adorning my arm. You need not fear that this will turn my head, or that I shall

---

*   Command to shoulder arms.

grow ambitious of further promotion. I should never have raised my hopes as high, and would gladly have remained a private of the second class. However, I feel more at ease now, for this morning I had an interview with the Chaplain, and that was a great encouragement to me. My mind is now quite made up to accept the cross God sends me. If I could not look at it from a Christian point of view, I should be at my wit's end, but He Who has supported me through the past year is still the same, and if dangers thicken around me, He will proportion His grace to my needs. If outward circumstances render my life a very material existence, I will in thought rise above the things of time and sense; I hope to enjoy the peace of a good conscience, and I mean from the first to show that I am a Christian, so that if the men do not respect my authority on account of my youthful appearance, at any rate they will respect my principles. If it is God's will that I should be at the depôt, I will endeavor to serve Him there. As soon as the stripes had been sewn on my sleeve, my good Angel inspired me with a happy thought. I went to the tomb of the holy Apostles, and kneeling there I consecrated them to them. One thing is a great comfort to me, and that is the kindness shown to me by my captain, M. Joubert, who is a good Christian, the Prefect of our Confraternity.

"I have now left the dear old 6th. I have much to be thankful for, and I shall take away with me many happy reminiscences. Farewell to the Vatican barracks, farewell to my old comrades. They were capital fellows, and I shall always think of them with pleasure. I do not believe there is a single other Company in which a better state of feeling exists amongst the men. Alas! The oldest members, who have been the pillars of the 6th, are being dispersed on all sides. Some have returned to their families, others in the course of advancement are sent as corporals to other divisions of the regiment. It is to be hoped they will carry with them something of the virtues which distinguish the 6th, the dear old Company!"

To hear Theodore, one would fancy oneself listening to an old soldier of the First Empire, talking of his former comrades and of the grand old times, while he wipes away a stealthy tear!

Happily for our hero, life at the depôt turned out to be far less unendurable than his fancy had led him to conceive, and the horizon which from a distance presented so gloomy an aspect, looked quite bright on nearer approach. Amongst the corporals were several with whom he was glad to make friends. Of one, who had entered the Papal service as a voluntary expiation of the sins of his youth, Theodore says: "He was converted all in a moment, an irresistible force holding him back when he was on the point of committing suicide. He finds military service exceedingly wearisome, I can perceive that each day costs him fresh struggles and fresh sacrifices. Of a night when everyone else is asleep, he lights his trusty pipe, and we sit and chat together, or rather he talks and I listen. He is the best man alive; he often speaks of his wish to do penance for his past life. His great desire is to enter La Trappe; who knows upon what brilliant worldly prospects he will be turning his back!"

Another unexpected piece of good fortune connected with life at the depôt was that the whole of Sunday was free, and thus every one was more at liberty there than elsewhere to follow the bent of his devotion. The reader scarcely requires to be told that the newly-made corporal availed himself of the opportunity thus afforded him to enjoy the spiritual delights of Christmas to his heart's content.

"On the 24th of December, while sounds of rejoicing were to be heard on all sides, my thoughts reverted to my native land and my far-off home. I said to myself that on the morrow distance and separation would be done away with, for all will meet, filled with the self-same love and joy to celebrate the birth of the Infant Christ. How many Masses will be said throughout the world, how many prayers offered up at the Saviour's crib! Christmas is indeed the festival that of all others appeals most strongly to the heart. The weather was most suitable, one of those clear, cold nights, so common in the north; an icy wind, the stars excessively bright, I think it must have been like that at Bethlehem."

Theodore's new duties obliged him to be very frequently in the Square of St. Peter's, and thus they became the means of his often obtaining the Pope's blessing. No sooner did he descry the Papal carriage than he ran to post himself on its route, taking care to choose a spot where there were no other people, so as to get a blessing all to himself; then hastening to the Vatican, he used to mount the steps with long strides, and arrive quite out of breath, in time to place himself on his knees where Pius IX. would have to pass. "I really think," he said, "that in this way the Holy Father will get to know my face at last." But this distant acquaintance did not content him; for some time past he had been soliciting a private audience, and in the commencement of 1868, the favor so much wished for was granted him. No new year's gift could have been more welcome. He writes:

"I have a grand piece of news for you, such good news! and a very precious gift besides, nothing less than the blessing of the Holy Father. You ought to be highly delighted. My great wish, and yours for me, has been fulfilled; God has in His goodness given me more than I could venture to ask and hope. For at least ten minutes I remained kneeling at the Holy Father's feet, I kissed his hand, listened to his gentle words, and talked to him as freely and as unreservedly as I should have spoken to a father. Oh! I only wish I could give you some idea of my delightful interview.

"About a fortnight ago, I wrote a letter to Mgr. Pacca. It was rather an audacious thing to do perhaps, but I thought the strength of my wish would be my best excuse. I expounded all my reasons to the Cardinal, mentioning the great sacrifice I had made, what good Catholics all my family were, and how devoted to the Holy See; I pleaded the long time I had already waited, the desire you constantly expressed, my slight services, my youth, my struggles to do right, my sore need of help. Lastly, I told him that the 26th of December was my mother's feast, and nothing would delight me more than to be able to offer her on that occasion some trifling souvenir and a blessing from His Holiness. It seems the justice of my cause made me eloquent, and my words appear to have found their way to his heart. However, the days went by without my receiving an answer, and I had begun to give up all hope, though I did not cease to pray.

"Yesterday, January 3rd, I obtained what I wanted. At Mass that morning, the thought that I might perhaps have an audience suddenly occurred to my mind, and about ten o'clock, while I was quietly sitting in my quarters at St. Calixtus, one of my friends in the 6th came running in, exclaiming, 'Here's good news for you! you have got an audience!' and handed me—blessed sight!—the card of admission. It was with real emotion that I read the lines which announced my good fortune.

"I had plenty of time to get myself ready and make some little purchases, but I hardly knew what I did, I was almost beside myself with joy. I kept saying to myself: If I could only let my dear parents know that in a few hours' time I shall be in the Holy Father's presence! My first thought was to give thanks to the Giver of all good, and at the same time to ask for the wisdom I should need for this interview. A little before five I went up the marble staircase of the Vatican, and after having put off my saber in an antechamber, I was ushered into an audience-room, simply but handsomely furnished. In it there was a splendid throne covered with velvet, and opposite to this a magnificent crucifix. Six Zouaves were waiting there, and at first I was afraid that the audience was to be general, which would have been a terrible disappointment to me; but it was nothing of the sort.

"After I had waited for what appeared to me a very long time, in reality about half an hour, they began to call us each one in his turn. Even now as I write, something of the excitement comes back to me which I felt for a few minutes before I was summoned. I trembled from head to foot, not from timidity but for joy, for every one who came out said to the others: 'Oh, he was so kind to me!' At last my name was called, I was the last but one. The Monsignor who came for me smiled at me as if I had been an old acquaintance, he seemed pleased to see me look so happy. We went down a long and very narrow corridor, I was half afraid to go on, for I expected at every turn to see Pius IX. himself appear. My guide had to tell me to follow him; when we got to a small room leading into the one where the Holy Father was, I stopped there, while the Monsignor went into the inner room, and after exchanging a word or two with His Holiness, said aloud: 'M. Wibaux,' and then withdrew.

"I raised my heart for a moment in prayer and went, kneeling at the threshold before entering for a first benediction. The Holy Father was sitting at a writing-table in a small study; as I walked in he held out both his hands to me, saying, 'Come in, my dear child.' I kissed the hand he held out to me. 'Let me see,' he said,' where is it you come from?'

" 'From Roubaix, your Holiness.'

" 'That is near Lille, is it not?'

" 'Yes, in the diocese of Cambrai.'

" 'Ah, to be sure, Mgr. Régnier.'

" 'A most excellent bishop, who has sent your Holiness a great many Zouaves.'

" 'Oh, yes!' then touching my sleeve, he added with a smile, I see you are a corporal.'

"I looked up at him, and said, 'Holy Father, you will give your blessing to my family, will you not? If you only knew how my father and mother love you, how they think of you and pray for you! 'He smiled and nodded his head, and I continued: 'My grandmother, too, has bought a very fine likeness of your Holiness, and every evening she asks your blessing.' When I had finished speaking, he gave me a tap on the cheek, saying: 'Now I am going to

Blessed Pope Pius IX.

give you a little souvenir—a picture of St. Peter and St. Paul.' After looking about for some time in his desk, he found one, and gave it to me. I told him I would send it to my mother as a special souvenir from him, as her feast was St. Stephen's day. 'That will come just right,' he replied, 'now you can stand up.'

"I brought out a large photograph of Pius IX. which I had bought, and beneath which I had written the request for an Indulgence to be granted to myself, my parents, and my relatives to the fourth degree. I had been told that this was never given for more than the third degree, but I intentionally left it as it stood. Before I had time to proffer my request, Pius IX. took the photograph out of my hand, and took up his pen. I told him I had made a slight error, and pointed it out to him. 'That is of no consequence,' he said, 'I will set it right myself.' Then he read aloud what I had written, and when he came to the place corrected the figure, as you will see; afterwards he signed it.

While he was doing this, I kept saying, 'Oh, Holy Father, if you only knew how happy you have made me! This is indeed a day to be remembered!' I saw him smile as he was writing. Then I held out a small box filled with rosaries and medals, which he blessed, making a large sign of the Cross over them. One of the Zouaves of my old Company had given me sixty francs to take to the Holy Father; when I put them down on the table His Holiness appeared quite touched: 'I must send this good Zouave a little souvenir too,' he said, and looked about for a medal, but could not find one.

"All this time I was still kneeling. 'Have you any brothers and sisters?' he asked. I replied that I had four brothers and four sisters; he made a gesture of surprise, and inquired if they were married? I answered no, they were all quite young still. Ah, little sisters, are they?' he rejoined. When I told him that all my brothers wanted to be Zouaves, but this could not be managed, he laughed. I added that my grandmother had had fourteen children, 'This seems to be a family which God has blessed,' he replied.

" 'I have great need of your Holiness' blessing,' I went on; 'I have my full share of little miseries, I am young and often exposed to danger.'

" 'What is your age?'

" 'I am eighteen and a half years old.'

" 'Poor child!'

" 'I often have to struggle hard, especially against temptations which assail the virtue of chastity.'

" 'Do you find yourself in occasions of sin?' he asked, with the utmost kindness of manner. 'The Zouaves keep clear of vicious ways, do they not?'

" 'Oh, yes, Holy Father, only sometimes the conversation is not quite what it ought to be. You know what young men are.'

" 'This is what it is," he rejoined, touching the tip of his tongue; then with the most fatherly solicitude he added: 'Have you got your—what is it called?' He laid his hand on my jacket, unable at the moment to remember the word he wanted—'your cloak with you? It is very cold.' And on my replying in the affirmative: 'Well there, now I will give you my blessing,' he added.

"I took the hand he held out to me in both of mine, pressed it affectionately to my lips for some time without his attempting to withdraw it. 'Now,' I exclaimed, 'I can die happy!' That was the last thing I said. 'Poor child!' he ejaculated, and followed me with his eyes to the door as I withdrew.

"Those whom I passed on my way out could not help smiling to see my face beaming with happiness; I could hardly myself believe in my good fortune. All the time the audience lasted I was on my knees close to the Holy Father's armchair, I touched his white soutane, his hand rested on mine. I saw nothing else in the room, for I could not take my eyes off his countenance. I am sure they expressed more than my lips could find words to utter. He too kept looking at me, and always with a smile. From the first he treated me as a father treats one of his favorite children, the Zouaves all are his Benjamins. I quite forgot he was a Pontiff, a King. I only saw a father in him and felt perfectly at my ease. All that I said came from fullness of my heart, I should have liked to stay a long time to tell him everything, and pour out my whole soul, to have held fast those precious moments for the remainder of my life, had that been possible.

"I am afraid I have given you a very poor account of my interview. This sort of thing cannot be described in words the charm of his smile, his excessive kindness of manner, the expression of his features, the simple majesty of his whole person, must be seen to be appreciated. I can boast of having been more privileged than any monarch, however great, for Pius IX. does not talk to them as he did to me, poor common-place Zouave that I am. Fancy the highest Potentate on earth asking the humblest of his subjects whether he has brought his cloak! What do you say to such thoughtful kindness? As we were leaving, one of the Chamberlains said the Holy Father was really too kind. For my part I think there is no such powerful weapon as kindness.

"Thus you see all my hopes have been realized. The Holy Father has given me his blessing, and I have got a few words in his own handwriting; may this blessing bear abundant fruit! I hope that from this day, the 3rd of January, may date the commencement of a life of greater detachment, more generous devotion. The future is in the hands of God; any day fresh complications may arise, and if we have to take the field again, I do not think I shall escape a second time. I always had a secret conviction that I should not die before I had seen Pius IX. Now I am quite prepared for death. My dear parents, you do not know how glad I am to think of the pleasure this news will give you. While I was with His Holiness you were not for a single instant absent from my thoughts."

The tidings communicated by Theodore created quite a sensation in the whole family. As soon as the welcome letter had been read at Roubaix, Stephen was despatched to Tourcoing, to take it to his relatives there. "Good news!" he cried, directly he caught sight of his grandmother.

"What, a letter from Theodore?"

"Yes, he has had an audience with the Holy Father!" The pious old lady wept for joy.

"He has seen the Holy Father!" she exclaimed, "*Deo gratias!*" The letter from Rome was read aloud during dinner-time, and afterwards all joined in the Litany which M. Motte recited as an act of thanksgiving.

A touching incident in connection with what has been related may be added here. The Zouave who sent the sixty francs by Theodore to the Holy Father, a Frenchman named Burel, had his jaw fractured and his tongue partly torn away by a bullet during the siege of Rome in 1870. Shortly before his death, being unable to articulate distinctly, he asked by signs for paper and pen, and wrote down the words: "I bequeath all that I possess to Pius IX." When this document, stained as it was with the blood of the writer, was brought to the Pope, he could not refrain from shedding tears. What better recompense could the Supreme Head of the Church have bestowed for this generous act on the part of one of his sons?

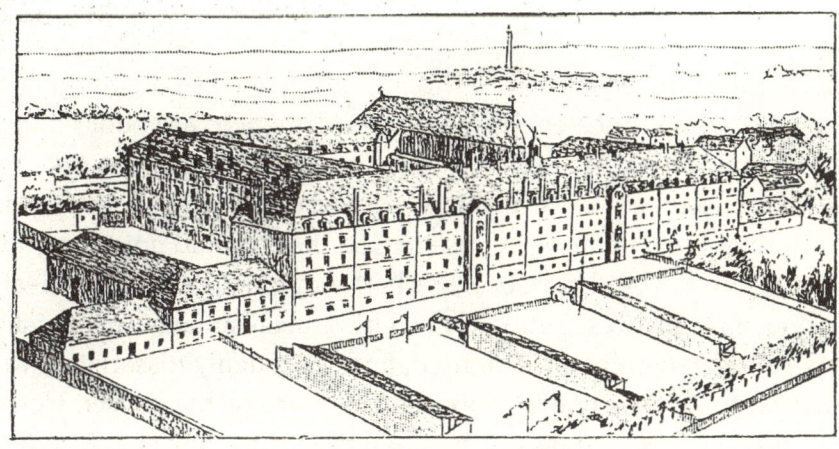
College of Our Lady of Boulogne.

CHAPTER XII.

1868.

The theater. Good counsel and its results. Theodore's nineteenth birthday. Unwelcome notoriety. Arrival of his brother and cousin. Excursions made in their company.

A FORTNIGHT had passed away since Theodore's audience, but his friends at Roubaix had not again heard of him. This was the first time that he had allowed so long a period to elapse without writing home, and it was evident that there must be some reason for his prolonged silence. An extract from his next letter will enlighten us as to its cause, for concealment of any kind was utterly foreign to his frank and loyal nature.

"You must be wondering very much at not having heard from me, the more so since I have twice received a welcome budget which it is a shame to leave so long unanswered. If one is not at peace with oneself, all goes wrong; affections and memories alike lose their hold over one. I have been terribly out of sorts lately, and have had hard struggles with myself; God in His mercy has enabled me to come out conqueror, though not without some measure of humiliation.

Alas for the weakness of the human heart, especially in the young! You little know what evil passions, bad desires, vain thoughts, lie dormant in my heart! I have three times yielded to the temptation to go to a small theater, where the performances are poor enough, but happily not very objectionable. One only goes for the sake of a little amusement; however, it was a wrong thing for me to do, for each time I had made a promise to God that I would not set my foot in it again. It would have been far better of me to resist. The theater is one of my greatest temptations. I have been sufficiently punished by feeling generally discontented, and thoroughly dissatisfied with myself, for unless one is more than human, or has ceased to take an interest in such plays, it is impossible that they should not fill one's mind with a crowd of thoughts of a more or less reprehensible nature. I found I could not pray properly, I did not care to write home, my whole tone was lowered.

"A good sergeant, a friend of mine, was the means of restoring my moral equilibrium, quite unconsciously to himself. One day he began to speak unreservedly to me of the struggles he had had to sustain; and I was quite struck by the uncompromising virtue, the high-minded devotion, the purity of sentiment he displayed. I felt heartily ashamed of my own weakness, when I saw how completely his conscience was at peace, and how he desired rather than dreaded death. I went to confession, and made a firm resolution from henceforth to be generous to the very utmost of my power."

The perfect absence of all reserve in Theodore's intercourse with his parents might occasion some measure of surprise, were we unacquainted with the prudent counsels which those parents gave in exchange for his confidence. Fully persuaded as they were that nothing would have induced their son to enter a theater which was known to be bad, or remain there during the performance of an immoral play, their answer to the foregoing letter was couched in the kindest terms and only aimed at cheering him, and encouraging him to proceed on the path which generous souls love to tread.

"My dear boy,—Though I feel deeply for your troubles, I am far from being surprised at them; such trials are unavoidable in the spiritual life, nay more, they are necessary to it. There is no great harm in going to the theater just to amuse yourself, the important thing is not to go alone, and to beware of any contact with persons whose reputation is at all doubtful." It was in accordance with counsels such as these, which without being in any way extreme, inspired the love of what is good and pure, that the young corporal shaped his conduct on entering upon his new functions at the depôt. His father, writing from Roubaix, speaks thus: "It is well for us to have an opportunity daily afforded us of overcoming our own likes and dislikes, and acquiring the virtues in which we are most deficient. Your position of command will teach you to be firm, it will give you strength of character, and make you see how important it is to be exact in little things. You must let it be seen that you can enforce obedience without being unkind, and that you can, as becomes a Christian, be firm in matters of discipline and yet indulgent to those under you."

No wonder that after receiving such letters Theodore is heard to exclaim: "Did I not always say that Papa was like the kindest of friends to us? And as for you, dear Mother, even if I was made Pope I should never be tempted to forget you, the remembrance of what you are to me will always be influential with me for good. The thought of Father, Mother, and home will hold me back from going far wrong; what vexes me most, what I really regret, is that my love for you is not what it used to be. It is as if a wall of ice were rising up round my heart, chilling my affections. Whether it is that I am getting older, or the effect of all this drilling, I certainly am growing indifferent, but nothing I hope will ever make me feel less deeply the need of prayer."

"The long hours of drill will have a very hardening influence on me," was Theodore's prediction on being appointed to the depôt. The following letter, written on the occasion of the death of an aunt, shows that there was no ground for any such fear. It shows us that his heart was unchanged, and that the all-absorbing occupations of the corporal on duty for the week, whose business it was to buy the supplies of vegetables, and see the barracks were properly swept out, left a place in his thoughts for affection, remembrance, and sympathy with the bereaved. "Alas! what a sad blow the loss of a mother is to a family! A Christian mother is an Angel guardian whose presence is the light of the domestic hearth. She always knows how best to comfort you, she always guesses aright the secrets of your soul, she never fails to give help and guidance just when they are wanted. No one knows this better than I do, who am so often the prey of evil passions. If I cannot pray, my memory often serves as a source of strength to me. I am indeed truly sorry for those poor children, who have lost so great a treasure; and at their age, too, they want someone to love them!"

In the opening weeks of 1868, Rome had cause to hope and to rejoice as she beheld volunteers hastening in hundreds to enlist under the Papal flag, drawn from all lands by the hope of a second Mentana. The prospect of sacrifice has an irresistible attraction for souls which are cast in an heroic mold, and the blood of martyrs acts as a powerful loadstone in regard to hearts which are given altogether to God. France and Belgium sent many of their sons, but Holland was especially generous; indeed it seemed at last as if all the Catholics whom her limited territory contained had devoted themselves to the service of the Holy Father. From across the sea too, came one hundred and fifty Canadians, all picked men; they met with a splendid reception in Rome, and many others speedily followed their example. In the midst of the stir caused at the depôt by these various arrivals, those in authority had to equip the newcomers and find quarters for them, to make all necessary arrangements, and what was most difficult of all, to remain calm and self-possessed amidst the general excitement. In such a school as this, Theodore was obliged whether he would or no, to learn how to make haste; an art which to a nature so independent and dreamy as his, is not easy to acquire.

But there was ample compensation to be found for the *ennui*[*] inseparable from his present occupations. Numerous occasions for doing good presented themselves in connection with the recruits, and the young corporal was only too glad to make his stripes a means of promoting the cause he had so much at heart. He would point out to his subordinates the dwelling of the Chaplain, tell them

---

*   Feeling of dissatisfaction.

about the Conference and the Confraternity, and on Sunday, after having escorted them to Vespers in their own chapel, serve as guide to any of their number who desired to inhale that perfume of piety which pervades Rome. It was delightful to see how at the sound of the Angelus, the corporal was the first to bare his head, and repeat the familiar words in honor of our Blessed Lady; and how, when the hour came for innocent recreation, he was the first to lead the sports, not blushing to lay aside his saber and his dignity, to play at hide and seek in out-of-the-way corners of the ancient circus. Truly the ghost of Romulus must have marveled to see these peaceful gladiators amusing themselves in so harmless a manner! When evening came, and the party had returned to barracks, Theodore used to say the night prayers aloud in the presence of about thirty conscripts; and his men would shake him by the hand, and smilingly tell him that at any rate he took good care they should not forget their devotions.

It is easy to understand that such an Apostle found numerous opportunities of serving the good cause; hence it is not wonderful that on the 2nd of February, which was a solemn festival for the Confraternity, Theodore was promoted to a post of honor, being appointed one of the counselors. "I like this title," he says, "much better than that of Corporal. As I am stationed at the depôt, it was no doubt thought that I am in a position to be useful."

Not many days later we find him saying, on the occasion of his birthday: "To think that I am already nineteen, and I still have withal both the face and the feelings of a child; it is only in regard to my faults that I have anything of the young man about me, and certainly I am not without the caprices and the passions of that perilous age. I am indeed oddly constituted, it would not be easy to find a character more inconsistent than mine! I wish you could see me now; I think myself so fine with my Mentana cross on my breast. Really I am very proud of it, the little blue and white ribbon recalls the triumphs of my school-days. I send it to you just as it was given to me, and I beg my dear father to accept it, it was dearly purchased. This. decoration constituted me ipso facto, a knight of the Immaculate Conception, and the Senate has, as an expression of gratitude, conferred upon us the title and privileges of Roman citizens. *Civis romanus sum!*"

Many years have passed away since 1868, yet Theodore's correspondence has remained as fresh and bright and attractive, as on the day when it was penned; for a style like his can never grow old-fashioned, any more than the sentiments that he expresses in so admirable a manner. Whether he relates his adventures, or dwells upon his own failings, whether he speaks of his love for God or his affection for his relatives, whether he describes a battle or a fatigue-party, we cannot but take pleasure in looking down into those depths of his heart which the pellucid stream of his flowing phrases allows us to behold so distinctly. And what could be more interesting than to watch the secret struggle between the Creator and His creature, which these pages bring to light? We see infinite tenderness and thoughtful foresight on the one side, and generous fidelity on the other; the work of grace sustaining that ceaseless warfare with fallen nature which keeps alive humility and her helpmate prayer in the heart of the young man who is so desirous to remain pure. If extracts from Theodore's letters have power to charm us even now, in spite of the lapse of years and the distance of space, which must inevitably tend to detract from their interest, it is not difficult to imagine what an impression they must have made on their first arrival, when they contained the echo of yesterday's occurrences. Their advent was quite a little event at Roubaix; they were copied, they were passed from hand to hand, for Theodore's friends and relatives were unwilling to lose one of these dainty morsels, and thus the circle of his readers became a continually increasing one.

Theodore happened to get wind of this, and at once took alarm. With the childlike simplicity and sincerity which characterized him, he immediately wrote home about it, showing how repugnant to him was the bare thought of such publicity. "It is always best to speak openly, and from you at least I need conceal nothing. I cannot help suspecting that my letters have been shown about pretty freely, and the idea of this cannot fail to restrain my pen when I am writing to you. I should be so terribly annoyed to find that my letters had gone beyond the circle of my immediate relatives. They are merely the expression of my feelings, and often of feelings which I desire to have, but do not possess in reality. Sometimes I speak as if I already were what I heartily wish to be, and thus I unconsciously represent myself as ten times better than I actually am. Besides, I often express private opinions about persons and things which may be utterly erroneous, for I never think I need be very cautious when I am writing to you. You will forgive me for speaking freely; it so much detracts from the pleasure of letter-writing if one must weigh all one's words."

This remonstrance did not content him. He reverts to the subject in a letter to Willebaud, his eldest brother and trusted counselor, opening his whole heart to him. The worst of the matter was that friends and relatives visiting Rome, and some of his comrades from the neighborhood of Roubaix who had been home on furlough, had seen his letters; and doubtless admiring his style and sentiments, either from mistaken politeness, or a mischievous pleasure in making him blush, had paid him some compliments about them. For the Zouaves this means of teasing him was a perfect godsend, they could hardly speak to him without bringing it into the conversation and reminding him what a saint he was.

Poor Theodore! what a mortification this publicity was to him, especially as it was supposed to be flattering! "I try to laugh at this thread-bare joke," he writes to his brother, "and devour my chagrin in secret. Those who judge of me from my letters are quite out in their reckoning, and the whole affair is a bitter annoyance to me. I appeal to you, because you can enter into my feelings, and even if you think me silly, you will not be hard on me. You know what a quantity of letters I have written, sometimes for the sake of the relief it afforded me, frequently only because of the promise I had made. It strikes me that I have not always been sincere in what I said, and that the words which flowed from my pen, were not the outpourings of my heart, but the effusions of imagination and inexperience. It appears that my letters contained beautiful sentiments so at least I am told *ad nauseam** by persons who have read them, and who, with an utter want of all good feeling, make this return for

---

*   Something that has been done repeatedly.

the kindness of those who unluckily were so thoughtless as to show them the letters.

"Hearing what people say of me, and knowing that it is quite false, naturally makes me think I must be an impostor, who says what he does not mean. I am afraid I have misrepresented my feelings, and more than once I have confessed to God the sorrow and the scruples this occasions me. I do not think I can accuse myself of insincerity; rather let me hope that the fervor my letters, seem to display was wholly the effect of God's grace, of a grace granted me at the time, but which passed away when I laid down my pen. My conduct doubtless sadly belies my words, but I fully meant them when I wrote them, and perhaps flattered myself that the dispositions I wished so earnestly to possess were already mine. Of one thing I can assure you, that.I never wrote a single line in the hope of being thought good. Well, I must console myself with the knowledge that God sometimes makes use of the most feeble instruments to benefit others."

And as he was then thinking of asking leave of absence in order to revisit his family, he adds: "I thought I had better tell you these wretched scruples before making my appearance amongst you, lest you should be disappointed when you see me as I really am, not by any means a model of virtue, but an ordinary mortal, endowed with an ample share of the passions and frailties of human nature. I must expect all manner of interior humiliations, and therefore make up my mind beforehand to accept them. I wanted to make a clean breast of it to someone who would understand me, now I have done so, and I feel all the better for it. I mean to banish all such thoughts from my mind henceforth, they are perhaps only a temptation, and to be resisted as such; I shall bury them under a heap of stones and mark the spot with a cross. And you, my dear brother, will not think any more of what I have said, but only remember it in your prayers."

But an unexpected pleasure was in store for Theodore. Willebaud, to whom he had turned for sympathy in the fresh and unlooked-for annoyances that had overtaken him, was on the point of setting out for Rome, accompanied by their cousin Henry, in order to assist at the ceremonies of Holy Week, and sing the Easter Alleluias with Theodore, for whom that family life in which he so delighted was thus to be renewed in the very heart of Rome. He was almost beside himself for joy at the prospect of a month's real holiday, a month during which military science was to be replaced by confidential conversation, the stifling barrack room by the open air, wearisome drill by enjoyable excursions. Theodore was to act as guide and interpreter to the merry trio, while Willebaud was to be the confidant and counselor of his younger brother, and teach him from his own experience how incessant a warfare must be waged by the young man who desires truly to serve God. On account of his rare intelligence, cultivated mind and fervent piety, he was calculated to be of the greatest service to Theodore, over whom his advantage in regard to age, and his more practical manner of viewing men and things, gave him a decided ascendancy. As for Henry, he was an enthusiastic artist, a persistent explorer of museums, and a passionate admirer of antiquities.

In order not to lose a single moment that might be employed in affectionate intercourse, they preferred to sleep all three in the same room, and the famous bolster fights, formerly a favorite amusement of Theodore's, began to be once more carried on as of yore. "How old habits cling to one!" he writes. "Will is quite a snare to me, for no sooner do I find myself with him again, than I fall back into my bad trick of teasing. When it is time to get up, there is just the same uproar there used to be when we all four slept in the large dormitory. In the midst of it all, I remember how a piteous voice was often heard proceeding from under the blankets of Stephen's bed, begging that he might be left in peace to sleep. Then a chorus of three voices, each pitched in a different key, would make answer. An end was generally put to it all by a pair of hands vigorously applied to Joseph or Stephen, or by one of us being forcibly turned out of bed. Willebaud does not make as free with me now, he seems to stand rather in awe of my saber, and I think he finds my fists are stronger than they used to be.

"We have made an excursion to Naples; Naples, whose azure sky and balmy air are so much belauded. We all are of opinion that the poets have drawn largely on their imagination, for the wind is positively cold, very unlike the soft zephyrs of their songs. However, I find nothing to complain of, for spending so many nights in the open air has hardened me, and I am able to enjoy the magnificent panorama to my heart's content. Liberty is after all the greatest boon to me, and I am only too glad to lay aside my dignity, and, together with my two dear friends, get all the pleasure I can."

In spite of visits to ruins, museums, and beautiful scenery, in spite of the physical and mental fatigue inseparable from such incessant coming and going, Theodore did not wish to enjoy all this pleasure in an egotistical manner, and remained faithful to his former habits. It was to his parents that he owed the companionship of his favorite brother, and how could he give them a more practical proof of gratitude than by enabling them to share in the varied enjoyments and experiences of each succeeding day? Hence the numerous pages written during this period, for the pen which the heart inspires can never know fatigue. Theodore leaves nothing untold; Pompeii, Vesuvius, Caprea, are all described by turns; nor does he omit amusing details concerning rickety conveyances, insolent beggars, and disputes with guides and innkeepers. He recalls and renews classic associations, and does not fail to visit the tomb of Virgil, "the old friend of my schoolboy days," as he terms him; adding, "he is buried on the very spot where he composed the Georgics. It is a pity that the poetry of one's thoughts should always clash so disagreeably with vulgar reality in the shape of the clamorous and incessant demands put forward by one or more of the custodians of the place."

On their return to Rome, the travelers continued their sight seeing, and the different characters of the trio furnished an unfailing source of amusement. "Henry's enthusiasm is quite provoking; when once he gets into a gallery of *chefs d'auvre*,[*] he is oblivious of all else. Wille baud is more earthly minded; it is most comical to see him if we stay out beyond a certain time, his face begins to look pinched, his eyes grow hollow, he can take interest in nothing; we can guess in a moment what ails him, poor fellow, he is desperately

---

[*] A masterpiece in art.

hungry!"

One day the desire to see everything worth seeing took them to the church of a convent, where a celebrated fresco adorns the walls, but alas! it was Holy Week, and a thick veil concealed the painting. While Willebaud and Theodore were engaged in making an act of adoration, they were startled by hearing a noise behind them, and turning round to discover the cause, they saw Henry absorbed in contemplation of the fresco. Carried away by his love of art, he had drawn aside the curtain, the supports of which had given way, so that the whole fell to the ground with a loud clatter. This incident so provoked the risible faculties of the two brothers that they had to decamp hastily, hardly able to suppress a hearty fit of laughter till the church door had closed behind them!

CHAPTER XIII.

1868.

Loretto and Castelfidardo. Month of May in Rome. Theodore's promotion. His quarters at St. Augustine. Another change. The feast of Corpus Christi.

THE brightest days must come to a close, and the time arrived for the travelers to make preparation to start on their homeward journey. One more pleasure was however in store for Theodore, he was to accompany them as far as Loretto. "I did not at all expect this happiness," he writes home, "I owe it entirely to our Lady. How many permissions I have asked for lately, and though I am quite at a loss to account for the favors shown me, all have been granted me without the slightest difficulty, even this last, which I hardly liked asking for, and which I had not the least expectation of obtaining. Today I have received my passport in due form. I mean to make this excursion as a pilgrimage, in company with the Blessed Benedict Labre, who often traversed the same road, though after a far less comfortable fashion than ourselves. Henry and Will are. snoring; it is their last night in Rome. Tomorrow I must bid farewell to the snug little room, the cheerful evenings, my dear friends, and my happy careless life! God's will be done,"

First of all, the travelers visited the spot hallowed by the memory of the seraphic St. Francis. "The heavens were bright with innumerable stars as we climbed the hill whereon Assisi stands, shedding all around the odor of sanctity; the night was deliciously cool. The next morning the birds woke us with their songs, perhaps they are the descendants of those who listened to St. Francis' exhortations. We said the *Gloria Patri* with Will; I remember papa used to wake us on Sundays with these words."

But the tourists hastened on in order to reach Loretto; night had already closed in when they arrived there. Once more they repeated together the familiar night prayers of their home in which each one had his accustomed part; Theodore saying the *Pater* for the Propagation of the Faith as naturally as if the habits of his childhood had never been broken off.

"The next morning we wended our way to the *Santa Casa*. On entering we saw beneath the dome, encased in white marble, the Holy House wherein our Lady dwelt. In the course of centuries a hollow place has been worn away in the marble all round by the knees of the pilgrims who have come to venerate the sacred relic. We were admitted into the interior of the Holy House itself, and there, uniting in spirit with the multitude of Pontiffs and Saints who, like ourselves, had knelt in worship within those hallowed precincts, we prostrated ourselves and kissed the sacred walls. Could they but speak, how entrancing the tale they would tell! They heard the angelic salutation, they saw how Mary was troubled, they witnessed the triumph of her humility. Here it was that Jesus lived for thirty years in obedience, subject to His parents, tasting in anticipation the bitterness of His Passion. What marvelous memories, what wonderful associations are these!

"How much I thought of you all in the Holy House, of my brothers and sisters, my friends and relatives. Trusting in the greatness of Mary's mercy, which one seems to claim with more confidence on the spot where once such miracles were performed, I exposed to her all my wants and all my hopes. I remembered the soldiers who

The Church of the Holy House of Loreto.

were defeated at Castelfidardo when I went to Communion; what a privilege for them in the midst of their sufferings to be able to turn with looks of love to their Mother's house, to have their thoughts raised to Heaven by the sight of it, and to breathe their last on the very threshold of her temple, with her dear name upon their lips!

"On leaving the Santa Casa we descended the hill and found ourselves upon the battlefield of Castelfidardo, whence the glistening dome of the Church of Loretto can be seen. When we got to the station, there was still an hour to spare; Will and I took a walk together arm in arm, and had one more confidential talk. I shall never forget the conversation as we paced along the lovely pathways of the valley, overlooked by Our Lady of Loretto, who, it seemed, was listening to what we said. Then I embraced my dear Will for the last time, and stood watching the departure of the train that was bearing him back to France. Before it got out of sight we waved a final adieu. I did not feel very sad while I could still see him; the time when one's heart sinks within one, is when one looks around and nowhere sees the face of a friend. I told myself I would spend another day at Loretto, there at least I should have the Madonna, to her I would confide all my sorrows and by her be comforted. I shall also revisit the plain of Castelfidardo and the spot where my friends lie buried, and kneeling on the soil that covers them I shall gain a fresh supply of strength.

"Here I still am. This morning I heard Mass in the Holy House, where the ineffable mystery of the Incarnation was accomplished. I thought of the *Fiat* Mary uttered, and repeated it after her, rejoicing to have something to offer her in the separation from my friends. Now I am off to visit my beloved martyrs, I have so much to say to them. Good-bye till evening.

"I have been fondly over the field of battle, and said a prayer there; I have seen the tree riddled with shot beneath which Pimodan received his death-wound, and the farm where a score of Zouaves held at bay the whole Piedmontese army. General Cialdini would not allow the prisoners to go and identify their comrades' remains, he ordered a trench to be dug into which all the dead were thrown indiscriminately. Happily the place of their interment is known; a grave indeed of touching simplicity, merely a square plot of ground in a cultivated field, at the edge of a rock. The peasants, as a sign of respect, never drive the plough over it. In the midst of the plot stands a piece of wood, once a cross, but every one who comes to pray here carries away a morsel as a relic. You can fancy what were my feelings as I stood on this hallowed spot; though ignorant even of the names of those who are interred there, I felt a pleasurable certainty that they could hear me when I addressed them.

Site of the battle of Castelfidardo.

"The grave where the Piedmontese soldiers are buried produces a very different impression. It is, like that of the Zouaves, a mere strip of earth, and there are the remains of a cross in the center; but no one ever goes to pray there, the very ground seems accursed. By the side, on a little hillock, a few stones have been set up in the form of a pyramid, with some sort of funereal inscription, a poor attempt at a monument! There was no money to do the thing properly, and the weather has already destroyed some of the stones, as if to mark the displeasure of Heaven. I said a prayer at this grave too, for death puts an end to all hostility.

"There is much to make this place attractive to me both as a Christian and a Zouave. My room commands a view of the hills and the battlefield. Last night there was a regular storm, the clouds were heavy and as black as ink, the wind came in furious gusts, making the windows rattle, I looked out on to the plain, all was perfectly dark, my thoughts had dwelt so long on the dead who lay buried there that a kind of horror seized on me, and as I continued to stare out into the blackness, it seemed as if some phantom form must come down from the hillside, or some deep voice break the silence of night. Today the battlefield is lit up with brilliant sunshine, the quiet, peaceful beauty of the landscape makes one think of Heaven. The face of nature smiles all around Loretto, it is truly a country worthy of our Lady. The sunset over the Adriatic has been glorious, I watched the light die away gradually behind the Appenines. My thoughts reverted to the evening of the battle; I said my evening prayer at the window, looking in the direction of the Frenchmen's grave, as the people here call it.

"(In the train). As the train carries me back swiftly towards Rome, the remembrance of the friends from whom I have so lately parted haunts me continually, but do not suppose that this makes me melancholy, or that I regret returning to the prose of every-day life, in comparison with which the past month seems a delightful dream. I like looking back on pleasures that are past, and it is better for me to be a little sad sometimes, for then I feel more inclined for prayer"

"Rome, May 1st.

"In entering upon this sweet month, let us unite together in prayer, and meet at the feet of the Blessed Virgin, to draw freely from the fountain of her mercy. I mean to spend this month as piously as possible, and I know, all I do for Mary's sake will be amply rewarded. Still I miss the sweetness I used to experience. Is this the effect of age? At any rate I can willingly resign myself to part with sensible devotion, so long as my fervor does not diminish. Tomorrow my visitors will reach home again. Two months' absence is enough to make one very glad to get back to home and friends, what will it be after two years? Will has doubtless plenty to say about his brother the Zouave, and the fun we had together; he will tell you that I am far from forgetting you, and that, thanks to your prayers, I manage to keep up, though my will is deplorably weak; he will tell you, too, that though I am by no means what I would wish to be, it is my earnest endeavor to become a true soldier of the Pope.

"Happy days, that have sped by only too swiftly! for me they are now only a dream that is past. The awakening has been rude, for I have passed by an abrupt transition from an atmosphere of delightful freedom to the irksome duties of a corporal of the week, which means being kept close prisoner to barracks for that space of time. I ought to congratulate myself on it, for by this means I am plunged at once into the thick of the service, and must break off short with the past.

"Here almost every hour of the day there is something to remind me of Willebaud and Henry. Going down a street, or passing some object of interest, I say to myself: They were with me the last time I saw this. Then I take out my notebook and look for the date, and read what we did on that day. Thus memory keeps alive in our hearts pleasures long since departed.

"Every evening quite regularly we have devotions for the Month of Mary. This is one of my greatest pleasures. When our work is finished, and the noises of the day are hushed, we assemble at our Lady's feet, we sing hymns in her honor, and then have Benediction of the Blessed Sacrament. What comfort these devotions afford to those whose life is so uncertain as ours. Last year Lieut. Guillemin played the harmonium at the Month of Mary services; this year he keeps her feasts in Heaven."

Theodore had only been a corporal for five months, when to his great astonishment his worsted stripes were exchanged for gold lace; but the new-made sergeant paid dear for the honor, since he was sent away to a fourth depôt which was being established. "I am falling from Scylla into Charybdis," he writes; "now my fate is sealed for the rest of my days. I am destined to become one of those wooden old drill-masters, who never speak except in phrases borrowed from the military text-book. And just fancy, if we should take the field, how shall I like to be forcibly detained within the enclosure of a depôt? The best of it is, the Captain of the new Company has asked specially for me, though I have not so much as ever spoken to him. He will repent nicely of his choice, when he discovers how incapable I am. God help me! Pray that I may not give way to vainglory, and that I may do my duty faithfully. I am glad of this advancement more for your sake than for my own."

As was the case in every change, Theodore regretted breaking off with the past; he knew the evils of what he was leaving, and he shrank from encountering those which were unknown. His new quarters, his superior officers, his comrades, all such doubtful matters were so many bugbears to him, huge and formidable in the distance and uncertainty. But happily all turned out as well as possible; Theodore was certainly a spoilt child of Providence. We will let him tell his own tale.

"Here I am installed in a pretty little room with four companions, all capital fellows. One of them is a bearded veteran, already beginning to get bald, an old African Zouave, very proud of wearing five or six medals. A second has made the Italian campaign, the others are beardless boys who have only seen fire at Mentana, and are glad to learn from the experience of their seniors. We get on excellently together, we are merry and quite at our ease; the conversation is never objectionable; indeed I could wish for nothing better. I have now got over the dreaded time of being corporal; the kindness of my friends did much to alleviate the disagreeables; on the whole, I have every reason to be thankful.

"These stripes change one completely. It is curious to see how an additional row of buttons down the waistcoat, a stripe of gold lace on sleeve and képi, will smarten up a man who only the day before was one of the dowdiest of corporals. Besides, as a non-commissioned officer one enjoys a host of privileges which certainly contribute largely to render life agreeable. The change is a very rapid one too; there is not a more unenviable lot than that of a corporal, he is a regular beast of burden, whose back ought to be wide enough to bear a great deal, for everything is laid on him; he is responsible for the mess, responsible for the appearance of his men, responsible for a thousand other things which are a constant source of anxiety to the unhappy creature. Now the sergeant stands on his dignity, and rarely comes into direct communication with the men, he acts through the medium of the corporals; if anything goes wrong, it is the corporal who is reprimanded. The sergeant is to the soldier what the superintendent is to the police; he is never in the wrong, when he speaks everyone is silent, everyone bows down before him. Surrounded by the halo his position gives him, he has no difficulty in making his authority respected, none of his subordinates would venture to disobey so distinguished a personage. When the sergeant appears, all discussions cease, disputed questions are referred to him, his dictum is law, his orders are sacred and violable as is his person. 'The sergeant said so,' is in every case the most convincing of arguments."

The new sergeant's barracks were situated close to his favorite Church of St. Augustine, in which, he says, "on the right of the chief entrance there is a miraculous image of the Blessed Virgin, resplendent with jewels. Seated on a marble throne, and wearing a crown on her head, she holds in her arms the Infant Jesus; her countenance is extremely beautiful, combining dignity and gentleness; it represents her in her double character of Queen and Mother.

All day long this image, entitled the Madonna of Mothers, is besieged by a crowd of pious worshippers; old men and little children, the miserable and the afflicted, come to kiss her feet; many make a cross on their foreheads with oil from the lamp which burns in her honor. So numerous are the wonders worked through her intercession, that room cannot be found for all the ex-votos. This is my favorite Virgin, whom I invoke in all my necessities with the utmost affection and confidence. I feel powerfully drawn to her, and go to her with all my troubles and all my wants.

"Besides this, the barracks themselves are no unknown country. Buildings, courtyard, and fountain are quite familiar to me; they recall one of the most stirring episodes of my military life, soon after our return from Albano. As I ascend the wide staircase, I fancy I hear the call to arms ring dismally in my ears. How many times has the alarm resounded within these walls! Everyone used to snatch up his bag of bread, his cartridges and his rifle, each trying to be downstairs first, while the air was full of a confused clamor of voices and clash of arms. Then we would sally forth, uncertain each time whether we should ever return, and defile proudly through the streets, carrying our heads high. The 6th was really a fine sight at that time. Several members of the nobility were in it, and it is no vanity to say it was considered the tip-top Company of the whole regiment. I used to slip out of a day to pay a visit to the Madonna; we were forbidden to leave the barracks, but I knew of a little door by which one could get into the church through the monastery; it did not matter to the Fathers, and in fact their consent was not asked.

"I had never been inside the St. Augustine barracks since that memorable time. I wanted to go alone to see my old quarters again, and was quite pleased to find my name where I had written it myself, over my bed. Further on there were my comrades' names; we used to get together in this corner to talk of an evening. All souvenirs, however slight, are welcome to me. I should like to write you a good long letter, but circumstances are against me; the African Zouave is talking of his campaigns, and how can I help listening?"

No sooner had he settled himself at St. Augustine, than sergeant and depôt had to remove elsewhere. Now and again in the course of his life he found to his cost that we must not attach ourselves too much to what is subject to change; but whatever else changes, one thing is always the same with him, and that is the joyful alacrity with which he is ever ready to express his acquiescence in the will of God.

"Oh the inconstancy of the human heart! I am already a fanatic about my new barracks; at least no one can say the place is not poetic enough. Picture to yourself a white house on the Square of the Janiculum, surrounded by gardens in terraces, which load the air with delicious perfumes. Every morning I see the sun rise behind the Sabine mountains. To crown all, one of our little gardens joins the kitchen garden of the good Jeromite monks of St. Honofrius, where poor Tasso's oak tree is to be seen. An opening has been made in the hedge, and the sergeants are free to go there as they list, to dream or meditate. I avail myself daily of this permission, the view thence is enchanting. And besides, from the garden one can go into the church almost without leaving the barracks.

"Here the duties of military service almost cease to be irksome, though they impose restrictions on one's liberty; in so beautiful a cage, hung on the side of a well-wooded mountain, the bird warbles freely, forgetful that it is a captive. The prospect is not shut out by four tall somber walls, the eye and heart alike can roam at will beyond the lofty cupolas, over the vast campaign, towards the horizon closed by distant mountains. Of an evening I kneel at the window to say my prayers. Rome looks glorious by moonlight, the softened tints add an air of majesty to the buildings. Not a sound breaks the stillness of this queen of cities; she sleeps tranquilly at the foot of the Cross, the memories of the past giving her confidence in the future. On the summit of Fort St. Angelo I see the colossal figure of St. Michael, watching over the city with his sword drawn. People say that he has now sheathed his sword, but I am, on the contrary, of opinion that he has drawn it for the defense of the Church, and is making ready for battle."

And then by way of winding up this ecstatic description of his new abode, and as a counterpoise to his youthful rhapsodies, he adds: "Pray for me, my dear parents. Too often I seem unable to look beyond this material life. It is so easy to drop the habit of offering all one's actions to Him to Whom they belong, to lose sight of the serene countenance of Pius IX. I am afraid of becoming too much of a soldier; I assure you I have good reason for fear. As for the sweet emotions of my youthful days, I have parted with them long since, poetry and imagination have been stamped out by the drudgery of the parade ground."

Certainly one would never suspect such to be the case, to judge by the gay notes of the bird who was just now proclaiming the charms of his cage. At any rate, a slight diminution of exterior fervor is of no detriment to his interior piety; the love of God seems to gain strength when shorn of sensible consolations, and the devotional practices in which it finds expression are in no wise interfered with. Thus we find the business of the depôt does not prevent Theodore from remembering and recording the anniversary of his First Communion.

"I transported myself in thought to the little chapel where I received Holy Communion for the first time. I remember it as if it were yesterday; the sleepless night passed in expectation of seeing the Child Jesus, the emotions which agitated me before Mass, the scruples of an over-sensitive conscience which induced me to go to my director in order to confess some faults which I had overlooked, and of which now I should doubtless not dream of accusing myself; then the feverish longing, the tears of unfeigned happiness after Communion, and the pleasant meeting with my friends. I thought how other parents and other children were enjoying a similar felicity, and I endeavored to revive, albeit faintly, the delight of that gladsome day, confident that your hearts would unite with me in my petitions."

Some days after, the procession of Corpus Christi in all its magnificence suggests to Theodore's mind a comparison between the grandeur of the ceremony as he then witnessed it, and as it figured in the past, amid the cherished memories of his childhood. "It is impossible to imagine anything more imposing than this procession, composed of the Religious Orders, with their generals, and the seven Basilicas represented by their canons and choirs, then the bishops, the cardinals, and lastly Pius IX. himself kneeling on the *sedia,* holding aloft the Blessed Sacrament. It was indeed a splendid ceremony, but if I had to choose, I would rather have the simple processions of our own towns and villages; the hymns, the choirs of children and young girls, the waving banners, the *reposoirs* raised by pious hands, the concourse of Christian people flocking to pay homage to their Creator, appeal more fondly to the heart. I prefer the sweet to the sublime.

"Everything is grand in Rome, as benefits the capital of Christendom. Here at the fountain-head of religion, the ceremonial of the Church has naturally somewhat more of a divine and exalting character. Pius IX. was rapt in contemplation; his lips moved slightly, and he kept his eyes steadily fixed upon the Blessed Sacrament. On that day it is not his hand that is raised to bless the people who throng around, he yields the precedence to our Lord. Behold this old man, gazing fixedly at the Sacred Host, in appearance so insignificant a thing, but in reality the source whence alone he derives all his strength; it is the Supreme Pastor, the Bishop of Bishops, the King of Catholics Who thus humbles, annihilates Himself. Where, I asked myself, could a truer, more living representation of the Divinity be found?"

Castelfidardo.

CHAPTER XIV.

1868.

Theodore resumes his studies. Military maneuvers. Hannibal's Camp. The Pope's visit. A sham fight. Mentana. Leave of absence.

THEODORE'S duties as sergeant left him plenty of leisure, so that he was able to resume his favorite literary pursuits, which, during his first months of service, he had been forced completely to put aside. Judging from what we know of his cast of mind, one would have imagined that he would give the preference to modern authors, but this was not by any means the case; he knew little of any of the writers of the day, with the exception of Louis Veuillot, whose energy and originality pleased him, and whose enthusiasm for the Papal city he fully shared.

"I have turned my mind to serious studies, and feel real hunger and thirst for Bossuet, Bourdaloue, and the great writers.I have before me the little library—small in size but great in value—which you were so good as to send me. This kind present of books is most welcome. No sooner did they arrive than I took them up and turned them over as affectionately as a miser handles his hoard. Not only does my intellect revel in anticipation of the enjoyment of so generous and sustaining a diet, but my heart also is gladdened at the prospect of what is in store for it. You know how I love to go back over the happy past, and how joyfully I catch every breath of air from my native land. In these volumes every page, every line calls to mind some bright memories of my youth, of my school-boy days.

"Everything is going on well here; the non-com missioned officers of the fourth depôt are firmer friends than ever, and cheerfulness is the order of the day, though there are still the old disagreeables incidental to the service; for instance, turning out so early in the morning, and the fatigue and drowsiness one feels. In addition to these, a regular plague has now invaded our barracks, an army of fleas; we are eaten up alive; the only consolation is that we are all in the same boat. Excuse these trivialities."

In spite of the July sun the Papal army performed its exercises with unremitting regularity. The troops moved along burning roads, made forced marches, carried on mock hostilities in order to prepare themselves for real warfare. "I cannot help thinking," Theodore writes, "of the well-known argument Papa used always to bring forward whenever we grumbled at anything: If you were in Africa or Cochin-China, you would be only too glad of it; and our stereotyped rejoinder: But we are not there. This is very much the same in principle as what they say to us now, only no retort is allowed. 'My lads,' they tell us, 'any day you may have the Garibaldians down on you, you won't be able to take your ease then. You will have to go and encounter them, to fight them, to march long distances, to sleep when and how you can; it is well to get accustomed to this sort of thing a little beforehand.'

"With the idea of inuring us to fatigue our lieutenant invents all manner of whimsical schemes. Yesterday the fancy took him to make us get up at 2 a.m. and keep us out until 10.45, when we returned to our barracks under a tropical sun. Remember, the men carry all their household goods and earthly possessions on their backs, cartridges, brushes, bread-bag, etc. It was piteous to see the state to which the unfortunate recruits were reduced. Today we have had the same thing over again; we sergeants not having to carry our kit,

Pontifical Zouave and Jesuit.

Hannibal's Camp, according to a drawing by Captain de Gouttepagnon.

use our voices instead of our shoulders, and shout all our repertory of songs one after another. Nothing helps better on a march. The *Deux Gendarmes* is one of the favorite songs. I sing it at the top of my voice, till my lungs are quite. Exhausted."

But these partial manœuvres were followed by something better; a camp was formed not far from Rome, where the soldiers could live by day and night as if they were making a campaign. The site chosen for the camp was the plain where once the Carthaginian general, Rome's conqueror, pitched his tents; in consequence of this it still bears the name of Hannibal's Camp. "It is a vast plateau," so runs Theodore's description, "the crater of an extinct volcano, about eight miles in circumference, shut in by verdant hills, and commanded by the village of Rocca di Papa. We pitched our tents, the young forest-trees were ruthlessly cut down in their prime that their branches might make poles, while the bark served for the purposes of ornamentation. The Canadians, born foresters as they are, specially distinguished themselves in the use of the hatchet, officers as well as men handling it with dexterity and vying with each other as to which should construct for himself the most elegant hut."

There the days went by, one just like another, but the monotony was not felt to be wearisome; how could life be tedious where nature was so fair, and the sunny landscape was made more gay by free intercourse with congenial companions? "How I enjoy this idyllic life," Theodore writes. "At 4.30 a.m., when the trumpets of the several' companies one after another sound the *reveille,* ordinarily so unwelcome a summons, one's heart rejoices to greet the first rays of the sun. Even the drill—would you believe it?—is invested with a poetic halo. It is grand to see our fine battalions perform their manœuvres in the plain; the bayonets of the infantry flashing in the sun, the cavalry in quick trot, the artillery thundering along with their heavy field-pieces. Our regiment is proud of deploying its twenty-nine Companies; the colonel is commander-in-chief, and Lieutenant-Colonel de Charette carries animation everywhere, as he gallops about in all directions. In the evening, when the sun has set, huge bivouac fires are lighted, and seated around them in groups, in the pale moonlight, we sing in our native tongues the national airs of our native lands. The nights are somewhat cold, I confess, and we are too closely packed to be comfortable; as I am rather restless, I am afraid sometimes in my sleep I give my unfortunate neighbors a hard kick, but they only laugh at it as a joke.

"One thing I miss here, and that is my daily Mass. I feel being deprived of it keenly. On Sundays we have a military Mass, at which all the various corps assist; this is most impressive, but it is not enough for me; I want the altar and the tabernacle. The conclusion of my letter finds me no longer sitting in the cool and shady retreat where I established myself at first. The scene has wholly changed; masses of heavy clouds have gathered over the camp; the wind is tremendously high; we are literally amongst the clouds. I have sought shelter in my tent, but a few intrusive drops have found their way through the canvas to cool me. However, hurricane and downpour matter little to me; only the dripping of the rain makes me think of the comforts enjoyed under the paternal roof. When all looks bright I am less apt to think of what I have left."

"Hannibal's Camp, August 12th.

"How can I ever tell you what a happy day we had on the 10th! By eight o'clock we were all under arms. Shortly after the cannon sounded; its thunder, rumbling in prolonged echoes amid the surrounding mountains, seemed as if it would announce to all that the Holy Father was coming. In the center of the camp an altar, draped with red cloth, had been erected, and there Pius IX. proceeded to say Mass. It was a sublime spectacle! God Himself offered up by the hands of His Supreme Pontiff, the clarionettes playing and drums beating in this open-air temple, nature arrayed in her loveliest to honor the occasion, in the distance the far-stretching Campagna, Rome, and the glittering ocean; the hoary Monte Albano too with its Olympus, looking down upon this glorious regeneration, and to complete the scene, our whole regiment with its colors and forest of shining bayonets, prostrating itself to receive a two-fold benediction! The Holy Father took a slight collation in a hut very nicely decorated, the Italian Chasseurs meanwhile singing hymns in his honor; then he gave us his blessing again, and admitted the officers to kiss his foot. A great many Roman families had come over for the occasion. Afterwards Pius IX. inspected the camp, escorted by the staff officers. Several triumphal arches, made of branches of trees, with appropriate devices, had been erected. Amongst others, there was one representing a ship, on either side of which yawned the open jaws of a shark; above was a rainbow, and an image of our Lady with the motto of the Immaculate Conception.

"This visit was quite that of a father; one would have thought Pius IX. was some venerable patriarch, walking about with his numerous family around him, oblivious for a time of his own cares and anxieties. His attention was chiefly directed to the hospital, of which the Chaplains and the Sisters of St. Vincent of Paul did the honors. Would that I had been among the sick that day! Last of all, he went on foot through the village of Rocca di Papa, an astonishing thing for such an old man, especially when one considers how steep the descent is, and how stony and slippery the roads are. In our excitement and extravagant delight, we uttered shouts fit to deafen one; the Holy Father only laughed, and put his fingers in his ears. Then again, after bidding us be silent, he spoke to some old women in a jocular manner, listened to various requests, and distributed alms. The good gendarmes endeavored in vain, both by persuasion and the use of force, to restrain us from pressing closely upon him; when the inconvenience caused by the clouds of dust our feet raised was pointed out to us, he said: 'Never mind, it does not matter.' Where else would you find such mutual love between sovereign and subject?

"Yesterday, the 20th of August, we played at soldiering just as if we had been children. These sham fights are vastly amusing; we besieged and took Albano, in the presence of a concourse of spectators who had come to enjoy the spectacle. We broke up our camp at a very early hour, and the various battalions advanced by different roads on the devoted town. To begin with, Castelgandolfo, Ariccia, and several other heights were stormed, the cannon thundering angrily above the lake. After this first victory we marched triumphantly through the streets of Castelgandolfo, and then deployed as skirmishers. The discharge of musketry was fast and furious, the noise was really infernal; happily in all the uproar no cries of wounded men were to be heard. After an obstinate resistance of half an hour, the town surrendered; or rather, at the appointed time we entered it. It were well if all victories were equally tearless and bloodless. The inhabitants proved most hospitable entertainers, having got an excellent supply of provisions in readiness for their conquerors, who set to work as vigorously with the knife and fork as they had previously done with the rifle.

"I cannot write much today, for I have the week. There are a lot of things to worry one here; unless you are very careful you get guard-room days* as easy as not, without knowing in the least what it is for. We shall leave the camp very soon, the nights are getting so dreadfully cold as to remind one of descriptions of the Russian campaign. On Wednesday we are to have another sham fight; it is poor sport to have all this fatigue without any glory!"

"Mentana, Sept. 17th.

"Here I am at Mentana now, in the midst of lovely hills covered with vines and low woods. When the time of vintage comes, I shall live amongst grapes. From my room, a charming room, I assure you, I can hear the cocks crow, and see the sun set. I look around and behold nature rejoicing; I revisit the battlefield, and there revive the memories of the past; they are not too joyous, it is true, but they do one good. Yesterday we were sitting on the spot where the famous hay-ricks stood, nothing is left of them now but the poles, otherwise all is unchanged, the ground is still stained with blood.

"Our barracks are very picturesque-looking, flanked by round towers, with a portico of somewhat imposing appearance. The church is close by, a regular village church, as simple as can be, but open all day long from morning till night; what more can one want? The life we lead is quite free and informal, I hope being thrown together so much will make us all better friends. Our officers are most obliging and willing, they are almost all Frenchmen and Canadians. Our depôt has completely established its reputation already;

---

* Compulsory confinement to the guard-room for two or three days, as a punishment for some slight offense.

all the time we were in camp everyone congratulated us on our efficiency. You need not be afraid that we shall waste our time here in pernicious idleness; our commanders take good care that we have no chance of falling into that snare by keeping us hard at work with drill and maneuvers"

But when the military exercises were all finished, our sergeant still had a considerable amount of spare time at his disposal. What was there for him to do at Mentana? One cannot be always going for long walks, and to become a frequenter of cafés was not Theodore's taste; he was, it is true, by no means a man to despise a good dinner, and was as ready as anyone else to partake of good cheer; but when once his appetite was satisfied, no amount of pressing could prevail upon him to take anything which he considered as superfluous, if only a glass of wine. His books afforded him one means at least of filling up his leisure hours. "A rage for studying has taken possession of me," he says; "it is a strong reaction from my former state of mind, when I used sometimes to ask myself what was the good of reading and study." Was it not in itself a definite benefit merely to have resisted slothfulness, and also prevented his mental powers from deteriorating under the influence of a purely material existence? Contact with good writers will moreover give increased ease and versatility to his style, already so thoroughly French, and at the same time aid in preserving him from sinking to the level of what is utterly commonplace, which is unfortunately too often the result of life in garrison. In the center of the mess room stood a large table where he put his books, and there he established himself for the purpose of study, as far as this was possible considering the hubbub his comrades made, for he felt he had no right to impose silence on them, and indeed any expostulation on the subject would have been resented as an unwarrantable encroachment on every man's liberty to do and say what he pleased.

Several of the Zouaves, at Theodore's instigation, thought they would get up a choir, and therefore on Sunday at the High Mass they gathered in the organ-gallery, and with joyful heart and voice sang Dumont's *Royale,* to the utter amazement of the parishioners and the evident satisfaction of the priest. Thus the men, who under other circumstances had performed so ably the duties of infirmarian and soldier, showed themselves equally ready, when occasion required, to assume the part of choristers.

Sometimes, for the sake of change, a false alarm was given at night, and the men turned out to go in stealthy pursuit of invisible foes, marching on indefinitely in darkness and doubt. "My men," Theodore says, are raw recruits who have not so much as heard a bullet whistle by, but they are good-hearted, willing fellows, and I find they are not devoid of intelligence. In my character of a veteran, I give them advice founded on my own experience: Do not waste your cartridges shooting sparrows; fire seldom, but when you do take careful aim. The situation becomes more and more tragic, but alas! in what a pathos it culminates! We never get the chance of seeing so much as a Garibaldian, and we have to return to our quarters just as we left them, only *plus* a great deal of fatigue, and *minus* some few of our illusions."

"Mentana, November 3rd.

"The anniversary of the battle. This morning the sun rose in all its glory over Mentana, as brilliant, doubtless, as when it shed its splendors over the field of Austerlitz. We heard Mass under arms, and at the conclusion chanted a solemn *Te Deum* on the very scene of our victory, standing in the modest little church where, a year ago, wounded men writhed in agony, and the dying drew their last breath. As we uttered the beautiful words, *Te martyrum candidatus laudat exercitus,* it was as if all who had bled and suffered there joined with us in raising a hymn of praise to the Lord of Hosts.

"Happy day, the anniversary of a triumph due to the power of God alone, for He it was Who fought for and with us. We can boast of being nothing more than instruments in His mighty hand. It is now noon, just the time when the first shots began to be heard of the firing that was so warmly responded to. I do not know how matters are going on in Rome, but I know that serious apprehensions were entertained as to how this day would pass. It is glorious weather for fighting, but I should hardly think they would wreak their vengeance in broad daylight, they will rather concoct some devilish scheme to be carried out by night. I must leave off for a time in order to make my pilgrimage. I mean to go all over the battlefield to collect my souvenirs, and then to offer a prayer where the dead lie buried in the cemetery of Monte-Rotondo. The joy of our victory must not make us forgetful of the claims of charity.

"I kept the beautiful feast of All Saints as I desired, under less exciting circumstances than last year. It is a festival which appeals strongly to the heart, on which we taste alternate joy and sorrow. The Church has plainly intimated her intention that it should be so, for in her services she places these two emotions side by side, in the morning bidding us sing Alleluia, and in the evening chant the *Miserere*. This was always one of my favorite festivals; I loved the high wind moaning in the trees like souls sighing to be released, the sermons in the afternoon, the visit to the cemetery, the bells constantly calling on us to have pity on the dead. I did not forget my little brother Francis, now my intercessor in Heaven. I remembered how he passed away just at the moment when the *Gloria* was being sung; I shall always cherish his memory."

The agreement signed by Theodore had now nearly expired, and he could, had he been so minded, have chosen for himself another path in life. But since it had long been his only ambition to devote his life to the service of the Holy See, he felt neither doubt nor anxiety as to a future which seemed already marked out for him; to fight, and if needs be die, for the cause of the Church. At that period no imminent danger, no proximate peril menaced Rome: the volcano was, it is true, always there, ready to burst out at any moment, but who could tell when the eruption would take place? Pius IX, with the calm confidence of one who trusts in God, and whose soul reflects the peace of Heaven, had fixed the 8th December, 1869, for the opening of the Ecumenical Council. A temporary pacification might therefore be reckoned on, during which the Church would have leisure to accomplish her work. This appeared to be the right moment for our sergeant to revisit his family, to bask once more in the warm glow of the domestic hearth, and refresh his heart at that pure source of generous affection. Every circumstance, too, seemed propitious to the plan, for the men of the 4th depôt having just been drafted into the different Companies, the work of the officers who had been engaged in drilling them was ended, and they had quitted Mentana to return to Rome.

Theodore asked for a three months' furlough, and while he permission was working its way downwards by the necessary process of being handed on from the Major to the Captain, from the Captain to the Commandant and so on, he was drinking in deep draughts of the hallowed air of Christian Rome, and paying final visits to each of his favorite churches, in order that the impressions he carried with him to his far-off home might be as vivid as possible. His feverish impatience and delight almost deprived him of sleep: "Scarcely a night," he says, "but what I dream of my dear home, and in my dreams anticipate the joy of being there once more. Sometimes my dreams are little short of a nightmare; then I am back again at home, but so *blasé** by two years of military service, that the meeting with those I once loved so dearly finds me utterly cold and in different. But let us leave these fancies and talk common sense; I can hardly realize that I am to see again the home of my childhood. I have never dared to think of this as probable. I am perhaps too much given to presentiments, but in truth I fully believed I should die here. May God's holy will be done! It is for us to accept gladly the pleasures He sends us; I try to prepare myself for this by prayer, I wish to regard the matter from a Christian point of view. I hope my stay will profit me, and that the good examples I shall see around me may serve to strengthen my faith."

And while our Zouave is waiting for his leave of absence to be delivered to him, his heart flies forward in advance, pouring itself out in the following letter addressed to his mother; the mother whose remembrance was as much a part of his existence as each breath he drew, and whose letters every week brought him comfort and encouragement, with an echo of the fond familiar sounds of home.

"Dearest Mother, you have always been so good in writing to me with such regularity and with so much kindness that I am sure the others will not feel jealous if I address this letter exclusively to

---

*   The feeling of indifference.

you. You have given me such constant assurances of your love that I should be afraid of appearing ungrateful were I to utter no word of affection in response. The way in which the thought of you acts as a motive, inspiring me to make many a little effort both in regard to my general conduct and also in regard to the regularity of my correspondence, would in itself be ample proof of my affection; but I know a mother's heart wants something more, she likes to hear her child say as I do now, that he loves her as much as ever. Just as I never knew how fond I really was of you until the first time I was separated from you, so now it seems as if the consciousness that I am soon to see you again intensified my affection; in the former case it was sorrow at parting that deepened my feelings, now it is the hope of reunion. Not that I have ever wavered in my attachment to you, but habitual separation, the prosy duties of one's profession, and the certain something that always stamps the soldier whether he will or no, have to some extent blunted the sensibilities of my heart. How many times have I not bitterly regretted no longer possessing the fond feeling of former days, being obliged to force myself in order to say some kind thing! This dried-up state of my feelings has often been a bitter mortification to me; it is the same with fervor, one cannot have it by merely wishing for it. One may love God with all sincerity, and yet be unable to formulate a single prayer; the soul remains silent and cold as a stone. There is but one thing to be done in these times of trial; to remain steadfast in one's conduct and constant in prayer. You see I have never left off writing to you, although frequently I did not feel the least inclination to do so; on the contrary, I hated the sight of the paper, and used to beat my brains to find something to say. All the time there was no want of affection on my part; I was like one who when he finds himself without sensible devotion at the time of Communion, continues to repeat: My God, I love Thee! You will understand me I am sure, dearest Mother, and if I have not made my meaning plain, your own heart will suggest all that I have failed to say."

CHAPTER XV.

1868, 1869.

Three months at Roubaix. A week's retreat. The Golden Jubilee of Pius IX. Depôt at Monte Rotondo. Excursions in the neighborhood. Toulon.

By far the greater part of the Zouaves, when they succeeded in obtaining leave of absence, profited by the fact that they were in Italy, and loitered on their homeward journey, after the fashion of schoolboys going back to school. And certainly the attractions to be met with on the way were of no ordinary description, considering that their route led them through such cities as Venice, Milan, and Florence! But it was otherwise with Theodore; Roubaix and Roubaix only was the goal of his journey, and in his impatience to be there the railroad itself seemed too slow a means of conveyance. He traveled without stopping until he reached his beloved home, and no sooner does he cross the threshold than we may see him, his mother's hand clasped in his, surrounded by the other members of the family, kneeling at the feet of *Our Lady of the Staircase;* Mary's blessing must be asked on the happy days to which all are looking forward with so much delight.

The Zouave brother is just the same as ever, except as regards the proportions of his outward man; he thus jocosely describes his somewhat ungainly figure: "Fancy two gigantic crutches, on which is perched a small insignificant body, with a pin's head stuck at the top. "His tastes and wishes are more simple and innocent than ever, he asks nothing more than to be constantly with his relatives, to live with them and pray with them, and thus enjoy all the sweetness of quiet family life. Sometimes he spends half the day playing with his little sisters, sitting on the ground before them, letting them dress him up in all sorts of finery, and submitting to all the childish caprices of his feminine tyrants, who assign to him alternately the parts of puppet, pupil, and plaything.

Of one thing only he stands in horror, and that is of any visit or other occasion when he may be made prominent, and a complimentary allusion or word of praise will make him blush up to his eyes. When with his eldest brother, the time they spent together in Italy is often referred to, and this leads to the discussion of many questions of literature and art, of politics and social science between the two brothers, whose minds are so singularly fitted for mutual comprehension. The Ozanam Club, founded by Willebaud three years previously, an association of young men who were desirous of improving themselves from a literary point of view, used to meet every week, and of this Theodore became an active member. The archives of the association contain more than one of his poetical effusions, through which runs a strong vein of humor.

The old-fashioned family parties, on whose remembrance our Zouave had often dwelt fondly, were still held at Tourcoing, and still presided over by the venerable M. and Mme. Motte. During the two past years Theodore had gained a good deal of knowledge of mankind, and he was now better able to appreciate his grandparents, and estimate aright the sterling virtues he saw in them, virtues hidden from the light of day, foremost amongst which was their inexhaustible charity. To do good was their sole occupation from morning to night, it was the summary of their life. Sometimes quite late of an evening, when the family had gathered round the supper-table, Mme. Motte was told that a poor woman had come to beg. Then her husband would answer testily that these people would not even let her eat her meals in peace, and she was not to go; meantime, rising from table himself he went to speak to the applicant. "She will be no loser for not seeing me," Mme. Motte would remark on such occasions, "I should probably have given her two francs, now she will get five." These good people gave away with an unquestioning liberality, an almost lavish prodigality; the poor were aware of this, and took advantage of it. Witness an old man at the hospital, a sort of infirmarian, just able to get about and help the sisters a little; having observed that M. Motte came every week, went round to all the beds, and spoke to the occupant of each, accompanying his kind words with a more substantial gift of money, the old rogue used to put down broom or physic bottles directly the visitor was descried approaching, and slipping into the first empty bed draw a nightcap over his ears and begin to cough ostentatiously. When the coin was duly pocketed and the visitor had departed, he would get up and resume his work, prepared to enact the same farce a week later.

In such a school as this, Theodore was not likely to unlearn his lessons of generous self-sacrifice. An occasion for practicing this virtue did in fact soon present itself; before the expiration of the three months, a letter arrived from the chaplain of the Zouaves, recalling him to Rome. Theodore promptly obeyed this summons, although the prospect offered him was anything but inviting or attractive.

The last days of his leave were to be employed in making a retreat, and were to be spent in seclusion and silence. Hard as had been the first parting from home, this second parting seemed still harder, and the brave young soldier, who had not shrunk from exposing himself to the dangers of cholera, and had stood unmoved amid a shower of bullets, cried like a child when the time came to bid farewell to Roubaix. On his way back he stopped at Fontainebleau, to see his brother Joseph, who twelve months before had dedicated himself to the service of God in the Order of the Redemptorists. "Happy Joseph!" exclaimed Theodore, "he has already entered upon the road to Heaven." This visit had a soothing effect upon Theodore, for self-sacrifice is contagious, and the happiness of the novice seemed to restore serenity to the troubled heart of his Zouave-brother. When the latter found himself once more in Rome, under the shadow of St. Peter's, in close proximity to Pius IX, and in company of his former friends, the pain of parting had lost all its poignancy.

The first thing he did was to go and place himself in the hands of his spiritual guide, Father de Gerlache. It is not a pleasurable thing to look stern truths in the face, and view oneself in the unflattering mirror of one's conscience; happily for Theodore he did not consult his own tastes, but listened to the dictates of reason and faith. "Let us once for all," he says, "shake ourselves thoroughly free from the miseries of the past, and walk on courageously in the path of self-denial, keeping our eyes raised to Heaven. I am going to enter upon this retreat with the trustfulness of a child, without any previous preparation, but with an instinctive horror of meditation, which in my case soon degenerates into idle dreams and fancies."

And now behold him installed in a Jesuit's cell at St. Eusebius', bringing with him nothing but a good will, but this is in itself enough to ensure him the assistance of Divine grace. Only the evening before he was laughing merrily with his friends, and now the change to four silent white-washed walls seems rather an abrupt transition. "The rule of life marked out for me," he confesses, "took me somewhat aback. Four hours of meditation daily, not to speak of reviews and preparations, spiritual reading in my room, silence in the refectory, silence at recreation, silence always and everywhere; and this to go on for eight whole days! There is one comfort, from time to time one of the Fathers comes to talk to one." As Theodore did not go thither for amusement or diversion, he kept steadily to his purpose, though his thoughts wandered to the ends of the earth, and meditation proved anything but a congenial occupation.

At the outset he began making heroic efforts to prepare for his general confession. While he was laboriously ransacking his memory, searching out every little detail of his past life, putting his mind, as it were, on the rack, to his unspeakable relief Father de Gerlache knocked at the door. Theodore received him with open arms. "He at once put a stop to all the painful efforts I was making, bidding me kneel down then and there, and begin what I had to say without more ado. I obeyed with the docility of a child, and certainly I was only too glad to get the thing over; it is a pill that one likes to swallow unquestioningly, remembering that the doctor is responsible for the prescription he gives." A clear knowledge of the past helps him to provide for the future; he discerns the weak point in his fortifications, and sees where his batteries must be placed in order to defend it. Imagination and sensibility exercise too much mastery over him; he resolves at once to put these faculties back to their place, and without an hour's delay, he forthwith consigns to the flames certain trifling objects to which he thinks he clings too fondly. One recognizes here the man of prompt and vigorous action, the enemy of feeble compromise.

When the last day of the retreat came, he wrote home in a peaceful and calm state of mind, giving a summary of his impressions. "I am not writing to ask your permission to enter the Novitiate, though this would only be the natural thing to do according to the opinion of some people, who think it impossible for anyone to spend a week in the house of any religious order without being caught in their trap. The terrible Jesuits, with their Exercises of St. Ignatius, have not managed to turn my head yet. You will be fancying that the time spent here has seemed very tedious, but no, I have simply found it a time of trial. Of this I am glad, for to be tempted while in retreat is a good sign, at any rate it shows me that the devil thought it worth his while to take some notice of me. As I have definitely made up my mind to belong wholly to God, I am prepared for a life of conflict, of daily, hourly conflict, but a conflict from which I can always come out victorious, with the help of prayer. Moreover, though I have had more meditation than I exactly relish, I am ready to acknowledge that it is a necessary, not to say indispensable, thing, and I mean to make it one of my chief means of defense.

"Half an hour hence, I shall go to Communion for the second time since I came here; then I must bid good-bye to the solitude of St. Eusebius', and return to what is now quite a new world to me. Now is the time to arm myself with courage, and adopt some measures to make my head steady, that it may not turn and twist like a weather-cock with every wind that blows. The atmosphere within these walls is fresh and pure, and one may draw one's breath freely;

outside it is otherwise. I am sure I shall regret my cell and the large gardens, where the sight of the ruins and the mountains around speak to one so eloquently of the majesty of God."

Theodore had faithfully performed his part; he had done all that was within his power, and he could therefore look with confidence for the assistance of Divine grace. Nor was this denied him; Providence continued to shelter him with its protecting care, and smooth his path before him.

From this time forward Theodore's Company was almost always detached from the main corps, and employed outside the walls of Rome; and in virtue of his rank as sergeant he found himself exempted from those toilsome and laborious duties of the service, of which so large a portion fell to his share whilst he was a private. But how gladly would he have exchanged the greater liberty he enjoyed, and he prospect of promotion to which as a non-commissioned officer he could look forward, for the old times when all he had to do was to obey, and when the privation of everything that makes this world agreeable caused him frequently to utter the ejaculation which may be termed a summary of his inner life;" All for Thee, O my God!" Henceforward too the struggle to preserve his purity will be sharper, the sacrifice required of him greater; daily effort, continual vigilance will be needed, as was the case at Albano. Others in his place would have given way to discouragement, but he has recourse to prayer, and in prayer, he finds at the same time both strength and consolation.

On the 11th of April, 1869, the anniversary of the first Mass of Pius IX, the Golden Jubilee of the Pontiff-King was celebrated in Rome and throughout the whole of Christendom. "During the past week," Theodore writes, "a chorus of affectionate rejoicing has resounded through the Roman Campagna, and has been taken up and echoed back by the mountains. There is not a single village, how poor and insignificant so ever, but has striven to take part in the universal jubilation. The affection of the people, undeterred by the pinch of poverty or the difficulties of distance, has found its way to the feet of Pius IX, displaying itself often in the most touching manner. For three successive days, as if moved by a spontaneous impulse, carts might be seen entering Rome through all the different gates, adorned with colored hangings and drawn by six horses gaily decked with ribbons; some of these contained a large cask of wine, with gilt hoops; others some specially fine goats, or an ox of the best breed, round whose throat hung a collar formed of gold coins strung together; others were loaded with sacks of flour, or other agricultural products, bearing Latin mottos appropriate to the occasion. On a great barrel of oil were inscribed the words: *Oleum effusum nomen tuum*. Each of these vehicles was escorted by a deputation from the municipalities of the place whence the offering came, and they all wended their way to the Court of the Vatican Palace, which was soon completely filled. It appears that Pius IX, astonished at all these numerous arrivals, asked the meaning of it all, and on hearing the explanation, positively sobbed with emotion, and was unable to eat anything all the rest of the day. Do you not think that there is in reality something very pleasing about this primitive mode of expressing affection by gifts in kind, that appeals to the heart on account of its simplicity and sincerity?"

But not from the vicinity of Rome alone did all the offerings proceed; foreign potentates, and the faithful of every clime and race sent presents to the Holy Father, all of which being set out in the galleries of the Vatican made so imposing a collection, that Pope Pius IX. could boast that he too had an International Exhibition! Then the spring came, with its fresh, fair tints, to supply the decorations, forming a fitting frame to all the rare and beautiful things, and rendering the brilliant festivals still brighter. Theodore fully appreciated its glories. "Would that I had in my hands a magic wand," he writes, "I should make a most excellent use of it! I should wish for my dear mother some quaint corner of this immense Villa Borghese; one or two of the lofty pine-trees I see before me, or those heavy oaks, whose thick foliage would overshadow a whole village; one of these fountains with their crystal-clear waters; five or six of the little birds whose song gladdens the listener's heart; a corner of mossy turf studded with white daisies, or a bed of violets in the midst of a thick clump of trees; and lastly, a bit of real deep blue to brighten our gray northern skies."

But Theodore was not to be left any longer to enjoy Rome and its *fêtes;* he was wanted at Monte Rotondo, to resume his duties at the depôt, "to grind away at the barrel-organ once more," as he expressed it, "and make my marionettes move day by day to the same tune, the word of command."

"Monte Rotondo, April 27th, 1869.

"I am now wearing my uniform again, and heartily glad I am of the exchange, I assure you, for my civilian's clothes seemed to be a weight dragging on my shoulders, and to make me feel as if I were untrue to my colors. Now I feel quite proud of my stripes and my sword, and even of my hair, which is clipt as close as a convict's. I was anxious—so strong are my military instincts—to keep strictly to the regulations, so I ruthlessly submitted my locks to the hairdresser's scissors, and even experienced a certain satisfaction in witnessing the accomplishment of the work of destruction. With each lock of hair that floated to the ground, a portion of my vanity fell away, and at last with something of the air of a martyr I lifted up my head, bereft of its adornments. No fear that I shall captivate any one's fancy just at present. If you could but see my head! it is a ludicrous sight, like nothing so much as a Dutch cheese."

At the depôt the sergeant found his old colleagues, his books, his accustomed walks, and the church; that was all he wanted. "I am as happy," he says, "as it is possible for an exile to be. The prospect before me is calm and serene, an idyllic life, a life elevated by prayer and study, embellished by fond memories, illumined by glorious sunshine, refreshed by mountain breezes, shaded by verdant woods. Every morning we practice as skirmishers; we step out cheerily, marching along in time to a tune that helps one over the ground; no sooner are we out of the town, than we avail ourselves of the freedom of the country. With rifle slung across our shoulders, hands in our pockets, eyes fixed on the high mountains just lit up by the first rosy rays of the sun, we trudge on, singing some merry glee. The roads are stony and our feet get sore, but the view before us sustains our spirits, and long draughts of the fresh, pure air are most exhilarating. What can I say about the moonlight nights? Such evenings as we have here cannot be described, a mellow light sheds its soft radiance over the whole landscape, whichever way we look, on the snowy peaks of the Sabine Hills, the summit of Soracte, the vast plains around Rome. To this is added the melodious song of the nightingales. You may think how pleasant it is to say one's evening prayers in such surroundings. I shall rejoice in keeping the Month of Mary in this delicious spot, it seems to throw a halo of poetry and sentiment around the worship of our Lady that is singularly attractive."

The occasion of his mother's birthday calls forth the following effusion from the pen of our Zouave:

"May 3rd, 1869.

"I am glad that your birthday falls on this day, dear mother, as I like to associate your name with that of our Blessed Lady. The love of my Mother in Heaven, and that of my mother on earth, are two kindred feelings of filial affection which meet together and mutually strengthen one another. I wish I loved the former as well as I do the latter, but I am too earthly-minded as yet for that; yet, at any rate, I do not lack confidence in her. In one thing I do envy the Italians, that is their absolute and entire trust in the Madonna. The lovely sky above me makes me think of our Lady's blue mantle, while the dazzling whiteness of the snow-capped mountains reminds me of her immaculate purity. If I were a poet I would write a hymn in her honor. I did think of doing so, on the day before the 1st of May; I was going through a little wood to the Capuchin Convent, it is my daily walk: I like to sit and read in the cool shade of the lofty trees, to meditate, or sometimes chat with one of the Fathers. On the evening in question, I fancied it would be enough to touch a chord in my heart to awaken melodious sounds, but alas! nothing came of it, no music, at least, only a confusion of sounds. However, prayer is after all the best song of praise, and the offering of a pure and chastened heart is better than the sweetest incense."

When the recruits at Monte Rotondo had finished their course of military instruction, they were drafted into the regiment, bearing the stamp of the 4th depôt, and, thanks to the excellent training they had undergone, really having the deportment of soldiers who had been a long time in the service. Their departure procured the drill-sergeants a welcome holiday, a break in the dull monotony of daily routine. What more delightful than to set out on a country excursion, not one of their usual rambles in the immediate environs, with a fowling-piece on their shoulder, for the sake of enjoying a little liberty and fresh air, but a long expedition of some days, with the seven-leagued boots on their feet.

Monte-Libretti.

Theodore started for his first excursion in the company of two conrades, and Monte-Libretti, famous forever in connection with Lieutenant Guillemin, was the first stage on the journey undertaken by the trio.

"I had never seen Monte-Libretti before, and you can understand the interest it had for me, and how carefully I went over the ground, observing every trace of the conflict, which was indeed a battle of giants. I cannot imagine how it was that a single Zouave escaped alive. It is a regular citadel commanding the road; Guillemin was obliged to climb the mountain whilst the enemy opened fire on him from every window; it would have been quite possible to crush his party by throwing stones down on them. I saw the spot where he fell, truly a martyr to the good cause; and the place where De Quelen dropped down, mortally wounded; also the house where some of our gallant fellows held out during the whole night, and the city gates, riddled with shot. There were ninety of our men, and they attacked twelve hundred Garibaldians. People have often said that it was a mad thing to do, so it was, perhaps, but at any rate it was the same holy madness that prompted the Christians in the Coliseum to throw themselves open-armed into the jaws of the wild beasts. It is an action about which one cannot argue. Our officers almost all agree in condemning it, but I think in doing so they are hardly consistent with themselves. Put any of them in a similar position, and there is not one amongst them, even the most insignificant sub-lieutenant, but would electrify his men, and make them follow him. When, after marching eight whole days in pursuit of an enemy who retreated as fast as one advanced, one suddenly comes face to face with that enemy, what so natural as to shout 'Forward!' without stopping to think about numbers. Leonidas did not trouble himself at Thermopylæ about the numerical superiority of the Persians. And besides, *Sursum corda!* When one meets with an act of such noble heroism, it seems petty to stop to pull it to pieces. God required a pure holocaust, and it matters little how that holocaust was obtained; and if for the accomplishment of His will it was necessary that a whole band of men should be cut to pieces, it is not for us to cavil. Besides, after all, the defeat of Monte-Libretti was worth more than a victory, for it showed what a handful of men can do when actuated by the highest motives; it struck terror into the Garibaldians, and taught them better than anything else could, what there is beneath our uniform. If one remembers, too that the shedding of one's blood in God's service is the best and worthiest prayer, one cannot wonder that the divine protection was so manifestly extended over us throughout the remainder of the campaign. It was, perhaps, to the defeat at Monte-Libretti that we owe the victory of Mentana."

From thence the travelers proceeded to Montorio Romano. At the entrance of the village, Theodore relates, they came upon a little white chapel. "This was a delightful surprise, for we found it was dedicated to Our Lady of la Salette. She stands there on the highest point, overlooking on one side the plain wherein Rome lies, on the other, the magnificent amphitheater formed by the mountains of Piedmont. It was a welcome sight, a real ray of sunshine to the heart of the wanderer, who, finding Mary, seems to find in her both home and friends.

"I need hardly say that we meet with the kindest reception from the inhabitants of these country places at least, we always put the best construction on the signs of curiosity shown on our approach, and the smiling faces which appear at the windows; it may possibly be that they cannot help laughing at our appearance, which, be it re marked, is certainly peculiar our faces burnt as brown as a berry, revolvers in our belts, huge sticks in our hands, dusty boots, torn gaiters, in short, everything to proclaim the tourist in undress."

After having visited Nerola and Correze, these indefatigable pedestrians were compelled to enter the neighboring territory in order to cross the Tiber, and they asked themselves, not without some amount of apprehension, whether the Piedmontese would be likely to give them a very cordial reception. However, the best way to get out of a predicament is to display plenty of impudence; and as our Zouaves were certainly not wanting in effrontery, on this occasion they got off admirably. "We invited the Custom-house officer to have a glass of something with us, just as if we were harmless National Guards, then we hired a conveyance, an official from the Customs got up behind, like the servant of some great people, and away we went. Fancy seeing Papal Zouaves in full uniform, on Piedmontese territory, escorted by a Custom-house officer! On the way we were saluted, and let me observe, in full military style. After playing the part of deserters for three quarters of an hour, we reached the ferry, crossed the Tiber, and stood once more on Pontifical soil, not a little proud of our escapade.

We are going to attempt the ascent of old Soracte, whose form rises ghost-like before us in the far distance; it is, indeed, the chief goal of our wanderings. Instead of the hoary head, crowned with snowy locks, of which Horace speaks, and the sighing forests, it can boast a thousand memories which clothe it with perpetual spring.

No less than fourteen Pontiffs, flying from persecution, have found a shelter on its mountain sides, and several monasteries have successively been built upon its crest. The Fathers of the Holy Trinity live there now. We knocked at their gate, and met with the most hospitable and cordial reception. One of the Fathers, who is very fond of the Zouaves, showed us over the place; heaps of ruins lay about on all sides. Today is Saturday, the eve of Trinity Sunday, so by a fortunate chance, we shall keep the feast with the Fathers. The village bells are ringing a merry peal."

On his return from this expedition, Theodore's rambling propensities found fresh opportunity for exercising his pedestrian powers; he was invited to join another party of excursionists. "This time we were six in number; our chaplain, Father Doussot, a Dominican; M. de la Tocquenaye, my esteemed Captain; De la Celle, our sergeant-major; my friend Carlos; Henri de Villers, a Belgian; and your humble servant made up the party. I looked into the state of my finances, and found this further call on my meager resources would completely exhaust them; yet I did not hesitate on that account, even if I should have to live on poetry and clear streams. M. de la Tocquenaye, *le Père la Toc,* as he is called, is one of the most finished officers I know. In his official capacity, he is firm almost to inflexibility, cool, and impartial; but outside the barracks, he is a changed man, all his gravity is left behind, he is full of merriment, animation, high spirits; the soldiers adore him. At the time when our men were distributed in the various Companies, he met with a perfect ovation; the cheering, and shouts of *Vive le Capitaine!* were enough to deafen him. One of the men delivered an address—full of heartfelt feeling—in Dutch; he did not understand a word of it, but no matter, it was very touching all the same!"

Another, and a very important member of the party, must not be overlooked, *Loulou,* the Captain's dog, a most intelligent animal, who, at a word from his master, would salute, and go through a number of amusing performances: and who on one occasion, as we shall see, made himself of no small service to the whole party. Always on entering a village, the first thing the friends did was to call on the head priest; a visit prompted, it must be confessed, as much by motives of policy, as by the requirements of politeness. "The appearance in which we presented our selves," says Theodore, "dusty and travel-stained, with a handkerchief tied round our heads and panting with fatigue, said as plainly as possible: we are dying of thirst, for pity's sake give us something to drink." Moreover, considerations of economy induced them whenever they could to take up their quarters in a monastery, and they repaid the hospitality of the good religious by making their cloisters re-echo with the sound of their hearty laughter. One day they as usual rang the bell of a monastery, and were shown into the parlor; the Prior received them politely, but rather coldly; now what the Zouaves wanted was to be asked to dine, and they talked on, but without attaining their object. At last, observing that they wiped their faces, the Prior inquired if he might not offer them something to drink, and rising, said he would go and order coffee to be served. Coffee, indeed! this was poor fare to set before hungry men, and as soon as the Father Prior had left the room, our friends' faces became visibly elongated. It was decided that *Loulou* should be deputed to explain the state of affairs; so on the reappearance of the Prior, the dog was told to return thanks in the name of all present. His pretty behavior, the graceful way in which he gave his paw, and begged so long and so well, had the desired effect, bringing a smile to the Prior's grave face. All at once he exclaimed: "Perhaps you have not dined, gentlemen?" Everyone gave a sigh of relief, and half an hour later our friends were seated at a well spread table, at which, if *Loulou* had not the best place, he was certainly entertained with some choice morsels.

In this way they visited Subiaco, Alatri, Anagni, Pales trina. "We paid a high price, Heaven knows, for our pleasure," Theodore writes: "in exchange we got sun strokes, skins completely tanned, weary looks, baths of perspiration. My boots, the precious pair I brought from Roubaix, have almost dropped to pieces. I thought my long legs would have been worn out; I assure you they were not spared."

On their return to Mentana, Theodore was unanimously chosen to write an account of the tour, but how was he to find time to record all the impressions of this delightful expedition, for the depôt had meanwhile been formed afresh, recruits flowed in, and our sergeant was appointed to fulfill the duties of *Vaguemestre** to the little colony.

---

*   A *Vaguemestre* is, in the French army, an adjutant or non-commissioned officer, who does for his corps, or the garrison, the office of postman from the local post-office.

CHAPTER XVI.

1869, 1870.

Theodore's new duties. Description of his room. Farewell to Monte Rotondo. The heat in Rome. At Mentana again. Silver wedding of his parents. The Vatican Council. Visit of his father and other relatives.

"Monte Rotondo, June 12th.
"Every morning I go to the post to fetch the letters, and deliver them to the different Companies. I find this is a pleasant task, I assure you, and all the more so when I recognize your writing on one of the numerous envelopes. I have, it is true, all the responsibility of the registered letters, but as these do not ordinarily present themselves in serried ranks, nothing more is required on my part than a little extra care. The best of it is that these duties give me the right to a private room, a privilege of which I am only too glad to avail myself. There just happened to be an empty apartment left in this great Piombino palace, at the very top of the tower, and I obtained permission to make it my office; it is a regular nest, round which all the winds of heaven play, and whence the eye ranges over a vast sweep of country. I have the topmost landing all to myself, there I can philosophize, weave day-dreams, write verses, smoke

a quiet cigar, enjoy the coolness of the morning air, and the gentle melancholy of the evening hours; meditate upon the Heaven to which I seem so near, and look down with calm pity on the busy, troublous world at my feet, with very little fear of interruption, for the key is in my possession; and besides, everybody does not care to tire his legs by toiling up two or three hundred steps in order to delight his eyes with the sight of a fine view."

Let us follow Theodore to his Carthusian cell, of which he is about to do the honors, setting it before us with a few strokes of his skilful pen, and a few touches of delicate feeling.

"June 22nd, 1869. *From my tower.*

"Today, after devoting the requisite time to my humble duties, I hastened to ascend the stairs leading to my tower, and when I had carefully closed the door behind me, I settled myself in my little room to read, or rather to talk, for our correspondence is really nothing but a verbal interchange of thought, the converse of hearts. It was with sincere pleasure that I listened to you, for it is just three weeks since I last heard your voice; I felt as if I were meeting again a friend whom I had not seen for some time, and my thirsty soul drank in eagerly one by one your repeated assurances of affection, of which, when deprived of them, it feels the want so keenly.

"How delicious it is to be alone, when solitude is peopled with the forms of those one loves. My room is a great delight to me, because I can so often be there alone with you, without fear of being disturbed, although it is a very hermit's cell, consisting of four perfectly bare walls, and a flooring of planks, without the slightest decoration. of any kind, unless you reckon as such two rather shaky chairs, and a table whose frightful shabbiness is only concealed by the cover I have put on it.

"I certainly could not take a *journey round my room,* like Xavier de Maistre, for I cannot boast a nice arm-chair on castors, to serve as a means of conveyance, nor any paintings on my walls to suggest wise reflections. And yet, without stirring from my place, or leaving the table which I dignify with the pretentious name of my *bureau,* I could make a journey of several days, and fill a number of pages;

my affections, that is, would travel far, borne on the wings. of memory. But instead of that, let me show you my treasures; this is a box, given me by my sisters, containing several valuables, about which I could find a great deal to say. Here are my note-books; here the letters mother wrote to father when I was in Paris, on the eve of my departure for Rome; before me are your likenesses, with those of my brothers and sisters, and my dearest friends; all of these suggest thoughts of love and gratitude, and are a record of my happiest years. Here is a collection of songs, and some of the works of Joseph de Maistre. Here again are a few lines written by my brother Joseph (I could hardly help crying as I read them again just now), in which, when he became a Redemptorist, he bequeathed to me his beloved books: the word sacrifice does not appear on this page, but doubtless it is inscribed, and in golden letters too, in the Book of Life. I fancy I can see the trace of my mother's tears on the paper; it was, I doubt not, a hard blow for her maternal heart, but the tears she shed were all offered up to God.

"Lastly we come to my crucifix, which for more than eight years has been my constant companion, the witness of all my trials, my joys, and my conflicts; it is worn with being pressed to my heart and my lips. Many a time in the strife of passions, I have held it in my hands with an almost convulsive grasp, as a drowning man clings to a plank for safety! I wore it at Albano and Mentana, and I hope I shall still be wearing it when death overtakes me. Now tell me, may I not call myself a rich man? And I have not yet enumerated a quarter of my possessions! If you could look into my heart you would find there a wealth of feeling and affection; you would hear low strains of music, the key note of which is always love. Unfortunately I cannot quite unfold it to your sight, and in my inability to do so I must content myself with opening wide my windows, and calling on you to admire the panorama before you, a panorama which I have described a hundred times, but always imperfectly. It is a clear day, you can see St. Peter's on one side, and old Soractus on the other; all the surrounding country wears a golden hue. Let the fresh wind blow on you it rushes round my tower at full speed; it makes the same sort of noise as in our belfries at home, but you need not be alarmed, the walls are very thick. How do you like this glorious sun, and all the thoughts he awakens to life, like flowers, opening bright and fair in the early hours, growing sadder and yet sweeter when the shades of evening fall. Once more I ask, have I not every reason to be more than content with my quarters?"

It is all very delightful up there, but there is a drawback, one too which cannot be escaped anywhere in Italy." How awfully hot it is, and what crowds of flies! The fidgeting is intolerable; even while I am writing to you, I have to carry on a constant and most unequal warfare against these winged tormentors, who persist with provoking pertinacity in coming to embrace me. I would most willingly dispense with their caresses, as well as with the affectionate nips of the fleas who are amusing themselves with a game of play between my gaiters and my legs. What with one and another, I am not still a single moment; my arm travels incessantly from my head to my feet, and I twist round my *képi* quite viciously; I might just as well throw both pen. and ink out of the window, for as you must allow, the state of matters is not conducive to correspondence. I hear a comrade shouting my name at the foot of the tower, it appears that it is dinner-time; the boa constrictors are going to begin their meal, I must go too. Good-bye, dear Father and Mother, my letter is a short one, and my ideas are rather incoherent; but what have I done to these wretched insects that they should tease me so persistently? Perhaps they want to make me expiate the old faults of my youthful days. So let it be! My best love to you."

Outside the walls of his tower, Theodore found ample opportunity to give practical proof of the kindness of his heart, for in spite of the marked absence of friendly feeling on the part of the inhabitants, the Zouaves had established. a Conference of St. Vincent of Paul, of which Theodore was treasurer, and thus they returned the hostility, or at least the indifference displayed towards them, with acts of that charity whose property it is to console and forgive.

In the month of August, the soldiers quartered at the depôt received orders to pack up their things and return to Rome; "to be baked alive," as Theodore says, "in the Eternal City. I have just been up the stairs of my tower for the last time; for the last time I shut myself into the dear little room, so devoid of ornament, but enriched with thoughts of you. I have left on the walls the crayon drawing of the head of Christ. Farewell now to the sweet simplicity of the country, to family life; farewell to white trousers and white waistcoats; farewell to my walking-stick, my walking-stick which I lay aside with much regret, when I think of the many rough roads I have tramped over, with this trusty friend in my hand. It must now be superseded by a saber, a highly polished saber too! and you know what a bad one I have always been at polishing. Here one may safely have a little dust on one's boots without any remarks being made, but at Rome brushes and blacking are the order of the day. Farewell, too, to the shady woods of the Capuchin Fathers, where I have more than once had a conversation with a certain Father Bonaventure, a very agreeable man. A hasty farewell to all and everything, for the waggons are already in motion, they will soon be loaded with the baggage, each man will put his *lares* and *penates* on his back, and at the sound of the bugle set off on his way."

At Rome the day was divided between the barracks and the parade ground; fresh recruits were continually arriving, and they had all to be polished and got into shape by dint of incessant drilling and patient training; a most prosy and tedious process. "In the mess-room the clamor of voices is fit to shatter any ordinary tympanum; the name we give it is *mâcher de la paille,* in other words, speaking Dutch. It is bearable when two or three are quietly talking together, but thirty or forty in one room, all shouting at the top of their voices, is more than one can stand, it is enough to put the most importunate dun to flight! As to making yourself understood, you would be lucky if you could; the only answer you receive is *Niet verstaen!** over and over again, and with strong emphasis. If anything has to be explained, it is necessary to have an interpreter always at one's side. Get the same individuals outside the barracks and inter course is equally pleasurable, only now the parts are reversed; it is our turn to shout, and oh! what a terrible trial to one's patience! After going on at it for two hours and a half, I am fairly worn out, my chest is tired, my throat hoarse, my voice gone, my feet ache

---

*   I don't understand.

with standing on the flagstones—an attractive trade is this! I am sorry about my unfortunate voice, what will become of me if I cannot sing? Certainly I have no intention of going in for a prize at the academy, but it will go hard with me to resign myself never again to utter out of the fulness of my heart a note of remembrance or of hope, of sorrow or of joy."

Happily the Church festivals came in due course to brighten the dullness of this arid way; of them Theodore was never weary. Sometimes, too, a more worldly amusement came to contribute its quota of gaiety and pleasure. "Today the Prince Borghese, imitating the munificence of the magnates of Telemachus' time, has generously thrown open his splendid villa for some games, which are also on the model of the Greek pastimes. There will be chariot races and Heaven knows what else, as amongst the ancients; and a play in old style, in an old amphitheater, under a sky which is called old, but whose unclouded serenity is more suggestive of youth and springtime. There is, however, a strange anachronism in the programme of amusements, which smacks of the bad taste of the present day—a balloon ascent. This is essentially modern, and puts to flight all illusions; there is no mistaking it, the good old times of the Greeks are gone, a single word is enough to remind us that we are in the age of enlightenment and progress. And yet it is a pretty sight to see a balloon go up under a Roman sky; how majestically it takes possession of its aërial realm, and what a glorious panorama for those who are in the car!"

Owing to the number of new arrivals, the lists at the depôt were speedily filled up, and they set out for Mentana. Theodore was not sorry for this change; the atmosphere of Rome seemed to oppress him, and in a large city there were more distractions than he cared for. On returning to the town where he was in garrison a year before, he found his past impressions still so fresh that he appeared to have lost all conception of time and space. "Am I a year older or a year younger?" he inquires of his parents; "to me it seems that in reality I am both the one and the other; older when I look back on the days that are gone, younger when I look inwards on myself. I have returned to my old self of a year ago in returning to Mentana; two days ago I established myself there again, like a man taking possession once more of hearth and home. I still find plenty to do in revisiting all to which my heart clings, a task I fully enjoy, but one which takes up much time.

"I have had little short of a battle to secure the same room we occupied last year, and in that room the same corner for myself in which my nest was then made. My nest! that is a poetical name to give it, when one thinks of the plague of insects that infest it. But I have slept sweetly many a night in that corner and dreamt delightful dreams, dreams of happy anticipation then, for it was just a few weeks before I was going home; now dreams that revive the past, but with no bitterness. Sometimes I ask myself if all the events of the past year are not a dream? No, it is no use deluding myself, I am in reality a year older than I was then, but what do the number of one's years matter, if the heart remains as young as ever?"

Theodore was right, his heart had not changed; let us listen to the simple expressions of filial affection which escape his lips:

"Dearest mother, you are my best friend, you know you are, my very best friend. Why is it that when I hesitate between the call of duty and the clamor of passions, I strive to hear your voice interpose with sweet but irresistible authority? Because it is my ambition ever to offer to your kiss a cheek to which no unworthy deed calls up a blush of shame, because I want to have the right to meet your eye without a shade of confusion, because it would make me hopelessly miserable if my conduct ever caused you to shed a single tear. This is the reason I go on struggling, fighting, suffering, even when prayer itself avails not to help me, and no resource remains but to take refuge in the thought of you."

How his heart overflows with thankfulness to God on the occasion of his parents' silver wedding! "Today your two faces stand out in the family group with special prominence, shedding all around the radiance of a peace so sweet, that it makes one think of Paradise. I see the fond mother, more proud of the children who encircle her than a queen of her jewels; the Christian mother who continually looks up to Heaven, whose every word is a word of prayer. And at her side is the master of the household, at once the father and friend of his children, ruling by love rather than by fear, enforcing his authority with a firm though gentle hand. If I attempt to analyze the various emotions of my heart, I find gratitude fills the foremost place, since out of the twenty-five years during which you have been united in this close and sacred bond, for nearly twenty-one you have led me by the hand, and as far as possible, removed the stones from my path. Sad thoughts intrude upon me when I think of the future, for I know the day must come when the hand of time will add darker hues to the bright picture before me, and contrasting in imagination our present happiness with the sorrow that sooner or lately will surely come, I pray God that I may never live to see the accomplishment of what I dread. But gloomy thoughts ill suit a day like this, which should be one of unmixed gladness: *Sursum corda!* May we not each and all of us look forward to the bright day of eternal felicity!"

At the time when earth began to lay aside her winter garments, and bask in the warm rays of the life-giving sun, the training of the recruits was being hurried as much as possible, for it was very necessary to keep a sharp look out, and be continually in readiness. The enemy was on the watch, and might perhaps consider the opening of the Council a favorable moment to show himself." On two consecutive days, "Theodore relates, "I have had to represent Garibaldi at the head of twenty men; I allowed myself to be taken because it was an understood thing that Garibaldi was never to get the better of us, but I took care first to tire out the good Zouaves by leading them a fine chase for three livelong hours on the wooded heights about Mentana. At last I fell, fighting bravely to the last, cut to pieces with all my men, in a reedy meadow."

On the 8th of December seven hundred and sixty-seven bishops met together in Rome, in answer to the summons of their Supreme Head, and the Vatican Council commenced its labors. The Zouaves were stationed in the immediate vicinity, the post of honor having been assigned to them, and right happy they were to ensure tranquility to the Church at the cost of their personal fatigue. Theodore had just been promoted to the rank of sergeant-major; his new duties recalled him to Rome, but alas! they proved so arduous and engrossing as to leave him no leisure to take part in the festivities, or even to enjoy the society of his father, who had come to Rome for the purpose of assisting at them. "A sergeant-major ought to be always with his company; he is the pivot on which all turns. To tell the truth, if I take my own measure, I cannot say much for my efficiency; without an idea of book-keeping, deficient in energy—well, well, they must do as they like with me. For my part, I feel I have exchanged a comfortable, easy post for one encumbered with many cares and responsibilities. My list of misdemeanors to be punished, hitherto immaculate, will soon be defaced with ink-blots, here begins misery and actual suffering for me."

Nothing could be more uncongenial to the new Sergeant Major than the work to which he was condemned; he, who always held figures in abhorrence, who eschewed all acquaintance with them, who would always leave it to his comrades to see if a bill was added up correctly, even when they had regaled themselves at his cost, finds himself suddenly plunged head over ears in the most common-place calculations, in accounts of money advanced and payments made; this too, just at the time of the Council, and when his father was in Rome! "I know I ought not to complain," he says, "because I can see father every morning and evening, and I am sure he is enjoying his trip. But under such circumstances, it must be owned that the additional stripe on one's sleeve seems a vexatious burden."

He was, however, able to make several excursions in his father's company. One day when they were visiting Albano, a whole family, both parents and children, rushed forward, and almost overwhelmed Theodore with expressions of gratitude and demonstrations of delight, kissing his hands over and over again. They were some of the cholera patients, whom he had tended in 1867, and who had just recognized their former infirmarian. When these worthy people found out who M. Wibaux was, he, as the father of him who had saved their lives, came in for an ample share in their effusive proofs of affection; whilst each one began to tell something in praise of the Zouave, who had to listen with outward indifference, but inward confusion, to the unlooked-for revelation of much that his humility had hitherto kept concealed.

A single fact will prove how incessant a struggle with grace was going on in his heart. His father wanted to see the house and the cell where Theodore had spent a week in prayer and self-conquest; but as they traversed the streets of Rome arm in arm, his son always led M. Wibaux in an opposite direction; and whenever the latter recurred to his wish of visiting St. Eusebius', invariably he used to mention something of interest which ought not to be left unseen, situated in a different quarter of the city, dreading doubtless to find himself brought face to face with the serious thoughts which such memories could not fail to evoke for there are moments when the soul shrinks from contact with the supernatural. Perchance he had, in the dim and hazy distance, already caught a glimpse of the cross which in later years he was to carry with joy, and nature, fearing the burden, sought to stop her ears against the call of grace.

If the days of the Sergeant-Major, with their monotonous perspective of book-keeping, and their horizon bounded by the four walls of his office, offered him but little distraction, at least he had the sense to look on the bright side of things. What was the use of regretting the past? Was it not much better to enjoy the advantages, slight as they were, which the present offered, and glean here and there such pleasures as were afforded by his daily routine?

"February 8th, 1870.

"It is nine o'clock in the evening, we are sitting by the light of a petroleum lamp, quite a grand one too, I declare; I owe this to my dear father's kindness, and I think of him whenever I light it. We are enjoying the warmth of a good fire at very little cost; we took out two or three bricks which blocked up the chimney, and as for wood, nothing could possibly be easier to get, for some repairs are being done in the barracks now, and we carry off as much of the old wood as we please, to make a regular bonfire. It is raining, and the weather out of doors is dark and gloomy; and while sitting in comfort and at ease, I cannot help thinking of the un fortunate sentries on guard on the walls of Fort St. Angelo. I have had experience of such pleasurable promenades, when a bitter wind pierced you through and through, and the rain soaked you to your very skin; when sleep hung so heavy on your eyelids that in order to keep awake you had to pinch yourself till the blood came; or else when your ears were strained to distinguish the slightest sound, and your eyes peered into the darkness to detect the slightest movement; when your finger was always on the trigger, and you held your breath, ready to fire at any moment; when you felt like a man with a sword hanging over his head, for you were conscious that a ball, coming from you knew not where, might suddenly lay you low on the stones before you had time to utter a cry. One must have known the frightful monotony of spending two and a half hours on guard, *tête-à-tête* with one's rifle, alone with the mysterious horror of the darkness, the emotions a storm produces, the constant vigilance of a sentinel in the presence of dangers real though unknown; one must, I say, have experienced all this before one can fully appreciate the luxury of a quiet evening by the fireside, in the company of one's friends. The past is now but a dream, and the present is very much like the awakening after nightmare; an awakening as delightful as the night has been miserable."

Whilst discoursing after this fashion, busying himself with his accounts and his note-books, Theodore awoke one fine morning to the consciousness that he had on his shoulders the weight of twenty-one years; and having reached that stage on the journey through life which is commonly called "coming of age," he cannot refrain from turning to look back and measure the space he has already traversed. There are some memories which the heart holds fast, and with which it communes long and fondly; memories of a happy childhood, of a First Communion; memories of hard struggles and of generous sacrifices. There are others, mournful memories of weakness and of discouragement, which when they rise up before the mind's eye are dismissed speedily; then looking inwards, the heart takes note of the ruin time has wrought, grieving to see less generous impulses than in bygone times, less ready belief in the goodness of others, a germ of skepticism which spreads quickly, and destroys the simple faith which thinks no ill. "Alas for all the poor heart loses, for the faded flowers time leaves behind! Now let us interpose reason, and above all faith, to fill the gap between advancing age and departing youth; and since we really have come to years of manhood, let us at least strive to be men of sound heart and firm will."

Presently the Carnival came, to cast a ray of gaiety on the tedium of Theodore's dull life. He felt as if he had grown four years younger, whilst indulging in the harmless practical jokes which young men allow themselves to play off on one another. The victim in the present instance was an old acquaintance, *un pays*, to use their expression, who had recently arrived to join the Zouaves. "We were so mischievous as to take him with a grand, tall hat on, to the Corso; it was taking a lamb to the slaughter. Such headgear acts as a lightning conductor, and attracts all the thunderbolts. Of course he fell readily into the snare, and for the space of three quarters of an hour, whilst we proceeded down the long street, his chimney-pot hat was slowly undergoing the process of demolition. From every story of every house the *confetti* fell like showers of hail, thick and fast. I am sure no less than three pounds must have been rained down on his devoted head, not to speak of those which came from below, for our malice went so far as to point him out to all the acquaintances whom we met disguised as clowns or boatmen. At length he was compelled to retire from this unequal contest; saving his dignity as well as he could by retreating to the heights of the Pincio, as white as a miller from head to foot, accusing us of treachery, and the Roman people of childishness."

The arrival in Rome of his uncle and godfather, M. l'Abbé Wibaux, who for eleven years had labored for the conversion of souls as a missionary in Cochin-China, was a piece of good fortune for Theodore. Harassed as he still was by the assaults of temptation, he derived much spiritual benefit from the conversation of this good man, and the spirit of faith wherewith he was animated. "How well he knows how to set one's heart to rights!" was the admiring remark of his nephew. Moreover the good missionary, like the thoughtful man that he was, had provided himself with a good supply of excellent cigars; the visits of his godson were consequently frequent, and plenty of comrades were anxious to accompany him. And if the Abbé

Acquapendente.

chanced to be out, his visitors made themselves quite at home, and got out the box of manillas; prepared to make the humblest apologies on the owner's return. But these were soon cut short: "My dear friends," the missionary would say, "I only regret that I was not here to receive you; do take some cigars, I am sure you will find them good; "an invitation which his guests complied with as willingly as if they had not already laid the box under contribution.

To crown all, about the same time Theodore had a visit from his brother Stephen, his merry-hearted brother, the friend and companion of old times, or rather of youthful days. "For the last week we have been always laughing. When we two are together we get into one of those im moderate fits of laughter which one cannot stop; it must be owned that in what we have to tell each other there is often good cause for mirth. When the two brothers were out in Rome together, Theodore would frequently suggest that they should go into a church and say a prayer for their mother. And when dinner-time approached, his kindness of heart would manifest itself in another way. "Stephen," he would say to his brother, "if you wish to give me pleasure, ask—to dine with us, the poor fellow never dines out, he has not the means." Accordingly the comrade in question was invited to sit down to table with them, a treat which he had not known perhaps for many a long day. How this thoughtful kindness must have added relish to the meal!

It must however be acknowledged that this kindness, of which we have given one example amongst many, was sometimes carried to an excess; thus one may imagine in what a sad dilemma Theodore found himself placed when he was compelled to inflict punishment. After repeated warnings to the offender, he only brought it over himself to pass sentence on him in view of averting a more severe one on the part of the lieutenant or captain. This argument always prevailed with him. His subordinates were fully aware of this weak point in the character of their superior officer, and doubtless some took unfair advantage of it; but it may safely be asserted that the greater number were won by the kindness of the good Sergeant-Major, and obeyed from a sincere wish not to vex him. At any rate the result was satisfactory, since his captain was able to say that never had his Company done him more credit than since it had been under the command of Theodore Wibaux. He was fond of his men, and they returned his affection, so that the good feeling was mutual. When they were on a march, and the heat of the sun caused the perspiration to pour down their faces, whilst what with dust and what with singing their throats were parched with thirst, Theodore would be seen with his characteristic gesture, thrusting his hand down to the bottom of the wide pocket of his trousers, saying: "Let us see if there is anything left here;" and never did he fail to produce the wherewithal to treat his men to a glass of something to drink.

We should know a great deal more of his unostentatious kindness if *Brindamour,* the dog of the Company, a pretty little creature, could speak, or commit his reminiscences to paper. About the time of which we are now speaking, the Company was detached from Rome, and ordered to Acquapendente. *Brindamour* could not keep pace with the Zouaves, though he scampered as fast as his little legs would carry him: Theodore in consequence issued his orders, and *Brindamour* performed the journey either asleep in the cook's cauldron, or curled up in the hood of one of the Zouaves. Woe to him who should hurt the little favorite! He would have found out that the pacific Sergeant-Major had a rough side to his tongue.

During this march to Acquapendente, Stephen had taken his place in the ranks by his brother's side, in order to postpone the parting as long as possible, and profit by the last opportunity for conversation. "On arriving at the great Roman aqueduct the Captain ordered a halt, and I availed myself of it to leave the ranks. A glimpse of the past and of the future seemed afforded me, and a rush of varied emotions filled my heart. We bade each other a tearful farewell; the order to march sounded, again we exchanged adieus, and I sorrowfully followed my Company, turning round at almost every step to wave my handkerchief. The sort of desert all around me corresponded well with the solitude this parting made within my heart; the old aqueduct, through whose arches the cloudless sky could be seen, and in the distance the blue belt of sea—the road to France and the way my affections always travel—beheld through the tears which filled my eyes; this scene, and prominent in it all the form of my dear Stephen growing each moment more indistinct, will ever remain indelibly impressed on my memory." It was ordained that the two brothers should walk side by side, both along the flowery path of innocent mirth and the steep road of sacrifice; of this Stephen was soon to give proof. Theodore was now of an age to serve in France, and the idea of possibly being compelled to leave the Zouaves at a critical moment caused him many a bitter pang. It was decided in family conclave that Stephen, who was not yet old enough to be drawn in the Conscription, should serve in his brother's stead in order to set him free for the time. His parents felt that they were doing this for God, and it was the same as if Stephen himself had become a Zouave. Theodore never forgot this act of kindness, which later on became as it were a fresh link to bind together the souls of the two brothers yet more firmly. *A brother who is helped by his brother is like a strong city.*

Acquapendente.

CHAPTER XVII.

1870.

Acquapendente. Inspection by the General. The Lake of Bolsena. Outbreak of the Franco-German War. Retreat upon Civita Vecchia. Preparations for the Defence of Rome. Capitulation. Reluctant departure of the Zouaves. Embarkation on board the *Orinoco*.

LIFE at Acquapendente passed very pleasantly, under the command of Captain de Kermoal; he had never any reason to regret having chosen Theodore for his serjeant, whilst Theodore could only congratulate himself on his good fortune in being under so excellent an officer. Acquapendente is a pretty-looking town," he says; "the country is picturesque, the large, majestic lake of Bolsena is not far off; every face I meet is that of a friend. We are lodged in a monastery, the cells of the Fathers join the soldiers' quarters; we can even go into the organ gallery without going out of doors. The

Dutch sing their hymns and we sing ours: I think nothing is sweeter than these meetings in the Month of Mary; nothing is better calculated to recall to the soul the thoughts and holy aspirations of her happiest days. The people are good-hearted, full of piety and of frivolity. The choir-master of the place plays dance music from the operas, and embodies in valses and polkas the reminiscences of his youth; the faithful, when the singing is over, indulge in chattering to each other, and their tears of devotion rapidly give place to a smile of amusement, if through those tears they happen to descry some unhappy lizard running about the church."

Theodore had under his orders his fellow-country. man and friend, Sergeant-Quartermaster Adolphe Florin; Corporal Amoury, whom he was to meet again as a fellow religious in the Society of Jesus; and an assistant quartermaster. If their superior officer erred on the side of leniency, it must be confessed that this was a fault which his subalterns did not find it very difficult to pardon. The Sergeant-Major and the Quartermaster occupied the same room, and would sit of an evening, smoking their pipes and talking of Roubaix, until drowsiness put an end to the conversation.

During the day-time Theodore's bureau looked like a bower of roses, lilies, and carnations, thanks to the delicate attentions of some of the inhabitants of the place. "It is quite a pleasure to write," he says, "with flowers close about one. Everything here is charming, from the time we are awoke by the song of the nightingales, until the golden rays of the departing sun contend with the silver light of the rising moon. While I am writing in comes Adolphe, who has intercepted a lay-brother carrying a can of wine; this he requisitioned, and brought to the bureau for our benefit in a most unceremonious manner. We are now all engaged in making good use of the gift which—with in voluntary generosity—the Brother has bestowed on us, and I assure you we feel no stings of conscience. Bashfulness is a word which does not exist in the soldiers' vocabulary, either French or Italian."

In order that all might not be roses and flowery delights in this Eden, there as elsewhere, alarms were given, marches made, and last of all, reviews were held and accounts settled.

"May 16th, 1870.

"Farewell today to all poetic sentiment. Instead of the peaceful breeze rustling in our woods, there is nothing more or less than a warlike wind rushing through them. This morning the Lieutenant of Gendarmerie received a despatch containing intelligence which his marshal hastened to communicate to me, breathless with agitation. A band of eighty red-shirts had sacked a little village of Tuscany; they were being pursued by the regular army and were about to swoop down on our frontiers. Tomorrow, please God, we shall have more accurate information; for the present I must say good-bye, and go to sleep like Condé on the eve of Rocroy." This was assuredly by far the best thing he could do; he had served his apprenticeship in regard to expeditions of this sort, and knew them to be more productive of fatigue than of glory; in fact on the morrow the formidable band had vanished into thin air.

The idea of war with the brigands was not attractive, but a still more gloomy prospect loomed on the horizon, for there was to be an inspection of the troops. "General de Courten is coming, and with him all the disagreeables of the military service; inspection of the men's quarters, inspection in the open air, examination of the regimental accounts, and anything else the fancy for which may come into the General's head. What a curious notion it is to persist in paying visits where you are not wanted! I call it an abuse of power to force oneself on people who would rather be left alone. Why does he not leave us to our illusions instead of recalling us to stern realities by the sight of his cocked hat?

"It must be acknowledged that the less one has to do, the less one feels inclined to do. I never felt so strong an aversion for all that is connected with accounts and military service. One is always tempted to regard the time when one is detached from the main corps as holiday-time, and to consign drill-books and ledgers to temporary oblivion, as schoolboys do their Greek and Latin books. After all, it is the same principle applied to minor matters: a great sacrifice has an attraction of an irresistible nature, whilst a small misery utterly depresses you; a difficult, arduous task appeals to one's pride, and rouses one's courage, whilst things comparatively unimportant appear unbearable, and are like flies which worry one in the course of a charming walk.

"Our office has become a bee-hive; one has forcibly to confine to their seats legs addicted to roaming, and compel eyes which love to look about them to fasten themselves on their papers. It is not easy to put one's shoulder to the wheel all of a sudden after this fashion. My Quartermaster rose up like a lion roused from sleep at an unfortunate moment, storming at everyone and everything, and even wishing that the General might sprain his foot on the way. But for all that, he got his business done admirably well, and seems quite astonished at his own prowess."

General Kanzler
Minister of Arms of Pius IX.

And how about Theodore himself, who is ten times longer over his accounts than anyone else would be, and who yet, from love of duty, persists in doing all himself, even declining the proffered assistance of his Quartermaster? He too, at length, by dint of much writing and burning the midnight oil, had all in order, ready for the General. Let us hear what he says about the coming of the great man. "M. de Courten has a pleasant face, one of those countenances one instinctively likes. He expressed his satisfaction in so unequivocal a manner, that this visit which had been such a bugbear to us, is now amongst our most agreeable recollections. He was satisfied with everything, both as regards the condition of the men and monetary matters." On his return to Rome, the General, thinking he had hardly said enough in commendation, gave the Colonel a most eulogistic report of the Company at Acquapendente. "It really was a pleasure to see the delight of our Captain; he certainly well deserved that we should make some effort to do him credit, for no father could have been more thoughtful and attentive towards us. Thus our peace is re-established on a yet firmer basis, and now let the birds sing, let the sun shine, let the breezes blow from the mountain side, all we have to do is to add our voices to the universal chorus." Need it be said that there was a jollification in the bureau in consequence of the inspection? And the one who was slowest in emptying his glass had to pay for all the rest. As may be guessed, Theodore was the one on whom the penalty fell.

He was now at liberty to resume his daily visits to the Gonfalonier of the place, an excellent man, himself somewhat of a poet, in whose company the hours sped quickly by whilst studying the beauties of Dante's masterpiece; and also to enjoy the country and make friends with the inhabitants, whose primitive manners and customs had many points of interest to the intelligent observer. Their religious ceremonies and processions in particular had something typical about them. "They are performed in a most homely manner. After each psalm a miserable musician. plays a valse; then the singers begin again, and Heavens! what singers they are! One would fancy they were sitting on a gridiron made alternately hot and cold, according as their screaming voices are required to rise or fall. If there was not so much sincere faith in this grotesque surrounding, one would be greatly tempted to laugh at the performance."

And yet, in spite of the happiness of this tranquil life, Theodore looks back on the past with regret, as every generous heart regrets the time when sacrifices were required of it. "Speaking as a Christian, I would gladly exchange my present dignity and the leisure I enjoy, for the two years of hardship I endured as a private soldier. If I were allowed to go back over my past life, and choose a place for myself, I should unhesitatingly take up my position in the thick of the battle at Mentana; exposed to bodily dangers it is true, but at peace about my soul, for I believe that purified as it was by long months of suffering, it would have had little to retard its upward flight. But Providence had other designs; I was not wanted in Heaven just then!"

Lake of Bolsena
According to a drawing by Captain Gouttepagnon.

One day the Sergeant-Major and the Quartermaster went for a walk to the lovely Lake of Bolsena, situated in a delicious spot, with its girdle of ancient masonry, its crown of fortified castles, its veil of white smoke rising from the houses and mingling with the morning mists, and the music of its bells, ringing out a joyous peal, which, repeated from mountain to mountain, seem to fill the air with a very ecstasy of gladness. Whilst his companion, stretched at full length upon the grass, was quietly enjoying his pipe, Theodore was disporting himself amid the waters of the lake. An excellent swimmer, he was soon at a distance of some nine hundred feet from the shore, when suddenly his legs. became entangled in the regulation *caleçon*[*] he was wearing; he found it impossible to free himself, and still more impossible to gain a footing, owing to the depth of the water where he then was. Although exhausted by his efforts to liberate himself, he did not lose his presence of mind, but kissing his scapular, he raised his heart in prayer to his Mother in

---

[*] Undergarments.

Heaven, and all at once found himself standing upon a rock. But for this firm resting-place, he must inevitably have perished. Throughout his subsequent life, he ascribed his deliverance to a miraculous intervention, the more so as no rocks were known to exist in that locality. Shall it be said that the Protectress who had so often succoured him in spiritual dangers, was not equally able to save him from bodily perils?

The rumors of war then afloat in France and Germany at length reached, though somewhat tardily, the peaceful little town of Acquapendente; from that time all was changed to gloom and sadness for the soldiers of the Pontifical army. Even before the news of the calamities which befel their country reached them, the hearts of the French Zouaves were stirred to their inmost depths.

"July 22nd, 1870.

"For the last few days I have lived, as you will readily understand, in continual excitement; it is said that war is probable, that it is already declared! What a thunder-clap! The two announcements followed as close upon one another as the bolt follows the lightning flash. One would fain bear one's part with generous heart and active arm in the events that are taking place. You see the position in which I am, or rather, we are, for there are a good cluster of Frenchmen here, who all hailed the news of this national war with enthusiasm."

Somewhat later he adds: "I feel certain that I should do good service fighting for my dear country. To be thus compelled to hold aloof is enough to drive any one who has a drop of French blood in his veins to despair. I scarcely know how to contain myself. But what can be done under the circumstances? One can do nothing but chafe in futile impatience; it is enough to make me wish myself dead. But I must try and be calm, and not let my excitement carry me away; I will hold my tongue, for fear lest I should say too much. You will understand, and make allowance for the exaggerated expressions which may escape me in my patriotic ardor."

The effects of the war made themselves felt immediately in Italy. "Some plot is being formed against us; there is treachery at work; it is by no means impossible that we may be sacrificed to some new alliance, and that a second Castelfidardo may be in store for us. Woe betide France if she abandons the Church in her hour of greatest need! Any moment we may receive intelligence both of the final withdrawal of the troops and of the advent of the Piedmontese. These two events will follow close upon one another; everything moves with astounding rapidity now-a days, and all happens so unexpectedly, without a note of warning. We shall be the first to be exposed to danger, victimized, and cut to pieces. The Remingtons will play the accompaniment of the first dance; a delightful entertainment for the vacation! If we have all Italy down on us, we may as well prepare at once to depart to a better world; but if we have only to do with our amateur enemies of Mentana, there is not much to be afraid of. Come along, my pets, my little lambs; we have some *confetti* to give you. Our kits are packed, and for the last hour we have been in perfect readiness to take the field, waiting like machines for the hand which is to work them, prepared to march whichever way the wind of war may blow us."

Valentano
According to a drawing by Captain Gouttepagnon.

What Theodore foresaw came to pass; the contingent of French troops, which had withdrawn to Civita Vecchia after the battle of Mentana, finally quitted Italy. Well may it be said: "Woe betide France!" She refused her help to the cause of God, and the chastising scourge was about to fall on her.

In the event of a Piedmontese invasion it would have been useless for the little band stationed at Acquapendente to attempt the defense of the place, commanded as it was by the adjacent heights. The company therefore retired to Valentano, a village perched on the summit of a rocky peak, which Sub-Lieutenant Bardo, with fifty men, had sometime previously held against twelve hundred Garibaldians. Whilst there the news of the first battles on the Rhine reached them.

"These two successive defeats of Woerth and Weissem bourg have had the effect of a blow on the face, making one's blood boil, and recalling one to a true state of things. Poor France! I had a presentiment of these reverses, though I would not believe them possible; on the one hand I had a dread of the Divine chastisements, on the other a perfect confidence in our arms. Our fate is hard! I could name more than one man who has lost both spirits and appetite in consequence of the news. Words are quite inadequate to describe our grief.

Sept. 10th, 1870.

"Confirmations of the sad truth reach us daily, but by slow degrees, by means of despatches which drive one to desperation, so curt and laconic are they, and almost devoid of details; it is like poison which one is forced to swallow in infinitesimal doses. The Emperor taken prisoner, MacMahon severely wounded, his Corps surrendered to the enemy! Undoubtedly one must lower one's flag when Providence is against one; neither valor nor mitrailleuses are of any avail. A gloomy despair has come over us, I could weep my eyes out for sorrow. We must have done something very heinous to deserve such punishment, to deserve an humiliation unparalleled in the pages of history. My God! Thy judgments are indeed terrible!

In mercy do not compel us to drain the chalice to its dregs: *Parce Domine, parce populo tuo!* This touching supplication comes back to my memory as one of my early recollections; I have not sung it or heard it sung since the time when I used to go to Benediction at the parish church with my dear mother, whose countenance then so placid and trustful, now appears to me wearing a sorrowful and anxious expression.

"No, we shall lead the Prussians a fine dance yet! Of this I am confident, and a kind of rage, an uncontrollable longing to be face to face with them possesses me. Oh, how hard it is to go on living as we are doing now, to silence feeling and listen to reason! But our day will come, it must come. God will remember our patient and painful endurance, the difficulty with which we restrain our patriotic impulses for His sake, and His alone, for no merely human motive would have the power to hold us back another hour."

At the moment when France could tell of nothing but defeat, humiliations, and capitulations, Italy had the long desired opportunity for putting her schemes in execution, and laying hands at last upon Rome.

A force consisting of sixty thousand men simultaneously invaded the Papal territory at several different points, and seeing that they were six to one, they certainly could advance without fear! The little army of the Pope was immediately recalled to Rome, as the center of action; but as it was of the utmost consequence to retain Civita Vecchia, a portion of the northern detachments were despatched in that direction. General Bixio was however equally aware of the importance of the place, and was marching upon it in his hot-headed fashion at the head of thirteen thousand Piedmontese, eager to be beforehand with the Pontifical troops and intercept their advance, making forced marches in order to accomplish his purpose. It all happened in such a short space of time that the Zouaves, whose destination was Civita Vecchia, learnt in the same breath the fact of the invasion, and also how impossible it was for them to effect their retreat along the high roads. The company of Valen tano was therefore compelled to cover double distances by day and by night through woods, over fields, and along bad roads.

"We marched on without taking any rest, and with empty stomachs. During the night it was desperately hard to keep awake; we had to grope our way along over the stones, and during the day the overwhelming heat was enough to subdue the most determined energy. I learnt for the first time what the pangs of hunger and thirst really are. To give you some idea of the danger to which we were exposed, let me tell you that only an hour after we had left Toscanella several thousands of Piedmontese entered the place. If we had wasted time in making soup we should have been overtaken. Of course we should have made a stout resistance, but one Company against several regiments can do nothing, it must be cut to pieces.

"It is only justice to M. de Kermoal to say that he effected the movement in splendid style, showing a firmness that under other circumstances might have been called cruelty, but which in this case was indispensable. Yet every one who is acquainted with his character can readily imagine the pain it must have given him to witness the suffering of others. For my part, though I can boast of great powers of endurance, and am an excellent walker, at times I felt quite disheartened, and repented ever having enlisted. Finally, after having left behind not a few stragglers, who dropped like flies, we found ourselves at Civita."

The Pontifical soldiers employed in the defense of this place consisted of a mere handful of men, for the most part recruits; in Theodore's Company alone could be found well disciplined men, inured to fatigue, ready to do and dare anything; but all without exception, whether recruits or veterans, were fully prepared to do their duty without flinching. Never," writes Theodore, "did I see such eagerness to fight, or such disregard of death. There is nothing like being obliged to depend entirely on Divine assistance, it makes one feel ten times more powerful.

"From the room in which I am writing I have a view of the sea. Four or five large Italian frigates are cruising at a short distance from the shore; one of them just passed before the port at half rifle range. Do they want us to open fire on them in order to have a legitimate pretext for self-defense? This going to and fro as if on purpose to provoke us is most contemptible: it is not generally the lamb who seeks to pick a quarrel with the wolf; and if on the one hand we are resolved to hold out while we have a cartridge left, on the other we know that it would not do for us to take the aggressive, the forces are far too unequal. Leave matters to take their own course; tomorrow, perhaps today, an hour hence perchance, the bombardment by sea and the siege by land will commence simultaneously."

In expectation of these things Theodore collects his thoughts for a moment, they turn naturally in the direction of Roubaix, and then, raising his eyes to Heaven, he writes with a steady hand the following lines, which might almost be called his last words as a Zouave: "And now, dear father and mother, dear brothers and sisters, one last word with you, whom I love more dearly than ever. If I fall, I shall die in the hope that all your merits and your prayers will in some measure counterbalance my weakness and unworthiness. Although at intervals I have been sadly lukewarm and remiss, I trust that the voluntary sacrifice of my life, offered up to God, will obtain for me a full pardon. Once more I wish to repeat that the only motive of my coming here has been the simple and pure desire to die a martyr's death, and though oftentimes through thoughtlessness I have lost sight of it, I hope that God, and the intercessors who plead for me in His presence have not forgotten it. *Pro Petri sede!*"*

During the night of the 15th of September the Zouaves were suddenly roused. "We obeyed with exultant joy, thinking the decisive moment had come at last. Instead of this, M. d'Albiousse announced to us with sobs that all was now ended. Oh, the grief of that moment! and the fury that took possession of us all! The Captain vainly entreated permission to depart with his Company; we would have cut our way through the enemy's lines, some of us would have had the good fortune to get as far as Rome, and those who fell would certainly not have been the most deserving of commiseration. But it would have been a violation of the treaty; how could we attack soldiers who relied on the terms of the capitulation? My dear Kermoal, I appeal to your honor,' was the only reply."

---

*   For the See of Peter, a phrase that was important to the Papal Zouaves. After the 1860 campaign, the Papal Soldiers who partcipated were given the Pro Petri Sede medal, which featured the cross of St. Peter.

Then scalding tears, the expression of concentrated rage, rolled silently down each bronzed cheek, while sobs burst from every heaving breast. Not a blow had been struck; what had happened therefore to cause all this emotion? Colonel Serra, the officer in command of the garrison, when summoned by Bixio to surrender the town, had in hot haste called together a council of war. He spoke first, and declared there was nothing left but to surrender. The Commandant, whose name was d'Albiousse, rose at once to protest, and demand, in the name of the Zouaves, that they should at least be permitted the honor of dying a soldier's death; but no one was found to second him. Before the sitting was dissolved, the act of surrender was signed by the nineteen Italian soldiers who composed the council, the French officer alone refusing to add his name to the list.

The Piedmontese made their entry the next day, the populace meanwhile repeatedly shouting, "Death to the foreigners!" And in order to prove that these threats were not merely intended as an expression of delight in the triumph of might over right, their hatred soon passed from words to deeds. Theodore says: "The cowardly insults, the vulgar outrages which we had to endure at the hands of five or six hundred of the dregs of the people, who were let loose on us and even paid to throw mud at us, all the annoyances and humiliations to which we were subjected, seem like a bad dream or a nightmare to look back upon." He adds no more; it is to one of his friends that we are indebted for the following incident. The lofty stature of the Sergeant-Major attracted the attention of a band of Piedmontese soldiers, who, goaded to fury by the sight of his Mentana medal, threw themselves on him, jostled him rudely, and pinned him against a wall. As he remained unmoved amid their blows, standing upright as a pillar, his arms folded over his precious medal, the Italians, incited by the example of one of their sergeants, pointed their bayonets at his breast. Fortunately an officer who happened to pass sent these infuriated miscreants about their business.

Nothing was henceforward wanting to complete the glory of the soldiers of the Pope. They had had the honor of being vilified by a godless press, but calumny had only served to gain them a higher place in the esteem of all good men, and at the same time to procure for them the best blessings from Pius IX. They had known the assassin's dagger and the bursting bomb, dark plots and mines treacherously laid to destroy them; they had on the other hand known the triumphs of Mentana, the glories of martyrdom, and the acclamations of the whole Catholic world. Now they were to know the ignominy of the Prætorium, the crown of thorns, and the scarlet cloak. As soldiers all hope was dead within them; as Christians, every fiber of their being thrilled with joy because they were counted worthy to suffer reproach for the name of Jesus.

The bombardment of Rome took place on the 20th of September, and the Italians entered the town a few hours later. This was *consummatum est** as far as the Zouaves were concerned; but before quitting the city which had become to them home and family, the center of all their hopes and the object for which they lived, they wished to receive from Pius IX. a parting blessing. No sooner was his venerable countenance, with its expression of mingled sweetness and sadness, seen at one of the windows of the Vatican, than Colonel Allet waved his sword, and shouts of "Long live Pius IX!" ascended to Heaven for the last time in the midst of a city which was from thenceforth to be cold and silent as the grave. There was a strange blending of sobs, acclamations, and salvoes of musketry; then the Holy Father's blessing, pronounced for the last time, went straight to the hearts of his children, and the Pontifical troops filed out in the presence of the Italian soldiers, carrying their heads so high, meanwhile, as to look more like victors than vanquished.

They were marched to Civita Vecchia, whence they were to depart to their various homes. And so the gallant men, who had forgotten their different nationalities in order to remember only their common title of Christians, met together once again, but only to exchange mutual farewells, since they had witnessed the utter failure of the cause which had been the mainspring of their existence. The French contingent, numbering six hundred men, embarked on board the *Orinoco,* and there, on Sunday the 27th of September, after Mass had been celebrated on deck, the flag of the regiment, marked with blood and pierced with balls, was unfurled, these

---

*   It is finished.

stains and rents constituting so many proud memorials of Mentana. It was subsequently divided, each soldier receiving a small portion of what had been the very life of the regiment. Theodore treasured up the fragment with religious care, as one treasures up the relic of a martyr, and upon the paper in which it was wrapped he wrote the following lines, composed by a Zouave:

> Le Drapeau, by the Marquis de Beauffort.
> (The Flag, by the Marquis de Beauffort.)

> Nous aimions, saint et cher drapeau,
>   Avoir tes larges déchirures,
> Et comme un vieux guerrier, tu nous semblais plus beau,
>   Plus tu nous montrais de blessures!

This translates to:

> We loved, holy and dear flag,
>   To see your wide tears,
> And like an old warrior, you seemed more beautiful to us,
>   The more wounds you showed!

Valentano.

CHAPTER XVIII.

1870.

Toulon. Tarascon and Beaucaire. Tours. Theodore's dejection. The reorganization of the Corps. Campaigning. Wearisome marches. Sufferings of the soldiers. Patay. Colonel de Charette. Retreat upon Poitiers.

"Toulon, September 28th, 1870,
"On board the *Intrepid*.

"A PRISONER still! It is now nine days since I stood on *terra firma*.[*] I was not aware that I was destined to enter the marines. This life between Heaven and earth is beginning to grow intolerable; the deck of a frigate, and nothing but the deck of a frigate whereon to walk up and down, revolving in bitterness of heart present reflections and past recollections! We are longing to employ our forces in our country's defense."

This was in fact the one aim, the one desire of all the French Zouaves. Absolved by Pius IX. from the oath which bound them to the service of the Holy See, the only thing they wanted was to offer to France the affection and devotion they had vowed to Rome; the land

---

[*] Stood on dry land.

of their adoption did not make them forget the land of their birth. But whilst putting their arms and their blood at the disposal of their country, they claimed the privilege of fighting together, under the orders of their beloved leader, M. de Charette; they were too fond of their regiment to consent to break the bonds, so tender and so strong, which had united them together around the Papal throne. The Lieutenant Colonel therefore went in the name of all the others, to offer their services to the Ministry, whose official residence was then at Tours; and whilst awaiting the result of negotiations, the Zouaves directed their steps towards Tarascon and Beaucaire.

"September 30th.

"How strange it seems to find oneself at Beaucaire, at liberty, and respected, even made a great deal of by the inhabitants, just as the defenders of the country are customarily treated by a nation which is still alive to the feeling of patriotism. The people are kind, frank, and open-hearted, not given to fawn on the powerful and oppress the weak. It appears that the pestilential breath of the revolution has not swept over this part of the country; the principles of the Republic have not penetrated here. The women and children ask us to give them medals of the Pope, entreating us at the same time to run the Prussians through with our bayonets.

"I am indifferent as to the form in which we are organized, provided only that we are not dispersed. What I care most about, is keeping up the good spirit of the battalion; for the sake of maintaining this, I would gladly tear off my stripes, and cease to be Sergeant-Major. Everybody knows we shall not show the white feather in face of the enemy, and on that account they forget our character of Papal Zouaves, and only see in us defenders of the country. The revolutionary press willingly forgives us our past delinquencies, in the hope of future services. All that happens is for the best; if one has but faith in Providence, and the consciousness of having done one's duty, one can rise superior to circumstances. I can afford to be philosophical because I am a Christian, and instead of allowing myself to be depressed, I prefer to be joyous, whatever may occur, and always to live in hope."

After a week of weary waiting, wasting their time, and in want of everything, the Zouaves received orders to rejoin their Lieutenant-Colonel at Tours. The wish of all was realized; the regiment existed as before, with its staff, its commanders, and its uniform, to which all clung with the affection one feels for anything to which some grand association is attached; their name alone was altered, they were to be called the *Volunteers of the West*. All started in the highest spirits, but on their way what heart-rending sights met their view! "Thousands of men who from morning till night are shouting that one must die for one's country, are useless, either from lack of arms, or on account of mismanagement. At Nimes and Avignon we saw depôts where a considerable number of volunteers were congregated, lounging about the streets, almost in rags, destitute of everything, utterly undrilled. In the absence of officers, discipline has become a thing of the past, and most disorderly conduct is permitted. I heard some of the inhabitants say they would rather have the Prussians, they would have less to suffer with them."

At Tours the aspect of matters was still more to be deplored, as it plainly revealed the moral wounds of the nation. "It is a queer thing for us to be always encountering Glais-Bizoin, to be present at an ovation at the railway station in honor of Gambetta, or run up against Garibaldi's carriage; he arrived last night, and indeed the presence of the hero of Caprera was all that was wanting to the revolutionary festival! What a cruel mockery for a nation. if it has not entirely lost its self-respect! Mentana ought to be remembered, and the fact not overlooked that twelve thousand of these *feroci*[*] valiantly turned and fled before three thousand Pontifical troops; three thousand mere 'pasteboard soldiers!' "

But side by side with all this grief and vexation, keen joy found a place in the hearts of the Zouaves, because their beloved regiment, which they had reason to think doomed to extinction, had now risen to a new life in France, as full of Christian energy, of youthful vigor, of self-sacrificing devotion, as in its best days. "We really had no cause to expect so favorable a result. It had long been one of my dreams that we should unite together to fight for our country, after

---

[*] Voracious people.

we had fulfilled our duty as Catholics, but the idea seemed to me rather utopian."

This band of brave men was then reduced to the number of about three hundred, but such was their reputation for valor, that from the day of their arrival at Tours, they were wanted in three directions at once. Something in the shape of a battalion was hastily formed, the command of which was given to Captain Le Gonidec de Traissan.

"The Companies, composed of all the private soldiers we had, have been dispatched this morning to Fontainebleau. Singular destination! Explain it as you can, my friends, the fact remains that they are gone, and that in two or three days they will have found out what the Prussians are made of. You see all moves very quickly, and we are not considered cowards; all those who have been sent off have a spark of the sacred fire. Wyart is one of the number; we said good-bye at the station; all who were left of my old Company have flown."

There remained a small knot of officers, sufficient to form the staff of a regiment, if, as Theodore said, all the men had not been wanting. This was the first beginning of that gallant band of volunteers, who, at Cercottes, at Brou, at Patay, at Le Mans, made some compensation to France for the humiliations she endured at Sedan and at Metz. But as we have seen, everything had still to be done; not only were the men wanting, but there was an utter lack of money and equipments. It was like a soul without a body, or rather the heart alone remained intact of what had once been the regiment of Zouaves. But this heart still beat so vigorously that it soon restored life and animation to the mutilated body. Le Mans was assigned as its center to the regiment in course of formation, and they bade farewell to Tours and Garibaldi, without a single regret.

"Le Mans, October 19th.

"We arrived here safely, after a fairly pleasant journey. He who goes straightforward on his way towards the accomplishment of a plain duty, feels within himself a fund of contentment which comes from having a conscience at peace. Nothing exciting occurred on the way, we did not see the trace of an Uhlan. We are quartered in a Jesuit house, where the virtue of hospitality is practiced to the fullest and most Christian extent. There are Fathers here from all the other houses, many of them recognize amongst us old pupils of their own, the names of Motte and Wibaux seem quite familiar to them. Some of my comrades have determined on having a regular turn out of their consciences. The appearance of our recruits is highly creditable; in case of need, they would stand to their guns like veteran soldiers."

At the College of Ste. Croix, now transformed into barracks, the life they led was almost like the happy life of a family. The former pupils of the Jesuits felt themselves quite at home in the house, and conducted themselves accordingly; and as for their comrades, it was not long before they too spoke and acted in concert with them. Many an one can still remember the kind attentions shown to him there, and tell how those who had bad colds and coughs were doctored by the Rector of the College himself, the Rev. P. du Lac, who distributed lozenges and prescribed *tisanes*.*

Finding himself at Le Mans, Theodore availed himself of the opportunity afforded him to run home for a few hours to see his parents and ask their blessing, and at the same time to revive his own courage, and renew his offering of himself. But he returned immediately to his duties as Sergeant-Major, a post more important now than ever, for large numbers of volunteers had responded to M. de Charette's call, allured by the attractive title of Pontifical Zouaves, which, though officially abolished, lived on as a matter of fact, on everybody's lips. To have to organize this body of new-comers was no sinecure. "We might fancy ourselves in a beer-garden," Theodore writes; "all have to be equipped and instructed; M. de Charette is hard at work in the midst of it all, shouting orders right and left, now scolding angrily, now making good-humored jokes. That man is worth his weight in gold."

We are enabled to follow Theodore from stage to stage of his journey through the country around the Loire, by means of the long letters, which, despite the hubbub on ail sides, he continued to send home regularly this habit of writing, adopted in the first instance

---

* A type of medical drink.

through affection, must needs have become very deeply rooted, since he kept it up under the most disadvantageous circumstances. "I must beg you to be very indulgent on account of my poor bewildered head. I am no longer at Acquapendente, enjoying my rustic comforts; here things are different; there is nothing but confusion and disturbance, a complete upset of my moral and physical being. Fancy the Sergeant Majors, a brood of idlers, accustomed to have a whole retinue about them, and let their subordinates do all their work for them, now have not even a quill-driver to help them."

The 17th of October was a day of great joy for the regiment. M. Le Gonidec returned to Le Mans, after having successfully covered the retreat of the French army near Orleans. By means of their sang-froid, their steadfastness, and their excellent discipline, this band of one hundred and seventy men had been equal to, a force ten times their strength. "We have now established our reputation," Theodore writes, "a better beginning could not have been made. M. Le Gonidec has been promoted to be Commandant, in reward of his skillful tactics."

Alas! this was no time for rejoicing; the tidings of the capitulation of Metz struck every Zouave with stupefaction. "We seem no longer to have the energy to deplore the lamentable events that are occurring; we scarcely have courage left even to hope. One would think that Almighty God took a pleasure in turning the weapon in the wound, in order that it may bleed more profusely. *Sursum corda!* Humanly speaking, there is no more room for hope, and Gambetta's proclamations are nothing but offensive bombast. Our regiment is in a fair way of being formed, but the process is slow and difficult, as it must be in the case of everything that is to be solid and permanent. Today we have got our numbers up to a thousand."

At length, after the first weary days were over, the time came to go out against the enemy, to take the field, not as heretofore beneath the fair skies of Italy, where one could sleep under the open canopy of heaven without getting any harm, but on the snow, in intensely cold weather, with defective equipments, amidst recruits who had hardly been three weeks in the service. But in the hearts of these impromptu soldiers there had arisen something which could compensate for their imperfect training, viz., the desire to do credit to the uniform they wore, sentiments of faith and piety, of true devotion to their country, which calls for gallant deeds and blood gladly shed, not for boastful rhymes and meaningless manifestoes. The old Zouaves had reason to be proud of the new conscripts, for in them they felt that their spirit lived again; if the flag of Mentana existed no longer, the standard of the Sacred Heart was to replace it; and many a stainless victim now preparing for the sacrifice, was destined to mingle his blood with the drops which fell from the Sacred Heart on the pure white of its silken folds.

Theodore formed part of the 2nd battalion, of which Le Gonidec was commander, and de Kermoal captain. The Sergeant-Major's letters, brief but numerous, present a vivid picture of the life of a soldier on active service, who receives orders to advance and then to fall back, who has to keep watch night and day, to march without breaking his fast, and who knows nothing about the great movements in which he takes part. Alas! how many of the leaders at that time knew no more about them than the men! Shut up in their offices, some few members of the legal profession, birds of ill omen, took upon themselves, with unheard-of self-assurance, the heavy responsibility of saving France. They issued bombastic proclamations and delusive despatches; they made and unmade generals with a stroke of their pen; they cast the idols of the day down from the pedestals where they had been the means of placing them, and delivered them over to public derision; all this they did with the same unconcern as one would take a cup of coffee; such were the lucubrations of their wine beclouded brains!

"Chateaudun, Nov. 11th, 1870.

"Here we are surrounded by ruins; the freshly-made wound is still bleeding; it is pitiable to see the rows of bare walls standing amidst heaps of rubbish. Nothing edible is to be had; bread has become a thing of the past. We cannot complain of our own lot, seeing the greater misery around us, but I can assure you that since the day we left Le Mans, no one has felt inclined to sing *'Ah! quelplaisir* d'être soldat!"*

"I am not as badly off as some, because I am tolerably well accustomed to marching, but you will easily imagine that I do not sleep on a bed of roses. The day before yesterday we covered a distance of some fifteen miles on foot, from Nogent-le-Rotrou to Bazoches; it poured with rain the whole time; we spent a delightful night under canvas, lying in the mud, our heads in a pool of water; yesterday from Bazoches to Chateaudun, another twenty miles, always of course with the charming little adjunct called a knapsack on our backs; mine, by the way, is pretty tightly packed, *omnia mecum fero.*** We spent the night in a church, huddled together, our rugs and cloaks all soaking wet: I really expect one of these days a crop of mushrooms will spring up on our backs. I am always wet through. When I woke this morning my limbs felt like lead; I was aghast at perceiving that my feet were not a little swollen, and my boots not a little shrunken; it was only by a tremendous effort of will that I succeeded in forcing the greater into the lesser. Now I seem to be walking on pins and needles, and if, as they say, we have to go to Chartres or to Orleans, some ten leagues any way, I dare not think of the state my poor legs will be in by the evening.

"These miseries do not depress me: when I feel the cold snow lashing my face, or when I look into the distance in the hope of descrying the end of these interminable roads, I sometimes think with a certain longing of the tranquil life at home, but mind conquers matter, and we manage somehow to be cheerful and even merry. The best thing under the circumstances is to say: Suffering, thou art but a word! However, in order to do this we must take a firmer standpoint than mere philosophy. I am dirty, unwashed, black, encrusted with mud, but that is a matter of small importance. Let me have the benefit of your blessing and your prayers. If we fall, it will be wearing the uniform of the soldiers of the Pope, and I hope this may prove a passport to Paradise. Please excuse my manner of writing. I am frozen with cold and half-stupefied with fatigue. I

---

*   Ah! what fun is it to be a soldier!
**   I carry everything with me. In addition to physical things, this phrase implies that non-visible things such as experiences, knowledge, virtues, and faith are also being carried.

often think of you; it is at times of moral or physical suffering that the heart feels irresistibly drawn towards those whom it loves. God and my country! let this be our watchword."

It is a pleasure to hear such ingenuous, such Christian language; no studied phrases, not a word of self-commiseration; hardships are borne with a laugh and a song, and hearts are kept warm in spite of frozen limbs; and an upward glance, a word of prayer to God is sure to give consolation. Alas! why had France at that time so few soldiers of this stamp?

Three days later field service is shown us under another and a different aspect. After long fasts and endless marches, means are found of recruiting the exhausted powers of the soldiers, and of laying up provisions for days of dearth.

"Ferme de la Chalendrière, Nov. 14th.

"A few words of affection from the depth of this solitude. I hope they will reach you. I wish I could invest my letter with the picturesqueness of my surroundings. About the life we are leading now there is something essentially contradictory savagery side by side with luxury, apprehension of danger alternating with a sense of security, want of everything succeeded by abundance of all good things. You might as well fancy travelers eating a dish of oysters in the depth of an American forest! We are busy cooking, the poultry are about to migrate from the farmyard to our empty stomachs, with the accompaniment of the best imaginable sauce; there is nothing like a trooper on a campaign; the smallest turn for the culinary art develops into a positive talent, and in his hands onions and potatoes become inviting delicacies. At night we lie awake shivering with cold, listening to every sound, on the watch for surprises, until warmth and hope return with the sun. I like being here far better than in garrison, and but for the great anxiety to encounter the Prussians, and the frightful cold which stings one, I should not be at all averse to spend a few days in villeggiatura (prolonged stay). We are stationed four leagues from Chateaudun, in the direction of Chartres. All the companies are placed in echelon over à large tract of country, yet not too far apart to be concentrated if need be. It is said that we are co-operating in some great movement; I only hope that this may be true, but at any rate I know nothing at all about it. The soldier ought to be a machine, and I have less than no wish to be anything more."

In this aggressive movement of the French troops the post of honor was assigned to the 2nd battalion, for on the 24th of November it was sent to dislodge the Prussians from the village of Brou. On arriving at the summit of one of the opposite heights the column was received with a volley from the Prussian artillery, which tore up the ground about fifty yards in front of them; a second volley passed over their heads; a third proved the skill of the enemy in adjusting their aim, for it was poured into the ranks of the Zouaves, cutting down a number of men, amongst them the gallant Captain de Kermoal, who was wounded by the bursting of a bomb. As long as the cannon continued to roar the Zouaves remained under cover; about an hour later they entered Brou, which the enemy had evacuated. Then they fell into marching order again, going on from farm to farm, from village to village, through woods and along highways, sustained in all their disappointments and weariness by the inward satisfaction which results from the consciousness of having performed one's duty with unquestioning obedience.

"Coulmiers, December 1st.

"We are encamped on the ground where our first tardy victory was won, four or five leagues from Orleans. This morning I had the privilege of serving Mass and of receiving Holy Communion, the thought of you was present to my mind all the time; now I am ready to face the cannon, although it will be a miserable sensation to be shot at without being able to reply; but happily though a shell may come and knock my mortal frame to pieces, it will have no power to shatter the immortal hopes of my soul."

On the morrow, the 2nd of December, the regiment added to the record of its noble deeds the words Patay and Loigny, and side by side with the names of the brave men who fell as martyrs in Italy, were inscribed those of the soldiers who died in valiant defense of the standard of the Sacred Heart. While his impressions were still fresh, Theodore wrote as follows to his family:

"At three o'clock in the afternoon M. de Sonis came to the front of the 1st battalion and addressed them thus: 'My friends, two regiments have just run away; now is the time for you to show these cowards how brave men can fight; hurrah for the Zouaves!' A loud cheer was given for the General in reply; the companies immediately deployed as skirmishers in the direction of a wood where the Prussian artillery and infantry were firmly entrenched, but the fire was too deadly, and the General gave orders to carry the position at the point of the bayonet.

"It was a grand moment when M. de Sonis, Colonel de Charette, M. de Trossures, M. de Ferron advanced on horseback at a gentle trot amid a shower of bullets, followed by the whole battalion at double quick pace. The wood was literally taken by storm; it is impossible to give you an idea of the butchery; the Zouaves hacked and hewed as if they were beating butter, not to mention the shots they distributed liberally. The wood was carried, some hundreds of prisoners were taken, a mitrailleuse had fallen into our power, and we were on the point of storming the village when the Prussians perceiving how very small our force was, brought up several reserve regiments against us. The infantry saw us engaged with the enemy. and refused to reinforce us; the artillery, on whose support we reckoned, was without ammunition; we were obliged to fall back. The havoc in the ranks was frightful, it was like a scythe mowing down corn; mitrailleuses, grapeshot, shells came from all sides. The victims were so numerous that any attempt to enumerate them would be useless; the ground seemed covered with the bodies of the fallen. Out of fourteen officers only three returned to camp that evening; that will give you some idea of our loss!

"If only this movement had been supported it would have been a splendid victory, and undoubtedly the army of the Loire would not have been as it is now, completely routed. The 2nd battalion would perhaps have been enough, but unfortunately while our comrades were gallantly giving themselves up to death, we were occupying a position which had been assigned to us as being one of special danger; all we actually did, however, was to support the artillery without so much as firing a single shot. No one need wonder at our defeat. There is not a scrap of patriotism or a grain of religion left anywhere."

The 1st battalion had been composed of three hundred men; in the evening scarcely ninety answered to their names. Still these losses might have been got over, for the gaps in the ranks, far from being a disgrace, were so many glorious wounds, and men could be found to fill them, as wounds can for the most part be healed. But where could anyone be found to replace Colonel de Charette, who had been left upon the battlefield, struck by a ball, and perhaps taken prisoner? In the person of its head the whole regiment had received a mortal wound. "We shall never have a second Charette. He was the life of the regiment, the soul that informed it. Alas! how his voice is missed, his sonorous voice, now heard in angry and impassioned tones, now merry and playful, but always enforcing respect and obedience. We liked to feel his authority over us, sometimes a little harsh perhaps, but always to be trusted; we liked to see his fearless countenance, his decided features, bearing the stamp of his energetic and loyal character. His influence was unbounded; we would have followed him through fire and water. Never did I see anything like the discouragement that prevailed when the sorrowful tidings became known: this then was to be the result of all that we had undergone! Everyone seems to feel an oppression as if the atmosphere would stifle him! There is nothing to be done but to call religion to one's aid, and throw oneself headlong into the arms of Providence. Thus it is that faith gives strength and consolation, and converts what is grievous into a source of hope and confidence."

And to fill up the measure of their misfortunes, General de Sonis, the Commander of the 17th corps, was also among the wounded. The Zouaves had been proud to march under the command of this chief, whom they knew to be a man of honor, devoted to duty, as brave a soldier as he was a good Christian, and humanly speaking, all now seemed lost. But Theodore regarded things from another point of view: "*Le régiment est mort,*" he writes, "*vive le régiment!*"

How refreshing it is in the midst of defeat and ruin, when the very air seems laden with disgrace, despondency and distress, to find our Zouave hoping against hope, his only anxiety being to press onward, always walking in God's sight!

General Baron de Charette.

After Patay a retreat was the only alternative. It was a scene of confusion which beggars description, the Zouaves being almost the only troops who preserved a semblance of order they returned to Poitiers, where the depôt was, and Heaven only knows what that march cost them! "Our young soldiers had really been quite heroic, they kept up to the last, only a few being left behind on the way, and those not until their strength was completely exhausted. We who by this time have got pretty well inured to hardships, know from our own experience in bygone years what these poor fellows must have suffered. I am worn out with fatigue, and good for nothing; the cold is intense. Keep a good heart! 'God and our country!' this was our good general's favorite saying."

As for the remainder of the army, with some few exceptions of which one is only too glad to think, it afforded a sorrowful instance of the demoralization produced by the absence of religion, added to the want of all discipline and patriotic feeling. "If you take away the motive of patriotism, once so powerful an incentive, from men who have no religion, what is left them in presence of so dismal a scene as the battlefield presents, but profound horror and shrinking from death? The great mass of the soldiers believe neither in God nor the devil. They only open their mouths to blaspheme; no one who has not lived among them can have any idea of the real state of things. Three phrases serve to characterize the marching regiments: 'For God's sake!'—'Where is my regiment?'—'We are betrayed!' It is deplorable to see bands of soldiers wandering listlessly about the country or in the barns, their backs invariably turned to the place where the guns are posted. One wonders less, on seeing this, at the very cold reception they meet with from the people. These worthless fellows always make their way first into the villages; thus they get the bulk of the army into ill-repute before it arrives, and those who do their duty suffer on account of the good-for-nothing idlers."

To crown all, it happened more than once that the Zouaves were insulted by the French soldiery, who doubtless desired to cause the cowardice they had displayed in presence of the enemy to be forgotten, by showing that they were not afraid to insult brave men. It was some consolation at least for the Volunteers of the West, to know the esteem in which they were held by the remnant of true soldiers that remained, an esteem which they may truly be said to have conquered at the point of the bayonet, since they had won it by their gallant conduct and strict observance of discipline.

"The uniform of the Pontifical Zouave has taken the place of honor in the army: the Marines protested when they were separated from our regiment, and when it was a question whether we should be sent to Poitiers, the Artillery men declared they would not march without us. This shows you what a pass things have come to, since so much honor is paid to men who have merely done their duty. We give all the honor to Him to Whom it is due, and delight to think that it brings us nearer, if only in a scarcely perceptible degree, to the object of our hopes; and that in doing what we could for the cause of our country, we have been doing yet more for the cause of Holy Church."

CHAPTER XIX.

1870, 1871.

Recollections of Rome. Close of the year 1870. Stephen Wibaux joins the Regiment. Theodore receives his brevet. Willebaud's illness. Theodore's anxiety and distress. He returns home. Last days and death of Willebaud.

AT Poitiers the Volunteers of the West received a welcome such as true Christian charity alone knows how to give. Mgr. Pie set an example of those delicate attentions and that large-hearted liberality which invests hospitality with a double charm, and the inhabitants vied with each other in striving by means of kind offices, to make the Zouaves forget the fatigues of the campaign.

"December 8th, 1870.
"Today, the feast of the Immaculate Conception, our Blessed Lady grants me the unexpected pleasure of finding myself amongst you all once more. I am alone, and fancy conjures up your dear forms around me, while the burden of a thousand memories, sorrows, and hopes weighs heavily on me. After a month of incredible hardships I am enjoying a temporary respite, almost too good to be true. Can it be that all my recent sufferings were a dream? The

forced marches, the wintry cold, the painful impressions of the battlefield, the glorious death of the 1st battalion, were all these a mere vision of the night?"

Cardinal Pie.

And when our Zouave looks back further still to the days when he fought for the cause of the Church, the remembrance of that bygone time only increases his sadness, on account of the contrast between the happiness which was then his portion and the miserable state of affairs at present. "Alas!" he writes, "all is very different now to what it was in Rome; I can no longer go to battle with the same light-hearted joy, and the thought of receiving a Prussian bullet under the auspices of the Republic is most repugnant to me, though I should have deemed it an honor to receive any number of wounds under the paternal eye of the Holy Father, and for his sake. Now the scene, the times, our way of life, all are changed: prosaic realities take the place of poetic dreams, melodious song gives way to meaningless jargon. We all have the same feeling, the same sorrow of heart: then we fought for the cause of truth, the cause of God, and death was to us a welcome deliverer; now one does not really know for what one is required to lay down one's life, to endure such hardships. At the outset the idea of defending one's country was enough to arouse enthusiasm and inspire self-sacrifice; now it has become an empty phrase degraded by being found on the lips of poltroons. One is ashamed to speak of patriotism as one's motive for fighting, since those who talk the most about this sentiment, and who are never tired of proclaiming aloud their sacred love of home and country, are the very men who are content to see their fellow-countrymen massacred while they themselves refuse to strike a single blow."

He seems to take pleasure in directing a questioning glance towards the far-off horizon of Italy, in the hope of discovering there some ground for encouragement and consolation. "I often think of Rome, and if were not engrossed by the incessant occupation of a soldier's life, I should certainly feel homesickness for it; but we shall return thither some day; of this our most experienced men entertain a deep-seated conviction. Pius IX. is far from forgetting us; the following words, which M. d'Albiousse recently communicated to us, give us no little consolation: 'Tell Charette and his heroic sons as speedily as possible that my wishes, prayers, and remembrances constantly follow them wherever they go; that as they were, and still are, present with me, I am also with them in heart and soul, ever entreating the God of all mercy to protect and save both them and their unhappy country, and to bless them as fully and as specially as I do this day, in His name and with the warmest effusion of my heart.' Thus an echo reaches us of the *Benedicat vos,* which sounds from the balcony of St. Peter's."

In this manner the fatal year 1870 came to a close amidst the heavy boom of cannon. The new year was inaugurated by the battle of Le Mans, in which the 1st battalion once more saved the honors of France, in the celebrated charge at Auvours. It is a singular thing that during the whole of the campaign of the Loire, the three battalions of the Volunteers of the West were never together in action. In vain did the chief officers of the regiment endeavor to prevent the division of their forces; each General who had the command of a *corps d'armée,* wanted to have under his orders at least one battalion of the quondam Papal Zouaves, and when he had once got possession of these brave men, he took care to keep them as the flower of his forces. Theodore briefly sketches the history of the regiment in these words:

"The 1st Battalion is in process of being formed again; we have given it the name of the *Martyr's Battalion.* The 2nd, the *Parade Battalion,* has scarcely sustained any losses, although the men who compose it are just as willing as the others to have their heads broken for the sacred cause of the Republic; but chance, or rather Providence, decreed otherwise. The 3rd, the *Marching Battalion,* is the one which has had most to suffer from hunger, cold, and fatigue, and all without the satisfaction of firing a single shot. It is also the one of which the men present the most untidy and shabby appearance, their clothes are in tatters, their rifles rusty, everything about them testifies to their having been. exposed to severe and protracted privations. They have moreover that look of stoical resignation that misfortune often gives. To their credit it must be said that during this campaign they have acquired a quality of great practical utility, the power of soon getting straight again. *In medio stat virtus!* This proverb applies to us admirably, standing as we do between those who are filling up their decimated ranks, and those who are continually on the look-out for a somewhat lengthened period of repose."

It is not for us to give a detailed account of all the vicissitudes through which the regiment passed, nor to record its woes, its joys, and its glories. Ever since the first days of 1871, M. de Charette had been amongst his beloved Zouaves again, by his presence inspiring them anew with life and hope; his promotion to the rank of General was hailed with universal delight, and the whole regiment considered itself rewarded in the person of its chief.

Shortly before they left Poitiers for Rennes, Stephen Wibaux, who since the outbreak of the war had been serving in the Dragoons, came to spend a few hours with his brother.

"It is like old times to see Stephen again! How much has happened since we were in Rome together, since we last parted! We bade each other a tearful farewell, but under the bright Italian skies the tears we shed had no bitterness, they were only the expression of affection pained by parting, but happy in the consciousness that it sustained no injury from the smart of separation. Now we have other grounds for grief, but really sufferings have become such an every-day matter that one has got in a measure blunted to them; however, one is none the less eager to catch at anything which may light up the somber landscape with a gleam of sunshine. I am divided between the great pleasure it will give me to have him again for a part of my daily life, and the dread of seeing him confront with me all the dangers of war. I can imagine no more heartrending case than that of two brothers, together exposed to the enemy's fire, if one should be struck and the other spared; it is a thing I cannot bear to thing of."

However, since at any moment they both might be called on to go into action, they preferred to fight side by side than in different regiments, thinking anything was better than to be separated. By dint of persevering applications at head-quarters, Stephen obtained leave to change his dragoon's uniform for that of the Zouaves; this involved giving up the rank of Quartermaster to which he was about to be advanced, a sacrifice he gladly made, and for which he was amply rewarded by being nominated to the post of Assistant-Quartermaster, under his elder brother. "The firm of Wibaux Brothers now manages the office of the 5th Company of the 2nd Battalion. You can imagine that all goes on very harmoniously, and not many differences arise between superiors and subalterns."

No disunion was to be dreaded in that quarter; separation was however to come, and to come speedily and ruthlessly.

"Rennes, February 4th, 1871.

"It is with much pleasure that I announce my promotion to the rank of officer; I received my brevet this morning. This undeserved distinction does not awaken in me a feeling of pride, but only of gratification at the thought that it will make you happy. It is an important thing to be put in command, and it is well to have previously learnt obedience. I pity the man who gets hold of his epaulets all at once; those who have first undergone the trial of passing through the inferior grades will find their impressions of the past stand them in good stead as a guide to their future conduct. I have exchanged my rifle for a sword, the biggest blade I think in the whole regiment has fallen to my share, and this is only right, for I am nearly, if not quite, the tallest of the officers. It remains to be seen in whose company, and for what cause, I shall draw it for the first time.

"We are now passing through a crisis of which the most clear-sighted are unable to predict the issue. One thing I know and am sure of, that my sword shall never be dishonored, that it shall always be unsheathed on behalf of right and justice, when they assume a definite shape. Where are right and justice to be found now? This is a question we cannot answer at present. My God, I can no longer see clearly, I feel that nothing is stable, that all things around me are ready to crumble away, support me with Thy help and guide me in the right way! It would indeed need a vigorous hand to obliterate the memory of all we have suffered."

Theodore's promotion did not in any way diminish the happy simplicity of his character, or that joyous lightheartedness on which the secret of good fellowship so often rests, as we see from the humorous tone of a letter written at this time to his friend Victor Crombé, who had been severely wounded at the siege of Rome." Many thanks for your kind congratulations, which I received with the dignified gratitude becoming my new rank. For the five months we have been in France, we have lived constantly in the smell of gunpowder, and still more in the smoke of incense; we are past being dazzled by or astonished at anything. We are like the Madonnas or statues of saints which are carried solemnly through the streets in Italy, and who never change their countenance or move a muscle amid discharges of artillery, and fragrant clouds of incense: *Evviva la Madonna! Evviva sant' Antonio!*

"You may be quite sure that I would far rather have your bullet wound than my gold lace and big sword. This unfortunate blade is doubtless destined ere long to rust in an out-of-the-way corner, unless one day, when I am hard up, I walk off with it to an old curiosity shop, in which case there would be a chance of seeing it flash in the hands of some captain of the Fire Brigade. Now you on the contrary will always retain your scars as an honorable decoration, a title to public esteem; they will give you the right to expect fair maidens to smile on you, old men to bless you. I can quite fancy how interesting a young man who has been wounded in the war will be, especially as he is already very charming in himself; how sympathizing papas will squeeze his hand, kind mamas overwhelm him with condolences.

"We are now at Fougères, rather a pretty sea-port, in the midst of a flat but well wooded country. The programme of our amusements is not very elaborate, the greatest diversion is the mid-day drill; our future is a blank; our past alas! only too full of recollections, all suggestive of keen regret."

The above lines, in which the merry comrade of old days indulges once more in his former view of pleasantry, contrast strongly with the general tone of the letters he wrote at this time, and which bear the stamp of acute suffering. The departure from Italy was an abiding sorrow; to this, and the yet greater sorrow of having daily to blush for his country's shame, it pleased God to add another grief, more poignant and more personal, doubtless with the design of purifying his soul in the crucible of affliction and rendering it more perfectly His own.

Theodore's eldest brother, Willebaud, the cherished confidant of his hopes, his joys, and his struggles, was suffering from a painful illness, consequent on a sprain of his right arm. Ever since September he had been unable to obtain any relief from an agonizing pain in the shoulder: one remedy after another was tried with the hope of allaying it, but in vain; the swelling continued to increase, and finding the use of natural means inefficacious, Theodore, in union with the rest of his family, earnestly entreated from Heaven that supernatural aid which alone could restore health to the much-loved sufferer. In November 1870 we find him writing: "I could make myself happy enough in spite of all these physical hardships, were it not for the anxiety about Willebaud's illness. The thought of this pursues me everywhere, and spoils everything, it is far harder to bear than bodily suffering."

The disease made such alarming progress, that the medical advisers judged amputation necessary; in this decision the patient acquiesced with the docility of a child and the courage of a Christian. The sorrowful tidings reached Theodore on the day after the battle of Brou.

"Chateau des Coudreaux, November 28th:

"Dearest Willebaud,—I have just heard from my uncle of your terrible sufferings; I have been crying my eyes out over the sad news. And I hoped so confidently too in the prayers that have been offered; I need your example, and father and mother's, to prevent my being quite cast down and disheartened. I am more grieved than I can say, but this is not the time to give way to faintheartedness; I require all the force of will that I possess, in order to keep up in these troublous days. I am grateful to you for having taught me how to suffer, and to my dear parents for teaching me how to practice resignation; no doubt on many a future occasion I shall find these lessons useful. I will say nothing of my own miseries, they are indeed insignificant compared with your trials.

"Yesterday there was a battle, we repulsed the Prussians at Brou; our battalion sustained the heaviest loss, for it was all the time within range of the enemy's shells. It was probably owing to your prayers that I got no harm. If it should be the will of Providence that I should at any time undergo, as you have done, a painful amputation, the thought of you, always present to my mind, would help me to bear it. Your example seems to call me to more faithful devotion to duty, to greater generosity, to the cultivation of those Christian sentiments which can alone impart courage such as yours. Pray for me, my dear brother, for in time of war the soldier's life is a hard one."

Willebaud's existence was now one of unbroken suffering; he sought to distract his mind by means of reading, study, and prayer; he translated Virgil, learned parts of Tacitus by heart, wrote French and Latin verses, and sent letters to encourage his absent brothers. In answer to one of these, Theodore writes from Poitiers: "I have just received a letter, dated January 1st, containing good wishes for the New Year, written by Willebaud with his left hand. These few words, dictated by affection at a time of acute bodily suffering, are very precious to me; the shaky handwriting tells a sad story of sacrifice."

Somewhat later the two Zouaves were cheered by the sight of another letter from their sick brother.

"Rennes, February 11th,
"Your letter of the 24th of January contained three pages in our dear Willebaud's handwriting, one of his writing-lessons, as he says. We were glad to see how well he is getting on, his patience does him great credit, as well as his kindness in making this effort on our behalf."

But no nursing, no remedies, no prayers were of any avail to arrest the disease or abate the agonizing pain. Willebaud, always happy with that happiness which is not of this world, accepted his sufferings as a precious means of sanctification. "If it pleases God to cure me," he said, "it will be in order that I may become a saint. The best prescription for me is patience, it saves one's purse here and lays up treasure in Heaven." Far from hardening himself against suffering, he only sought something that he could offer to God, to purchase patience and resignation; and as the self-immolation of the religious life had always had an attraction for him, he resolved to begin by taking a step that rough and thorny road, whose very asperities seemed to allure him: "It is the will of God that I should renounce all thoughts of becoming a father of a family, and should devote myself to good works; I have trifled with grace too long, I will now do so no more;" and in the presence of his confessor and of his parents, he took a vow of chastity.

One day when the Lives of the Saints were being read to him, he remarked in reference to some martyrs who had been put to death by the sword, "They were fortunate, indeed, but after all, it is within everybody's reach to do the will of God. "He used earnestly to entreat, not to be relieved from his sufferings, but to be enabled to bear them aright: "My God," he would sometimes exclaim, "give me patience, for I can bear this no more!"

In this manner the first three months of 1871 passed by. Now, ever since the 1st of March, when the preliminaries of peace between France and Germany were signed, Theodore and Stephen had been at liberty to return to their family, where their coming was eagerly anticipated; still, any day some unlooked-for complication might arise, and no one could predict what the morrow would bring forth, for France could not resign herself to give up all for lost, and was still buoyed up with the hope of speedy reprisals. Considering the unsettled state of affairs, therefore, Theodore thought it his duty to remain with the army, and Stephen set out for Roubaix without him.

"If the regiment has a mission to fulfill in the maintenance of order and the vindication of honor, I shall be at my post to represent you and the principles you profess. It would hardly do for me to leave so soon; I ought not, as an officer, to be the one to give the signal to decamp, just at a dangerous crisis, too, when M. de Charette finds it all he can do, with his authoritative manner and persuasive words, to rally right-minded men around him. Besides, I have before me too many admirable examples of self-abnegation in fathers of families and many others, whom their individual taste and even imperious duty calls elsewhere, but who stay on here from a sense of duty, and of the responsibility of their position. As far as I am personally concerned, you know quite well that I thoroughly detest the service. Stephen is to leave tomorrow. I shall be very sorry to see him go, but I must not be selfish, and I am glad to think of his being in some measure a help and a comfort to you, and perhaps, please God, the means of cheering you up a little. We began a novena to St. Joseph together, tomorrow we shall both go to Communion, and he will finish the novena with you. How grieved I am at being thus parted from you! and how grieved, too, at the humiliations of our unhappy country, at the wounds she has received and which are yet unhealed, and the dark uncertainty that hangs over the future!"

The next day he adds: "Now I am alone, quite alone. I shall no longer have the pleasure every morning of descrying the figure of my dear Quartermaster in the office. We used to exchange a familiar greeting, and then read your letters together, making common cause of our sorrow and anxiety. It is easier to bear a great trouble when there are two. Now I must confess I am thoroughly miserable; a kind of moral and physical inertia, a wretched depression of spirits has taken possession of me, and I am utterly without any occupation to distract my thoughts."

The accounts Theodore received from Roubaix became more and more alarming, causing him the greatest distress; and frequently the absence of all news increased his uneasiness, and led him to fear the worst. "I am waiting for the post with impatient anxiety; I long for tidings of Will, and yet am afraid of what those tidings will be. Please tell me about him, tell me all about him. What you say makes my heart bleed, but the cry wrung from it shapes itself into a prayer. Pray do not conceal your uneasiness from me, indeed, you could not do so; if I suspected for a moment that you kept anything from me in order to spare my feelings, I should not remain here another hour. I have a right to know the whole truth, and I cannot think that you disguise it in writing to me.

"Thank you very much, my dear brother, for thinking of me, in spite of your agonizing pain. I need all that your merits and your influence with God can obtain for me; you ought to obtain from God all that you ask, since suffering cheerfully accepted gives one a right to His favors. It seems so unfair that I who have made a campaign, and am of no earthly use, should be perfectly well, while you have a monopoly of pain. I ought not to pity you, because you do not pity yourself, and you look on your couch of suffering as a kind of step to raise you nearer Heaven. Forgive me for not having shown more courage with such an example of mortification as yours before me; your prayers will cure me of that moral malady which is called tepidity of soul I confess with shame that my spiritual life is in a poor kind of way, desiring as I do the highest good, whilst I dread the cost of the conflict; but thanks to your unconscious influence, I feel that every day finds me walking more firmly in the right way, that my resolutions take more definite shape, and will ere long be fully carried out. It is a great thing at any rate not to have fallen, and I am convinced that I owe this in a great measure to you!

"Would that I could take on myself Willebaud's pain! The dear boy did not need so much suffering to make him see things in their right light. How insignificant all the interests of this world must appear from a bed of sickness. Grant, O my God, that I may not postpone returning to Thee with my whole heart until suffering drives me to Thee!" These letters from Theodore were one of Willebaud's greatest pleasures; he set himself to re-peruse all the letters that had been received from him since his first arrival in Rome in 1866, and when thus brought again under the influence of the spirit of self devotion and piety which we have seen at work, the sick man felt himself better able to bear his sufferings bravely.

At that time there was some question of sending the Volunteers of the West to Paris, where the Commune held sway, and the regiment was prepared to do its duty in any case.

"Rennes, March 30th.

"This morning I went to Communion for the close of the retreat, as did all the men who are left of our regiment, with the General at their head. After such an act, it seems as if our forces were increased fourfold; we feel like giants, able to swallow all Montmartre at a single gulp. Our poor little regiment! always at death's door, and always returning to fresh life and more than renewed youth; it reminds me of the shrubs that are cut down in order that they may send out new and more vigorous shoots. You would hardly believe how strong the *esprit de corps* is amongst us and what wonders it works."

Theodore's return to Roubaix now appeared to him a more remote hypothesis than ever; meanwhile Willebaud daily grew weaker. Of his own accord, with the calm joy of a soul awaiting her deliverance, he asked that he might receive the last sacraments, acquainting, the doctors himself of his wish to that effect, and requesting his mother to explain all the ceremonies to him. Then Extreme Unction was administered in the presence of his relatives, whom he had invited to assist, as if on a festive occasion.

Afterwards with perfect self-possession he dictated to his mother a profession of faith, which might have been a martyr's last words, wherein he offered himself as a holocaust to God; and whenever the pain became more intense, he held this paper, to which he had confided the inmost thoughts of his heart, tightly clasped in his hand. Then he expressed a desire to see Theodore, who on the receipt of the telegram sent to summon him home, immediately left his regiment, intending however to return to it at the slightest wish of his Commander. When he arrived, the whole family was assembled in the sick-room, reciting the rosary; Theodore would not interrupt the prayers, and remained outside until they were finished.

What a meeting it was between the two brothers! The big tears ran down poor Theodore's cheeks, but Willebaud knew how to comfort him with words of kind consolation. For some time they remained alone together, Willebaud speaking seriously to his brother about his future life, and exhorting him to aim at greater generosity of spirit; Theodore left the room sobbing, and saying over and over again that Willebaud was quite a saint.

The sufferer was to linger for two more months, during which he had not an hour's respite from the excruciating agony he endured; his shoulder was enormously swollen, and literally honeycombed with open abscesses. Throughout this time Theodore nursed him, watched by him, and anticipated his wishes with the tenderness and skill of one who had been trained in the hospital at Albano: "I cannot help admiring the way you do it," Willebaud said to him one day while he was changing the bandages. And seeing that, despite all his efforts to restrain them, the hot tears would drop from the Zouave-nurse's eyes on to the wound he was dressing, a sad smile passed over the patient's face as he added: "Never mind, old fellow, don't cry." Theodore managed to keep the mastery over himself while they were saying the psalms or the rosary, but often when he had repressed his tears for a long time, he was obliged to give them free course, and going into the next room, he would rest his elbows on the writing-table his brother had been in the habit of using and bury his face in his hands. "There," he afterwards wrote, "I laid bare all the misery of my heart, sometimes complaining, sometimes thankful; sometimes overcome with a kind of disgust, ennui, and spiritual lethargy, at other times praying with a fervent faith which seemed as if it must gain its point." Every day he repeated a long prayer to our Lady he had himself composed, entreating that by means of her intercession Willebaud's life might be spared, and promising that were his request granted, he would thenceforth lead a life of self-denial and prayer, in exact conformity to the revealed will of God.

But God had better things than the earthly cure his brother prayed for in store for Willebaud, who was prepared by suffering to take a high place in Heaven. On the 31st of May, in the early morning, he breathed out his soul to God, with his profession of faith clenched fast in his dying grasp, while his mother uttered aloud the words: "Mary, I give you my child!"

"I am heart-broken with grief," Theodore writes to his friend, M. Cordonnier," and yet I am not without abundant consolation. From this time forth Willebaud will be the guardian angel of the family. I wish you could see his countenance, it is that of a martyr, it is that of a dead Christ! Instinctively one drops on one's knees to invoke him. Poor fellow, he did so much wish to celebrate the feasts of May in Heaven; this was denied him for the perfecting of his patience, but he will not be the loser for it. Today is the feast of the Sacred Heart of Mary; he always had a picture of Our Lady of the Sacred Heart on his bed. It is quite crumpled with being held in his hand. When it was sent to him, he was told that it would bring him a blessing, and I am sure it has done so. The thought of my brother's happiness is so great a consolation to me that I scarcely feel the void his death has made. But I know what keen anguish I shall feel when I can no longer gaze upon his features."

Again, a few days later, he writes: "Since his death a great many tears have been shed by us all, but they were without bitterness when shed by his beloved remains. His countenance wore an expression of such resigned sorrow, that it consoled us as much as any words could have done had he been able to speak to us. His beautiful eyes remain wide open, seeming to gaze into the infinite depths of eternity. My mother tried in vain to close them after he had drawn his last breath; and his fixed, immovable gaze appeared to contemplate things that we behold as yet by faith alone. And on his half-open lips the sublime words he so often pronounced amid his tears: 'Thy will be done,' seemed still to linger, as if they had been the last words articulated with his departing breath. For two whole days we could not tear ourselves away from the couch on which he was laid; my mother and sisters prayed by it continually.

"It was heartrending when the coffin was brought. We were all overwhelmed with grief, as if the real separation had only come then. My father took the white hand in his—the hand which, as if to show his lamblike docility, remained flexible to the last—and raised it to his lips, saying: 'Farewell, dearest son, we thank you for all the good you have done us, the example you have set before us; pray for us that we may be re-united to you one day. *Au revoir!*' Stephen and I stayed behind to prepare him for burial; I felt that I owed him this last service, whatever it cost me to perform it, for it would have seemed almost a profanation had I allowed any but loving hands to touch the remains of one so dear to me. So I lifted him up once more in my arms, as I had done so often during his illness, and gently laid him in the coffin. At other times when he had to be moved, which always occasioned him acute pain, the principal part of the suffering and the resignation was on his side, now all suffering was over for him, but I had to endure a martyrdom. When he was wrapped in his shroud, leaving only his sweet and saintly countenance exposed to view, my hand again sought his, and I commended my spiritual needs to him for the last time. Then I left the undertakers to do their sad work, and on the morrow the last sorrowful journey was made from the paternal roof to the church, and from the church to the cemetery. A whole lifetime is summed up in this brief journey. Our sweet May-blossom! It is as if our Lady had taken pleasure in tending it with her own hands until the last day of her month in order that its beauty might be more perfectly developed, and when she found the flower fully expanded, she gathered it herself and carried it to Heaven."

CHAPTER XX.

1871.

Return to Rennes. Garrison life. The Zouaves are disbanded. Theodore's hesitation as to his future course. Death of M. Pierre Motte. Theodore starts for Amiens.

It may seem surprising to find Theodore setting out again for Rennes in order to rejoin what was left of his regiment, since one would have thought that pacifications having been made in France, his relatives might have been spared the pain of another parting, at a time, too, when his presence with them would have been a consolation and a help. And yet neither the Zouave nor his parents hesitated for a moment; Theodore had been given to God, and they would not reassert their claim to him. His place was with his regiment, and to that he would return, desirous to follow out the leading of Providence to the end.

"In this determination," he says, "I am not influenced by motives of ambition, and certainly not by the desire of tasting the delights of *farniente*. When the day comes for me permanently to resume my place in the family circle, I shall recoup myself amply, with compound interest. I mean to do my utmost to be useful, to make up for all the years in which I have not been able to take my share of work and care, until it pleases God to manifest His will to me in an unmistakable manner, and point out plainly the path in which I must walk in order to reach Heaven."

The thought of Willebaud, ever fondly present to his mind, was formulated in songs of thanksgiving, filling his heart and flowing from his pen. And yet he had hoped so confidently for his brother's recovery, he had prayed for it so earnestly, that to one whose faith was less strong this remembrance might have given rise to thoughts of melancholy and discouragement. "Yes," he writes, "I fully believed that a miracle would be wrought, and said to myself, Here is an excellent opportunity of showing how powerful is the prayer of faith, of opening the eyes of unbelievers, of strengthening those who are in the right way. Do not imagine that I am disappointed, far from it; the long martyrdom and holy and beautiful death I have just witnessed bear undeniable evidence of the work of Divine grace, and to the eye of the Christian the guidance of Providence is apparent in everything. It was not that God turned a deaf ear to our entreaties, or thought scorn of our simple faith and of our confidence, unwarranted indeed by human probabilities, it was that He answered our prayers in accordance with His own designs. We can trace His hand on that bed of pain, now strewn with roses; we can perceive the celestial fragrance grace sheds around. We can see more clearly than before, even through our tears; our brother's death does more to strengthen our faith than a miraculous cure would have done; we can truly say, 'the finger of God is there,' and our prayers have been heard.

"Do not forget to scatter some roses on his bed, and take some flowers to the cemetery. Think of me when you stand beside his last resting-place; I may be mistaken, but it seems to me that prayers offered by the grave of our loved ones have more chance of being granted, that is why I made a sort of pilgrimage of this visit to the cemetery. Pray for me, that I may not continue to live in neglect of grace, and that I may not always be so unworthy to call myself Willebaud's brother."

At Rennes the Volunteers of the West continued in the monotonous groove of garrison life, in which manœuvres, drill, and the usual military service of the town formed the sole diversions. Behind all there loomed the miserable uncertainty respecting the future, casting an additional gloom over an existence which was already by no means bright. Would it ever be granted them to return to Rome? And whilst awaiting the issue of events, would it not be better to disband the legion, rather than waste their best days in barracks? But before deciding upon so extreme a measure, it was at any rate their duty to make quite sure that there was nothing to be done at present.

"From another point of view, it may be said that a soldier's affection for his regiment is no ordinary affection; those who leave it for a time come back to it they know not why; it is a thing about which one cannot reason. It is the family feeling, the colors, Rome, a crowd of associations and fond affections which possess for us an attraction impossible to resist.

"I vegetate, we vegetate, they vegetate. Our case is much the same as that of a man waiting in an antechamber for an audience; he may be called in at any moment, and therefore does not care to engage in any serious occupation; not unfrequently the time of waiting seems terribly long, as I know by experience. Do you know the wretchedness of groping along in doubt as to your way, the tedious ness of walking on without aim or purpose, with no other guiding star than an undefined or ill-defined sense of present duty? And even this motive loses its power over one in the long run. As far as I go, I am far from being one of those magnanimous Christians who are proof against everything. I may have been one in the days of my early fervor, when I desired suffering quite as much as joy for my portion, and abandoned myself to Providence with the blind reliance of a child. That time is over and gone, and I regret it with all my heart. Perhaps though, I might in some measure return to it, through Willebaud's prayers, and a good deal of personal sacrifice on my own part. Just now my faith is at a sadly low ebb, almost every one has grown faint-hearted, and I am like the rest. I begin to despair about everything; the future of the regiment, the restoration of France to her true greatness, the re-establishment of the Papacy.

We meet on every hand with insults, revilings, jealousy; the worst papers already no longer keep any bounds. Here calumny is in the habit of dipping her poisoned arrows into the ink horn of a certain petty journalist, an unfrocked religious; there is not a single disreputable story of which we are not made the heroes, our persecutors always posing as the victims, and representing us as the tyrants. But enough of this; it ill befits those who profess to be the servants of Christ's Vicegerent, or rather the servants of Jesus Christ Himself, to complain of humiliation and of suffering."

It was only natural that the Volunteers of the West should have to put up with ill-treatment of various kinds from the Communist party at Rennes; the mere fact that the Zouave uniform spoke of devotion and served to maintain order in the city, sufficed to stir up a feeling of jealousy and hatred towards those who wore it. Happily for Theodore, prayer, correspondence with his family, and the ever present image of Willebaud, served to mitigate the sadness wherewith his heart was filled.

"Sunday, July 9th, 1871.

"I no longer care to write at any length on Sunday; I used to delight to do so in my peaceful solitude, in the happy days that are no more, indeed Sunday was my favorite day for writing to Willebaud, because I then had more leisure for self-scrutiny, and was consequently better able to paint a faithful portrait for him of my inner being, with its various tendencies. Those times are past; and he is no more who so thoroughly understood me because he had passed through the same experiences. But it is now no longer necessary for me to draw a sketch of all the misery that I endure—a sketch moreover which could not but fall far short of the reality—for he knows me better than I can know myself; he sees the depth of my weakness and blushes for me; yet, on the other hand, his sympathy is more availing, since the source whence it draws its healing power is the infinite mercy of God. My brother and friend, do thou ever watch over my spiritual welfare!"

But it became necessary to make some definite arrangement, and with a view to this, the Minister of War about this time proposed to

General de Charette that the Volunteers of the West should be constituted a regular regiment, and incorporated into the French army. It was the reward offered them for a past full of heroic courage and military glory, the memory of which was to be handed down by perpetuating the race of Zouaves. Charette called his officers together in order to communicate the proposal of the Minister to them." His voice trembled with emotion, for it is not easy for a man to give up, even temporarily, what has always been his cherished dream, the one aim and purpose of his life; nor, when men have been associated together for eleven years, when they have together confronted dangers, won laurels, borne humiliations and trials, finding their mutual friendship a help and a support, is it possible to sever the bonds that unite them without tearing asunder their very heart-strings, even though the separation be only for a time. But his manly countenance—slightly contracted, perhaps, by the struggle between devotion to duty and natural grief—expressed no desire except that of acting in strict accordance with the laws of honor.

"In accents which went to one's heart, so intense was the conviction which breathed in every word, he said: 'Gentlemen, I felt I had not the right to make over our uniform to the French army; this uniform is the property of the whole Catholic world, whose belief we represent; it is the livery of Rome, it is not ours to be disposed of at will, and linked to the fortunes of an unstable government.' His reply to the Minister was extremely dignified. He thanked him for the honor he had done us in making us this offer, and since he was unable to accept it, he requested that we might be disbanded. He laid a stress on the word *requested,* in order that we might have the satisfaction of feeling it was our own hand that signed our death-warrant. He made it a stipulation that in the event of war with Italy, our regiment should be one of the first to be called out, and also that, as a public recognition of the services we had rendered to our country, the officers and subalterns should be authorized to take the same rank in the army of France as they had held in the regiment of Zouaves. On this last point he specially insisted, bidding us consult our own heart and our own conscience as to the course it became us to follow."

Each one was to send in his decision in writing, giving at the same time his reasons for it. We subjoin Theodore's answer, for it shows him as he was, a single-hearted and magnanimous soldier of Christ.

"My dear General,—I fully share your conviction that our regiment has still a future before it; our career will not cease when we are disbanded. I shall be anxious to respond to the first call, and shall therefore enter into no engagement which would shackle my freedom of action. I think I can say that all my efforts, and all the aspirations of my life will in the future be directed, as they have been directed in the past, to one single end, the triumph of the Papacy. With God's help I hope never to deviate from this line of conduct, which is the same you pursue. In unaltered devotion to my regiment, I have the honor to remain, etc."

"I ought to tell you," Theodore adds in acquainting his family with what had occurred, "that the General only half accepted my proposal, and that he had doubtful written against my name, on account of my age, and ostensibly not to mar my future prospects. To tell the truth, if I am obliged to serve, I should prefer the rank of a private soldier to any other, and if required I would expound my reasons for this preference; but the last hour of the regiment has not yet struck, so we need not be in a hurry to pronounce its funeral oration."

The whole of Theodore's life as a soldier is comprised in this answer to his Commander; his one wish is to serve the Pope in the uniform of the Zouave, and if for a time the regiment is to be suppressed, no alternative presents itself to his mind but to wait patiently until in God's good time the clarion shall again sound, and then at its first note he will start up, don the well-worn uniform, shoulder the rifle rusty with disuse, and go forth to rejoice the Church of God by the repetition of deeds of self-devotion such as those which Albano and Mentana witnessed.

The progress of the matter in question was wearisomely slow, it might have been compared to the protracted agony of a courageous soul, rivetted, so to speak, to the body.

"Rennes, July 29th, 1871.

"At last we now know what we have before us! The suspense we were in was becoming intolerable, as all felt, from the General down to the lowest cook. Our regiment is definitely disbanded; the order to this effect has not yet been officially proclaimed, but it has been issued, and M. de Charette received it this morning; I know this on good authority. It is supplemented by an order of the day from the Minister of War, of a very flattering nature, in which M. de Cissey pronounces over us a most eulogistic funeral oration, enumerating our services, and heaping our tomb with laurels. I say funeral oration, but I am wrong, people do not inter those who still show some signs of life, lethargy is not death, and this is what M. de Cissey means by saying that he hopes soon to appeal to our patriotism, calling us to take part either in foreign wars or civil strife.

"You must not be astonished if I come down on you some day like a bombshell. In fact, for my part, I am very much surprised to find myself still here. Everybody is mystified, and everybody is growing impatient: from day to day we expect the official order to disband, which is to ratify M. de Cissey's order and fix the day of our departure. The newspapers have lost no time in announcing that we are defunct; some have availed themselves of the opportunity to show their delicate sympathy, they have wept over and bewailed us, they have composed eloquent panegyrics, and behold! we are still amongst the living. It is not a common thing for a man to assist at his own obsequies. One ceremony still remains to be performed before we are finally laid in the grave, namely, the blessing of the coffin, in other words, the confirmation of the decree. M. Thiers, who is the officiating priest, seems to hesitate, his hand, they say, usually so prompt, shrinks from accomplishing this function; meanwhile the relatives and friends of the departed, the journalists and reporters, weep around the open grave. Can it be that the universal grief has actually touched his valiant heart? or by a sudden and inexplicable revulsion of feeling, does he feel inclined to attempt a second edition of the great miracle of the raising of Lazarus? *Surge et ambula*—Arise and walk! But whither? If he should bid us turn our face Romewards, what a shout of jubilation would arise from every heart, with what glad *Alleluias* should we shake off the dust of the grave, and cast aside the lugubrious shroud! If, on the other hand, we are to go on groping in the dark as we have done for several months past, I am afraid our *Te Deum* will sound very much like a *Miserere*. Seriously, I believe the good old man does not half like giving us our dismissal. Perhaps he sees the gathering clouds which are only too perceptibly darkening the heavens. One need not be much of a politician to be aware that momentous events are imminent; if the storm were to burst over our heads, he might be rather glad to make use of us as lightning conductors."

"August 13th, 1871.

"All is settled now, our dissolution is close at hand, the Sunday bells seem all to be tolling our funeral knell."

On that day the Regiment attended Military Mass for the last time, and before the close, their valued chaplain-in chief, Mgr. Daniel, spoke to them a few farewell words full of sorrow and yet of hope. On leaving the church, the men formed in a square in the courtyard of the Seminary, and General de Charette announced the formal disbanding of the Regiment. It was the second time within a year that these gallant men had been forced to go through this painful scene; but the occasion of which we are now speaking was not merely a renewal of the first sad parting on Italian soil, it was doubly sorrowful, for the recent campaign in France was rich in recollections, and the blood that was shed at Patay and Le Mans, beneath the banner of the Sacred Heart, had served to knit together in closer sympathy hearts already united by no fragile bond. Thus when Charette uttered the words: "Farewell, dear comrades; it is with heartfelt grief that I now take leave of you, for it is a hard wrench to part after eleven years, "tears stood in every eye, and every voice joined in re-echoing the General's words, and raising as a last adieu the shout of *Vive la France! Vive Pie IX!*

"We have ceased to exist," writes our Zouave, "and we have found death very bitter. In a moment all has gone from us. But not so, we bear away with us the cherished hope of meeting again in Rome, and then hurrah for the azure sky and sun-lit plains!"

From that time forward all was changed for Theodore. Hitherto his path has been so plain that, as he said, he could follow it blindfold; now he finds himself at a spot where many roads meet, each leading he knows not whither. He cannot tell which to choose, in what direction to turn his steps. He only admits two alternatives: "Either I must serve my time in the army, or obtain a substitute, and make choice of some calling for myself. If I determine on the former course, I must gulp down the pill resolutely, and go back to the fatigue and daily toil of a private soldier, which I prefer to any higher rank: in the second case, I shall implore guidance from on high, making a careful retreat, and appealing to Willebaud for his intercession on my behalf, which he promised should never be wanting."

He does not express himself very plainly, but anyone who knows how to read between the lines can see that his heart remains unchanged, and that nothing common-place can ever satisfy him, as far as the service of God is concerned. Nor can we, who have followed him in each step of his course, feel surprise at this, for how could a nature so athirst for sacrifice be satisfied with compromises and half-measures? And yet, by one of those strange contradictions so frequently to be met with in the spiritual life, in the case of persons who are over-impressionable, Theo dore, instead of hastening to form a decision, adopting some definite line of action, and seeking in a docile spirit to know whither God was leading and drawing him, deliberately closed his eyes and remained deaf to the Divine voice. The truth was that he dreaded to see and hear; he was entering on an untried path, and the most critical period of his life was close at hand; a season of clouds and dark. ness, of struggles against grace, of want of energy, of lack of decision when confronted with obvious duty.

It seemed as if his soul were just then weary of sacrifice, and as if he lacked courage to turn a deaf ear to the importunities of nature, which was hungrily clamoring for a season at least of indulgence, and as if he felt the time was come for him to enjoy himself at will. It is deeply interesting to watch the progress of this drama, to behold the conflicts, the defeats, the infidelities, which in the final act, issue in the ultimate triumph of Divine grace.

When Theodore was again at home, he made a feint of initiating himself into business matters, but in reality, he would sit doing nothing before a table covered with papers and ledgers; and he suffered so intensely from ennui, that he slipped away as often as he possibly could, in order, during a long country walk, to give free course to the vague sadness that haunted him. "I must leave the world," he would say to his intimate friends, "for I feel that I shall lose my soul if I do not." His parents put no constraint upon him, to bias his decision, they only insisted that for the present he should not remain idle. Meanwhile the disgust he felt for everything, himself included, was becoming almost alarming. Sometimes he would go up to Wille baud's room and remain a long time there; on one occasion his mother followed him thither, and found him in tears. "What good is it," he exclaimed, "for me to go to Confession and Communion, since I am none the better for it? "The only reply his mother made was to seat herself by his side, and putting her arm round his neck, bid him let his tears flow freely.

Fortunately at this juncture something occurred to turn the current of his thoughts; an invitation came from M. Carlos Cordonnier to breathe with him the air of the Ardennes, and revive the memories of the past whilst enjoying in the present the delights of friendship and the charms of nature. Theodore set out with a light heart, for he felt that this plan gave him a temporary truce from his enemy, the enemy consisting, according to his present view of things, in any serious resolution. In the heart of the dark forest and amid the mountain paths he was able leisurely to enjoy the present; to endow with fictitious life the past, so full of charm for him; to avert his gaze from the future, so full of terror for him; and as he foresaw that he would ere long have to lay aside the mantle of youth with all its illusions in order to assume the garb of manhood with its austere realities, he sought at least to delay the dreaded moment, glad if he could in this way prolong awhile the period of careless freedom. Had his soul been cast in a less heroic mold, had the importunities of grace been less pressing and incessant, this crisis in his life would have left him, as it leaves so many others, with weakened energies and diminished strength, a stranger from that time forth to all idea of tasting the mystic joys to be found in sacrifice.

In order to recall him from the cloud-land of his dreams, God caused a fresh blow to fall within his family circle. The beneficial impressions which Willebaud's death had produced were gradually fading away, and Theodore had perhaps already almost forgotten that he had promised his brother on his death-bed to make a retreat before deciding upon his future course. The news of the decease of his saintly uncle, M. Pierre Motte, obliged him to take a hasty leave of the country, and to return to Roubaix and to serious reflection.

M. Pierre Motte was no ordinary Christian; pious, talented, humble, and charitable, he possessed all the virtues which distinguish a true servant of God, and seemed made for an apostle. His days and nights were devoted to good works, to the service of the poor, to the welfare of his native town, which still honors his memory and regards him as one of its benefactors. Theodore thought very highly of his uncle, for it was in a great measure owing to his instrumentality that he had entered the Papal service, as may be seen from the following extract from a letter which he wrote to him soon after arriving in Rome.

"I shall never forget, my dear Uncle, what a help you have been to me, how you guided me in perplexity and encouraged me to hope, how kindly you pleaded my cause with my father, and told him of my longing and my aspirations. You spoke for me, you prayed for me, you entered into my wishes, and I should indeed be ungrateful if I did not acknowledge that it was very much through you that I am now here, so near to the Holy Father. I remember our long talks together, when you used to say how gladly you would shed your blood for the Church. Oh! pray for your poor nephew, who sorely needs your prayers."

This pious uncle did much more for Theodore, for during his last illness he made it his earnest entreaty that God would take complete possession of his nephew's soul, offering all his sufferings for this intention. Doubtless as Theodore knelt by the mortal remains of his beloved benefactor, he reiterated his request more fervently than ever: "Oh! pray for your poor nephew, who sorely needs your prayers."

"There is nothing like death to make us see things in their true light," he writes to his friend Carlos. "As one misses one fond familiar face after another, one feels the want of some bond which cannot be broken, and this can only be found in God. I am a prey to the most miserable uncertainty; I am far from happy, I have no enjoyment in my life, I drag on from day to day. I need some fixed rule to control my impulses and subdue my imagination, or I shall be useless to others, and only a burden to myself.

"I am writing you a letter as lugubrious as my own thoughts, they are black like the ink I write with; nor is all very bright around me. My cheerfulness is changed to melancholy, my peace of mind to agitation; I have got quite bewildered, and scarcely know where I am. But I am perfectly persuaded that I must do something, whatever it cost me, I foresee that I shall have to suffer acutely, and must cast to the four winds of heaven all the follies that hitherto my heart has rejoiced in.

"In less than an hour's time I am leaving for St. Acheul* to seek enlightenment from on high. If I could only think that the result of this retreat would be what I desire; but that is more than I deserve. An oppression seems to weigh on me; the church-bell is tolling for a funeral; it is as if all my hopes were being borne to the grave. I am going with a heavy heart; if I find the way to be happy, you shall hear what it is"

As may be guessed, Theodore's journey was none of the brightest. The prospect of a retreat in the Jesuit Novitiate represented itself to him in the most somber colors: even after he had fairly started, he debated in himself whether he should not turn back, or at least go in some other direction. But then had he not given his word to Willebaud, and thus fettered his own liberty of action?

His cousin Henry, whom we have mentioned as visiting him in Rome, was then at St. Acheul, where he had just taken his vows. Madame Wibaux had written to apprise him of her son's coming,

---

* The Jesuit Novitiate at Amiens.

naming the very day and hour when he would arrive. That day passed, and the next too, and Theodore did not make his appearance; on the third day Henry, when out walking, encountered his cousin sauntering idly through the streets of Amiens. For the last two days he had spent his time in this manner, lounging about the cafés, going to the theater, reading novels. But it was no use trying to stifle thought and forget the object for which he had gone thither; there was no escaping from God, Who claimed his soul for His own.

Saint-Acheul.

CHAPTER XXI.

1871.

Retreat at St. Acheul. Struggles between nature and grace. The final victory. Theodore enters the Jesuit Novitiate. His devotional practices. First Vows.

GREAT as was the astonishment of Brother Henry at thus unexpectedly meeting his cousin, the embarrassment Theodore evinced was greater still. When urged to repair at once to St. Acheul, as had been arranged, he refused at first, alleging that he had an appointment; a former comrade, he said, had invited him to dine with him that evening, and he would therefore defer going to the Jesuits' house until the morrow. But this and other flimsy excuses, invented on the spur of the moment, and proffered with considerable hesitation, melted away when Henry, as a last resource, mentioned Madame Wibaux's name; Theodore finally gave in, through with a very bad grace. How great is the influence of a good mother, even when absent!

Although the old house of St. Acheul abounded in hallowed associations, it possessed no external attractiveness, and had been made the subject of many absurd stories invented by enemies of the Society. The brick walls, darkened by time, the narrow windows, the large, gloomy courtyard, which the gray sky of Picardy caused to look gloomier still, did not tend to inspire a cheerful frame of mind; but it was the exterior alone that was dreary, for no sooner had one passed the portals, than one found oneself surrounded by a number of young men, whose countenances beamed with holy joy, and who, by means of obedience and generous self-sacrifice, were forming themselves to become good soldiers of Jesus Christ. The halls of St. Acheul are now empty and deserted; but there is con Isolation in the thought that the wind of persecution, by wafting the seed to a foreign shore, has but rendered the harvest more plenteous. Theodore only saw the surface of things, and the sight chilled him at first he declared that he would leave the house for the present, and return the next morning to begin his retreat. But it was the 8th of December and the bell was ringing for Benediction: how could Theodore take his departure so abruptly, without offering a prayer to his Mother in Heaven on the feast of her Immaculate Conception, the anniversary too of his entrance into the Pontifical Zouaves? So he remained; and whilst he was kneeling in the church, the past rose up before him; those happy days, brightened by the pure flame of sacrifice, transformed by the steady light of unceasing prayer; he fixed his eyes on the Blessed Sacrament exposed above the altar, and as long as the service lasted, his tears fell freely, tears of regret, of contrition, of hope, tears which relieving his heart of its load of misery, made room in it for the Divine Master Who had come to take up His abode there.

Who can tell on what the future of a soul, or perhaps its eternal salvation, may depend? How different Theodore's future might have been, if he had put off going to St. Acheul for a single day? The concession made for our Lady's sake was the first link in the chain which was to bind him irrevocably to his God. After Benediction he was quite calm, and on being installed in his room, wrote the following lines to a former Zouave:

"Here I am, imprisoned for God knows how long. The prospect is frightfully alarming, alone with my own thoughts, confronted with all my frailties, my memories, my doubts, I now perceive how strong has been my attachment to the world, how powerful those bonds of whose existence I was hardly conscious, those habits which must now forthwith be broken off. Please pray a great deal for me. I do not want to go away in a despairing state of mind, my wish is to remain here, but I feel how unworthy I am, I feel that I have squandered the graces God has in mercy bestowed on me."

Saint-Acheul.

Meanwhile the enemy of souls did not consider himself defeated, but like the skilful strategist he is, he kept out of sight for a few days, lying in wait for a favorable opportunity to carry the fortress by storm. The retreat began with dryness, aridity, lassitude, obstacles which the retreatant combated with the weapon of good will; being too much perturbed for peaceful meditation, he spent the time allotted to mental prayer in imploring the saints of Heaven to intercede for him, whilst in his free time he strode in feverish excitement up and down the garden walks, now with his hands in his pockets, now telling his beads, now conversing with his cousin.

When the day of election came, it found him perfectly tranquil, desirous only to know and follow the path in which he was destined to walk. No Divine arm arrested him as it did St. Paul on the way to Damascus, no voice clearly articulated to his heart the *Sequere me* which our Lord addressed to the Apostles. Taking pen and paper, he wrote out on one side the motives which inclined him to remain in the world, on the other the reasons which influenced him in favor of the religious life; he saw that the latter pre dominated, he felt that he need look no further, for the problem of his life in future was solved; he would enter the Society of Jesus because he wanted the restraint of a rule to curb his wayward will, he feared the seductions of the world, he desired to keep beyond the reach of danger, it was the instinct of self-preservation that principally dictated his choice. Ten years later he thus expressed himself in reference to the grace he received at the time of which we are speaking: "I could bring nothing worthy to offer, only a heart of clay, unbounded love of self, inability to appreciate the honor done me. What thanks are due to our Lady who stooped to raise me out of the mire, and conducted me, like a shipwrecked mariner, unto this haven of safety. *Misericordias Domini in æternum cantabo.*"

This was the moment on which the devil had been counting in order to renew his attack. When the time came for Theodore to apprise his parents of his decision, his heart failed him; a flood of discouragement overflowed his soul, he could not resign himself to break altogether with the past, he could not renounce all possibility of ever again wearing his uniform, of drawing the sword in defense of Rome or of France; he declared he had been deceived, and burst into angry invective against the Fathers, so much so that not one of those who had till then been directing his retreat was willing any longer to undertake the charge of so intractable a soul.

Was he not, one feels inclined to ask, at perfect liberty to depart? The doors of the house were open, none of its inmates sought to detain him, why then does he continue to linger in a place the very atmosphere of which he said seemed to stifle him? The fact was that when prayer had for a time restored calm to his troubled mind, and dispelled the gloom, he was heartily ashamed of himself; and besides, the lengths to which he had gone under the influence of temptation revealed to him what he really was, filling him with alarm at the prospect of encountering the many dangers wherewith life in the world must inevitably be beset.

At this moment of struggle and faintheartedness, his cousin, who was the only person whom Theodore would then listen to, came in, bringing a letter from his mother. That enlightened and valiant woman had foreseen all that awaited her son, the choice to be made, the conflict to be undergone, the resistance to be maintained. "Keep up your courage, dear boy," she wrote, "think of your all powerful Mother in Heaven. Rather would I never see you again than know that you had left St. Acheul and lost your vocation." The faith displayed in these words, together with the terms of endearment in which his mother addressed him, melted Theodore's heart, and brought tears to his eyes; meanwhile his cousin, sitting by his side, commented on the storm on the Lake of Genesareth, when St. Peter, walking upon the waters, felt his courage fail, and cried out in alarm; he reminded him of the mercy shown by the Divine Master, of the prompt rescue of the Apostle; was not this narrative a recapitulation of the Zouave's own experiences?

In the evening Theodore was fairly worn out; tired of struggling against the will of God, conquered indeed by grace, though as yet no willing captive, he dropped on his knees, and opened the Imitation which was lying before him on the table; his eyes happened to fall on the words: *Ubi est fides tua? sta firmiter et perseveranter.*[*] This was an answer from above; in an instant, as if by a breeze from on high, the clouds were swept away, the light returned, and with it his courage revived. Taking up his pen, without rising from his knees or wiping away his tears, he wrote to tell his parents what great things God had done for his soul: "Give thanks with me," he wrote, "the voice of Jesus has spoken. You know with what lovingkindness, with what patience He has waited for me to come and cast myself at His feet, and implore pardon and mercy. When He called most urgently, I persisted in flying from Him; not un frequently I even tried to stop my ears so as no longer to hear the importunate appeal. At length, weary of the strife, almost by main force He brought me here.

---

[*] Where is your faith? Stand firm and preserve it.

"I have fully learnt to know my own misery, the dryness the sterility, the impotency of my heart. From doubt and anxiety I almost fell into despair; but no, I never went as far as that, I always hoped, because I always trusted in our Lady, I turned to her, and besought her help most earnestly, I may say I compelled her to have pity on me. In times of the greatest distress, there is nothing like the rosary to set one right. In a word, I waited in faith until God should manifest His mercy and now, despite my unworthiness, I am going to become a member of the Society of Jesus. My adorable Master vouchsafes to admit me into the number of His disciples, His chosen friends, those who are called to share more largely in His labors and His sufferings now, in order one day to share more largely in His glory.

"I owe it to you, my dear parents, to your prayers and to the Christian education you have given me, that I have at length been enabled to find fullness of peace and fullness of light. May God reward you for the good you have done me; I shall never be able to thank you for it aright, until I do so in Heaven, the final meeting-place of souls. I know you and love you well enough to be sure that you will place no obstacle in the way of my happiness; what do Christian parents desire more than that all their children should walk with them along the heavenward path? I shall take the most direct road; what matter whether I reach my journey's end sooner or later than you, provided we all meet there at last.

"Our dear Lord has given me grace to feel keenly the sacrifice I am making. For this I thank Him from the depths of my crushed and bleeding heart; it is much best to go to Him with the cross upon one's shoulders, for this is a mark of His faithful followers. Yes, I know full well how much I am giving up, but I know too by anticipation all that I shall receive in exchange.

"Dear Father and Mother, on my knees I beg your blessing, and, since Almighty God has freely forgiven me all my transgressions, I entreat that you too will forgive all my failures in duty and my ingratitude towards you, and the pain I have sometimes caused you. I promise to expiate all by my prayers. All for Jesus! this was the thought constantly present to the mind of our dear sufferer, may it also be our strength, our consolation, our hope. Please pray for me and get others to pray for me too. I am not abandoning the cause of the Papacy, only henceforth I shall fight for it with weapons that are peaceful, but not on that account less efficacious.

"Shall I make my dear mother jealous by showing her that I can love God even better than I love her? No, of this there is no fear; indeed, I now love her more dearly than I ever did before.

"Henry has really been like a guardian angel to me."

The struggle was now to all appearance happily ended, and the triumph of grace seemed complete; but human nature, and the enemy of our salvation were not yet finally silenced. After the seclusion and the agitation of the last few days, Theodore stood in need of recreation and change. Accordingly the two cousins set out together with the intention of visiting the Cathedral of Amiens. As they passed the railway station on their way thither, an uncontrollable impulse suddenly seized upon Theodore, a temptation more violent than any that had gone before, caught him in its vicious clutch; as if yielding to a superior power he turned to his cousin, and coldly informed him that he was about to return home, having finally made up his mind to enlist in the *Chasseurs d'Afrique*. Henry, at a loss what to answer, merely remarked that if that were the case, it would hardly be courteous to go off without taking leave of the Father Rector, whose guest he had been for the last week. Theodore acceded to the suggestion, and retraced his steps in moody silence. The Superior had gone out, so it was necessary to wait until he should return.

Henry tried hard to convince his recalcitrant cousin that in acting thus, he was false to God and false to himself; he bade him remember his mother, Willebaud, the uncle whom had recently lost; but all was in vain, he resolutely refused to see with his eyes, or hear with his ears. After all, was he not the principal person concerned? Let him go his way then, and keep his liberty, and make what use he pleased of it to offend God! At last Henry, finding all his arguments of no avail, went away and left him to himself.

Theodore's eternal salvation seemed at that moment to be quivering in the balance; but God looked down from Heaven in compassion on the unhappy waverer who, with despair in his heart, was walking up and down in the retreatant's garden, under the very shadow of a large image of our Lady. Mechanically he took out and began to say his rosary, framing the words with his lips while the one wish of his heart was to get done as soon as possible. But all this time grace was carrying on its work, acting on a secret inspiration, to every *Ave* which he uttered he added in imploring accents: "Willebaud, Uncle Pierre, pray for me!"

Then he bethought him of the day when he laid his much-loved brother in the coffin, and remembered how he had slipped into the lifeless hand a folded paper, to which he had committed his sorrows, his fears, his wishes, his passions, adding an urgent entreaty that Willebaud would aid him in choosing a state of life. Doubtless Willebaud had presented that petition to the Virgin-Mother, and she had been moved to compassion; for behold, before Theodore had done weaving his garland of prayer, his distractions took flight, despondent thoughts gave place to generous resolves, self-devotion and self-sacrifice began to wear a winning aspect. Just as his fingers touched the last bead of the chaplet, he caught sight of his cousin at the further end of the garden; hastening up to him, he threw his arms round his neck, saying, "Tell me, if I enter the Novitiate, shall I really love our Lord?"

"Most assuredly you will," replied Henry, himself deeply moved. What a lesson have we here for those who imagine that all is consolation, sweetness, and light in this important matter, which we call the vocation of a soul to lead the life of perfection.

Before long Theodore was to be seen wearing a cassock, and when evening came, as he crossed the threshold of the Novitiate, he declared that day to have been the happiest day of his life. At any rate it may be said to have been the day of his greatest victory.

Theodore had done well to place his trust and his strength in her who is all mercy and loving kindness; after this signal favor what could she henceforth refuse to her humble suppliant? "It must be confessed," he writes, "that the Blessed Virgin is incurring a heavy responsibility, and taking upon herself a great burden, by thus thrusting a soldier who has deserted in amongst a body of picked men. A place which many pure and generous souls would have coveted has been, I may say, forced upon me. But in making me scale the walls in this surreptitious way, she pledges herself to look well after me, if it is only to justify herself for what she has done."

Might not the pages we have just read be justly called the story of a soul? or better still might they not be entitled: The story of God's mercy towards one of His elect? Theodore had been in fault; he knew this, and was prepared to make amends like one to whom sacrifice can be nothing short of a holocaust.

On learning his decision his parents, true to what they had always shown themselves to be in times past, answered in the language of faith; a language incomprehensible to those whose paltry ambition forms for their children only such hopes and fears as range within the narrow limits of their world's low horizon, and who would make of their selfish feelings a virtue, of their fondness a tyrant. From the admirable letters Theodore received at this period, we see what Christian sorrow, resignation, and gratitude, really are. His father writes thus:

"I trust that ere long it will please God to give us strength to thank Him as you do: as yet we only feel the sacrifice, and feel it acutely; we do not rebel, but our hearts are broken. It is hard within six months to have had to part with Willebaud, with your Uncle Pierre, and now to be called on to give you up, my dear boy; you of whom we have always been so fond, and of whom we have as yet seen so little. Thy Kingdom come, O my God, Thy will be done! Do Thou reign in our hearts as their sovereign Master, and bring every thought into conformity with Thy good pleasure, and enable us to accept joyfully whatever trials Thou mayest see fit to lay upon us. Farewell, dear boy, I cannot as yet read your letter without tears, but I am conscious that my affection for you is not selfish, it is in God that I love you."

And Mme. Wibaux added these lines:

"My darling Theodore, many and many a time I have offered you to the Sacred Heart of Jesus; you are the child of Pius IX. I freely and gladly confided you to the safe keeping of our Immaculate Mother; and I cannot refuse to let you go, when our Lord asks you of me. Although natural grief must make itself heard, my stricken heart can echo your words of thankfulness to God. My God, I thank Thee! This is the uppermost feeling of my heart."

General de Charette, to whom Theodore communicated the step he had taken, expressed in a letter addressed to M. Wibaux, the feelings entertained by all his brothers in arms in regard to the soldier who hesitated not thus to leave God for God. "Perhaps it is selfish of me, but I cannot help regretting to see so fine a character lost to our regiment. The departure of your son is so great a blow to us all, that we cannot accustom ourselves to the thought of never seeing him amongst us again. But we shall still have his memory, and his prayers will procure for us the privilege of returning to Rome, and restoring the Sovereign Pontiff to his rightful position."

A fortnight after Theodore entered the Novitiate, his father went to see him, and found him rejoicing in his victory, although still bearing the traces of the severe struggle through which he had passed. The son wished to conceal nothing from his father, and whilst relating to him the various phases of the conflict he had undergone, he showed him the garden set apart for retreatants, terming it the scene of his agony, or rather that of his merciful deliverance.

The distinguishing characteristic of our novice was from the very outset an extraordinary fidelity to grace. In his new surroundings no great opportunities for self-revelation any longer presented themselves, as was formerly the case amidst arduous fatigue-work, forced marches, or under exposure to the enemy's fire; but all the small things which from a merely human point of view might be regarded as unimportant minutiæ, became in his eyes so many valuable gems, of which he made an extensive collection. He had indeed no longer the saber and bayonet to fear, but the courage of which he gave proof upon the battlefield now enabled him to endure the thousand pin-pricks which the new rule he had adopted daily inflicts upon nature in order to subjugate her completely. "The days," he writes, "go by like a flash of lightning, and everything here is so well ordered and arranged that one has no leisure to note the progress that has been made. We are led onward from one moment to another, and each fresh step in the spiritual life brings us imperceptibly nearer to the Sacred Heart of Jesus. It is there that I have cast my anchor, and although from time to time some storms will rise and rough winds will blow, I shall be tossed by the waves and enveloped in darkness, still I need fear no danger, for my timbers are sound and I can outride the gale."

His principal failing, both then and later on, was a sort of over-eagerness, induced by the fear of doing wrong, by an incessant aspiration towards perfection, by the remembrance of what he called his infidelities and the desire to atone for them; all these things were doubtless good in themselves, but were occasionally allowed to engross his mind to an extent which could not be otherwise than prejudicial. Owing to this cause he passed at first many sleepless nights, the result being an undue strain on his mind, which lasted for months, and but for the wise care of his superiors, might have had serious consequences. He was moreover obliged repeatedly to renew the sacrifice he had made in taking a final leave of his beloved uniform, conscious the while that though the regiment might perhaps be formed anew, his place there would know him no more. He might have sundered all other ties with comparative facility, but that which bound him to his regiment was riveted to the very center of his being, and when the time to break it came, the severance could not be effected without lacerating his heart-strings.

After the lapse of several weeks he wrote: "My head is not yet very clear, but the mist will gradually disperse; as for my heart, that is decidedly improving. Why should I not say that it is in perfect health? How indeed could it be otherwise in such an atmosphere of graces, prayers, and good examples? And if my imagination prove somewhat recalcitrant from time to time, by the help of grace I shall at length succeed in laying it, bound and captive, at the feet of my crucified Lord." One of his fellow-novices having remarked to him that all this excessive effort was not good for him, "Your task, "he replied, "is a comparatively easy one; with me it is different, I have lived in the world and been in the army, and have far greater efforts to make."

His life was pre-eminently a life of struggle; in the early days of his novitiate his countenance bore traces at times of the multiplied attacks to which he was subjected by the devil, who seemed determined to leave him no respite, but perpetually beset him with temptations to ennui, temptations to discouragement, temptations against the faith; these latter suggesting perforce to his mind the distressing doubt whether Mary was in reality our Mother!

But ere long he gained the mastery over himself, and his habitual expression was one of gentleness and recollection, his face being lighted up by the pleasant smile with which he greeted every one, and which so perfectly revealed the beauty of his soul. Even strangers were attracted by his appearance; one visitor who happened to see him pass, could not refrain from asking who the tall novice was that might have been taken for an angel, so recollected was his manner, and so devout the way in which he kissed the medal of his rosary. Thus in the midst of his adoptive family did he continue to exercise the silent. influence of a good example, which he had exerted with such happy results whilst serving with his regiment. Theodore had but changed his uniform, he was still the "holy young man," in regard to whom it was remarked during his French campaign, "Look at that officer, he is as pure as an angel."

Accustomed as he was to military exactitude, he thought that sanctity might be learned as one learns to handle a gun. Many an urgent "summons" did he address to his dear St. Joseph and the beloved saints who had been his patrons in Rome, in order that he might acquire without delay this or that virtue, grace, or favor. If, as is proved by the example of the saints, those who desire to attain perfection must be unremitting in their efforts, Theodore was a model in this respect. Ever on his guard against himself, he made his life one long succession of devotions, novenas, and other pious practices. Some men would have lost their way amid such a labyrinth, Theodore, however, not only threaded its paths in safety, but found there precious fruit for the nourishment of his soul. What could be more thoroughly in keeping with the spirit of the Church, who seeks to sustain the interest of her children by providing them with constant variety in the cycle of the liturgical year? Here again, however, Theodore could not at first avoid a little exaggeration, but where is the fervent novice who did not at the commencement go somewhat to an extreme before the happy medium was attained? Thus on one occasion, in his anxiety to prevail with St. Joseph, and obtain from him some particular grace, he took it into his head to carry about continually in his hand a small statuette of the Saint, until one day, whilst helping himself to soup, he chanced to let it fall into the tureen, thereby provoking a roar of laughter from the assembled novices.

The reader may perchance like to form some idea of the pious practices which regulated, so to speak, every pulsation of his heart. His day was an unbroken series of rendezvous in the morning with his Mother, in presence of the Blessed Sacrament; at each of the three times the Angelus rings, with one or more of his brothers, in the view of obtaining a greater love of our Lord; between the hours of eleven and twelve, with his grandmother, in order to give thanks to Our Lady of the Immaculate Conception for the many blessings he owed to her bounty; and in like manner every hour of the day, from the time he rose in the morning until he retired to rest at night, was consecrated to some special protector through whose intercession he hoped to procure some special grace.

In addition to the protectors whom he had in common with all the Church's children, he had his own particular patrons, whom he selected by preference from amongst the members of the Society. How carefully, how fondly, he searched the annals of his Order for some name to add to a calendar he was drawing up, in execution of an idea of his own, which well merits adoption, as being conducive to the promotion of *esprit de famille;* this is the plan which he submitted to one of his Superiors: "Every day we will commemorate on the one hand some memorable event or act connected with the Society, and on the other the names of those who have died a holy death; these are very numerous. How many martyrs we have of whom nothing is known, how many saintly Fathers whom we do not think of invoking because mention is never made of them; two or three lines would be sufficient to give an outline of their life. I consider that I owe a great deal to the intercession of these eminent servants of God."

Never was there such a man for anniversaries, dates, novenas;

on every page of his note-books, his memoranda, his letters, we find jottings such as these: "Blessings on Pius IX, our Pontiff-King!", "To. . . . who was my dear friend and companion in arms.", "Venerable Father Bellarmine, pray for us! ", "Today, the anniversary of Mentana," etc.

There is something very charming about the familiar intercourse which he maintained with his angel guardian; witness the following extract from a letter to his mother: "From time to time I send my good angel to you, to remind you to pray for me, and I often have a visit from yours, especially of a morning, just about the time when you go to Communion. What a beautiful devotion this is to one's guardian angel! How it helps to smooth one's pathway through life! Everything that contributes to our spiritual joy comes from our good angel: how sweet to think of this kind friend and brother whom God has placed at our side to protect us! I love to invite him to be present whenever I go to Communion, and then I pray Jesus and His Holy Mother to rejoice him with their loving notice; I think how happy this must make him, and I fancy I hear the gentle flutter of his wings. Then in return he suggests all manner of good thoughts to my mind." At another time he writes: "Now the month of October has begun, let us make good use of our good angels as messengers."

For a long time past he had besought St. Anne to obtain for him a filial affection for the Blessed Virgin, and it was with this object that he paid a visit to Auray during his sojourn in Brittany in 1871. Every night too, desiring that his last waking thought should be the thought of Mary, he invoked St. Anne with this intention.

On account of the infidelities and falls, as he termed them, of his past life, he cultivated a devotion to St. Mary Magdalen, besides other penitent saints; once every month he received Communion in her honor. Five days of each month, from the 8th to the 13th, he dedicated to the commemoration of the Blessed John Berchmans, his brother in religion; in this manner keeping the day of his birth into the world (the 13th of March), and also that of his entrance into a better life (the 13th August), the five preceding days of prayer were in memory of the five years which the Blessed Berchmans spent in religion.

He made St. Joseph his head "man of business"; on one occasion he said of him: "The illustrious plenipotentiary of the Holy Trinity has given us a grand surprise." Again: "The 19th of March. This feast is a double of the first class in Heaven, in Purgatory, and for all poor sinners on earth. Everyone ought to be in affluent circumstances, for this great Prince of Heaven is ready to distribute untold largesses; one has but to present one's petition, and he will sign it without even reading it. . . . All the most weighty matters are entrusted to him, he is the Patron of the whole Church, of Christian families, of the dying, of hopeless cases. I do not think that one thing more will make much difference to him. Go to Joseph: Lay all your concerns before him, this is a case for him, if ever there was one. I am employed in the household of the Holy Family during this happy month, busy from morning to night. I have every facility for speaking to him about you."

In this way he excused to his relatives his silence during the month of March. The origin of his tender devotion to his dear St. Joseph may be traced back to his childish days. Subsequently to his First Communion, he had the misfortune to fall into some intricate perplexities of conscience; a false shame paralyzed his tongue in the confessional, and his Communions became a misery to him. This went on until 1866, when, in the course of his efforts to merit the signal favor of serving Pius IX, he resolved to put an end to so unsatisfactory a state of things, and with this intention made a novena to St. Joseph, on the last day of which a good confession of his whole past life restored peace and tranquility to his heart, and the remembrance of the happiness he then enjoyed lent a tender charm to his thoughts of St. Joseph up to the last hour of his life.

Whilst serving in his regiment, Theodore had been a favored child of our Lady, and the heart of the, Jesuit proved no less affectionate than that of the Zouave had been; indeed, his feelings towards her were ever those of a loving son. "I am resolved," he says, "to cling to a fold of Mary's mantle until my latest breath, being fully assured that she will never let me go. Whilst holding me with one hand, she bestows on me maternal caresses with the other, as if to win me over to the service of her beloved Son. I am fully aware that as yet she cannot venture to bind me to the Cross, for I know how I shrink from it. Alas for the Mother who has such a son, and alas for the son, who is unworthy of such a Mother! However, her compassionate condescension will greatly redound to the glory of her mercy. An earthly mother would have lost patience, and troubled herself no more about me."

To his mother he writes: "It used to be the greatest relief to me to go and sob out my grief with you, dearest mother; now when I feel somewhat down-hearted, I betake myself to our Lady, and entreat her to fill the place of my earthly mother. I can truly say that never have I had recourse to her in prayer without obtaining consolation. Oh! how much I love the Blessed Virgin! and how I long to make others love her too! When I cannot see my way clear, when all seems to go hopelessly wrong, when I am in despair about myself and about others, she is always there, shining amidst the gloom; and even if I cannot utter a word of prayer, I can always find something to say to her. Indeed, it is through her I live; she is never weary of giving, and condescends to enter most kindly into all the minutiae of my daily life. I put all down in the great book of accounts, in the depths of the Sacred Heart, knowing that my debts will be paid in unalloyed coin. I do not know how I shall ever thank her, but I rejoice to think that the Heart of Jesus will love and bless Mary throughout all eternity." Every day, during the month of May, he contrived to find time to put into rhyme some words of petition, of remembrance, of affection, of desire, to be laid at the foot of our Lady's statue. Every Saturday he went to Communion in her honor, and before each of her feasts it was his habit to make a novena, and invite his friends to make it with him.

Shortly before his death he wrote out a list of all the benefits he had received through her mediation; this spiritual bouquet was at the same time a recapitulation of his whole life. To our Lady he attributed his successes at school, the prizes he had obtained, especially the medal for the Latin speech; his vocation to the Zouaves, the sacrifices he made before his departure, the farewell to home at the feet of Our Lady of the Staircase, the pilgrimages to Notre Dame des Victoires and Notre-Dame de la Garde, his arrival at Rome on the 8th of December—"a happy day for me, who am now a child of the Immaculate Conception and of Pius IX. to all eternity!" Each and all of these, as he enumerates them in turn, suggest thoughts of gratitude to his filial, loving heart. Then there were the Madonnas of Rome, who helped him to preserve his purity; the feast of the Assumption at Albano, when the cholera was at its height; and last of all, after the close of the war, the Benediction at St. Acheul, when a new life commenced for him, and the rosary which finally put an end to his vacillations; these are but a few of the many favors and graces where with page after page is filled. Amongst others he mentions the fact of his having escaped being killed at Mentana by a French soldier's clumsiness in discharging his rifle. One feels that he has indeed reason to say: "I am head over ears in debt to the Blessed Virgin." And at the end of all he adds: "In case of my death, I should wish thanks to be given to our Lady for me in every possible manner, by offering *Magnificats,* by Communions and Masses in honor of the Immaculate Conception."

His brother Jesuits used to tell him that every one of the saints who people Paradise was his favorite, and really to hear him talk one might have imagined that each of his celestial protectors was the one on whom all his affections were centered. In fact his heart seemed so large as to be capable of admitting all, and assigning to each a place in the foremost rank: the list would indeed be a long one, were we to enumerate all whom he selected as the objects of his special reverence, from St. Gertrude, known for her devotion to the Sacred Heart, to his patron, St. Theodore, soldier and martyr. One can plainly see that amid all these multifarious devotions and pious practices, he never turned aside or paused to draw breath in his onward course; for one of his temperament, strongly imaginative and extremely sensitive, this multiplicity of devotions, the external manifestations of his interior love of God, seemed almost a necessity, while a colder nature might have found them an intolerable burden. Let each do what is most conducive to his spiritual health.

As for our hero, there was no fear that he would get on a wrong track, for he never began anything of the kind without the approbation of his Superiors, to whom he invariably submitted his projects and his wishes, accepting with an equally good grace either a sanction or a refusal.

Such was Theodore in his relation to the unseen world; was it not a practical exemplification of the Apostle's words: *Our conversation is in Heaven?*

After his two years' novitiate, the recruit became a soldier of St. Ignatius, passing into the ranks of the regular army.

"My dearest parents," he writes, "this is the last letter I shall write to you while I am in the world. Pray do not be alarmed, and do not fancy that I am stretched upon a sick bed. I am in wonderful spirits for a man who is about to take the irrevocable step. The time has come for me to leave the world, and to leave it forever; I do so most gladly; at midnight on Christmas Eve I am to have the happiness of being born to a new life, born with the Divine Child, and taken like him, into the arms of the Blessed Virgin, my Mother. I have said before, my dear parents, and I cannot repeat it too often, the nearer I draw to God, the stronger does my affection for you become. I know enough already to feel that hitherto I have never rightly appreciated the inestimable blessing of having a father and mother who think more of the eternal welfare of their children than of their own affection and their temporal interests." Thanks be to God, this race is not extinct; there are still clear-sighted and Christian parents who are willing to devote their children to the special service of God, and who find in those children the reward of faith, consolation under the trials of life, a foretaste of celestial bliss!

CHAPTER XXII.

1872—1882.

Theodore at recreation-time. At the bedside of the sick. His correspondence. Love for his old regiment. Intercourse with former comrades. General Charette's fête.

"No more songs or dreams for me henceforth," wrote Theodore to a friend, also a Zouave, when he left St. Acheul after the Benediction on the 8th December, 1871. Will this prediction be verified, think you, reader? Must we, too, bid farewell to mirth and gaiety, if we would follow him as he goes onward along the somewhat rugged road of religion, and the thorny path of self-sacrifice? No, the high spirits of the Zouave are not incompatible with the fidelity. of a novice to his vocation; though Theodore dies to the world, his own joyous self will not be dead. Let him part with his day-dreams, if you will, but his merry songs must never be hushed.

Just listen to him at recreation-time, and when out walking; he is never tired of relating anecdotes for the amusement of his companions, he will keep them entertained for hours without once allowing the conversation to flag. Reminiscences of his old regimental days are recalled with an animation and power of description which seems to set scene and actors before the hearer; one might fancy oneself at Albano, in Rome, in the midst of a group of soldiers, in the presence of Pius IX. He had the gift of talking so as to instruct and edify, without allowing the conversation ever to become wearisome or unprofitable. Sacrificing his humility to the desire to please his brothers in religion, and the simplicity of his character triumphing over all considerations of false modesty, he did not shrink from giving an account of his interviews with the Holy Father, his talks with Louis Veuillot, Charette, and other distinguished personages, on account of the prominence which unavoidably appertained to himself in the narrative. How glad his companions were if they could start him off on the subject of his experiences in Italy and on the Loire! but how vexed he was if any one took the occasion to compliment him on the part he had himself enacted! One day, when the novices were asked in public whether they had any remarks to make about the rule, Theodore stood up and said: "I think one ought to try not to pride oneself about anything in the past, such as the notice taken of one by some distinguished person, or anything of that sort. One finds plenty to be vain of without that." This speech was highly approved of.

In free time and during the vacations, the indefatigable story-teller liked to turn poet, and amuse himself with writing verses, according to the bent of his fancy; sometimes they were humorous, but always refined, and never sarcastic. One day he got a friend to read aloud what he had written; it was not much admired. When the next recreation-time came, he was seen going about from one group to another, asking in the most natural manner: "Well, how did you like that piece of poetry?" "Oh, I thought it rather poor." "So did I," he answered, "I wrote it." He was desirous to preserve a strict incognito as long as there was any chance of success, but when he found the general verdict was unfavorable, he was ready and willing enough to claim the authorship.

No one was more scrupulous than Theodore in observing silence, for he always made use of signs if it was possible thereby to avoid speaking, and carried out the rule on all points most rigorously, yet, when the time for relaxation came, no one gave himself up more unrestrainedly to light-hearted mirth, or took a more active part on all festive occasions. During one vacation he sent for his text books of military science, in order to amuse his companions by putting them through various exercises. Of course large sticks had to take the place of muskets, but what matter, so long as the suspicions of the too curious neighbors were not aroused, who might easily have imagined—for what limit is there to human credulity?—that the wily Jesuits were secretly and silently preparing for a *coup-de-main*.[*] And in fact, there was the ex-officer to be seen drilling his men, ordering them about with the blunt familiarity of an old trooper, going the rounds at night and patrolling the garden walks in true military style, to the air of a military song!

But whatever character Theodore assumed, whether he sang songs, wrote verses, acted the commandant, or narrated his former adventures, he was never known to offend against charity, or to speak in a depreciating manner of others, and criticize their conduct. On the contrary, he invariably saw the best side of men and things, and represented them in the same aspect to others; and even where it was impossible not to blame, his kind heart suggested something to excuse. But the sick knew best how tender and thoughtful he was; in the infirmary more than elsewhere, his powers of diverting, cheering, and edifying came into play, and he consequently acted as infirmarian oftentimes out of his turn; indeed, he had not served his apprenticeship among the cholera patients at Albano to no purpose. If the contagious nature of the malady precluded him from visiting the sufferer, every day he would write and send him a few lines, containing an account of whatever incidents had occurred in the course of the day, or some pious thought connected with the saint whom the Church commemorated, or mentioning the name of any deceased Jesuit whose anniversary occurred just then. And if nothing of interest suggested itself, he would promise the sick man to present himself in his stead before our Lord, and say to Him: *Behold, he whom Thou lovest is sick.*

It is not our intention to follow Theodore step by step through the course of his classical, philosophical, and theological studies, as

---

[*] A surprise quick attack.

we followed him through the different stages of his career as a Zouave; nor shall we do more than glance at the years he passed among his pupils at Boulogne and at Amiens, for a minute and detailed account of this period, however interesting to his immediate friends, would only serve to weary the general reader, without enabling him to form a better idea of the character of the man himself. Who does not prefer a portrait sketched in with a few rapid strokes, a few bold touches of light and shade, to a miniature so elaborately worked up that the effect of the whole is thereby impaired? And in truth, there is nothing more to be said about Theodore during this time, than that his thoughts being centered in God and His interests, in the observance of the rules and in the performance of his daily duties he in no wise distinguished himself from his fellows, unless it were by the most scrupulous fidelity, and a sort of prestige attaching to him on account of his antecedents. What is so good a sign for a religious community as the fact that a man whose past would ensure for him a post of distinction in the world, disappears in the crowd when once he has enrolled himself amongst its members?

During the long years devoted by the Society of Jesus to the training of its militia, how well was Theodore forming himself for the apostleship, and preparing to be an instrument in carrying on the work of God! He desired his piety, like all true virtue, to be a shining as well as a burning light; and here mention must be made of his correspondence, which he looked upon as a means of doing good. While glancing at the innumerable letters he penned, and turning over page after page of the closely-written sheets, one asks himself how he could possibly find time thus to become all things to all men, since he only wrote at chance moments, or at night, if his Superior granted him permission to do so. And throughout all these letters, in which an erasure betraying hesitation or mistake on the part of the writer rarely occurs, there breathes something of the supernatural; the reader feels his own soul stirred by the zeal which glows in the heart of the apostle, and communicates itself to him.

"It makes one feel quite ashamed to read Theodore's letters," remarked a friend of his, himself a religious. The originality of his mind, and his fervent piety, were sure to find something new to say about Jesus and Mary, the saints, the festivals of the Church; he gives counsel and comfort, suggests some pious practice to be adopted, some novena to be made. Yes, it is true, his letters make one ashamed of oneself, and they make one desirous, too, of becoming better. From the members of his family, who are all so pious, he expects much more than from others; the following extract is from a letter in which he proposes they should take a journey to Lourdes. "All difficulties ought to be removed, and all obstacles to disappear in presence of the sweet and loving invitation of the Virgin Mother, whose arms are held out to clasp her pilgrims in a fond embrace. My advice would be to make a slight *détour* so as to visit Paray-le-Monial, and pass from the arms of the Immaculate Mother into the Saviour's Sacred Heart. I wonder very much that mother seems to hesitate about the advisability of undertaking the journey. . . . When you are there, do not be so selfish as to keep all for yourselves; do not forget the absent, and above all remember the spoilt child of Mary Immaculate, and be sure to lay my special request before the Sacred Heart." If it were not that affection takes no count of distance, he could, hardly speak of making" a slight *détour*" from Lourdes to Paray.

Writing to his brother Léon, he says: "You have your lessons to do, my little man, and you find Greek a tough morsel. Well, the only thing to be done is to offer all to the Sacred Heart of Jesus as best you can, and then this disagreeable Greek will be changed into all sorts of pleasant and precious things. Who knows but what it may be just what is wanting to procure the happiness of some sinner throughout eternity?"

Again at the new year he writes: "Let us determine to give the whole of this year to God. We must not be too modest when Heaven has to be won. There are some people who say: 'So long as I get into Paradise, it does not matter if I am very near the door; I am not afraid of the drought.' We ought to aim much higher than that. It is true that *tempus breve est*, but an upright heart and the love of God will impart to all we do in time a value for eternity."

"I have wept with you and for you," he writes on the occasion of the death of a little niece. "Our poor little darling! I can see her now, her pensive expression always struck one. Perhaps her ear already caught from afar the sweet melodies of Heaven. May I not add that she seems nearer to me now than she ever did before; she appears to my mind's eye in the form of a shining angel, reflecting the radiance of Paradise. I fancy I see her at our Lady's feet repeating her *Hail Mary* without interruption and without end. Happy little one! welcomed by the angels, smiled upon by our Lord! Blessed Jesus, Thou hast taken from us the child of our affections; while she rejoices in the light of Thy countenance, do Thou heal the wound of our hearts. Thou hast said: 'Blessed are they that mourn, for they shall be comforted.' Fulfill Thy promise, for we look in vain for consolation from any other than Thee. Happy little angel, pray for us who still suffer here below."

Chapel of the Visitation in Paray-le-Monial.

Even to this day, those who possess Theodore's letters find pleasure and profit in their perusal. It is needless to dwell any longer on this subject; the reader has had an opportunity of forming an opinion of them for himself. One touch is still wanting to the picture; a few selections from the exhortations he addressed to his little sisters will supply the lack.

"Far from praying less, you ought to try and pray more every day if you can. I have heard prayer compared to a vessel filled with a precious liquid, to which there is a tap; and if the tap is turned on just a little, a small stream trickles out; if it is turned more, the stream runs faster; and if the tap is turned quite on, it pours out abundantly. Thus when we pray a little, a tiny stream of grace flows down from Heaven; if our prayer is greater, I mean more fervent, the little stream of grace increases; and if we pray with our whole heart, trying to avoid all distractions, the stream of grace will become a torrent, inundating the soul, and filling it to overflowing. I send you a little picture of the Sacred Heart; set it before you when you are at work; every time you kiss it, or even look lovingly at it, that is as good as a prayer, and will not pass unrewarded. It makes no difference whether you put your arms round Mama's neck and kiss her, or whether you look at her fondly; she understands what you mean and is just as well pleased."

"This morning, when I received our Blessed Lord in Holy Communion, I thought of you. I fancied I heard a voice whisper to me: 'Theodore, suppose you were to write to your little sister and remind her that the great day is drawing near. I want to have a nice dwelling-place prepared for Me in her heart, and I think I have every right to expect this, after all that I have done for her. Remember how kind a Mother I have given her in Heaven, and another kind mother on earth too. Do you think, Theodore, that she loves Me very much, Who have done so much for her?' I answered, 'Yes, certainly, Lord Jesus, I am sure she loves Thee dearly, and would be truly sorry to do anything to vex Thee. Has she ever vexed Thee? I must say I should be astonished to hear that she had.' 'She has sometimes.' 'Is it possible! in what way?' 'Well, she is not always as obedient as a little girl ought to be; she is fond of dawdling, and often thinks of other things at her prayers.' 'Is that all, Lord Jesus?' 'Yes, that is about all. But tell her from Me to try very hard to be good before the time comes for her First Communion, for if I find her well prepared, I shall fill her heart with graces as full as it will hold.'

"There, dear child, is the message our Lord gave me for you. Try to have some little victory over yourself every day to offer Him; write them down in your note-book; then when the happy day arrives, you can add them all up, and give the sum total to the Blessed Virgin, that she may herself present it to our Lord. And when the Divine Child Himself comes to your heart, He will knock gently at the door, and say: 'My darling sister, do you love Me very, very much?' And when you have answered, 'Yes,' He will add: 'Dear sister, may I have your heart? Will you give it Me? Then you must answer directly: 'I will indeed, sweet Jesus; take it ail, and keep it all to the end of my life. I do not want it any longer, I mean it to be Thine forevermore.' "

And at Christmas he adds:

"You must be a great favorite with the Infant Jesus. He made me a sign with His little hand (for he cannot speak plainly yet) to tell me He wanted me to write to you for Him. I put my ears as close as I could to His Heart, and held my breath and listened; I could perfectly understand what He wished to say. Theodore, tell My dear sister that I am longing most anxiously to take up My dwelling in her heart, I am sure I shall find a better resting place there than this crib. Oh, you do not know how dearly I love her! She will have a nice little bed ready for Me, made soft and warm with virtues, and so white! not a single spot to be seen! Tell her, Theodore, that Mary My Mother is very much pleased to see the preparations she is making to receive Me, and if you would like it, she will go and help her a little.'

"Mind you accept the offer Jesus makes you. Go and stand before a statue of the Blessed Virgin, and say to her: 'Dear Mother in Heaven, you see that my mother on earth is very very kind, and has been doing all she can to prepare me for my First Communion; how I wish you would be so good as to come too.'

"But wait; I feel a little hand pulling my cassock; it is the Infant Jesus again. He has something more to say, so I must put my ear to His Heart again. 'Tell Stéphanie that she makes Me happy when she repeats the beautiful prayers of the rosary that My Mother likes so much to hear; each bead is in Heaven a pearl that the angels carry away and add to her crown. Good-bye, Theodore; I am going to sleep a little now, if I can, but before I shut My eyes I must repeat the names of My little friends once more: Stéphanie and Josephine. Good-bye, I shall soon be asleep.'

"Now we must be quite quiet not to disturb our Infant Lord; He is tired. Let us kiss Him very gently, and then go and sit down by the side of St. Joseph and our Lady, and wait until He wakes up again."

It has been said, and said truly, that the power of stooping to the level of children is a special gift. Theodore possessed this talent in an eminent degree; he was able to speak their language as if it was his own, to give intelligible form to abstract truths, and by captivating their imagination, to win their childish hearts for God.

His old regiment furnished a fertile field for exertion, and provided ample room for the exercise of his zeal. Although timid and sometimes almost shy in his manner, he retained the martial bearing of a Zouave, and never lost the affection of an old soldier for his regiment. This need not surprise us, for he had the spirit of the Society before. he entered St. Acheul, and is there not something of the soldier about every Jesuit?

The Regiment! magic word suggestive of heroic self devotion, magnanimous sacrifice, noble patriotism; recalling in its literal sense, the standard and the strife, commanders and comrades, glorious victories and ghastly wounds! Speak to the invalided veteran seamed with scars, to the old Zouave tanned by the sun of Africa, to any man, in fact, whose heart ever beat high with true martial ardor, of his old regiment, and he will instantly rise to the subject; you have touched a responsive chord, and while a tear sparkles in his eye, he will launch out on the entrancing tale of the feats of prowess achieved by his valor. And if the regiment is so sacred a thing to men whom mere chance or military compulsion brings together, what must it be in the eyes of the soldiers of the Pope, united of their own free will in a common bond to defend the cause of God and the Church?

"Long live the Regiment!" Theodore constantly wrote these words at the end of his letters or on the pages of his note-books. He took the greatest interest in everything about it, in its past history and its future prospects. "Though I have put off the uniform," he writes to a former comrade, "I have by no means divested myself of my affection for it. Notwithstanding every appearance to the contrary, I am convinced of the reality of the mission entrusted to the Zouaves; and I believe that the generous manner in which the regiment has been dedicated to the Sacred Heart is more than anything else, a pledge that it will not cease to exist, but is destined to bear a part in the regeneration of France. Would it not be well for the Zouaves to beg our Lady's blessing upon their flag? A pilgrimage to Lourdes might easily be organized, and if only the regiment were officially represented, it would be quite unnecessary for all its members to be present in person.

"Our battalion constitutes, so to speak, the crew of St. Peter's bark, and its lot is to experience the same afflictions, be tossed by the same tempests, shaken by the same storms as that much-enduring vessel. Its glory is to suffer with the Church; but it will likewise arise again as she will, and share the triumph of her resurrection. Our cause is God's cause, let us learn how to wait, how to suffer, how to be patient. The Holy Father bears his captivity without a murmur, praying, hoping, believing. The blood which was shed at Patay is no less the seed of martyrs than that which moistened the soil of the Coliseum, and we have confided the germ of our future life to the safe-keeping of the Sacred Heart. Happy those who, when the time comes, will answer to the call, and respond: Here I am! They will never think that the honor of fighting once more for the love of Christ can be bought too dearly; the best thing left for us to do at present is to pray."

He wrote letter after letter, in order to interest his parents and his friends, those Jesuits whom he knew personally, everyone, in short, with whom he was ever so slightly acquainted, in finding a home for some Zouave who was without employment, or rendering a service to some former brother in arms. "My Zouaves," such are his words, are dearer to me than ever; there is one in particular whose conversion I am most anxious to obtain from the Sacred Heart. He is a noble-hearted young fellow, if ever there was one, and devotedly attached to the Church, France, and—the Republic! The foundation on which his affection for the first of the three rests is sadly defective, for he has got hold of some wrong-headed notions, and is thus led to act in a painfully inconsistent manner. Several others of my old comrades cause me no small anxiety, but I commend them all to the Sacred Heart. The majority, however, are delightfully orthodox, as much so as anybody I know. They cling closely to the Rock of Peter, their hearts are there, united more firmly than ever by the same undying hope, *in spem contra spem!* How dearly I love my gallant regiment!"

One of his favorite walks was to the Castle of Prousel; the distance was, it is true, great, but what effort would he not have made in order to pray in the very room where General de Lamoricière breathed his last, and to kneel before the same crucifix which had been pressed to the dying lips of the father of his regiment?

When Lallemand, his former commander; was struck down by sickness, Theodore was unremitting in his exertions, begging prayers, novenas, Communions, and Masses from all quarters; and when he heard of the death of this model Zouave, his grief was deep and lasting, although his confidence remained unwavering, as far as the future was concerned. "The loss of our gallant friend is a great blow to our hopes from a merely human point of view, but it ought not to shake our faith. He will not do less for our cause now that he is in Heaven, than he did while upon earth."

Theodore's old friends often went to see him at St. Acheul, and he used to call it a red-letter day when he could talk about his regiment. But a mere flying visit did not satisfy him, he would endeavor to induce his old comrades to prolong their stay in order that they might hold converse with God in silence, by meditation and prayer. "Do you still," he asks an old friend in a letter, "feel the same strong aversion to my proposal that you should make a short retreat at St. Acheul? Three days at the most would be of incalculable benefit to you, and I think the devil is making you see things in a wrong light for his own interest. X. struggled long against the idea, yet he found at last within these walls the solution of the problems which had been perplexing him."

To another friend, who was making a retreat in accordance with his advice, he writes from Boulogne, in order to inculcate confidence in God. "Have you not been consecrated to the Sacred Heart of Jesus, with the whole of our regiment? You will see the garden walk where Divine grace and mercy triumphed over my weakness and cowardice. There it was that, after having said my beads, I united myself to Jesus Christ for all eternity. I feel sure that Willebaud and my uncle were praying for me in Heaven. Do you take courage; remember how many prayers are offered for you. I speak from my own experience, for I am perfectly certain that had I not been supported by a more than ordinary measure of grace, I should have fled before the enemy. Happily, our Lady did not forsake me, but helped me to pray almost without ceasing, that was my salvation. A spirit of prayer does everything. Place perfect confidence in your spiritual guide, open your heart entirely to him, in spite of the repugnance you naturally feel for this. Have confidence, my dear friend; not that sensible confidence which is based on frames and feelings, but the confidence which is of faith. You will have to endure a good deal of ennui, at least I know I had, but every work which is of God must be stamped with the seal of suffering."

He failed not in thought to follow his comrades from afar, giving them consolation, encouragement, advice. To one he says:

"Above all, teach your little Joseph to love the Queen of Heaven. In a hive of bees, if one only has the queen bee, one is sure of all the others, and it is the same with the Queen of Heaven. If your little son ever happens to come my way, I will teach him *The Flag of the Regiment,* and several similar ditties, and I will relate his father's exploits to him."

Shortly after he had entered the novitiate, he was joined there by a friend of his, likewise a Zouave, Captain Mauduit. This latter was a man of few words, tall and thin, with an expressive face and a smile that was full of meaning. He was remarkable for devotion to the Blessed Sacrament, and was accustomed to spend an hour every evening in adoration before It, which caused him to be known in his regiment as *le Monsieur de cinq à six*. At the siege of Rome this brave officer might be seen standing upright on the ramparts, directing the firing of his men, with his field glass in his hand, as cool all the time as if he were at the theater. Later on in the same day he was sent to unfurl the white flag, in order to stop the firing of the Piedmontese troops, who meantime, taking him for their mark, poured a perfect volley of balls upon him. Like so many of his comrades, he ended by asking of God leave to exchange, that he might thus continue to enjoy the honor of still serving the Church, though wearing a different uniform. For him the novitiate proved a still harder school than it had been for Theodore; sometimes he was seen to clench his fists and grind his teeth. The ci-devant Captain was, however, most edifying in his character of novice; his attachment to his former companion in arms was so great that when, thirteen years later, he lay upon his death-bed, he said in his old forcible manner, though with a radiant smile, "I shall soon see Theodore again."

The two old comrades were, during their novitiate, fond of seeking each other's society, in the hope of finding, in this brotherly intercourse, a fresh incentive to zeal in the service of our Lord. Upon one occasion, as they were returning in company with a third novice, from a distant pilgrimage to some shrine of our Lady, they were met by a group of laborers. The sight of their cassocks stirred up the gall of these horny-handed sons of the soil, who greeting them after their own fashion, exclaimed: "There are three idle fellows for you! That is not the stuff out of which soldiers are made!" Such language was meant to be offensive, but the insult was so singularly inappropriate that the incident developed a comic side, and provoked a smile from the three individuals referred to, for as it happened, the companion of the Zouaves had also served as an officer in the campaign of 1870. This manner of returning insults suited Theodore's humility when his personal honor was alone at stake, but the moment the honor of his regiment was concerned, he threw off his reserve and laid aside his meek bearing; and surely he was justified in doing so, since the flag of the Zouaves has never been stained except by the blood of the brave men who fought under it. Let us hear what he himself says in reference to this subject, after the expulsions which had taken place in accordance with the decrees of 1880.

"I have read in this morning's *Univers* an article entitled *Renegades,* from which I learn that two quondam Pontifical Zouaves have acquired a shameful notoriety by aiding in the execution of the decrees. I could not help crimsoning with shame, for the honor of my regiment is no less dear to me than that of my family. Were I not a Jesuit, and therefore an interested party, I would never rest until I had discovered some way of publicly effacing the shame of this disgrace to my regiment. Some one must do so, for I assure you I feel this as a personal attack upon my honor as a Zouave. I have no recollection of these two wretched tools of the Government. Did you know them in the regiment, and what position did they hold there? I altogether disown them as Zouaves."

In 1878, on occasion of the annual banquet at which, upon the name-day of General de Charette, year after year the old companions in arms met together, Theodore's muse inspired him to send a poetic bouquet, composed of unfading blossoms of memory and hope. Taking his idea from the *Sergent* of Paul Déroulède, he represented an aged Sergeant of Zouaves engaged, when stretched upon his death-bed, in recalling to a comrade the past exploits of his regiment.

> "The old sergeant was silent... then, bowing his head,
> he seemed to evoke a distant memory.
> Was it a battle, was it some celebration?
> Where was his uncertain gaze fixed?
> Did he still see himself at Viterbo, at Farnese,
> In Rome, in one of those fierce battles?
> Or under the tall pines of Villa Borghese
> Did he march proudly, keeping step in a parade?
> Then, as if under the effect of a sweet thought,
> He was seen lifting with a trembling hand
> His humble crucifix: "If the feast is over,
> Has there ever been a feast without a tomorrow?
> Do you know, Bernard, do you know what makes me

smile when I feel death so close to me?
You might assume it was delirium...
No, what transports me today is my faith!
So I will see them again, those valiant victims
Whose lives has traced a wide furrow
Of glory and virtue... I will climb the peaks
Where the ranks of the battalion have reformed.
Soon I'll be shaking hands with all these brave men,
Guillemin, Lallemand, Guérin, the Dufournels...
I'll have to name all our dear Zouave martyrs...
I am going to present arms to our colonel!
Oh! Just thinking about it fills me with such joy,
To celebrate cheerfully up there, what a feast!
And then I'll tell them about Pope Leo XIII,
I will tell them... it's true: The Pope does not die."

This simple and graceful effusion gave much pleasure to the distinguished Commander to whom it was addressed, and Theodore shortly afterwards received a letter full of grateful appreciation, in which General de Charette warmly thanked him, in his own name and that of all the guests assembled at the banquet, for these appropriate and touching lines. He wrote:

"My Reverend Father, my good and dear friend," replied General de Charette to Théodore, "yes, I wept! We were all deeply moved reading the death of the Zouaves Sergeant, because every thought in it echoed a thought from our hearts...

"Do you know what the regiment has represented and still represents? It is a much forgotten word: honor.

"Yes, honor for commitments made; remaining faithful in hardship as well as in prosperity, that's the honor of the good old days... As for us, the regiment, what role are we called to play? I don't know, but I only ask one thing: not to fail in honor!

"I went to ask the Holy Father for his blessing; he gave it to me. I count also on you, dear friends, on you who have chosen the best part, that of prayer and sacrifice; I challenge anyone to find hearts more devoted than yours and those of the Zouaves, my good and dear friends. You, who so clearly lay out my duty, bless you and thank you.

"I embrace all my old friends with all my heart.

Charette."

Beyond and above the place reserved in Theodore's heart for his regiment, his General, and his comrades, there was a chosen niche for his beloved protector, Pius IX, whom he was in the habit of constantly invoking. In order to renew his confidence in this revered Father, he was in the habit of frequently reperusing the account of the audience during which he had, as a youthful Zouave, passed ten minutes of unalloyed happiness in the presence of the saintly Pontiff.

"February 7th, anniversary of the triumphant death of Pius IX. Union of prayers and thanksgiving to Our Lady of the Immaculate Conception. Would that I could kneel beside his tomb, and water it with my tears! But I have no cause to grieve; he does no less for me now than he did formerly; and as for us Zouaves, who have received so much, nay all, at his hands, I must say that in order to acquit ourselves of our debt to him, we are bound to make him known and loved by others: *habemus Pontificem;* we have a Father who intercedes for his children."

And, since a mere expression of feeling, however touching and however true, can never satisfy real affection, Theodore undertakes a crusade of prayer to our Lady in order to obtain the canonization of Pius IX, and he expresses his confidence that she will not refuse this favor, but is rather ardently desirous to bestow it. He proposed to have a small picture printed, symbolizing the pontificate of Pius IX, to be distributed wholesale. He collected and spread everywhere accounts of extraordinary favors obtained. through his intercession, and we shall see that, when stretched upon his own death-bed, he frequently, pressed to his lips a relic of the Father whom he had so loved as to offer him his own life.

When Theodore signed his letters to his parents: Your Jesuit Zouave, he did indeed speak out of the fulness of his heart, for now more than ever he was a soldier of the Pope, a defender of the Church!

General Baron de Charette.

CHAPTER XXIII.

1874—1880.

In the College at Boulogne. Theodore introduces a military spirit among his pupils. Portrait of Pope Pius IX. Return to Amiens. Tour in Switzerland. Dispersion of the community at Amiens. Theodore is sent home.

HENCEFORWARD the sole desire of the former Zouave was to be an apostle of Christ, and to sow the seed of truth wherever he went. In October, 1874, when the school term began, he was sent as a professor to the College of Notre Dame at Boulogne.

The imposing structure, which from its position upon the summit of the cliff, looks out over the channel towards England, was not yet inhabited, and the pupils were crowded together in a house which was formerly the Bishop's palace, and which, though amply capable of accommodating a prelate and his suite, proved somewhat close quarters for three hundred boys. And yet not a single complaint was heard, for all day long its inmates inhaled the fresh sea-breezes, and lived in the very shadow of Our Lady of Boulogne. Theirs was a simple family life, carried on under the auspices of Mary, elevated, divinized by her. Nothing but a single door separated the College from the well known church, which may truly be described as an act of faith and love carved in stone, raising, as it does, the image of our Lady aloft to the very vault of Heaven. Pilgrims flock thither in crowds: fishermen to pray for a blessing on their nets, fishwives to implore protection for their absent husbands.

It may be imagined how delighted the young Jesuit was to find himself in the town which our Lady had honored with her preference a thousand years ago. Before he so much as crossed the threshold of the College, he hastened to implore the blessing of his celestial Patroness.

His new duties had nothing very brilliant about them, for he who had been head of his class at Roubaix, who had carried off the gold medal at Marcq; the attractive writer, the skilful versifier, was appointed to teach-the sixth class! Is it not to this virtue of obedience that the great Religious Orders owe their continued strength and perpetual youth, this virtue which enables him who deserves a post of honor to accept with joy the lowest place? There was much to be done too, besides actual teaching, since the professor was expected to exercise a sort of general supervision, especially in the dormitory; but this latter duty he accepted with great delight, since he found the head of his bed was in close proximity to the sanctuary of our Lady.

The ice was speedily broken between the tall Father* and his thirty-five little pupils, and when the latter had heard some episodes of his military life, and it had been agreed that a specially interesting story was to be the rewards of lessons perfectly repeated, and exercises specially well done, the eager enthusiasm became general. The class-room was turned into a battlefield, and thanks to the energy with which all the combatants sought to catch up their opponents, the most difficult rules failed not to find themselves ere long forcibly impressed upon the memory

All went on in military style. Two rival camps were formed, each with its own banner, one of these being an imitation of that under which the troops fought at Patay; the territory contested was the realm of classic authors and grammatical knowledge; the walls were covered with escutcheons bearing the names of the officers, and

---

* The Jesuit scholastics of the French Province are called "Father" previous to ordination.

when the great day of viva voce examination came, the whole school rang with the clash of the contending armies. To be guilty of a mistake was equivalent to being wounded, whilst inability to give any answer at all at once put the combatant hors de combat. At the word of command the mimic army marched in step, took up its position in battle array, laid ambushes; and a great deal was heard about volleys of grapeshot, skirmishes of the vanguard, armistices, and challenges. The séances were taken by storm, and finally to put an end to the hostilities, four of the strongest warriors on the conquered side were selected to bear the victor aloft in triumph, and while the decoration of some Pontifical order was solemnly conferred upon him, the whole class joined in singing a soldier's chorus. No one knew better than Father Wibaux how to keep both combatants and spectators wide awake while he gave his instructions.

But the part of teacher was in his eyes only a secondary one; indeed it was said of him by one of his superiors that Wibaux was the most perfect realization ever met with of the typical professor and apostle combined, according to the spirit of the Society. His ever-watchful zeal found in everything matter for some wise admonition or elevated thought. Day by day too, with untiring devotion, he made a pilgrimage to the shrine of our Lady, and remained kneeling there, engaged in reciting what he termed his class-litanies, consisting of an invocation addressed to the guardian angel of each of his pupils. "Above all things I try to induce the Blessed Virgin to take an interest in my affairs, without her I can do nothing. To her I have confided the direction of my class, and she is so kind that one might fancy she had nothing else to do in the midst of her numerous and pressing occupations, than to look after my petty concerns. Occasionally she deputes St. Joseph to take her place, and he seeks to execute all her wishes. In a word, the Holy Family helps us to get on wonderfully well together."

He calls Mary "Our beloved Commander-in-chief," and on the 8th December both professor and pupils publicly consecrated themselves to her under the title of Our Lady of the Immaculate Conception. "This gracious Mother," he says, "has consented to assume the direction of all our maneuvers, both spiritual and intellectual; industry, emulation, and piety are in consequence the order of the day."

From morning till night his rosary was in his hands, indeed he was sometimes spoken of as "the tall Father who is always saying his beads. "The long practice he had had drilling stupid recruits, and above all his perfect self-possession, prevented him from ever evincing the slightest sign of impatience, even in the case of the most tiresome pupils. He was still the kind Sergeant Major of former days, who never punished if he could avoid doing so, and who always inflicted the lightest possible penalty.

One of his pupils grieved him very much by his carelessness, and for him he offered up all his merits, his prayers, and his sacrifices. His discipline, which was discovered after his death stained with his blood, showed after what fashion he took Heaven by storm. Another of his scholars, a rough, churlish lad, offered him a direct insult; and for this culprit Theodore, said his beads more than four hundred times. Individual conversations, catechisms, the Saturday conferences, were all made use of by him as opportunities for attacking the weak points of his little regiment. There was nothing vague, nothing high-flown in what he said; he entered into details, pointed out the remedy for each evil, and invariably prepared beforehand the chief points of his discourse, leaving only the choice of expressions to the spur of the moment. In the MSS. notes of the instructions he delivered on the Catechism thirteen different authors are quoted and commented on. He employed illustrations and anecdotes, drawn for the most part from his personal reminiscences, to bring into relief the particular truth he desired to impress upon his hearers. When, for instance, he wished to speak of the happiness of Heaven, he would describe the magnificence of the festival services held at St. Peter's in Rome; or again, the contrast between the calm serenity of the Gulf of Naples, and the fiery outbursts of Vesuvius, which he had ascended during the famous eruption of 1868, would suggest some words about Heaven and Hell. Pompeii, the sanctuaries of Rome, his regiment and his battles, in a word, everything which he had seen and heard, was laid under contribution in order to give color and life to his addresses. Having known in his early years the tortures of a conscience ill at ease, and having had later on to make such desperate resistance to temptation, he recommended the habit of prayer, of trust in God, the practice of confession and of frequent Communion, with a warmth and earnestness which went straight to the heart of his hearers.

One day a splendid engraving of Pius IX. was sent to the quondam Zouave, with a special blessing on his pupils; beneath it was an entire sentence, written in the trembling hand of the saintly Pontiff. That day there were grand doings: the Rev. Father Couplet, the Rector of the College, came into the class-room, in order to hang the picture in its place with his own hands, and congratulate the delighted boys, telling them that there was probably no other class in the whole world as privileged as they, and that they must show themselves worthy of the honor bestowed on them. A few days later, the Professor, radiant with happiness, sent the following pen and ink sketch to his brother Léon: "The weather is splendid, the color of the sky resembling rather the deep blue of Italy than the pale grayish hue usually prevalent at Boulogne. The Cathedral with its dome reminds one of St. Peter's, and to render the illusion complete, a magnificent portrait of Pius IX. looks down upon our class-room, in the midst of the escutcheons of his advanced-guard. The likeness is in a gilt frame, and over it are the Papal arms. The gentle and saintly face seems to smile down upon my little flock and say: I am the good shepherd; whilst from her pedestal our Lady looks with affection upon the Pontiff who defined the dogma of her Immaculate Conception. I have been in much better spirits ever since Pius IX. has presided over the scene of my labors, and my children have shared with me the effect of his benediction."

From the sixth class he moved up with his pupils to the threshold of the third, no small advantage alike for the teacher, who was kept in constant practice by continually having fresh subjects to prepare, and for the pupils, whose education was thus carried on on the same system. "The old soldiers seem pleased to meet again their former Captain, and the recruits cannot do otherwise than follow the lead of the veteran warriors. I have ranked the last year's pupils under the title of *Zouaves*, whilst the new comers, and those recently moved up, are in the camp of the *Chevaliers;* but between ourselves, they are constantly being charged, and this amuses me not a little, because I can foresee that before long they will have to make a stout resistance, in order not to be overpowered by their adversaries: the Greek projectiles especially do deadly work. Meanwhile the Virgin Mother looks down placidly upon all this strife; indeed it is she who animates the combatants, cures the wounded, crowns the victors, and above all, up holds the authority of the commander-in-chief."

It was not without much regret that Theodore left Boulogne in 1877, in order to pursue his own philosophical studies at St. Acheul. But his influence continued to make itself felt from afar, by means of his numerous letters, and above all by his prayers. "I have abandoned my colors and my battlefield, I have been obliged to leave, God knows for how long, my brave little Zouaves and my Chevaliers, who march to battle like one man. Such is a soldier's life, one is obliged to shift one's quarters incessantly; and if one's heart becomes attached to any person or any thing, it has to be detached, at the risk perhaps of making it bleed a little, but that is soon over. I try to reconcile myself to the separation, by offering many prayers for these dear children, for whom I shall never cease to feel the deepest affection."

Two years later, he was appointed to superintend the older pupils at Amiens. The room assigned to him had formerly been used for the chemistry class, and was redolent of the odors left by sundry experiments; the ceiling too was so low that he could scarcely stand upright in it. However, he made the best of it, for it was a rule with him never to complain, and even if his bed was too short hé bore it philosophically; certainly it was not his first experience of the kind. His new duties obliged him to see that the rules were respected, to punish any infraction of them, and, in a word, from the height of his commanding stature, to dominate the whole situation. The boys committed to his charge found Father Wibaux at first very strict, not to say very formidable.

Ere long, however, stories of old times in Italy, tales of former campaigns, and above all long walks, greatly modified this state of opinion. "Our Superintendent," writes a pupil, seems to fancy himself a Zouave again, for when he takes us out walking, he treats us as if we were soldiers, making us march in step, or teaching us how to charge an imaginary enemy." One evening, instead of being back at five o'clock, in time for the hour's study, the party did not return till half-past eight. The Father Prefect is said to have been not too well pleased; the boys, on the other hand, enjoyed the excursion amazingly.

Theodore tried to, introduce among his pupils the practice of going to Communion on the first Friday of every month, as an act of reparation, and he so far brought into play their generous feeling that he collected every month, for the Propagation of the Faith several hundred francs more than they had been in the habit of giving; indeed, he constantly stirred them up to the performance of all good works by the marvelously attractive manner in which he spoke of holy things. One of his pupils has said: "Whilst telling us about his battles, and the banner of Patay, he exhorted us not to neglect Holy Communion, and to be devout to the Sacred Heart, in a manner so natural, so persuasive, and so original, that there was no resisting him. One winter evening, he asked me, as I happened to have a headache, to come out and help him pour water on the skating-ground. The sky was spangled with innumerable stars, and if I were to live a thousand years I should never forget the manner in which he commented in his cheerful way on the saying of St. Ignatius: *Quam sordet tellus dum cœlum aspicio.*"*

Towards the end of July, he was chosen to accompany three of his pupils on a tour in Switzerland and Italy. An indefatigable pedestrian, an ardent lover of nature, a practiced traveler, he was indeed a suitable person to play. the part of Mentor; yet notwithstanding the undeniable attraction which snow-clad mountains had for him, he confided to one of his Superiors that it cost him much to leave Amiens at so disastrous a period. The decrees had already been put into execution in regard to the Houses of the Society, and the turn of the Colleges would come shortly. Theodore feared lest the community should be expelled during his absence, and he should thus

---

* How vile the earth seems while I gaze at the heavens.

be prevented sharing in the sufferings of his religious brethren.

The little caravan set out, almost as free from baggage as it was from care. The tall Abbé did not look amiss, towering aloft above his three youthful companions, his knapsack on his back like the rest, a stout stick in his hand, the remainder of his equipment consisting of buff-colored gaiters, hob-nailed shoes, a traveling cap, and a soutane well fastened up.

The principal halts made by the party were at Annecy, the Lake of Bourget, Saint-Gervais, Chamonix, the great St. Bernard, Aosta, Lago Maggiore; but from these various points they made numerous excursions over mountains and glaciers, sometimes walking for twelve consecutive hours, and meeting on their way with those little adventures which may be termed the flowers of travel. However weary he might be, Father Theodore never omitted to note down each evening the impressions of the day; to do so had in fact

Road from Culoz to Lake Bourget.

become to him a second nature, owing to the habit he had contracted when serving with his regiment. Our tourists failed not to make fresh friends, and to renew their acquaintance with old ones, sometimes in an unexpected and delightful manner. It was a great pleasure for the quondam Zouave in the course of his journey to come across several of his old comrades, who were all rejoiced to entertain their former sub-lieutenant.

At Chamonix, amongst other places, the *table d'hôte** furnished them with odd types of character. "There is at present staying here," writes Theodore, "a portly inhabitant of Rouen, who invariably appears in a white cravat, and is traveling with his better half, seventeen bonnet boxes, and a mass of other luggage besides. He is forever boasting of the excursions he has made, and declares aloud that he was bathed in perspiration after he had merely been to the Glacier des Bossons. He carried about with him everywhere sheets and a provision of butter, because he was told at Rouen that sheets were never put on the beds, and that everything was cooked in oil!"

The heartfelt piety of Father Theodore everywhere found an opportunity for some outpouring of prayer and devotion; at Annecy, before the tombs of St. Francis of Sales and St. Jane Chantal; at the numerous sanctuaries of our Lady which he met with on his mountain wanderings; in Savoy too, the native land of Blessed Peter Lefebre, the first priest of the Society of Jesus, whom he incessantly invoked. His hand was always in his pocket, to distribute medals to the little shepherd-boys of the Alps, to the pious Savoyards, and to the guides; he calls them "baits to catch souls," and remarks upon the gratitude evinced by the recipients, who seemed to regard these trifling gifts as a perfect treasure. "It is well," he adds, "to be able to bestow so much pleasure at so small a cost! "

On their arrival at Chamonix, they all four repaired to the church to say their evening prayers. The next day Father Theodore heard several Masses; on Sunday they all went to Communion, and in order completely to sanctify the day, they made a pilgrimage to *Notre Dame de la Gorge,* a sanctuary which is situated at the bottom of a ravine, and is almost buried amid the snow. In this way the

---

*   A pre-fixed meal at a restaurant.

Chamounix.

Bourget lake.

thought of God served to supernaturalize their journey and elevate it into something above a mere pleasure-trip.

"Martigny. The church here is very nicely kept, and contains a beautiful statue of the Sacred Heart. I knelt alone before the Tabernacle, while someone was trying the organ, and playing in that dreamy style which suggests thoughts of Heaven. Here we have no lasting city. This is the reflection I always make when I see a crowd of tourists, wandering hither and thither in search of fresh excitement."

During the long hours spent in walking, the Mentor kept up the spirits of his companions by singing the *Ave Maris Stella* and other hymns. And when a difficult pass was reached, they invoked the help of the Blessed Virgin and their Guardian Angels, before the little caravan pushed on; for its members were full of courage, and did not shrink from encountering perils.

They were now going to descend the mountains on the Italian side, the only road being a ridge covered with snow and scarcely half a foot wide. "Only a first-rate climber could help turning giddy, especially as a high wind was sweeping the snow before us along the narrow track on which we had to walk. We were obliged to proceed a considerable distance in this manner, with the glacier and the rocks on either side; it was almost enough to make one drawback. First of all we repeated the *Memorare* aloud, then we were roped together. The head guide first made a place for himself to plant his feet on, and then cut steps as best he could for those who were following him. Every one of the guides watched carefully for the least slip; I did not look down at my feet, and kept on singing in order to forget where I was; twenty minutes of this work brought us on to the glacier."

Several other times our Lady preserved them in danger. On one occasion a wooden bridge gave way directly after they had crossed it. Another time their safety was entirely due to the interposition of Providence. Here is Theodore's account of the matter, taken from his note-book:

"Cabane on the Pass St. Théodule, the highest spot in Europe where a human habitation is found. At 2 a.m. I overheard our guides in consultation about the weather; the night was very dark, and snow showers were continually falling. However, our departure could not be deferred, today being Saturday; I silently invoked our Blessed Lady, for I felt somewhat uneasy. The cold is intense, and the immense glacier to be crossed on the Swiss side is full of crevasses from seven to eight hundred feet in depth. Everything is covered with newly-fallen snow, so that it will be necessary to make a fresh track, feeling our way very carefully at the risk of falling into the ravines. At last we set off, with the rope tightly stretched, having to plod through snow more than two feet in depth. The guide who went first proceeded with the greatest precaution, as if he were walking on eggs. For the first half-hour all went well, when all of a sudden he sank in the snow, those who followed him doing the same; some sank up to their armpits, but all made haste to extricate themselves as soon as they could. I came last, so I was likely to sink deeper where so many had sunk already, and it struck me at that moment as very odd to travel so far in order to seek amusements of such a nature; 'but happily it was not to please myself that I had come, so I said to myself that God was bound to protect us. We sank again several times in much the same manner, and thus passed two crevasses which were very deep, and others which were somewhat shallower. I thanked our Lord from my inmost heart every time that I again felt firm ground under my feet."

Our travelers also visited the Great St. Bernard, leaving Chamonix for the purpose early one morning in a carriage. "The road winds round the edge of a fearful abyss; it needs an experienced driver to thread safely this series of no less than fifty-two intricate routes, for it is no joke if two carriages happen to meet. In order to encourage us, various spots were pointed out to us where carriage accidents had occurred: in one place a lady had been overturned with her conveyance, and dashed to pieces against the rocks; in another equally cheerful reminiscences were revived. But surely our good angels watched over us, and except for the thought that at every step one is liable to break one's neck, the road is indescribably wild and magnificent. One certainly gets no notion of anything of that kind in Picardy!"

A little further on they were on the route by which Napoleon and his army once crossed the Alps. "I love to think that beyond that exquisite snow-clad peak, beneath that azure sky, lies Italy, and then Rome. How delightful to see Italy again, to hear the language and see the people! to catch a breath of Roman air, recalling my happy days with my regiment! I calmly recited my Breviary in spite of the jolting of the carriage. By a curious coincidence it was the Office for Our Lady ad Nives. In the first nocturn I read: 'The depths were not as yet, and I was already conceived, neither had the fountains of water as yet sprung out; the mountains with their huge bulk had not as yet been established; before the hills I was brought forth.'

"How can I describe our arrival at the great St. Bernard, and the reception we met with? I dine with the community, novices, and scholastics, and occupy a seat opposite to the Father Master. The stories the Fathers relate are most interesting; every evening I take tea with them." These excellent religious, whose truly Christian hospitality enjoys a world-wide renown, really strove to outdo themselves in kind attentions to the persecuted Jesuit.

Mount Saint-Bernard Monastery.

On leaving the monastery, the little party directed their course to Aosta, and after a series of fatiguing marches and some bits of difficult climbing, found themselves on Italian soil, where Theodore was able to talk freely with the kindly natives, who were not a little taken aback by the singular outfit of the travelers. They kept the feast of the Assumption on the shores of the Lago Maggiore, and visited Rome, Albano, and Bolsena, all which places evoked recollections dear to the heart of the Zouave. And yet all this enjoyment was in a certain sense a weariness to him, for he longed to be back in France, in order to bear his share in the persecution which had broken out against his brethren in religion. As soon as he had consigned his youthful companions to the care of their relatives, he repaired with all possible speed to Amiens, pausing only to lay his tribute of gratitude at the feet of Our Lady of Victories.

The decrees were to be put into execution towards the end of August, as far as the Colleges were concerned; and since the Jesuit professors were forbidden to live any longer under the same roof, the community at Amiens were dispersed in different directions. Theodore was sent home to his parents at Roubaix: "You must look on your mother as your religious superior," the Father Provincial said to him, as he took leave of him; Theodore interpreted these words in their most literal sense.

This sojourn of the religious in his family procured for all its members that quiet happiness which those who love and serve God alone can know. He was no longer the schoolboy of former days, or the Zouave on leave of absence, and yet he had not ceased to be his simple-hearted affectionate self; his love for his family was as tender as ever, though purified by contact with the Sacred Heart of Jesus, and it constantly showed itself by a thousand instances of delicate thoughtfulness in regard to the souls of those by whom he was surrounded. His virtue had the invaluable quality of knowing how to suit itself to circumstances, and fall in with the most opposite modes of life, without ever losing sight of the aim of the Society, namely the sanctification of one's own soul in sanctifying the souls of others. During this stay with his family, if he wished to make an excursion, write a letter, give away a little picture, he invariably went in the first place to ask leave of his mother, who had been appointed his superior. Whenever he had to take the tramway to Tourcoing or to Lille, he requested her to give him the few halfpence required for his fare, refusing to accept more than the exact sum. Upon one occasion he sought her out in order to ask that he might be allowed to give a glass of beer to a servant who had been doing some unusually hard work. When poor people came to the house, he first enquired what they wanted, and then went to tell his mother, respectfully advising her to practice liberality in their regard.

Such was the life he led at home, but his apostolic zeal required some field for its exercise abroad, and he therefore set himself to speak and preach in public, either at the workman's club, or to the old people gathered under the roof of the Little Sisters of the Poor. His addresses were full of life, abounding in illustration and imagery; with the greatest facility he made his audience laugh and weep by turns, while his genuine kindness, and compassion for human weakness, won for him all hearts. "What a splendid fellow he is! How well he talks!" exclaimed a workman after listening to one of his addresses; then turning to Stephen Wibaux he added, "You must be very proud of having such a brother." His success was due to his trenchant and well-chosen language, his somewhat florid diction, but above all to the Christian tone which he in variably imparted to his words. Several years before the time of which we are speaking, a young religious having preached a sermon before the community on the doom awaiting sinners, afterwards went to Theodore, and asked his opinion of it. He gave it with perfect frankness: "That is not the sort of sermon to do good," he said, "severity only repels; in order to win souls, we must imitate the compassion our Lord had for them. "But ere long the vacation came to an end, and the time arrived for Theodore to commence his theological studies; he therefore received orders to set out for Jersey.

Bourget lake.

Church of Saint-Matthew.

CHAPTER XXIV.

1880—1882.

The House in Jersey. Theodore commences his theology. The Apostle of the Sacred Heart. Pilgrimages to St. Matthew. Presentiment and preparation. Illness and death. A Jesuit's last will and testament.

THE following words written by Theodore after he had taken up his quarters in the barracks on the Janiculum might be used in reference to those Jesuits whose place of exile was Jersey: "The cage is so charming as to console the bird for its captivity!" And yet they are not altogether applicable, for whilst a change of quarters is a trouble for which consolation is easily found, it is impossible to bid adieu to France, to her colleges and her manifold works of charity, without experiencing deep and lasting regret.

In October, 1880, two hundred of the younger Jesuits who were studying philosophy and theology, met together from various quarters on the soil of Jersey. Scattered by the rude blast of the decrees, they had requested permission of the little island to take up their abode upon her shores, in order to devote themselves to study and to prayer; and faithful to her traditional hospitality, Jersey had

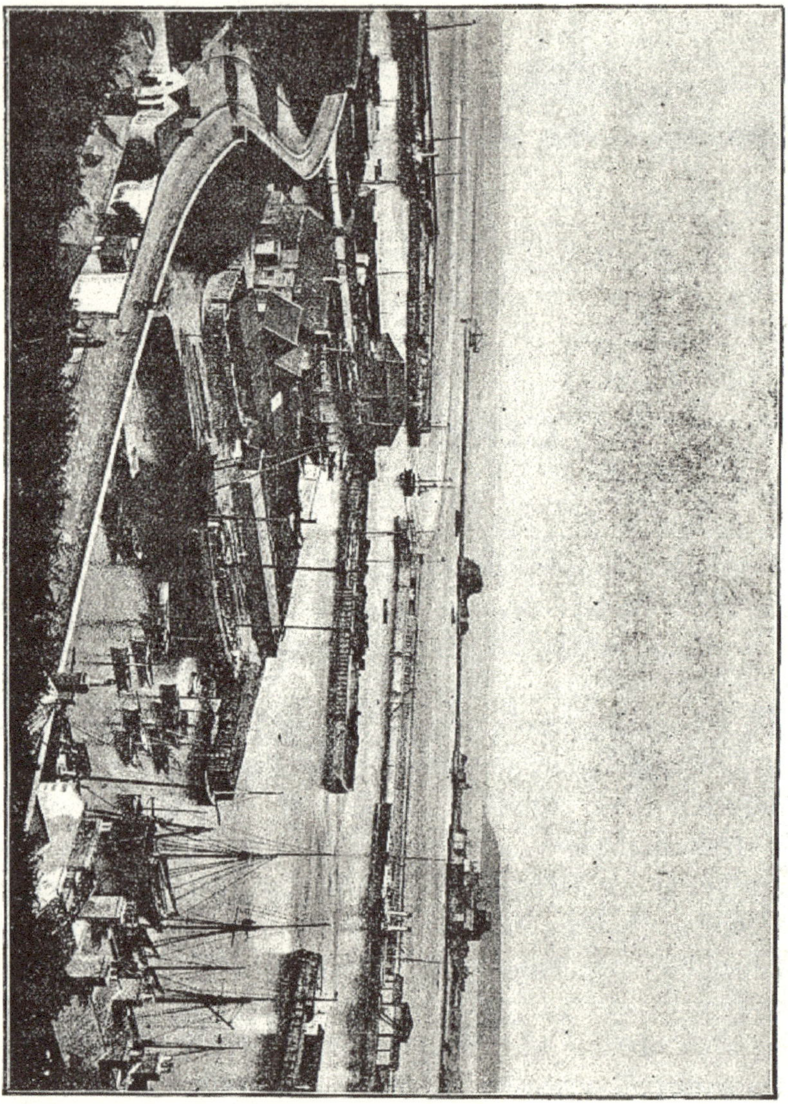

Jersey. - Port of Saint-Helier.

generously granted to the religious what France, once so truly Christian, had seen fit henceforth to deny them. So recently as the last century four bishops and two thousand priests owed their safety to this island. May she be repaid in blessings from above for the charity thus shown to proscribed ecclesiastics!

"Here I am at Jersey. From my window I have a view of the whole of St. Heliers, the capital of the island, which spreads in a sort of fan-like shape down to the shore opposite to us we see the sunset in the sea day by day. I can watch the different colored signals run up on the flag-staff to give notice of the arrival of the steam boats from Granville and St. Malo; they seem to bring a little bit of France with them. The cannon booms each morning and evening from Elizabeth Castle, reminding me of the cannon of Fort St. Angelo, which sounded at midday, in order to regulate all the clocks of Rome, and set the Angelus bells ringing."

Alas! in Jersey the Angelus is not rung, although church towers may be seen on every side; in former days, prayer ascended to Heaven from Catholic hearts, accompanied by the joyous sound of church bells, but now, as Theodore says," it is only sad to hear the Sunday chimes calling the people together to what they are pleased to call Divine worship."

What was formerly the Imperial Hotel, now the *Maison Saint-Louis,* seemed to have been prepared by Providence as a place of refuge for the exiles, when the storm should burst over their heads; and yet, in spite of its vast proportions, the new inmates found themselves somewhat pressed for room. Never, even in its most prosperous days, had it known such numbers of guests; it had, in fact, perished from inanition, before the coming of the exiled religious awoke it to new life. "Poverty is the rule everywhere, in regard to, furniture, books, and clothes. But on the other hand, what an abundance we have of fresh air, innocent mirth and brotherly charity, and how each heart expands under the influence of the mutual affection which our common exile serves to increase!"

Truly did the warm beams of charity shine upon the Maison Saint-Louis more brightly even than do the rays of the sun upon the little island; and this is saying a great deal when one sees the lovely

Saint-Louis House. (Former Imperial Hotel.)

flowers called into being under its influence, and finds how sweet is the springtime of the year in this island-garden of the Channel! "I can exclaim," writes Theodore, "with St. Francis Xavier: *O Societas Jesu, Societas amoris!* May my lot be with thee in life and in death, through honor and dishonor!"

Four years of theological study now lay before him, at the end of which shone the hope of the priesthood, ordained by God to give the Religious and the Apostle his final completeness. "Pray for me," he says, "that this slow and laborious process of formation may result in making me a priest after God's own heart. There will be so much work to be done in France when I return thither, and perhaps so much to be undone. Unhappy France! how often do my thoughts revert to her!

"My dear mother, I beg you to give me a special blessing, and I, too, on my part bless you, for having prayed so much and so often for your child; in spite of his manifold imperfections, he has succeeded in becoming a Jesuit. I consider myself as a conquest, made by my two beloved Mothers, one of whom is on earth, and the other in Heaven. I ask for grace to become both learned and holy, since it is for God's greater glory that I should do so. We are in the vanguard of the spiritual army; we must have our cartridge-boxes always full, and the bayonet fixed to the end of our guns must be sharp and bright."

Although he had never had any taste for abstract reasoning, he applied himself to study with a determination which might almost be termed exaggerated; so multitudinous were the notes he made, and the MSS. books he filled with close writing. One day when he was at St. Acheul, he expressed in his own quaint fashion how much taste he had for the niceties of scholastic philosophy. "Come along," he said smiling, and addressing his *bête,* as he playfully. called himself, "I must make you sit down to table and compel you to eat; if you have no appetite for your food, still we must force it down somehow."

Seated in the front row, his eyes fixed either on the professor or his note-book, or on a picture of the Sacred Heart, he made copious notes, which he afterwards copied out into a book, and never did he utter a single word or show the least inattention during the time the lectures lasted. The public disputations brought out his humility in no common degree; on one occasion when he had refuted one of his brethren in an argument with remarkable brilliancy, the latter came afterwards to congratulate him: "It was all your doing," Theodore replied, "you answered so well that I had only to follow your lead."

Exit from the cave of Plémont.

Simultaneously with his study of theology, he applied himself to the perusal of the works of the best preachers; he made notes of Bourdaloue, la Colombière, Texier; he analyzed the works of numerous ascetic writers, and thus laid up a store of materials for the time when he should himself be called to ascend the pulpit, without meanwhile neglecting his correspondence, which was more extensive than ever, and more than ever characterized by a supernatural and apostolic tone. Fortunately, the long walks he took on his free days counterbalanced to a certain extent the excessive mental strain which would otherwise inevitably have shortened his life. The indefatigable pedestrian found full exercise for his powers on the beach and among the rocks, along the roads which led to the lighthouse of Corbière and the caves of Plémont, past gaily painted cottages and gardens laid out with such precision and regularity, that one might almost fancy they, too, owed more to the painter's brush than the gardener's spade, amid a thousand Labyrinthine ways which intersect the island like fine net work, dividing one from another the vast plantations of potatoes. "Oh, the potatoes, the potatoes! one would think they were so many precious stones!"

Jersey. - Valley of Saint-Pierre.

As far as labors of an apostolic nature were concerned, the silent teaching of example was all that could be attempted, but this effected a great deal, and ere long the sight of these young *clergymen*, with their good-humored merriment, who appeared upon the various roads of the island twice a week for their accustomed walks, served to scatter to the winds the ludicrous calumnies associated with the mere name of Jesuit. But the salt of persecution is everywhere necessary, and the exiles were fortunate enough not to be left without it even in Jersey, and to perceive just sufficient of its flavor to prevent them from forgetting that they were under a ban.

"We oppose an imperturbable dignity to the snowballs wherewith we are assailed, and the elegant epithets by which we are designated, following the example of the senators of ancient Rome, who allowed the Gauls to pluck out their beards without stirring from their curule chairs." Orders had been issued to the effect that all provocations were to be met with silence. One day, however, when Theodore had been struck on the head with a clod of earth, his companion could not refrain from addressing a sharp reprimand to the aggressor, whilst the injured person quickly walked on without so much as turning his head.

However, he never ceased to desire something more tangible than this silent apostolate, and his zeal, ever on the alert, soon supplied him with a happy thought.

Towards the center of the island, upon a plateau which slopes down on either hand to the charming valleys of St. Peter and St. Lawrence, there rises a handsome granite steeple surmounted by a cross. The passer-by can enter, for the door stands always open, as befits the house of God; a lamp burns before the tabernacle, for it is a Catholic church, a place where light and repose await the Christian, since within his Father's house he cannot but feel at home. All around, alas! nothing but Protestant templesare to be seen, belonging to every imaginable sect, built in every imaginable style, cold and dreary as their own stone walls, closed against those who go to pray, open to the tourist who goes to stare, if the fancy takes him to look round, and he is willing to bestow a gratuity on the sexton. The inmates of the Maison St. Louis often made the little church of St. Matthew an object for their walks. Theodore used to repair thither as frequently as was possible, and if one of his companions proposed some lengthy excursion, he would generally make it a condition that they should visit the Church of St. Matthew on their way. One day on leaving this church, he told his companion of an idea which he had formed of establishing a place of pilgrimage there, whither people might resort to pray for the conversion of the island; on his return he went straight to his superior, and pleaded eloquently for the desired permission, which was granted. A statue being indispensable in a place of pilgrimage, a splendid image of the Sacred Heart was sent from France, and placed over the high altar, where it may still be seen. Thither week by week pilgrims repair from St. Louis to kneel at the Holy Table, and Theodore from his place in Heaven doubtless unites his prayers to theirs in order to obtain the conversion of the unhappy Protestants. And indeed, since the time we speak of, the parish of St. Matthew has undergone a transformation; through the zealous exertions of the French Oblate Fathers schools have been erected, and good works set on foot; can we doubt that it is the rays shining forth from the Divine Heart which are fertilizing this once barren soil?

Church of Saint-Matthew.

The devotion to the Sacred Heart also threw a radiance around the last period of Theodore's life upon earth; so great was his fervor, that it led him to form vast projects by means of which this favorite devotion might be propagated on an extensive scale, his chief desire being that France itself should by a formal act be consecrated to the Heart of Jesus. He kept this object in view in all his letters to his friends, to the editors of Catholic periodicals, to all in fact whom he thought likely to further this noble aim. As the first Friday of each month drew near he despatched missives in all directions to the more fervent among his friends, recalling to them the favors promised to those who offer their Communion on that day in reparation; and many an old Zouave received a reminder which, coming as it did from his former sub-lieutenant, had the force of a command: "Attention! Friday will be a day of general review and inspection; I count on you, let us meet at the Holy Table, and make reparation for sinners." "Send me a quantity of pictures of the Sacred Heart," he writes to his relatives;" you know how greedy I am in this respect. And do not fail to make yourselves apostles of this beautiful devotion: if one can but introduce into the dwelling of some poor family a picture of the Sacred Heart, it is a great thing done. Our Lord is so liberal that it is a pleasure to give Him the least thing; what costs but a single centime will be rewarded with notes for a thousand francs; these centimes are the little sacrifices of daily life accepted for His sake. "His distance from his family did not prevent him from arranging a plan for the consecration of his family to the Sacred Heart. On an appointed day, the Rev. Father Joseph said Mass, and after this Mass, at which his parents and all his brothers and sisters assisted, he recited in the name of all present a solemn act of consecration. Shortly after, a letter appeared in the *Messenger of the Sacred Heart,* exhorting all Christian families to do the same; it was signed "Theodore Wibaux," and was the means of inducing many persons in different lands to make a similar act of consecration.

In reward for these continual proofs of filial affection, a real pleasure was reserved for Theodore on the last feast of the Sacred Heart he was to spend on earth—General de Charette landed in Jersey on the evening before the day. "I threw my arms round his neck, and we embraced each other like old friends. On his mentioning to me his wish to receive Holy Communion with us on the following morning, I reminded him that he would have to come a considerable distance, and at a very early hour. 'Nonsense!' he replied, 'I mean to do the same as all of you.' In the parlor he unfolded the flag of the Sacred Heart, the beloved flag that I had not seen for ten years! how delighted I was to press it to my lips again, and how thankful to the Heart of Jesus for granting me this privilege! May the saintly victims who dyed that banner with their blood, obtain for us to fight like them under the shadow of the Sacred Heart, and be united to it in death."

Never had the fervent religious shown greater generosity in the service of God. He spent much time in the chapel, and made the Way of the Cross every day. He was always the first in any fatiguing occupation, and went daily into the kitchen to help in washing up the dishes. Those around him were oftentimes struck by his recollected air; the fact was that the thought of death was ever present to him. *Et vos estote parati,* he wrote everywhere among his notes; he was preparing to appear in the presence of his God, and felt a strong desire to offer himself as a living sacrifice, as is proved by the following extract from a letter written to one of his Superiors some time previously: "The impulse within me is stronger than ever to offer myself as a victim of expiation for France. This thought encourages me, and in seasons of trial my good angel whispers in my ear that the solemn hour is approaching. "We find the identical idea repeated in another letter: "I have the privilege of being permitted to go to Communion three times a week besides Sundays. This is not for nothing, I feel a sort of intuition that the hour of my departure is not far distant, and an interior voice cheers me with these words, *lætantes imus!*"

And when the 12th of February, 1882, his thirty-third birthday, came round, the fact of having attained the age at which our Lord suffered upon the Cross encouraged him to pray so earnestly and offer himself up so unreservedly, that his petition could not fail to pierce the heavens, and a secret voice whispered to him that it was granted. With all simplicity and frankness he hastened to acquaint his Superiors with his prayer, and with the conviction he felt that he would die that year. His last letters home are evidently intended to prepare his relations for the end which he knew to be fast approaching. "I hear more plainly than ever the voice that bids me hold myself in readiness to suffer and to die."

By a singular coincidence, only a few weeks previously the Sovereign Pontiff, when speaking to a Jesuit Father in private audience, had said that the Church stood in need of expiatory victims, who would freely offer themselves to appease the anger of God: "and these generous souls," he added, "will surely not be wanting, least of all in the Society of Jesus." Theodore had long since anticipated the idea to which the Holy Father gave utterance.

One evening towards the end of May 1882, he was busy getting all in readiness for the pilgrimage which was to be made to St. Matthew's on the following day, but his countenance betrayed such excessive weariness that he was advised to give up all idea of taking part in it himself. The next day he was unable to leave his bed, as a severe attack of inflammation of the bowels had come on; the progress of the disease proved so rapid and so alarming that in the course of a few days his father was summoned by telegraph. He started immediately. When Theodore was informed that he was coming, he requested the doctor to let him have a sleeping draught, in order that he might be able to give his father a cheerful welcome when he arrived on the morrow. A sudden change for the better took place, every one hoped that the worst was over, and the prayers that were being offered for his recovery were changed into thanksgivings.

Thus God graciously granted his heart's desire, allowing him to appear really better when his father arrived, accompanied by M. Cordonnier, the beloved friend of former days. But ere long a fresh attack came on, and the malady assumed a severer shape.

So calm and tranquil was the patient that one might have imagined him totally free from pain: only once or twice he remarked, "I feel as if I were being cut in two. It is a mark of our Lady's favor." When it was suggested to him that he should receive the last sacraments, he assented to the proposal in so matter of fact a manner that the Father Rector could not help asking him whether he had understood what had been said? "Indeed I have," he answered quietly.

It was truly edifying to see how absorbed he was by thoughts of the supernatural, and how constant was the union of his soul with God. Before taking his medicine, he would beg that a few drops of the water of Lourdes might be added, "not to benefit my body, but my soul," he would explain.

He frequently requested those who were watching by his bedside to repeat some prayer with him, or to give him his picture of the Sacred Heart; and after repeatedly kissing it, "that is my evening prayer," he would say.

He gave various commissions to his fellow-religious: "Would

you be so good as to pay a visit to the Blessed Sacrament for me," he said to one of them, "since I am deprived of that privilege. "He carried obedience almost to an excess, if such a thing can be, for whenever he was asked anything: "Just as Father Rector wishes," or "the doctor said so," was his invariable reply.

One of his brethren approached his bedside in order to give him various messages to be delivered when he should get to Heaven. "Please say this from me to our Blessed Lady, St. Joseph, St. Ignatius, and other saints." Theodore made a sign in the affirmative; and then, as the speaker was about to withdraw, he called him back, and said: "I shall also, ask that you may be an apostle of the Sacred Heart."

His suffering continued without intermission. In the night between the 9th and the 10th of June, Holy Communion was as usual brought to him; soon after his breathing grew shorter, and at five o'clock in the morning he gently expired. M. Wibaux repeated a *Pater* aloud, accentuating the words, *Fiat voluntas tua*. It was a Saturday, the day dedicated to the Mother whom Theodore had so fervently loved.

Before his body was carried to the chapel, it was laid at the feet of the statue of the Sacred Heart which stands in the vestibule of the Maison Saint-Louis. Only a short time previously, he had made every effort to have that statue sent from France, and it seemed only right that he who in his lifetime had so loved to kneel before it, should even in death, pay homage to it still.

He was laid to rest near his brethren in religion, in the place of his exile, and from his grave on the top of the hill, opposite St. Heliers, and looking over to France, he continues to intercede for the land whence he was banished, and for the isle which had been his home in the time of the proscription. General de Charette went to kneel in prayer at the grave of the Zouave-Jesuit, and in him as their representative, the regiment to which Theodore had belonged may be said to have paid military honors to their departed comrade.

On the self-same day on which intelligence of his death reached the sorrowing household at Roubaix, his brother Léon returned home from Jerusalem, whither he had gone on a pilgrimage to the Holy Places, bringing with him a letter which Theodore had intrusted to him, with directions to lay it for a few moments in the cavity of the rock wherein the Holy Cross had been planted. Léon had fulfilled his commission, but Theodore was no longer there to claim his property, his testament, as it might now be called. His mother opened it, and read with deep emotion, not unmingled with holy joy, the last words of the son whom God had just seen fit to take from her. We give the contents verbatim.

"Good Friday, April 7th, 1882.

"I Theodore, a most unworthy sinner, venture humbly to approach my beloved Master, Jesus Who was crucified, doing so with the same love which is felt by the Angels and the Saints.

"I am deeply grateful to my crucified Lord for having deigned to die for my sake, for having pardoned my failings, for having given me His own Blessed Mother and His Sacred Heart; I desire to love Him so fervently as to be willing to accept His Cross.

"I kiss in spirit the Sacred Mount of Calvary, where my salvation was wrought out; I desire to draw from the sacred cavity where the Cross was placed, on my own behalf and on that of all who are dear to me, an ardent love for Jesus Christ and His Blessed Mother.

"Standing at the foot of the Cross, I abhor my sins, and desire to weep for them with tears of blood: I implore my beloved Saviour Jesus Christ to grant me grace to atone for them by love.

"I confide my whole family to the Sacred Heart of Jesus, and desire to consecrate it to Him entirely. I implore Mary at the foot of the Cross to procure for me grace to make the Heart of Jesus the center of my life. I commend to her France, the Church, the Society; I implore the Mother of Mercy to assist me in my last moments and enable me to escape the fires of Purgatory.

"I entreat the Heart of my beloved Redeemer and His Blessed Mother mercifully to grant me, when my hour of suffering shall come, grace to suffer in a spirit of love, and even to rejoice in suffering, in order that I may thus glorify God and edify my neighbor. I accept everything beforehand in expiation of my sins: I gladly consent to become the suffering servant of Mary.

"Blessed be Jesus, Mary, Joseph, Ignatius, my good Angel, Gertrude my second mother, and all my beloved protectors in Heaven. Blessed be the Most Holy Sacrament of the Altar! May mercy and pardon be vouchsafed to me!

"I make my testament at the foot of the Cross: I give all to my Immaculate Benefactress, since to her I owe all.

"Beloved Savior, I place myself with my thirty-three years of life, in Thy Heart and upon Thy Cross, and there I bless my Immaculate Mother for all the benefits she has bestowed on me.

"*Virgo fidelis! Mater admirabilis!* obtain for me that Jesus' may take me to be with Him in Paradise, before I have the misfortune to grieve thee: I say this at the same age at which Jesus Christ deigned in mercy to die for love of me.

"One intention I earnestly commend to my beloved Saviour and His Blessed Mother; the consecration of France to the Sacred Heart.

"Upon this Mount of Calvary, I make the sacrifice of my life to the Sacred Heart; I offer it for France, for the Church, for the Society, for the Canonization of Pius IX, for the Regiment, for Charette, for the reigning Pope, and for all who are dear to me.

"Finally I entreat thee, my Blessed Mother, who didst assist and console Jesus when expiring upon the Cross, to assist and console me in my last moments, and grant me to die united to the Heart of Jesus.

"THEODORE,
"Child of the Sacred Heart to all eternity."

At the end he added, with childlike simplicity, the letters R.S.V.P. He had not long to wait for the answer: Jesus and Mary gave it him with their own lips, in Paradise.

In Madame Wibaux's heart no place was found for aught but grateful rejoicing. "Give thanks to God for me and for Theodore!" she wrote to one of her sisters. A few months later, unable any longer to bear the separation, she went to rejoin the son she had loved so dearly, and who had doubtless obtained from his Heavenly Mother the privilege of being united to his earthly mother in the country whither he had preceded her.

Jersey. - Montorgueil Castle.

Jersey. - Montorgueil Castle.

EPILOUGE.

THREE years later, on July 28, 1885, the regiment of the Zouaves celebrated its silver anniversary. The survivors of Italy and France had come from all over the world to gather around General de Charette, in the shadow of the standards of Rome and Patay, and, bowing under the blessing of Leo XIII, they acclaimed the Pope, still King even through he was a prisoner.

And in heaven it was undoubtly a great feast for the brave men of the regiment, for in heaven there are days of celebration. Lamoricière and Pimodan advanced at the head of their martyred soldiers, whose wounds shone more brightly than any decorations ever did here below, and all with one voice they sang to Pius IX a hymn of which the Seraphim would have envied if envy could enter paradise.

He was there, our second lieutenant; and Saint Ignatius, who was also a soldier, was proud of his son, the Zouave-Jesuit. And Theodore brought his flower for the crown of immortals shining on the regiment's front.

It was his story, written by himself, a story of his bravery and his piety, his battles and his victories, his filial affection for his family and for the Church; it is the life of the young Zouave that has just been read. As long as he lived on earth, humility imposed silence on him; from the heights of heaven, he could speak, for the blessed in paradise know no vanity.

FIN

Tomb of Theodore Wibaux and his religious brothers.

On the right crouching, Theodore Wibaux; on the left, his brother-in-law Carlos Cordonnier sitting on the chair; in the second row Victor Combré and Adolphe Florin. Taken sometime between 1868-1869 when Theodore was a sergeant.

Theodore Wibaux with his brother Stephen, taken sometime between 1869-1870 when Theodore was a sergeant-major.

Made in the USA
Columbia, SC
28 February 2026